WELFARE REFORM IN CANADA

The Johnson-Shoyama Series of Public Policy

Taking a comparative and international perspective, the Johnson-Shoyama Series on Public Policy focuses on the many approaches to major policy issues offered by Canada's provinces and territories and reflected in their intergovernmental relationships. Books in the series each explore particular policy issues, and while research-based, are intended to engage informed readers and students alike.

WELFARE REFORM IN CANADA

Provincial Social Assistance in Comparative Perspective

Edited by
Daniel Béland and
Pierre-Marc Daigneault

Higher Education Division

www.utppublishing.com

LIBRARY AND ARCHIVES CANADA CATALOGUING IN PUBLICATION

Welfare reform in Canada : provincial social assistance in comparative perspective / edited by Daniel Béland and Pierre-Marc Daigneault.

Includes bibliographical references and index.

Issued in print and electronic formats.

ISBN 978-1-4426-0972-3 (bound).—ISBN 978-1-4426-0971-6 (pbk.).—
ISBN 978-1-4426-0973-0 (pdf).—ISBN 978-1-4426-0974-7 (epub).

1. Public welfare—Canada—Provinces. I. Béland, Daniel, editor. II. Daigneault, Pierre-Marc, 1981–, editor.

HV105.W3765 2015 361.6'80971 C2014-907906-0
C2014-907907-9

We welcome comments and suggestions regarding any aspect of our publications—please feel free to contact us at news@utphighereducation.com or visit our Internet site at www.utppublishing.com.

North America
5201 Dufferin Street
North York, Ontario, Canada, M3H 5T8

2250 Military Road
Tonawanda, New York, USA, 14150

ORDERS PHONE: 1-800-565-9523
ORDERS FAX: 1-800-221-9985
ORDERS E-MAIL: utpbooks@utpress.utoronto.ca

UK, Ireland, and continental Europe
NBN International
Estover Road, Plymouth, PL6 7PY, UK
ORDERS PHONE: 44 (0) 1752 202301
ORDERS FAX: 44 (0) 1752 202333
ORDERS E-MAIL: enquiries@nbninternational.com

Every effort has been made to contact copyright holders; in the event of an error or omission, please notify the publisher.

This book is printed on paper containing 100% post-consumer fibre.

The University of Toronto Press acknowledges the financial support for its publishing activities of the Government of Canada through the Canada Book Fund.

Printed in the United States of America.

Contents

Illustrations

Figures

Tables

Contributors

Rick August is a Regina-based analyst with over 38 years of experience in the strategic development of social policy. He was an original policy negotiator for the government of Saskatchewan in the development of the National Child Benefit, and designed or led policy development on a number of initiatives that increased employment and reduced poverty among low-income households in that province. He has consulted with numerous governments on social policy reform and has published several articles on behavioural social policy, employment-based anti-poverty strategies, disability income support, and other topics.

Ken Battle is president of the Caledon Institute of Social Policy. Educated at Oxford University and Queen's University, Battle is one of Canada's leading social policy thinkers. He has played a key role both inside and outside government in the reform of social policy, including in the development of the new National Child Benefit and the proposed Seniors Benefit. He served as a member of the Ministerial Task Force on Social Security Reform in 1994 and as policy advisor on child benefits reform to the Minister of Human Resources Development in 1996 and 1997. Battle has published widely on social policy, including income security programs, taxation, medicare, social services, poverty and income inequality, social spending, and the politics of social policy. In 2000, he was awarded the Order of Canada (social sciences category), and, in 2005, the government of Saskatchewan awarded him its Distinguished Service Award.

Daniel Béland holds the Canada Research Chair in Public Policy (Tier 1) at the Johnson-Shoyama Graduate School of Public Policy at the University of Saskatchewan campus. A student of comparative fiscal and social policy, he has published 12 books and more than 90 articles in peer-reviewed journals. Recent books include *What Is Social Policy?* (Polity Press, 2010), *The Politics of Policy Change* (Georgetown University Press, 2012; with Alex Waddan), and *The Oxford Handbook of U.S. Social Policy* (Oxford University Press, 2014; co-edited with Christopher Howard and Kimberly J. Morgan). Professor Béland has also held visiting fellowships at Harvard University, George Washington University, the National University of Singapore, the University of Helsinki, the University of Southern Denmark, and the Woodrow Wilson International Center for Scholars.

Gerard W. Boychuk is professor and chair of the Department of Political Science at the University of Waterloo. He is the author of *Patchworks of Purpose: The Development of Provincial Social Assistance Regimes in Canada* (McGill-Queen's University Press, 1998) as well as *National Health Insurance in the United States and Canada: Race, Territory, and the Roots of Difference* (Georgetown University Press, 2008), which was awarded the Canadian Political Science Association Donald V. Smiley Prize for the best book relating to the government and politics of Canada. His current work focuses on examining the new politics of income redistribution in Canada.

Robert H. Cox is director of the Walker Institute of International and Area Studies and a professor of political science at the University of South Carolina. An expert on European politics, he has published extensively on the history of social policy in Europe and the reform of welfare states. His recent work examines the politics of sustainability in Europe, focusing on renewable energy programs. He co-edited, with Daniel Béland, a recent special issue of *Governance* on policy paradigms (2013), as well as the volume *Ideas and Politics in Social Science Research* (Oxford University Press, 2011).

Pierre-Marc Daigneault is assistant professor of public policy and public administration in the Department of Political Science at Université Laval. He was also a research fellow at the École nationale d'administration publique (2014–15) and a postdoctoral fellow at the Johnson-Shoyama Graduate School of Public Policy at the University of Saskatchewan campus and at Québec's Ministère de l'Emploi et de la Solidarité sociale (2012–14). Trained as a political scientist, he has an academic interest in social policy generally, and in social assistance and activation policies in particular. In addition, he has a keen interest in questions related to governance, policy paradigms, program evaluation, and research methods. His research has been published as book chapters and in various peer-reviewed journals such as the *American Journal of Evaluation, Canadian Journal of Political Science, Canadian Journal of Program Evaluation, Evaluation and Program Planning, Evaluation Review, International Journal of Social Research Methodology, Journal of European Public Policy, Political Studies Review*, and *Journal of Mixed Methods Research*.

Kathleen Flanagan has broad and comprehensive experience in child, family, and social policy, with a concentration in early childhood education. She has extensive policy experience at a senior director level in government, having participated in interministerial initiatives, led various government task forces, and negotiated intergovernmental agreements. A social policy consultant since 2005, Flanagan has undertaken research and evaluation;

strategic policy consultation and advising; and curriculum program development at the provincial, regional, national, and international levels. She has recently designed the plan for Prince Edward Island's innovative redesign of the early childhood system and developed PEI's Early Learning Framework. Flanagan is currently a PhD candidate in developmental psychology and education, with a specialization in the early years, at the Ontario Institute for Studies in Education (OISE) at the University of Toronto.

Kelly Foley is assistant professor in the Department of Economics at the University of Saskatchewan. She earned a PhD in economics from the University of British Columbia in 2009. Before commencing her doctoral studies, Foley was a research associate at the Social Research and Demonstration Corporation, contributing to the evaluation of a number of random-assignment, social-policy pilot projects, including the Self-Sufficiency Project. Her research has been published in journals such as the *Canadian Journal of Economics* and *Industrial and Labor Relations Review.*

Amber Gazso is associate professor in the Department of Sociology at York University. She completed her PhD in sociology at the University of Alberta in 2006. Her current research interests include citizenship, family and gender relations, poverty, research methods, and social policy and the welfare state. Her recent journal publications focus on low-income mothers on social assistance. She is currently working on two major research projects, funded by the Social Sciences and Humanities Research Council. In one project, she is exploring how diverse low-income families make ends meet by piecing together networks of social support that include government programs (e.g., social assistance) and community supports on the one hand, and informal relations within families and with friends and neighbours on the other. Another comparative project explores the relationship between health and income inequality among Canadians and Americans in mid-life.

Peter Graefe is associate professor in the Department of Political Science at McMaster University. He holds a PhD from the Université de Montréal. His research focuses on social and economic development policies in Ontario and Québec, as well as on intergovernmental relations in social policy. His publications include peer-reviewed articles in journals such as *Canadian Public Policy*, *Global Social Policy*, *Publius*, and *Theory and Society*. He sits on the Social Assistance Working Group of the Hamilton Roundtable for Poverty Reduction.

Andrew Heisz works with the Income Statistics Division of Statistics Canada. He has written extensively on income inequality, low income, and labour market issues. His research articles have appeared in peer-reviewed journals such as the *Canadian Journal of Administrative Sciences*, *Canadian Journal of Urban Research*, *Canadian Public Policy*, *Journal of Human Resources*, *Relations industrielles / Industrial Relations*, and *Review of Income and Wealth*. He is currently the survey manager for the Longitudinal and International Study of Adults.

Ron Kneebone is professor of economics and director of economic and social policy in the School of Public Policy, both at the University of Calgary. His published research has dealt with issues pertaining to the political economy of government deficit and debt reduction; the history of government fiscal and monetary relations in Canada; and the characteristics of Canadian federal, provincial, and municipal fiscal policy choices. In addition to continuing to work in those areas, he has more recently published examinations of the demand for homeless shelters and support payments to persons with disabilities.

Hélène LeBreton is a senior policy analyst with the New Brunswick Department of Social Development. She has provided advice in the area of income support policy development since 1999. Her work has been informing the provincial policy debate in the area of social assistance reform since 2007. She holds a BA in philosophy from Saint Thomas University and an MPhil in policy studies from the University of New Brunswick. Her graduate thesis was a quantitative investigation of factors affecting the duration of completed income support episodes in New Brunswick.

Stella Lord has an MA in political science and a PhD in sociology. She has over 30 years of experience working in various capacities with community, women's, and social development organizations at national and local levels; 20 years of experience as a university lecturer in the fields of sociology, political science, and women's studies; and 10 years of experience as a policy researcher and analyst with the Nova Scotia Advisory Council on the Status of Women. Lord has a passion for progressive social policy change and for developing community capacity to effect change. Now retired from paid employment, she is a research associate with the Canadian Centre for Policy Alternatives–Nova Scotia and works on a voluntary basis as coordinator of the Community Society to End Poverty in Nova Scotia.

Patrik Marier holds the Canada Research Chair in Comparative Public Policy at Concordia University and is the scientific director of the Centre de recherche et d'expertise en gérontologie sociale (CREGÉS). His research focuses primarily on the role of bureaucracy in developing and reforming the welfare state within the context of an aging population. His publications include articles in the *American Journal of Political Science*, *Governance*, *Journal of European Public Policy*, *Journal of Policy History*, and *West European Politics*. He is the author of *Pension Politics: Consensus and Social Conflict in Ageing Societies* (Routledge, 2008), and he is currently completing a manuscript on how Canadian provinces are developing policies and strategies to face the challenges of population aging.

Jennifer Mitchell has an honours BA and a child and youth worker diploma. Her interest areas focus primarily on counselling, self-care, and coping mechanisms. Through her work experience, Mitchell has become an advocate for marginalized populations, particularly people of minority groups and women who have experienced violence and abuse. She currently works as a Family Court support worker for women fleeing violence in Toronto.

Matthieu Mondou holds a PhD in political science from the University of Toronto. His research currently focuses on the politics of emergent technology policy in advanced industrial states. He is currently pursuing this focus as a postdoctoral researcher at the Center for Science, Technology, Medicine, and Society of the University of California, Berkeley. His research has been published in the *Journal of Public Policy*, *Policy Studies Journal*, and *Lien social et politiques*. From 2009 to 2012, he was co-editor of the monthly newsletter *PolitiquesSociales.net*. He has done background research reports for the Centre Léa-Roback and the Fondation Chagnon on the causes of poverty and for the Canadian Agricultural Innovation and Regulation Network (CAIRN) on biofuel policies.

Brian Murphy is a special advisor with the Income Statistics Division at Statistics Canada. For over 25 years, he has worked in the area of income distribution, economic well-being, and social policy research. Using a wide variety of large datasets and micro-simulation models, he has conducted studies and published reports examining income distribution and redistribution in Canada and the United States.

Alain Noël is professor of political science at the Université de Montréal. He works on social policy from a comparative perspective, as well as on federalism and on Québec and Canadian politics. His latest book is *La gauche et la droite: Un débat sans frontières*, (with Jean-Philippe Thérien; Les Presses de l'Université de Montréal, 2010). The original English version, published by Cambridge University Press, won the 2009 International Relations Prize of the Canadian Political Science Association. Between 2006 and

2014, Alain Noël was president of the Centre d'étude sur la pauvreté et l'exclusion of the Québec government, and, in 2013–14, he was president of the Canadian Political Science Association.

Martin Papillon is professor of political science at the Université de Montréal. His recent work centres on the intersection of Aboriginal governance and Canadian federalism, with a focus on intergovernmental relations, social policy, and economic development policies. He is the author of a number of journal articles and book chapters on Aboriginal governance and is the co-editor of two recent volumes on Aboriginal politics and Canadian federalism and Aboriginal-Québec relations.

Michael J. Prince is the Lansdowne Professor of Social Policy in the Faculty of Human and Social Development at the University of Victoria. He teaches courses in public policy, and his current research interests include Indigenous-Canadian state relations, federal-provincial relations, psychologically wounded veterans, and disability policy. He has over 200 publications and has been an advisor to various governments, four royal commissions, and many parliamentary committees. He is the co-author, with James J. Rice, of *Changing Politics of Canadian Social Policy*, 2nd ed. (University of Toronto Press, 2013); co-author with Bruce Doern of *Three Bio-Realms: Biotechnology and the Governance of Food, Health, and Life in Canada* (University of Toronto Press, 2012); and the author of *Absent Citizens: Disability Politics and Policy in Canada* (University of Toronto Press, 2009).

Jane Pulkingham is professor of sociology and chair of the Department of Sociology and Anthropology at Simon Fraser University. She received her PhD from the University of Edinburgh in sociology and social policy. Her work adopts a critical social policy focus and concentrates on contemporary welfare state restructuring, social policy, and inequality, particularly as it relates to women's income security and well-being. Her recent publications include *Human Welfare, Rights, and Social Activism: Rethinking the Legacy of J.S. Woodsworth* (University of Toronto Press, 2010), as editor; *Public Policy for Women: The State, Income Security, and Labour Market Issues* (University of Toronto Press, 2009; co-edited with Marjorie Griffin Cohen); and articles appearing in journals such as *Social Politics*, *Critical Social Policy*, the *Canadian Journal of Sociology*, and *Citizenship Studies*.

Anne-Marie Séguin is an urban and social geographer. She obtained her PhD from Université Laval. She is Professor at the Center Urbanisation Culture Société of the Institut national de la recherche scientifique (a network of research centres affiliated with the Université du Québec system). She is the chair of the research team VIES (Vieillissements, exclusions sociales et solidarités) and member of the CREGÉS (Centre de recherche et d'expertise en gérontologie sociale). Her main research interests are aging, urban social policy, poverty, and social exclusion. She is the co-author of a collective book titled *Vieillissement et enjeux d'aménagement. Regards à différentes échelles* (Presses de l'Université du Québec, 2012). She has published articles in *Applied Geography*, *Urban Studies*, *The Canadian Geographer*, *L'Espace géographique*, and *Housing Studies* (forthcoming).

Wayne Simpson is professor in the Department of Economics at the University of Manitoba. He is a graduate of the University of Saskatchewan and the London School of Economics. He is a specialist in labour economics, urban and regional economics, applied microeconomics, quantitative methods, and social policy, and has worked for the Bank of Canada and the Economic Council of Canada. He is the author of *Urban Structure and the Labour Market: Analysis of Worker Mobility, Commuting, and Underemployment in Cities* (Oxford University Press, 1992) and co-author of *Income Maintenance, Work Effort, and the Canadian Mincome Experiment* (Economic Council of Canada, 1991; with D. Hum) and *Maintaining a Competitive Workforce* (Institute for Research of Public Policy, 1996). He has published more than 50 refereed articles in economics and policy journals as well as numerous technical and research reports, book chapters, and other articles.

Tracy Smith-Carrier is assistant professor at King's University College, Western University. She received her PhD in social work from the University of Toronto in 2011. Her program of research touches upon a number of different fields in the social policy arena, including access to social welfare benefits; social assistance receipt; and health-care administration and the experience of service utilization, specifically for frail, homebound older adults. Her interest in social policy centres on examining welfare state retrenchment and the experience of marginalized groups in accessing the programs and services of the post-welfare state. Current research projects involve a mixed-methods study exploring integrated, home-based primary care models in Ontario and research interrogating "welfare dependency" and the potential of intergenerational trends in social assistance receipt.

Luc Thériault has been trained as a sociologist both in the French and Anglo-American traditions. He holds a PhD in sociology from the University of Toronto. He is currently professor of sociology at the

University of New Brunswick in Fredericton. His field of expertise is social policy and third sector studies, with a focus on the interactions between governments and social economy organizations involved in the delivery of human services. He has published on social assistance and other related social policy issues in Québec, Ontario, Saskatchewan, and New Brunswick. At UNB, he teaches courses in various areas including research methods, program evaluation, Canadian society, sociological theory, the sociology of science, the family, and Canadian social policy.

Sherri Torjman is vice-president of the Caledon Institute of Social Policy. She was educated at McGill University and has written in the areas of welfare reform, disability income and supports, caregivers, long-term care, employment policy, and community-based poverty reduction. She is the author of the book *Shared Space: The Communities Agenda* (Renouf Publishing, 2006). In 2012, she was awarded the Queen Elizabeth II Diamond Jubilee Medal for her policy work on caregivers. She received the Champion of Human Services Award from the Ontario Municipal Social Services Association in 2011 and the Top 25 Canadians Award from the Canadian Association of Retired Persons in 2010. She taught a course in social policy at McGill University and is a former Board Member of the Ontario Trillium Foundation.

Katherine G. White is Assistant Deputy Minister of the Economics and Fiscal Policy division at Alberta Treasury Board and Finance. She currently leads a team of professionals who forecast Alberta's population, economy, and income tax revenues, as well as advise on federal-provincial fiscal relations, tax policy, and fiscal policy. White also has responsibility for the Office of Statistics and Information. Her research interest and peer-reviewed published work is in the field of social assistance policy. In 2009, with Ronald D. Kneebone, she published "Fiscal Retrenchment and Social Assistance in Canada" in *Canadian Public Policy*.

Donna E. Wood is adjunct assistant professor in the Department of Political Science at the University of Victoria. She has a master's of public management from the University of Alberta, and completed her PhD at the University of Edinburgh in 2008. Before embarking on an academic career, she worked for the governments of Alberta and the Northwest Territories for over 25 years, providing policy advice and directing provincial and territorial income support, social services, apprenticeship, training, and employment programs. She has published on labour market policy in Canada, the United Kingdom, and the European Union; and has worked with the OECD to compare employment services in Canada, Denmark, the

Netherlands, and Belgium. She is currently undertaking research on the governance of work and welfare programs in Canadian provinces.

Xuelin Zhang is a senior research analyst at Statistics Canada. He has a PhD in economics and specializes in labour economics. More recently, his research has focused on poverty and low-income measurement. His research has been published in book chapters, peer-reviewed journals, and Statistics Canada publications.

Preface

The impetus for this volume dates back to the summer of 2012. Pierre-Marc Daigneault had recently started postdoctoral research at the Johnson-Shoyama Graduate School of Public Policy on welfare activation in the Canadian provinces under the supervision of Daniel Béland. We quickly came to the realization that there was no recent book available that systematically examined the state of provincial social assistance in Canada from coast to coast; the only comprehensive source available, Gerard W. Boychuk's (1998) *Patchworks of Purpose*, had been published almost 15 years earlier. To be sure, there were plenty of articles and reports published by economists, political scientists, social workers, sociologists, and advocates on various aspects of social assistance in this or that province, as well as a few excellent social policy textbooks, such as *Changing Politics of Canadian Social Policy* by James Rice and Michael Prince (2000),[1] but there was no state-of-the-art reference that provided comprehensive and up-to-date coverage of this important policy and research area.

At the same time, one of the few sources of comparative data on social assistance in the country, the National Council of Welfare (NCW), was about to close its doors. Indeed, a few months earlier, the Conservative government in Ottawa had decided to cut its funding. The decisions to abolish the NCW and the mandatory long-form census, as well as the muzzling of federal scientists, are troubling, to say the least. The Caledon Institute of Social Policy has recently revived this data source (see Tweddle, Battle, and Torjman 2013), but the need for systematic knowledge about social assistance is stronger than ever, considering the ongoing talk about activation, social investment, and economic inequalities in Canada. In this context, we felt, scholars had a special obligation to do as much as they could to fill the gaps in the available knowledge about provincial social assistance in Canada.

We already, therefore, had excellent reasons to work on this edited volume, but the fact that Michael Atkinson, executive director of the Johnson-Shoyama Graduate School of Public Policy, and Michael

1 Since then, *Inequality and the Fading of Redistributive Politics*, by Keith Banting and John Myles (2013), as well as the second edition of *Changing Politics of Canadian Social Policy* (Rice and Prince 2013) have been published. We see these books as complementary to ours.

Harrison, vice-president of the Higher Education Division at University of Toronto Press, were so enthusiastic about our project definitely motivated us. The project also fitted nicely within the new Johnson-Shoyama Series on Public Policy from the University of Toronto Press, which focuses primarily on the role of the provinces in policy development.

We did not rush, however, as we felt that the objective of assembling high quality contributions into a coherent volume would surely be easier to attain if we first convened a workshop on this topic that would draw together specialists with a diversity of disciplinary and policy perspectives on social assistance. Consequently, an important step leading to the preparation of this volume was to organize a workshop featuring our excellent team of contributors. The workshop was held in Regina in October 2013, and it featured a keynote address by Sherri Torjman (written with Ken Battle) and a public panel on welfare reform in the provinces. The event was a clear success, and, afterward, we provided feedback on the various draft chapters before putting our volume together. The manuscript was then forwarded to Harrison, who found a way to review it during the late spring and summer of 2014. The reviews proved very positive, but they also provided useful advice about how to improve the manuscript. When we forwarded the final draft of the manuscript to our editor in the late fall of 2014, we felt that we had accomplished something important in a relatively short time, at least by academic standards. We hope this book will prove valuable to researchers, university teachers, students, civil servants, policy experts, journalists, advocates, and informed citizens. We do not see this book as an end point; rather, we hope that it will stimulate further research and policy thinking on social assistance.

Many people helped make this project successful. First, we wish to thank our dedicated and knowledgeable contributors, who enthusiastically agreed to participate in this project from day one and graciously enacted changes based on the suggestions they received from us as well as the reviewers. Second, we thank these reviewers for their positive assessment and their excellent suggestions. The fact that the reviewers took only a few months to read and comment on such a substantial manuscript is also worthy of praise. Third, we thank our editor Michael Harrison for his dedication and professionalism. Michael is a most experienced editor and working with him is a true pleasure. Fourth, thank you to Nick Falvo and Chuck Plante for their feedback, at the Regina workshop and beyond. Fifth, at the Johnson-Shoyama Graduate School of Public Policy, we thank Michael Atkinson and Gregory Marchildon for their advice, as well as Karen Jaster and Andrea Geisbauer for their assistance in putting together the 2013 Regina workshop. The School also provided financial support to this project, for which we are grateful. Sixth, thank you to both copy editor Rachel Hatcher for her assistance and the members of the production team at the University of Toronto Press—Anna Del Col, Ashley Rayner, and copy editor Karen Taylor—for their work. Finally, Daniel Béland acknowledges support from the Canada Research Chairs Program.

Daniel Béland and Pierre-Marc Daigneault

Introduction: Understanding Welfare Reform in the Canadian Provinces

PIERRE-MARC DAIGNEAULT AND DANIEL BÉLAND

Social assistance, also known as "welfare," has admittedly a bad reputation among the public—in Canada and beyond. For instance, few Canadians think that the government should spend more on welfare, which suggests that this term has become a "dirty word" (Harell, Soroka, and Mahon 2008; see also Andersen and Curtis 2013). Public support for social assistance depends to a large extent on perceptions of deservingness and on the belief that these programs could have a negative impact on the attitudes and behaviour of clients (Larsen 2008; Somers and Block 2005; van Oorschot 2006). Yet, as last-resort income support programs, social assistance, including disability benefits, is a key component of the contemporary welfare state. Social assistance is indeed the "last safety net" (Bahle, Hubl, and Pfeifer 2011) in that it provides basic support to members of some of the most vulnerable segments of the population. In Canada, in 2012, 1,868,565 people—including dependents—were relying on welfare (Kneebone and White 2014, 4; see also their chapter in this volume). The social assistance rate, calculated by dividing this figure by the size of the population aged 0–64 years, was slightly higher than 6 per cent in 2012. This number is significant and, with the exception of Ontario, does not include First Nations people on reserve relying on social assistance (170,000 people according to Papillon, in this volume). Without social assistance, these people would have to rely on their families, private charity, and community organizations for their subsistence, with the result that many would fall into destitution. Indeed, welfare programs *do* mitigate poverty and inequality (Kenworthy 1999; Murphy, Heisz, and Zhang, in this volume), although less so in recent years than in the late 1980s (Haddow 2013). Now, social assistance is clearly insufficient in that respect: 12 per cent of the Canadian population was considered low-income in 2011 (Québec 2014, 3). For all their failings, however, welfare programs remain a means to alleviate poverty and inequality. Moreover, social assistance has become central to citizenship and social inclusion, in discourse at least. Indeed, according to the dominant narrative of the postwar era (1945–75), social assistance was understood as an entitlement that was part of the larger social rights granted to every citizen in a political society (Marshall [1950] 2009; see also Daigneault, 2014). There have been criticisms of this perspective, to be sure, for instance that social inclusion is exclusively centred on employment (Levitas 2004). Nevertheless, social assistance is much more than a simple income support program; it is central not only to the material well-being of the worst-off in our society but also for social citizenship. But, first, it is important to take a step back to examine the international socio-economic forces that have contributed to bringing the issue of *welfare reform*—defined here as a significant policy-led change to the social assistance regime of a state—to the fore of political debates in the 1980s and 1990s in most developed countries, including Canada.

The socio-economic origins of welfare reform

Many interrelated factors are responsible for the perceived need for welfare reform that has characterized developed countries for the last 30 years or so. The first is the emergence of "new" social risks (Jenson and Saint-Martin 2006; Mahon 2013; Taylor-Gooby 2004). As it crystallized in the post–World War II era, the modern welfare state was designed to protect certain categories of "deserving" poor, such as veterans' widows, from risks prevalent in an industrial, male-breadwinning society: unemployment, illness, old age, invalidity, and destitution. These "old" social risks were tackled with horizontal transfers equalizing employment income between age groups, supplemented with limited vertical transfers to poor minorities (Taylor-Gooby 2004). "New" social risks, in contrast, "are the risks that people now face in the course of their lives as a result of the economic and social changes associated with the transition to post-industrial society" (Taylor-Gooby 2004, 2–3). Whereas old social risks affected relatively easily identifiable class-based or demographic constituencies, new social risks are more elusive in that the precise boundaries of the affected groups are often unclear and constantly evolving. New social risks, for instance the growth in female part-time work in the service sector, exert a disproportionate toll on particular subgroups and at particular life stages (Jenson and Saint-Martin 2006; Taylor-Gooby 2004). These new risks are understood as highly individualized, which implies that the individual is responsible for them (Gazso and McDaniel 2010). Previously, governments used to shield individuals from risks; now, they only manage them (Edwards and Glover 2001, quoted in Gazso and McDaniel 2010). Put simply, social assistance has evolved from "security as protection *from* change, to security as the capacity *to* change" (Banting 2005, 422; emphasis in original).

Other factors have contributed to put welfare reform on the political agenda including the productivity slowdown associated with a shift towards the service sector, an aging population, and the fiscal stress caused by processes of welfare state maturation (Pierson 1998). The transition to postindustrial society was also marked by the massive increase in female employment; a rising divorce rate and the prevalence of lone-parent families; as well as various economic changes, such as globalization and the transition to a skill-based economy, that have polarized the labour market (Esping-Andersen 2002; Jenson and Saint-Martin 2006; Taylor-Gooby 2004). In such a context, governments have faced new challenges that sprang from these social, economic, and technological transformations. They have had to tackle child poverty, invest in human capital, help parents balance their work and family life, support the working poor, and boost the activity rate to ensure the sustainability of old-age pension schemes to address accelerated population aging. Simultaneously, however, governments' capacity to undertake initiatives aimed at tackling these new challenges has been seriously impaired by the large accumulated budget deficits and the constraints on increasing taxes posed by international competition that came to characterize the 1980s and the 1990s (Rice and Prince 2013). In short, governments in developed countries now face a context of "permanent austerity" (Pierson 1998).

The politics of welfare reform

The so-called Golden Age of welfare centred on the concept of entitlement is over—if it ever existed (see Wincott 2013). Indeed, harsh criticisms directed at this conception of social assistance have come from many quarters since the 1980s but, in particular, from neoconservatives and neoliberals (for the United States, see Mead 1992; Murray 1984; for Canada, see Crowley 2009). Critics—mainly neoconservatives in this case—have emphasized that individuals should be held responsible for their situations and that there is a need to fight a "culture of dependency" and the lack of work ethics of recipients (for an insightful analysis of the cultural model, see Bane and Ellwood 1994). Moreover, they have insisted on establishing firm distinctions between "deserving" and "undeserving" poor and on controlling recipients through the imposition of harsh work-related obligations, including workfare (Daigneault 2014; Herd, Mitchell, and Lightman 2005). The concerns about the deleterious consequences that welfare may have on recipients' attitudes and behaviours, as well as on recipients' perceived moral worth, are clearly not new. In fact, the distinction between "deserving" and "underserving" poor can be traced back to the English poor laws and their successive reforms in the late eighteenth and early nineteenth centuries (see Polanyi [1944] 2001) and remains the implicit background of many contemporary welfare debates in North America and Europe (Boychuk 1998; Rice and Prince 2013; Somers and Block 2005; Steensland 2008; van Oorschot 2006).

Other critics—including people on the centre-left and proponents of the Third Way—have highlighted the need to "activate" clients, by which they mean tightening the relationship between social assistance and the labour market so that public spending becomes more "productive" (Barbier and Ludwig-Mayerhofer 2004; Daigneault 2014, 2015; Dufour, Boismenu, and Noël 2003; Huo 2009; see also the chapter by Robert Henry Cox, in this volume). Activation ideas propose to restructure the contract between individuals and the state around values of reciprocity and mutual obligation (Daigneault 2014). The general thrust of this argument is that, collectively, we have gone too far in granting rights and entitlements to citizens and that, consequently, we must either cut back those rights or balance them with new responsibilities: "One might suggest a prime motto for the new politics, *no rights without responsibilities*. Government has a whole cluster of responsibilities for its citizens and others, including the protection of vulnerable people. Old-style social democracy, however, was inclined to treat rights as unconditional claims" (Giddens 1998, 65). There has been a transition from a conception of social assistance as an unconditional, universal social right to a conception that defines the receipt of benefits as contingent, conditional, and selective (Cox 1998; Dufour, Boismenu, and Noël 2003; Gazso and McDaniel 2010). Moreover, critics have pointed to the mounting costs involved in maintaining relatively generous social assistance programs and to the "welfare wall" problem (see Battle and Mendelson 2001), that is, the work disincentives generated by the interactions among the level of the benefits, the tax system, and what can be earned in a full-time job at the minimum wage. Interestingly, though curtailing benefits can contribute to reduce the work disincentives for social assistance clients, so do various "making work pay" measures such as a generous income supplement for low-income workers. In terms of policy instruments (see Bemelmans-Videc, Rist, and Vedung 1998), the goal of activating welfare clients is primarily achieved through "carrots" (e.g., monetary and fiscal incentives given to beneficiaries who seek and take employment) and "sermons" (e.g., information on the labour market, career counselling services). However, "sticks" are also an instrument of activation; examples are the obligation to be looking for work and time-limit policies (Daigneault 2014; Serrano Pascual 2004).

A different, albeit related, line of criticism holds that welfare reform should take the path of social investment and human capital development (Banting 2005; Esping-Andersen 2002; Jenson 2011). This trend significantly overlaps with activation when the aim of social investment is to foster—sometimes enforce—the acquisition of skills related to the labour market (Daigneault 2014). The aim is to build up the knowledge and skills of social assistance clients in order to increase their labour market productivity now and into the future. Social investment can also be conceived more largely; by investing in citizens and in children, in particular, it is possible to prevent various costly social problems such as crime, educational underachievement, health problems, poverty, and social exclusion.

Under the impulse of these—partly conflicting, partly reinforcing—strands of reform, social assistance has generally been the object of multifaceted transformations in the last three decades. Although many governments have made significant cuts in their welfare programs, the concept of "retrenchment" does not adequately describe the complex and diverse reforms enacted in most countries (Béland 2010; Pierson 1994, 1998).

The three "I"s of welfare reform: Ideas, institutions, impacts[1]

A full understanding of social assistance reform requires studying its various dimensions, namely *ideas* (what people think and believe and what they say about reform—a broad concept that includes policy preferences, political ideology, and culture; see Béland and Cox 2011), *institutions* (what changes are brought by reform at the institutional level and day-to-day practices), and *impacts* on social assistance clients in terms of their numbers, characteristics, and experiences of well-being.

Although it is easy to forget them because they are often less visible than institutional features, "ideas" constitute an important facet of social assistance regimes (Béland 2005; Daigneault 2014, 2015; Hemerijck 2002; Huo 2009; Somers and Block 2005; Stryker and Wald 2009; Surender 2004; van Oorschot 2006):

> . . . social policy making inevitably proceeds within a broad conceptual framework that defines the critical problems facing society, the goals that should guide government action, and the range of relevant policy alternatives. These underlying assumptions about the domain of social policy need not always

1 The three "I"s is only a "catchy" way to organize our analysis of welfare reform. Therefore, the absence of "interests" should not be over-interpreted.

> be comprehensive, internally consistent, or explicitly elaborated. Nonetheless, they are critical; decision making is inevitably guided by a general conception of the social role of the state. (Banting 1987, 147, quoted in Rice and Prince 2013)

Ideas matter because they provide scholars with a yardstick to characterize welfare and because they influence when, how and what type of welfare reform is enacted.

Yet, there is often a gap between what policymakers say (and think) and what they do in practice—a "policy dissonance" (Imbeau 2009; for an example in the field of welfare, see Dostal 2008). Therefore, studying the institutional characteristics of social assistance is essential to understanding welfare reform. Indeed, benefit levels, eligibility rules, target groups, modes of delivery, and governance arrangements represent the backbone of social assistance regimes. A close examination of these features provides information regarding "who gets what, when, and how" (Lasswell 1936). Reform has been particularly active on the "how" issue as the delivery of social assistance has increasingly been characterized—although with significant variations across jurisdictions—by interagency cooperation, privatization, public-private partnerships, decentralization, and the tailoring of services to the specific circumstances of each individual (van Berkel and Borghi 2007).

Third, the impact of reform on social assistance caseloads (number of recipients and characteristics) and on the well-being of clients should not be neglected. Welfare reform embodies ideational and institutional changes that, in turn, have an impact on social assistance clients and society and the economy more generally. Studying the impacts of reform has acquired a renewed importance in light of the focus on "what works" in terms of interventions that aim at putting people back to work, increasing their skills, and reducing dependency rates. "Evidence-based policy" is characterized by two developments. First, policy decisions must be based on, or at least informed by, "evidence" rather than anecdotes, hunches, and ideology (Heinrich 2007; Learmonth and Harding 2006). Second, although all types of evidence are useful to inform policy decisions, each type has its comparative advantage. Thus, it is important to match the right type of evidence to the right question (Hansen and Rieper 2009; Petticrew and Roberts 2006). For instance, quasi-experimental methods are best suited to evaluate policy impact whereas the added value of qualitative methods lies in assessing issues such as policy relevance; clients' perceptions, experiences, and satisfaction with service delivery; and unintended effects. The key point to remember here is that, from this angle, policymakers are increasingly interested in learning what has been done in their jurisdiction and elsewhere and with what level of success (or failure), although they are sometimes more interested in caseload reduction and cost control than in gauging clients' well-being. Nevertheless, these assessments require, in turn, access to quality data.

The convergence-divergence debate

The multifaceted nature of social assistance reform, in addition to path-dependent processes of development that are specific to each jurisdiction (Béland 2010), complicates any attempt to compare what happens in different jurisdictions and assess processes of convergence or divergence. These challenges have been highlighted by others who study activation (e.g., Barbier and Ludwig-Mayerhofer 2004; Eichhorst and Konle-Seidl 2008; Serrano Pascual 2004; van Berkel and Møller 2002). For instance, Eichhorst and Konle-Seidl (2008) have found a "contingent convergence" of activation strategies and instruments across a number of countries. However, *convergence* (a process) does not necessarily mean that all social assistance regimes instantaneously become identical; significant differences may subsist, especially if regimes were very different at the outset. In any case, it remains to be seen whether provincial regimes are converging in Canada, especially as it is reasonable to expect more convergence for jurisdictions within the same country. Whereas the differences between provincial social policy regimes may not be as consequential as those existing between countries such as the United States and Sweden, they nevertheless remain significant (Bernard and Saint-Arnaud 2004; Boychuk 1998; Haddow 2013; Proulx, Faustmann, Raïq, and van den Berg 2011).

Welfare reform in Canada

The general movement toward the reform of social assistance regimes has definitely not excluded Canada. Though social assistance falls under provincial jurisdiction according to the constitution, the federal government has always had a standard-setting and funding role (Boychuk 1998). In 1996, a key reform occurred. The Canada Assistance Plan (CAP), whereby the federal government funded half of provincial spending on social assistance and imposed several country-wide standards in exchange, was replaced by the Canada Health and Social Transfer (CHST), a conditional, block transfer payment that funded health care, postsecondary education, and welfare. It is important to stress that not only the funding formula changed but also the amount of money received by provinces, which was considerably less. The advent of the CHST effectively eliminated all but one of the standards previously embedded in the now-defunct CAP (the provinces are still unable to impose arbitrary residency criteria). A significant implication of the replacement of CAP was that the right to unconditional assistance (i.e., given without recipients participating in work and training programs) and to a "reasonable"[2] level of assistance disappeared (Gazso 2007). In 2004, the CHST was further divided between the Canada Health Transfer (CHT) and the Canada Social Transfer (CST), the latter being the component that contributes to the funding of social assistance, certain child and family services, and postsecondary education (McIntosh 2004).

Although the replacement of CAP did not seem to generate a "race-to-the-bottom" in the field of social assistance (Boychuk 2006), this institutional change has been significant for federal-provincial relations and the governance of social assistance regimes. Yet, following Gerard Boychuk's provocative contribution to this volume, the impact of the 1996 abolition of CAP should not be exaggerated, as other factors have played a direct role in shaping the evolution of provincial social assistance in Canada since the 1990s.

In the 1990s, for instance, a major federal-provincial-territorial initiative, the Canada Child Tax Benefit (including the National Child Benefit Supplement), was launched to fight poverty among children and to lower the welfare wall (Battle and Mendelson 2001). As a general trend, cash benefits administered through welfare were increasingly replaced by benefits administered through the tax system. Needless to say, this policy epitomizes the trends of social investment (in children) and activation (of parents and mothers in particular). Many provinces have indeed taken the turn toward activation, albeit with a different emphasis (Daigneault 2015; Proulx, Faustmann, Raïq, and van den Berg 2011). In addition, studies of various provincial social assistance regimes have found that, overall, the balance between an individual's rights and responsibilities has shifted toward responsibilities (Dufour, Boismenu, and Noël 2003; Gazso 2007; Morel 2002).

This volume

These changes, as well as the previously mentioned international trends, make it more urgent than ever to pay close attention to the diverse and

2 However, "need" was up to interpretation in each province, and "unconditionality" was blurred by the actual provincial practices. We are grateful to Stella Lord for bringing this point to our attention.

changing provincial landscape in the field of social assistance reform. Furthermore, as quite some time has passed since these developments first unfolded, we are now in a better position to assess their direction and significance. Because our comparative knowledge of the current state of social assistance reform in the provinces remains patchy, at best, there is a clear need for a systematic comparison of provincial social assistance systems, particularly as more than 15 years have passed since the publication of Gerard Boychuk's (1998) seminal book *Patchworks of Purpose*. This need is especially true because the federal government has not provided social assistance caseload data in a timely fashion since 1996 (Wood 2011). Moreover, the National Council of Welfare (NCW)—an independent body created in 1969 by the federal government to advise the Minister of Human Resources and Skills Development on issues of poverty and a precious source of comparable data on social assistance benefit levels in Canada—was dismantled by the Harper government in 2012. Although the Caledon Institute of Social Policy has recently revived this data source (see Tweddle, Battle, and Torjman 2013), the need for systematic knowledge about social assistance is stronger than ever, considering the ongoing talk about activation, social investment, and economic inequalities in Canada.

For precisely these reasons, we put together this edited volume, which is centred on detailed accounts of the state of social assistance in each province, accounts that do not lose sight of broad trends and cross-cutting issues. More broadly, throughout this volume, we address the following questions. In terms of ideas, institutions, and impacts, what are the broad trends that characterize the recent evolution of social assistance in Canada? Have policies and caseloads significantly changed over the last three decades and, if so, how? How can we assess the impact of the dismantlement of CAP on welfare reform in the provinces? Have provincial social assistance systems converged over the last three decades, and, if this is the case, do significant policy differences remain among the 10 provinces? Finally, how have welfare reforms in the provinces interacted with and affected issues such as gender, immigration, and income inequality? In order to address these issues and map the evolution of provincial social assistance in a systematic and coherent way, this volume is divided into three main parts.

The four chapters comprising Part I respectively offer international, historical, and quantitative perspectives on social assistance reform. In his chapter on international trends in welfare reform, Robert Henry Cox argues that a new, coherent vision of the welfare state has emerged in recent decades. According to him, this vision has clear consequences for social assistance while displaying a number of problematic blind spots that need to be addressed. In the following chapter, Gerard Boychuk takes an historical perspective on provincial social assistance in Canada, focusing primarily on the 1980s and, especially, the 1990s. One of the key lessons of his chapter is that we should not overemphasize the importance of changes in federal-provincial fiscal arrangements, such as the 1996 abolition of CAP, when we look at what remains a diverse provincial social assistance landscape, despite broad trends such as the clear rise of the social investment perspective, both at the federal and the provincial level. In their chapter, Ronald Kneebone and Katherine White offer a high-level, quantitative overview of provincial social assistance in Canada. One of their main findings is that, even when using a conservative—and controversial (see e.g., Williamson and Reutter 1999)—measure of poverty, such as the basic necessities model by Christopher Sarlo (2001), most provincial social assistance benefits in Canada fail to meet the "very basic needs" of recipients. Finally, in their chapter, Brian Murphy, Andrew Heisz, and Xuelin Zhang, offer a statistical overview of changing low-income and inequality trends in Canada over the last four decades. Their analysis shows a clear increase in income inequality while stressing the enduring role of social transfers, such as welfare benefits, in mitigating inequality and low-income incidence.

Part II is devoted to an in-depth analysis of the state of social assistance in the Canadian provinces. Each of these 10 case studies explores social assistance developments in a particular province, through a presentation of basic historical background, recent reforms, trends in caseload and benefit levels, and current issues and challenges. Part II features one chapter per province, starting with the four most populated provinces before moving to the six less populated ones and moving from the Prairies to Atlantic Canada: Ontario (Peter Graefe), Québec (Alain Noël), British Columbia (Jane Pulkingham), Alberta (Donna Wood), Saskatchewan (Rick August), Manitoba (Wayne Simpson), New Brunswick (Luc Thériault and Hélène LeBreton), Nova Scotia (Stella Lord), Newfoundland and Labrador (Matthieu Mondou), and Prince Edward Island (Kathleen Flanagan). Based on these 10 cases, which are assessed comparatively in the conclusion of this volume, we observe that similar trends are currently taking place across all or most provinces. These trends include the growing number of single individuals on welfare rolls and the enduring and frequently growing gap in benefit levels among categories of social assistance recipients. Despite these trends, differences exist among the provinces in crucial areas such as benefit levels and eligibility rules. From this angle, in the field of provincial social assistance, it is possible to talk of common trends but not of genuine and systematic convergence in policy rules and outcomes.

The seven chapters comprising Part III address key issues and clienteles of social assistance in the Canadian context: gender relations, disability, immigrants, Aboriginal peoples, seniors, housing and homelessness, and, finally, the impacts of activation programs. These chapters all offer important insight into social assistance by providing readers with different lenses through which provincial programs can be understood and assessed critically. In her chapter, Amber Gazso shows that social assistance intertwines ideas about gender with discursive shifts in entitlement to social assistance and new(er) rules of activation. She also establishes that welfare reform has gendered consequences. In the first of his two chapters, Michael Prince demonstrates that, in most provinces today, people with disabilities are the single largest category of clients within the social assistance caseload. As for Tracy Smith-Carrier and Jennifer Mitchell, in their chapter, focusing mainly on the Ontario case, they explore the fate of immigrants within provincial social assistance systems. In his contribution, Martin Papillon turns to the important issue of social assistance for Aboriginal peoples, focusing on First Nations living on reserves. He shows how the unique institutional configuration of social assistance on reserves, where benefits are delivered by the federal government according to *provincial* welfare rules, limits program adaptability and flexibility. In their chapter, Patrik Marier and Anne-Marie Séguin map the field of social assistance for seniors in the context of accelerated population aging. Their analysis focuses on provincial housing subsidies and pension top-ups for low-income seniors. In his second chapter, Michael Prince contends that social assistance policies have important implications for housing and homelessness, contributing to both the security and insecurity of shelter for many Canadians. Another important issue in social assistance policymaking is activation. In her contribution, Kelly Foley reviews the quantitative evidence derived from two major Canadian activation experiments: the Self-Sufficiency Project (SSP) and the Community Employment Innovation Project (CEIP). She shows that social assistance recipients are willing to choose work over welfare, if offered an income supplement, job search, and employment-support services or a job in a community project.

As suggested in this edited volume, the changes that affect social assistance are significant and consequential. This is why the following chapters offer nuanced and detailed perspectives on social assistance reform in the 10 Canadian provinces. By looking at each province while stressing the impact of broad issues such as aging, disability, immigration, gender, and the status of First Nations, this volume offers a unique assessment of the state of provincial social assistance in Canada, with a focus on changes that have been taking place since the 1990s.

References

Andersen, Robert, and Josh Curtis. 2013. "Public Opinion on Social Spending, 1980–2005." In *Inequality and the Fading of Redistributive Politics*, ed. by Keith G. Banting and John Myles, 141–64. Vancouver: UBC Press.

Bahle, Thomas, Vanessa Hubl, and Michaela Pfeifer. 2011. *The Last Safety Net: A Handbook of Minimum Income Protection in Europe*. Bristol, UK: The Policy Press.

Bane, Mary Jo, and David T. Ellwood. 1994. *Welfare Realities: From Rhetoric to Reform*. Cambridge, MA: Harvard University Press.

Banting, Keith. 2005. "Do We Know Where We Are Going? The New Social Policy in Canada." *Canadian Public Policy* 31 (4): 421–29.

Barbier, Jean-Claude, and Wolfgang Ludwig-Mayerhofer. 2004. "Introduction: The Many Worlds of Activation." *European Societies* 6 (4): 423–36.

Battle, Ken, and Michael Mendelson. 2001. "Benefits for Children: Canada." In *Benefits for Children: A Four Country Study*, ed. Ken Battle and Michael Mendelson, 93–186. Ottawa: Caledon Institute of Social Policy.

Béland, Daniel. 2005. "Ideas and Social Policy: An Institutionalist Perspective." *Social Policy & Administration* 39 (1): 1–18.

Béland, Daniel. 2010. *What Is Social Policy? Understanding the Welfare State*. Malden, MA: Polity Press.

Béland, Daniel, and Robert H. Cox, eds. 2011. *Ideas and Politics in Social Science Research*. Oxford: Oxford University Press.

Bemelmans-Videc, Marie-Louise, Ray C. Rist, and Evert Vedung, eds. 1998. *Carrots, Sticks and Sermons: Policy Instruments and Their Evaluation*. New Brunswick, NJ: Transaction Publishers.

Bernard, Paul, and Sébastien Saint-Arnaud. 2004. "Du pareil au même? La position des quatre principales provinces canadiennes dans l'univers des régimes providentiels." *The Canadian Journal of Sociology / Cahiers canadiens de sociologie* 29 (2): 209–39.

Boychuk, Gerard W. 1998. *Patchworks of Purpose: The Development of Provincial Social Assistance Regimes in Canada*. Montréal: McGill-Queen's University Press.

Boychuk, Gerard W. 2006. "Slouching Toward the Bottom? Social Assistance in the Canadian Provinces, 1980–2000." In *Racing to the Bottom? Provincial Interdependence in the Canadian Federation*, ed. Kathryn Harrison, 157–92. Vancouver: UBC Press.

Cox, Robert H. 1998. "The Consequences of Welfare Reform: How Conceptions of Social Rights Are Changing." *Journal of Social Policy* 27 (1): 1–16.

Crowley, Brian L. 2009. *Fearful Symmetry: The Fall and Rise of Canada's Founding Values*. Toronto: Key Porter.

Daigneault, Pierre-Marc. 2014. "Three Paradigms of Social Assistance." *Sage Open* 4 (4): 1–8. http://dx.doi.org/10.1177/2158244014559020.

Daigneault, Pierre-Marc. 2015. "Ideas and Welfare Reform in Saskatchewan: Entitlement, Workfare, or Activation?" *Canadian Journal of Political Science / Revue canadienne de science politique*. (Published online ahead of print, April.) http://dx.doi.org/10.1017/S0008423915000098.

Dostal, Jörg Michael. 2008. "The Workfare Illusion: Re-Examining the Concept and the British Case." *Social Policy & Administration* 42 (1): 19–42.

Dufour, Pascale, Gérard Boismenu, and Alain Noël. 2003. *L'aide au conditionnel: La contrepartie dans les mesures envers les personnes sans emploi en Europe et en Amérique du Nord*. Montréal: Les Presses de l'Université de Montréal/P.I.E.-Peter Lang.

Edwards, Rosalind, and Judith Glover, eds. 2001. *Risk and Citizenship: Key Issues in Welfare*. London: Routledge.

Eichhorst, Werner, and Regina Konle-Seidl. 2008. *Contingent Convergence: A Comparative Analysis of Activation Policies*. IZA Discussion Paper No. 3905. Bonn: Institute for the Study of Labor (IZA).

Esping-Andersen, Gøsta. 2002. "Towards the Good Society, Once Again?" In *Why We Need a New Welfare State*, ed. G. Esping-Andersen, 1–25. New York: Oxford University Press.

Gazso, Amber. 2007. "Balancing Expectations for Employability and Family Responsibilities while on Social Assistance: Low-Income Mothers' Experiences in Three Canadian Provinces." *Family Relations* 56 (5): 454–66.

Gazso, Amber, and Susan A. McDaniel. 2010. "The Risk of Being a Lone Mother on Income Support in Canada." *International Journal of Sociology and Social Policy* 30 (7/8): 368–86.

Giddens, Anthony. 1998. *The Third Way: The Renewal of Social Democracy*. Cambridge: Polity Press.

Haddow, Rodney. 2013. "Labour Market Income Transfers and Redistribution: National Themes and Provincial Variations." In *Inequality and the Fading of Redistributive Politics*, ed. Keith G. Banting and John Myles, 381–409. Vancouver: UBC Press.

Hansen, Hanne F., and Olaf Rieper. 2009. "The Evidence Movement: The Development and Consequences of Methodologies in Review Practices." *Evaluation* 15 (2): 141–63.

Harell, Allison, Stuart Soroka, and Adam Mahon. 2008. "Is Welfare a Dirty Word? Canadian Public Opinion on Social Assistance Policies." *Policy Options / Options politiques* 29 (8): 53–56.

Heinrich, Carolyn J. 2007. "Evidence-Based Policy and Performance Management." *The American Review of Public Administration* 37 (3): 255–77.

Hemerijck, Anton. 2002. "The Self-Transformation of the European Social Model(s)." In *Why We Need a New Welfare State*, ed. G. Esping-Andersen, 173–213. New York: Oxford University Press.

Herd, Dean, Andrew Mitchell, and Ernie Lightman. 2005. "Rituals of Degradation: Administration as Policy in the Ontario Works Programme." *Social Policy & Administration* 39 (1): 65–79.

Huo, Jingjing. 2009. *Third Way Reforms: Social Democracy after the Golden Age*. New York: Cambridge University Press.

Imbeau, Louis M., ed. 2009. *Do They Walk Like They Talk? Dissonance in Policy Processes*. New York: Springer.

Jenson, Jane. 2011. "Redesigning Citizenship Regimes after Neoliberalism. Moving Towards Social Investment." In *Towards a Social Investment Welfare State? Ideas, Policies and Challenges*, ed. Nathalie Morel, Bruno Palier, and Joakim Palme, 61–90. Bristol, UK: Policy Press.

Jenson, Jane, and Denis Saint-Martin. 2006. "Building Blocks for a New Social Architecture: The LEGO Paradigm of an Active Society." *Policy & Politics* 34 (3): 429–51.

Kenworthy, Lane. 1999. "Do Social-Welfare Policies Reduce Poverty? A Cross-National Assessment." *Social Forces* 77(3): 1119–39.

Kneebone, Ronald D., and Katherine White. 2014. *The Rise and Fall of Social Assistance Use in Canada, 1969–2012*. SSP Research Paper 7, no. 5. Calgary: School of Public Policy, University of Calgary.

Larsen, Christian A. 2008. "The Institutional Logic of Welfare Attitudes: How Welfare Regimes Influence Public Support." *Comparative Political Studies* 41 (2): 145–68. http://dx.doi.org/10.1177/0010414006295234.

Lasswell, Harold. 1936. *Politics: Who Gets What, When, How*. New York: Whittlesey House.

Learmonth, Mark, and Nancy Harding. 2006. "Evidence-Based Management: The Very Idea." *Public Administration* 84 (2): 245–66.

Levitas, Ruth. 2004. "Let's Hear It for Humpty: Social Exclusion, the Third Way and Cultural Capital." *Cultural Trends* 13 (2): 41–56. doi: 10.1080/0954896042000267143.

Mahon, Rianne. 2013. "Childcare, New Social Risks, and the New Politics of Redistribution in Ontario." In *Inequality and the Fading of Redistributive Politics*, ed. Keith G. Banting and John Myles, 359-80. Vancouver: UBC Press.

Marshall, Thomas H. (1950) 2009. "Citizenship and Social Class: Classical Works on Social Stratification and Inequality." In *Inequality and Society*, ed. Jeff Manza and Michael Sauder, 148–54. New York: W. W. Norton and Co.

McIntosh, Tom. 2004. "Intergovernmental Relations, Social Policy and Federal Transfers after Romanow." *Canadian Public Administration / Administration publique du Canada* 47 (1): 27–51.

Mead, Lawrence M. 1992. *The Nonworking Poor in America: The New Politics of Poverty*. New York: Basic Books.

Morel, Sylvie. 2002. *The Insertion Model or the Workfare Model? The Transformation of Social Assistance within Québec and Canada*. Research and publication funded by Status of Women Canada's Policy Research Fund. Available from Research Directorate Status of Women Canada, Ottawa.

Murray, Charles A. 1984. *Losing Ground: American Social Policy, 1950–1980*. New York: Basic Books.

Petticrew, Mark, and Helen Roberts. 2006. *Systematic Reviews in the Social Sciences: A Practical Guide*. Malden, MA: Blackwell.

Pierson, Paul. 1994. *Dismantling the Welfare State? Reagan, Thatcher, and the Politics of Retrenchment*. New York: Cambridge University Press.

Pierson, Paul. 1998. "Irresistible Forces, Immovable Objects: Post-Industrial Welfare States Confront Permanent Austerity." *Journal of European Public Policy* 5 (4): 539–60.

Polanyi, Karl. (1944) 2001. *The Great Transformation: The Political and Economic Origins of Our Time*. 2nd ed. Boston: Beacon Press.

Proulx, Christine, Samuel Faustmann, Hicham Raïq, and Axel van den Berg. 2011. "Internal Diversity in Social Policy Regimes: The Case of Canada's Four Major Provinces." In *Social Statistics, Poverty and Social Exclusion: Perspectives from Québec, Canada and Abroad*, ed. Guy Fréchet, Danielle Gauvreau, and Jean Poirier, 176–89. Montréal: Les Presses de l'Université de Montréal.

Québec. Centre d'étude sur la pauvreté et l'exclusion. 2014. *Synthèse—La pauvreté, les inégalités et l'exclusion sociale au Québec: État de situation 2013*. Québec: Ministère de l'Emploi et de la Solidarité sociale. http://www.cepe.gouv.qc.ca/publications/pdf/CEPE_Etat_Situation_Synthese_2013.pdf.

Rice, James J., and Michael J. Prince. 2013. *Changing Politics of Canadian Social Policy*. 2nd ed. Toronto: University of Toronto Press.

Sarlo, Christopher. 2001. *Measuring Poverty in Canada*. Critical Issues Bulletin. Vancouver: Fraser Institute.

Serrano Pascual, Amparo. 2004. "Are European Activation Policies Converging?" In *Labour and Employment Regulation in Europe*, ed. Jens Lind, Herman Knudsen, and Henning Jørgensen, 211–31. Brussels: P.I.E.-Peter Lang.

Somers, Margaret R., and Fred Block. 2005. "From Poverty to Perversity: Ideas, Markets, and Institutions over 200 Years of Welfare Debate." *American Sociological Review* 70 (2): 260–87.

Steensland, Brian. 2008. *The Failed Welfare Revolution: America's Struggle over Guaranteed Income Policy*. Princeton, NJ: Princeton University Press.

Stryker, Robin, and Pamela Wald. 2009. "Redefining Compassion to Reform Welfare: How Supporters of 1990s US Federal Welfare Reform Aimed for the Moral High Ground." *Social Politics: International Studies in Gender, State, and Society* 16 (4): 519–57.

Surender, Rebecca. 2004. "Modern Challenges to the Welfare State and Antecedents of the Third Way." In *Welfare State Change: Towards a Third Way?* ed. Jane Lewis and Rebecca Surender, 3–24. Oxford: Oxford University Press.

Taylor-Gooby, Peter. 2004. "New Risks and Social Change." In *New Risks, New Welfare? The Transformation of the European Welfare State*, ed. P. Taylor-Gooby, 1–28. Oxford: Oxford University Press.

Tweddle, Anne, Ken Battle, and Sherri Torjman. 2013. *Welfare in Canada 2012*. Ottawa: Caledon Institute of Social Policy. http://www.caledoninst.org/Publications/PDF/1031ENG.pdf.

van Berkel, Rik, and Vando Borghi. 2007. "Editorial: New Modes of Governance in Activation Policies." *International Journal of Sociology and Social Policy* 27 (7/8): 277–86.

van Berkel, Rik, and Iver H. Møller. 2002. *Active Social Policies in the EU: Inclusion through Participation?* Bristol, UK: Policy Press.

van Oorschot, Wim. 2006. "Making the Difference in Social Europe: Deservingness Perceptions among Citizens of European Welfare States." *Journal of European Social Policy* 16 (1): 23–42.

Williamson, Deanna L., and Linda Reutter. 1999. "Defining and Measuring Poverty: Implications for the Health of Canadians." *Health Promotion International* 14 (4): 355–64.

Wincott, Daniel. 2013. "The (Golden) Age of the Welfare State: Interrogating a Conventional Wisdom." *Public Administration* 91 (4): 806–22.

Wood, Donna E. 2011. *Using European Governance Ideas to Open up Canadian Federalism: The Case of Labour Market Policy*. Policy Brief. Ottawa: Canada-Europe Transatlantic Dialogue.

PART I

International, Comparative, and Multilevel Perspectives

one

International Trends in Social Assistance

ROBERT HENRY COX

Introduction

Welfare states around the world have undergone dramatic change in recent years. This is perhaps nowhere more visible than in the reforms that have been introduced into programs of social assistance. Despite the wide variety of programs and the unique pressures in different countries, we can identify a few recurrent themes in these reforms. At their most basic level, reforms represent a shift in emphasis from the alleviation of poverty toward more vigorous efforts to move recipients into paid employment.

This general trend demonstrates a third stage in the evolution of welfare states. The first stage, which we can date from the middle of the nineteenth century to the end of World War II, was characterized by the adoption of poor laws, or measures of last resort for the most destitute in society. The postwar period ushered in a second phase. This phase of welfare expansion was characterized by the designation of welfare assistance as an entitlement, guaranteed by the state and afforded to all citizens (Esping-Andersen 1996).[1] Today, two seemingly contradictory changes are underway. On the one hand, austerity has led many countries to cut back on spending for social assistance, pushing down levels of support and limiting the ability of these programs to alleviate poverty. On the other hand, many countries have increased spending in programs that provide targeted assistance rather than cash benefits (e.g., Cox 1998a; Dwyer 2004; Taylor-Gooby 2001; for examples in this volume, see chapters by Rick August, Wayne Simpson, and Matthieu Mondou). These trends appear less contradictory when we think of them as representing a repurposing of social programs so they serve a developmental purpose, helping to return people to a productive role in society, that is, paid employment (see Cox 1998b; Daigneault 2014).

This developmental phase of welfare states is guided by a few ideas that frame understandings of the policy problems and their likely solutions and,

1 Though the idea remains dominant that the postwar era was a golden age of welfare expansion, Daniel Wincott (2013) makes a persuasive case that welfare in this time was less expansive than many scholars believe.

in terms of specific programs, have their largest impact on social assistance. The majority of this chapter strives to outline these ideas and the policy innovations they have given rise to. Briefly, the ideas are balancing welfare rights and responsibilities, labour market activation, balancing work and welfare (flexicurity), and the notion of a "social investment state." Some of these ideas are used to legitimate austerity measures in social assistance. Others are used to legitimate new initiatives that represent the developmental components of welfare states. The purpose of this overview of trends is to outline what these new policy instruments are and how they represent a repurposing of the welfare state. The basic message here is that social welfare in the new millennium seeks to address the situation of the disadvantaged in society less by providing cash assistance to raise them out of poverty and more by expecting citizens to be proactive about ensuring their own welfare. As we shall see, the degree to which developmental objectives are achieved varies greatly.

The drivers of welfare reform

My contention is that this new vision of the welfare state has coherence and represents an adaptation of welfare states to contemporary reality. The need to adapt means, of course, that reality has changed, which in turn compels policymakers to reform welfare policies. The drivers of reform are the growing problem of program sustainability, the need to adjust welfare states to the demands of a technological and service economy, and the challenge of both a society that is more geographically mobile and ethnically diverse and one in which the traditional family unit is not the basic economic foundation for most households.

Concerns over the sustainability of welfare systems are perhaps the most prominent. The "greying" of society, a trend happening in most advanced industrialized nations, is one aspect of the sustainability problem. The growth in the retired population is driven by two factors. First, the retired population is living longer in retirement, thereby placing demands on pension and health systems that those systems were not designed to accommodate. Second, many industrialized societies have experienced a decline in their birth rates, leading to fewer people entering the workforce at the same time as so many are in retirement. Within the European Union, for example, the ratio of retired to working persons is expected to rise from 26 per cent in 2010 to 50 per cent in 2050 (European Commission 2009).

The transition from an industrial to a knowledge economy is also driving changes to welfare states. During the golden age of welfare states, education was intended to train someone early in life for a career they would practice until retirement, often with the same employer. Today, old jobs are disappearing from the economy at an alarming rate, and new jobs require greater technological skills. Indeed, many workers today are holding jobs in sectors of the economy that did not exist when they were students. In addition, today's workers are likely to change employers, even careers, several times over their working life. Preparing students for jobs that do not exist and for unpredictable career paths places a heavy burden on education.

Globalization has ushered in an unprecedented degree of mobility. Refugees, as well as economic migrants, comprise a larger share of society in many Western countries. Although labour mobility often brings great economic benefits to those who move for a job, as well as to the economy of the country where they are employed, it often brings another form of social exclusion to the welfare system. Unskilled migrants, especially if they do not speak the language of their host country, are at greatest risk to be unemployed or underemployed. Many of these immigrants suffer the classic first generation problems of poor language skills, placement in jobs that are below their skill level, and even outright discrimination.

By the second generation, however, living and attending school in the country often gives the children of immigrants a better ability to function in society. Though they might still face racial discrimination, usually their circumstances improve. Recently, however, some have noticed a "perpetual first generation problem" among immigrants, especially among Turkish and Moroccan immigrants in Europe, who comprise a large portion of the immigrant population in many European countries. The problem arises when the children of immigrants marry someone from their parents' country of origin. If they also raise their children in an exclusively Turkish- or Arabic-speaking house and neighbourhood, their children might grow up no more assimilated into the European society than were the parents. Such non-EU immigrants have more difficulty finding jobs. In Belgium, more than in any other EU country, children of immigrants are more likely to live in a household where neither parent works (Platonova 2013).

Ethnic minorities within a country, especially those whose host nation has a history of discrimination, often face a form of welfare exclusion similar to that faced by foreign workers. Both in Canada and the United States, Native Americans, or First Nations, suffer the same problems of higher poverty, higher unemployment, and social exclusion that other sectors of the population face (see Papillon, in this volume). The financial and social pressures to assimilate immigrants and to help both immigrants and citizens with minority ethnic backgrounds participate fully are forcing reformers to do more than simply provide benefits to those with identifiable needs.

These excluded groups also need services that help them to realize their full potential as citizens and residents.

Finally, changing family dynamics are placing great pressure on welfare states. Fewer households fit the traditional pattern that includes one income earner, one provider of care within the household, and dependent children and grandparents. Today's traditional households are more likely to have two income earners, creating greater pressures on the provision of care within the household. Also, the traditional household itself is disappearing as more households are headed by a lone parent. These trends have forced reformers to consider the gendered character of welfare programs. Yet many observers of these programs have noticed that reformers fail to notice how responsibilities to care for others fall more heavily on women than on men (Kan, Sullivan, and Gershuny 2011; Sainsbury 1996; see also Gazso, in this volume). Consequently, many reforms, such as the requirement to seek work, are more easily met by men than by women, who are the major caregivers in their households. Some countries have sought to balance the gendered impact of welfare programs; others have adopted reforms that only exacerbate the differences.

Welfare systems that operate on principles of gender-blind equality often have higher incidences of women-headed households in poverty. Indeed, the best way to raise children out of poverty appears to be for a family to have both parents earning an income. However, in many countries, the rules for how household income is calculated often provide a disincentive for the mother to seek paid employment (Bäckman and Ferrarini 2010), with the result that the welfare benefit works contrary to the notion of welfare activation. As several of the contributors to this volume note (see especially Gazso), reforms in Canadian social assistance have often failed to take full account of the implications for women.

Balancing rights and responsibilities

The most prominent reform in social assistance evolved from a critique of the way social citizenship was extended during the age of welfare expansion. Beginning in the 1960s, reformers in many countries strove to establish social assistance as a right of citizenship (e.g., Daigneault 2014; Huo 2009; White 2004). By establishing a right to social assistance, reformers sought simultaneously to remove both the stigma that has been associated with charity aid and the discretion that allowed different levels of support to go to the "deserving" and not the "undeserving" poor. Though generally considered a progressive advancement, the right to social assistance soon came under criticism because of two unforeseen consequences.

First, cash transfers were widely adopted as the mechanism for distributing social assistance. This manner of delivering assistance was criticized for putting the state in a "passive" role. By simply awarding cash, the state was unable to ensure that the assistance actually helped poor people (Cox 1998b; Dwyer 2004). Indeed, this broader criticism had two distinct strands. The first was a complaint that cash transfers allowed people to make inappropriate choices. In the United States, popular media was filled with images of "welfare queens" who drove to the social assistance office in their Cadillac automobiles (Cassiman 2007). In Europe, more compassionate discussions focused on "social exclusion" as a consequence of welfare passivity. The term originated in France (Béland and Hansen 2000) and identified an unintended consequence of the system of cash transfers. Though benefits were designed to provide a sufficient level of existence, social workers discovered that many people receiving benefits still were unable to participate fully in society. Many suffered from substance abuse or depression. Cash transfers enabled these perverse effects and did little to give help where people needed it.

Despite these distinct differences in tone, American and European critiques generally agreed that, in establishing rights to welfare assistance, reformers had not paid enough attention to the responsibilities that balance those rights. Depending on the political tone of the criticism, some argued that those who received social assistance needed to accept more responsibility. Others argued that the state had responsibility for the well-being of citizens that went beyond simply providing cash benefits. This debate resulted in two types of changes to social assistance. One type of reform strove to place more responsibility on the recipient by imposing limits on how long one could receive benefits, lowering the levels of benefits, and stiffening the requirements to seek work. The first and most prominent example was the American Personal Responsibility and Work Opportunity Act, passed in 1996 and popularly known as "Welfare to Work." The law was quickly emulated in several other countries, most notably Britain (O'Connor 2004).

The other thrust of reform added responsibilities to the state to make sure those in need were given the resources that could help them become independent of social assistance. Countries that have followed this approach have expanded programs such as job counselling and assistance with household budgeting. Two of the early leaders in this reform were Denmark and the Netherlands (Green-Pedersen 2001). Indeed, many of these new programs intervene quite substantially in people's lives. Assistance with household budgeting, for example, might require people to allow a social worker to scrutinize their finances or force welfare clients to change spending habits. Welfare assistance during the "golden age" was based on the belief that individuals in a liberal society are morally autonomous. The state's role was to provide them the resources to be independent, not to instruct them on how to live their own lives. The new attitude, by contrast, suspends the principle of individual autonomy and empowers public officials to intervene in the best interests of the welfare client. Moreover, both forms of state intervention reflect, in a fundamental way, a specific sense of what it means to be a good citizen. These changes in systems of cash transfers might be motivated by outrage as well as compassion, but, in either case, they called for more active state involvement to help the person on assistance.

Activation

Activation is a shorthand term for "active labour market policies," or policies designed to move able-bodied people back into the labour force (Barbier 2004; Barbier and Ludwig-Mayerhofer 2004). The appearance of active labour market policies coincided with the general critique of passive welfare assistance, and stemmed from a similar concern. Basically, in the area of employment, unemployment assistance had come to be treated like another passive form of welfare assistance. Though most countries require that those receiving unemployment benefits also be "actively seeking work," beginning with the expansion of welfare states in the 1970s, many governments stopped enforcing these requirements, with the result that, in many European countries, unemployment benefits could last for several years. Efforts to reform unemployment assistance followed a path similar to that taken by the reformers of social assistance: reductions in the generosity of benefits and stronger incentives and penalties designed to get people back into the workforce. Moreover, as in social assistance, the responsibilities for moving people back into the workforce have been taken on by the state as well as individuals (Ferrera, Hemerijck, and Rhodes 2001).

Reductions in unemployment benefits have been designed to provide strong incentives for people to return to work. Whereas, in an earlier time, relaxing the requirements to seek work was intended to protect the unemployed from the stigma of being on social assistance, today, more countries are limiting the time one can receive benefits and more quickly moving the long-term unemployed onto social assistance. In return, however, they are expanding opportunities for job counselling and occupational retraining (OECD 2007). Thus, as is the case with reforms to social assistance benefits, the changes in unemployment benefits are intended to encourage citizens as well as states to be proactive.

Indeed, what is novel about the notion of activation is that the term applies in equal measure to the unemployed and those receiving social assistance. In many countries, the enhanced work- and job-training requirements apply equally to both groups, and the distinction based on the origins of one's need for assistance is breaking down. The aim today is to ensure that all those of working age who are able to work do so. Activation programs in countries such as Denmark, Sweden, and Germany are now designed to help people whose jobs have been replaced by technology learn the skills for a new job, help mothers whose children are in school enter the workforce for the first time, and even place disabled individuals in jobs suited to their abilities.

Activation programs vary across countries, and, to a large degree, these variations correspond to cross-national differences in type of welfare state (Carcillo and Grubb 2006; Lødemel and Trickey 2001; Serrano Pascual 2007). In Scandinavia, for example, where there are long traditions of state-sponsored job training and placement, activation programs have been competently staffed and are viewed with high regard. In countries with laissez-faire labour market traditions, such as the United States and the United Kingdom, activation programs have been seen as make-work programs; often the training is poor or badly matched to the needs of employers. In a study that asked British and Danish employers how valuable they found the activation programs in their countries, Cathie Jo Martin and Duane Swank (2004) found that Danish employers valued their participation in the programs and preferred to hire workers who had been "activated" through a public program. British employers, on the other hand, viewed these programs as a waste of their time because the workers who came out of the training still lacked the skills they needed. As a consequence, British employers either avoided the activation schemes entirely or participated because they thought doing so would help them to curry favour with government officials.

Decentralization is an important characteristic of the administration of activation programs. Traditional social assistance was characterized by universal entitlements that applied equally to all citizens (Béland and Lecours 2007; Minas, Wright, and van Berkel 2012; Scott and Wright 2012). In many countries, benefit levels were calculated based on formulas established by central authorities. For activation programs to work effectively, however, local authorities need a greater degree of authority and discretion. On the one hand, local control empowers local officials to establish agreements with welfare clients that are suited to their own skills and training needs. On the other hand, local control allows these officials to match their training programs to the needs of local employers and to negotiate labour contracts with those employers and their clientele. This local orientation is a good example of the trend in welfare states to decentralize control and adjust assistance to individual needs (Minas, Wright, and van Berkel 2012).

Flexicurity

In the early 1990s, a Danish government coined the term "flexicurity." The term quickly became a catchphrase for efforts to adapt social security, especially pension systems, to the new changes in social assistance and to active labour market policies. From the perspective of the Danish government, flexicurity represented a combination of a strong safety net, a flexible labour market, and an active citizenry. In concrete terms, this approach meant a series of labour market reforms designed to allow more part-time opportunities and make it easier for employers to expand or reduce their labour force. In return, the strong system of social support would soften the adverse effects on peoples' incomes. Finally, several new programs for retraining and skill development would allow people to remain active and able to move back into the labour market, rather than simply exiting out because their skills were not in demand.

Outside of Denmark, especially in countries with Christian democratic welfare states, this vision proved attractive but difficult to implement. The problem in countries such as the Netherlands, Belgium, and Germany was that their social security systems had been built on the "breadwinner" principle (Sainsbury 1996). This principle assumed that the basic social unit was a family with a man working outside the home. The male breadwinner needed a guarantee of full-time employment that provided enough compensation for him to support his entire family. Moreover, because the family was dependent on his income, his insurance needed to provide a high level of income replacement in the event he became injured, unemployed, or otherwise unable to provide for the family.

The breadwinner principle was the basis for highly regulated labour markets, but it proved difficult to reconcile with the changes in unemployment and social assistance, as well as outdated in the face of significant social change. The breadwinner model, which provided generous benefits in return for a lifetime of full-time work, was not able to easily accommodate people who were returning to work after long periods of unemployment or women who wished to take on part-time work so that they could better balance work and family duties. In addition, an uncertain economic climate made employers less willing to hire new workers into full-time and lifelong jobs. Flexicurity reforms allowed individuals working part time to enroll in social security programs. These reforms were expected to improve the incomes of pensioners, as, in most countries, pensions were more generous than public assistance benefits (Madsen 2004).

Flexicurity reforms also signal another important change in welfare states. By trying to make public assistance, activation schemes, and pensions all work more seamlessly together, flexicurity reforms also help to make different programs work more effectively with one another and to reduce administrative duplication. Similar efforts to create a more efficient welfare administration were also popular in the UK, where they were part of the notion of "joined up government" (Hood 2005). Better coordination across programs has allowed for more efficient service delivery and greater degrees of satisfaction, both among welfare clients and social workers. A related administrative reform, which also illustrates the potential for better program management at the local level, is the idea of a one-stop shop. This administrative reform swept through Western countries in the early 2000s, primarily at the municipal level. The idea was to create a first point of contact where citizens could learn about all the offices they needed to visit. This arrangement was a great improvement over the old system of individual offices, not clearly coordinated, which forced an applicant, for example, to visit different agencies to apply for housing, health care, and income assistance. In many countries, such reforms led to increases in take-up rates for programs because the simple and user-friendly systems no longer discouraged clients from seeking assistance (Daigneault, Jacob, and Tereraho 2012). In some cases, one-stop innovations involved the creation of a single application that would free an individual from repeating the same information at each office. The increased use of technology has facilitated this sharing. Indeed, technology has made flexicurity easier to manage in an age when the model of lifetime employment is disappearing and increasing numbers of workers have several employers over the course of their careers.

It should be noted that flexicurity has been least relevant in those countries that had either weakly regulated labour markets or residual models of welfare support. But, in the countries that have implemented flexicurity reforms, people with irregular working profiles can still enjoy basic levels of security, and people can interrupt their work histories to attend to family emergencies.

The social investment state

The "social investment state" (Jenson and Saint-Martin 2003) is a term designed to evoke movement away from the old idea of a social security state. The idea of social security arose during the golden age of welfare expansion and denoted a state that provided protection against the vagaries of market forces. Social security provided income support for people who fell outside the labour market due to such social and occupational risks as unemployment, disability, and old age.

Instead, the social investment state treats its human capital (i.e., citizens) as valuable resources to be developed both inside and outside the labour market. At the centre of the social investment state are social services, especially education. Indeed, what sets apart the social investment state is a vastly expanded array of social services, such as day care, occupational retraining, and in-home elder care.

This array of services does two things that the benefit-based social security state did not. First, to help people focus on the ways they can be active citizens, it provides assistance sensitive to those issues that usually cause people to leave the workforce. Sometimes known as "new social risks," the new threats to people's well-being include inadequate care for children and elderly family members, the growing need for households to have two incomes, and the disappearance of jobs for people who have skills suited to an industrial rather than a technological economy (see, e.g., Taylor-Gooby 2005). Second, this emphasis on activation is concerned with more than economic productivity; it is also concerned with each citizen's dignity. In-home care for the elderly is a good example. The services themselves provide a great deal of employment that otherwise (and in many other countries) is absorbed by the household.

The social investment state also follows logically from the move away from welfare passivity. In this formulation, the poor are not a disadvantaged group in need of care; rather, they are undercapitalized resources that need investment from the state to raise them to their potential. The social investment state places a strong emphasis on the development of skills, and welfare states that focus on skill development do not simply distribute benefits but also provide a large array of services.

In terms of education, the social investment state marks a new vision for the role of education, often called "lifelong learning." Lifelong learning is based on the idea that formal education and training should not end when one enters the workforce; it assumes that people will occasionally exit the workforce to undergo retraining, either for a new career or to refresh skills in their current job. To enable lifelong learning, the state needs to build education and training into the expectations of the welfare system.

Sweden has long been one of the world's leaders in using education in support of its welfare state by sponsoring an extensive system of retraining programs that help unemployed people prepare for new careers. For many people, this educational initiative makes Sweden the best example of a social investment state. In Sweden, the investment in citizens is not simply a form of commodification of human capital. Instead, investing in citizens helps to ensure the dignity of each citizen (Andersson 2006). The wide array of social services that comprise the social investment state include some programs that help people stay in the workforce, to be sure. Retraining programs move the unemployed into jobs, and childcare programs make it easier for mothers to work. But the programs that comprise the social investment state also work to combat social exclusion. For example, programs that allow the elderly to remain in their homes rather than move to nursing communities may not make them productive workers, but such schemes do help to protect the dignity of citizens.

Conclusion

Recent reforms to social assistance represent a repurposing of welfare states. The changes are designed to adapt and adjust welfare policies to the demands of a technological and service economy, to a more geographically mobile and ethnically diverse society, and to a transformed family structure, one that no longer has at its centre one breadwinner supporting multiple generations. As reforms have been designed to respond to the new pressures, people are also rethinking the way they understand the purpose of the welfare state. I argued in this chapter that four new ideas are at the centre of this reconstruction of welfare states; balancing rights and responsibilities, labour market activation, flexicurity, and the social investment state. To conclude, I would like to offer three observations about these new ideas—ideas that give welfare states a developmental purpose, by which I mean that these states strive to improve the conditions for people to contribute in a positive way to society. First, the shift in the normative foundations cuts across political ideologies in ways that the old notions of the welfare state did not. The emphasis on work and the criticisms of passivity, for example, are shared by the left and the right. And, though this shift occurs across the political spectrum, there are differences in ideological emphasis. Generally, actors on the ideological left articulate a broader conception of rights, not simply rights to assistance but also rights that uphold the dignity of citizens. Actors on the ideological right, by contrast, tend to emphasize the responsibilities of individuals, stressing the punitive consequences of failing to meet those responsibilities. Yet, despite the different orientations of these actors, the debate about rights indicates a new belief that, for social rights to be fully realized, citizens must actively engage in society through work and education.

The second major change is a trend to integrate disparate programs and make them work more effectively together. In some instances, integration aims to break down the stigma associated with some forms of support, such as when social assistance recipients are treated like the unemployed for retraining and work. Sometimes the trend is expressed as an administrative imperative to make government services operate more purposefully. National standards once ensured that citizens would be treated equally according to uniform rules. Decentralization, however, allows local officials to exercise more discretion, to tailor assistance more specifically to the individual needs of clients. The developmental purpose here is clear; public officials have obligations to their fellow citizens, not only to process their claims but also to think broadly and comprehensively about how each person can play a meaningful role in society.

Finally, the reforms of welfare states still exhibit surprising blind spots in how effectively they recognize the special challenges that affect women or ethnic minorities and immigrants. Because these problems seem to persist over time, programmatic adjustments may have little effect, and a more fundamental change in social attitudes might be needed to bring about recognition for the way some groups in society continue to be treated differently. Social assistance is at the centre of a growing irredentist sentiment sweeping many Western countries.

Some critics of activation programs have argued that they were designed to satisfy a neoliberal agenda and erode the social rights of citizenship that are central to welfare states. To be sure, activation programs are favoured by neoliberals who generally place stronger emphasis on the responsibilities and not the rights of citizens. However, activation programs were a key feature of welfare reforms undertaken by two moderate left-leaning governments: Bill Clinton's "Welfare to Work" in the United States and Tony Blair's "Workfare" in the United Kingdom. Moreover, in many Scandinavian countries, particularly Denmark, activation has been undertaken vigorously by social democratic governments motivated by a concern with the negative consequences of social exclusion. One could say that activation programs represent a repurposing of welfare states in a way that depoliticizes the programs, making them appeal to people from across the political spectrum.

The aim of this repurposing is to adapt welfare systems to the demands of a more globalized and competitive world. Yet the reforms do not happen willy-nilly. Policymakers need to provide justifications for the reforms, and citizens need to believe that these changes establish or uphold a coherent system. The repurposing is as much a battle of ideas as it is of responding to real pressures. Changing the way people think about their welfare state also changes the way they behave. Thus, as policymakers make changes, they are simultaneously changing their citizens' expectations about what their governments can provide, and what individuals need to provide for themselves.

We might ask if these changes are good or bad. This chapter has sought to make sense of the observable trends and to argue that people—policymakers and the public—are reconsidering what the welfare state means in light of these policy changes. People desire to have cognitive frames that fit their empirical realities, and, as welfare programs change over time, we alter our understanding of what they mean. The question of whether the new notions of the welfare state are good or bad likewise depends on these normative frames and on the empirical realities to which they refer. In some countries, the United States in particular, the changes barely hide a rather severe conception of what society owes to those with the least advantages. In northern European countries, by contrast, the reforms have a pragmatic theme and represent an adaptation to growing fiscal and demographic constraints. Moreover, within each country, the reforms and what they mean are constantly being contested by people who argue that some types of reforms would be good and others bad. Politics is the struggle to achieve outcomes that people believe are better than the alternatives.

References

Andersson, Jenny. 2006. "The People's Library and the Electronic Workshop: Comparing Swedish and British Social Democracy." *Politics & Society* 34 (3): 431–60. http://dx.doi.org/10.1177/0032329206290472.

Bäckman, Olof, and Tommy Ferrarini. 2010. "Combating Child Poverty? A Multilevel Assessment of Family Policy Institutions and Child Poverty in 21 Old and New Welfare States." *Journal of Social Policy* 39 (2): 275–96. http://dx.doi.org/10.1017/S0047279409990456.

Barbier, Jean-Claude. 2004. "Systems of Social Protection in Europe: Two Contrasted Paths to Activation, and Maybe a Third." In *Labour and Employment Regulation in Europe*, ed. Jens Lind, Herman Knudsen, and Henning Jørgensen, 233–53. Brussels: Peter Lang.

Barbier, Jean-Claude, and Wolfgang Ludwig-Mayerhofer. 2004. "Introduction: The Many Worlds of Activation." *European Societies* 6 (4): 423–36. http://dx.doi.org/10.1080/1461669042000275845.

Béland, Daniel, and Randall Hansen. 2000. "Reforming the French Welfare State: Solidarity, Social Exclusion and the Three Crises of Citizenship." *West European Politics* 23 (1): 47–64. http://dx.doi.org/10.1080/01402380008425351.

Béland, Daniel, and André Lecours. 2007. "Federalism, Nationalism, and Social Policy Decentralisation in Canada and Belgium." *Regional & Federal Studies* 17 (4): 405–19. http://dx.doi.org/10.1080/13597560701712643.

Carcillo, Stéphane, and David Grubb. 2006. *From Inactivity to Work: The Role of Active Labour Market Policies*. OECD Social, Employment, and Migration Working Papers, No. 36. Paris: OECD.

Cassiman, Shawn A. 2007. "Of Witches, Welfare Queens, and the Disaster Named Poverty: The Search for a Counter-Narrative." *Journal of Poverty* 10 (4): 51–66. http://dx.doi.org/10.1300/J134v10n04_03.

Cox, Robert Henry. 1998a. "The Consequences of Welfare Reform: How Conceptions of Social Rights Are Changing." *Journal of Social Policy* 27 (1): 1–16. http://dx.doi.org/10.1017/S0047279497005163.

Cox, Robert Henry. 1998b. "From Safety Net to Trampoline: Labor Market Activation in the Netherlands and Denmark." *Governance: An International Journal of Policy, Administration, and Institutions* 11 (4): 397–414. http://dx.doi.org/10.1111/0952-1895.00079.

Daigneault, Pierre-Marc. 2014. "Three Paradigms of Social Assistance." *Sage Open* 4 (4): 1–8. http://dx.doi.org/10.1177/2158244014559020.

Daigneault, Pierre-Marc, Steve Jacob, and Maximilien Tereraho. 2012. "Understanding and Improving the Take-Up of Public Programs: Lessons Learned from the Canadian and International Experience in Human Services." *International Journal of Business and Social Science* 3 (1): 39–50. http://www.ijbssnet.com/journals/Vol_3_No_1_January_2012/5.pdf.

Dwyer, Peter. 2004. "Creeping Conditionality in the UK: From Welfare Rights to Conditional Entitlements?" *Canadian Journal of Sociology* 29 (2): 265–87. http://dx.doi.org/10.2307/3654696.

Esping-Andersen, Gøsta. 1996. "After the Golden Age? Welfare State Dilemmas in a Global Economy." In *Welfare States in Transition: National Adaptations in Global Economies*, ed. Gøsta Esping-Andersen, 1–31. New York: Russell Sage Foundation. http://dx.doi.org/10.4135/9781446216941.n1.

European Commission. 2009. *The 2009 Ageing Report: Economic and Budgetary Projections for the EU-27 Member States (2008–2060)*. Luxembourg: Office for Official Publications of the European Communities.

Ferrera, Maurizio, Anton Hemerijck, and Martin Rhodes. 2001. "The Future of the European 'Social Model' in the Global Economy." *Journal of Comparative Policy Analysis: Research and Practice* 3 (2): 163–90. http://dx.doi.org/10.1080/13876980108412659.

Green-Pedersen, Christoffer. 2001. "Welfare-State Retrenchment in Denmark and the Netherlands, 1982–1998: The Role of Party Competition and Party Consensus." *Comparative Political Studies* 34 (9): 963–85. http://dx.doi.org/10.1177/0010414001034009001.

Hood, Christopher. 2005. "The Idea of Joined-Up Government: An Historical Perspective." In *Joined-Up Government*, ed. Vernon Bogdanor, 19–42. Oxford: Oxford University Press. http://dx.doi.org/10.5871/bacad/9780197263334.003.0002.

Huo, Jingjing. 2009. *Third Way Reforms: Social Democracy after the Golden Age*. Cambridge: Cambridge University Press. http://dx.doi.org/10.1017/CBO9780511581045.

Jenson, Jane, and Denis Saint-Martin. 2003. "New Routes to Social Cohesion? Citizenship and the Social Investment State." *Canadian Journal of Sociology* 28 (1): 77–99. http://dx.doi.org/10.2307/3341876.

Kan, Man Ye, Oriel Sullivan, and Jonathan Gershuny. 2011. "Gender Convergence in Domestic Work: Discerning the Effects of Interactional and Institutional Barriers from Large-Scale Data." *Sociology* 45 (2): 234–51. http://dx.doi.org/10.1177/0038038510394014.

Lødemel, Ivar, and Heather Trickey, eds. 2001. *"An Offer You Can't Refuse": Workfare in International Perspective*. Bristol, UK: Policy Press. http://dx.doi.org/10.1332/policypress/9781861341952.001.0001.

Madsen, Per Kongshøj. 2004. "The Danish Model of Flexicurity: Experiences and Lessons." *European Review of Labour and Research* 10 (2): 187–207.

Martin, Cathie Jo, and Duane Swank. 2004. "Does the Organization of Capital Matter? Employers and Active Labor Market Policy at the National and Firm Levels." *American Political Science Review* 98 (4): 593–611. http://dx.doi.org/10.1017/S0003055404041371.

Minas, Renate, Sharon Wright, and Rik van Berkel. 2012. "Decentralization and Centralization: Governing the Activation of Social Assistance Recipients in Europe." *International Journal of Sociology and Social Policy* 32 (5/6): 286–98. http://dx.doi.org/10.1108/01443331211236989.

O'Connor, Brendon. 2004. *A Political History of the American Welfare System: When Ideas Have Consequences*. Lanham, MD: Rowman and Littlefield Publishers.

OECD (Organisation for Economic Co-operation and Development). 2007. "Activating the Unemployed: What Countries Do." In *OECD Employment Outlook, 2007*, ed. Raymond Torres, 207–42. Paris: OECD.

Pearson, Noel. 2000. "Passive Welfare and the Destruction of Indigenous Society in Australia." In *Reforming the Australian Welfare State*, ed. Peter Saunders, 136–55. Melbourne: Australian Institute of Family Studies.

Platonova, Anna. 2013. *Labour Market Integration of Immigrants in the EU: Key Trends and Policy Issues*. Brussels: Itinera Institute. Accessed January 10, 2015. http://www.itinerainstitute.org/sites/default/files/articles/pdf/20130312discussion_paper_platonova_eng.pdf.

Sainsbury, Diane. 1996. *Gender, Equality and Welfare States*. Cambridge: Cambridge University Press. http://dx.doi.org/10.1017/CBO9780511520921.

Scott, Gill, and Sharon Wright. 2012. "Devolution, Social Democratic Visions and Policy Reality in Scotland." *Critical Social Policy* 32 (3): 440–53. http://dx.doi.org/10.1177/0261018312444420.

Serrano Pascual, Amparo. 2007. "Reshaping Welfare States: Activation Regimes in Europe." In *Reshaping Welfare States and Activation Regimes in Europe*, ed. Amparo Serrano Pascual and Lars Magnusson, 11–34. Brussels: P.I.E.-Peter Lang.

Taylor-Gooby, Peter. 2001. "Sustaining State Welfare in Hard Times: Who Will Foot the Bill?" *Journal of European Social Policy* 11 (2): 133–47. http://dx.doi.org/10.1177/095892870101100203.

Taylor-Gooby, Peter, ed. 2005. *Ideas and Welfare State Reform in Western Europe*. Basingstoke, UK: Palgrave/Macmillan.

White, Stuart. 2004. "Welfare Philosophy and the Third Way." In *Welfare State Change: Towards a Third Way?*, ed. Jane Lewis and Rebecca Surender, 25–46. New York: Oxford University Press.

Wincott, Daniel. 2013. "The (Golden) Age of the Welfare State: Interrogating a Conventional Wisdom." *Public Administration* 91 (4): 806–22. http://dx.doi.org/10.1111/j.1467-9299.2012.02067.x.

two

Federal Policies, National Trends, and Provincial Systems: A Comparative Analysis of Recent Developments in Social Assistance in Canada, 1990–2013

GERARD W. BOYCHUK

Sketching developments in social assistance policy in Canada in broad brushstrokes on a national canvas inevitably collides with an inescapable reality—social assistance in Canada is predominantly a provincial and territorial responsibility. There are 13 distinct social assistance regimes in Canada rather than one single national system. National trends in social assistance can only be adequately understood as the culmination of developments within individual provinces, and overemphasizing the effects of either federal policy or national trends in policy discourse often obscures this reality.

First, the most interesting questions relating to social assistance in Canada are to be found not in examinations of broad national trends but, rather, among instances of provincial divergence from them. To a significant degree, broad national trends in indicators of social assistance provision (e.g., recipiency rates, overall expenditure levels) are, as this chapter argues, primarily driven by changes in economic conditions. As such, instances of provincial divergence only become evident by isolating, to the degree possible, policy effects from the effects of shifting economic conditions. Second, effects of federal policies in this area have been multiple and complex, variable across provinces, and contingent on the interaction of these policies with other policy dynamics at both levels. Finally, while new policy ideas—including, most notably, the social investment perspective—have emerged to challenge the pre-existing concepts on which provincial social assistance systems were variously based, cross-provincial consensus on these ideas has not clearly emerged and important differences between provinces in these regards remain.

The Canada Assistance Plan—initiation and dismantling

Provincial social assistance in Canada is conventionally seen as largely shaped, until the mid-1990s, by the Canada Assistance Plan (CAP; for an overview, see Rice and Prince 2013). Instituted in 1966, CAP consolidated various cost-sharing programs for categorical assistance under one umbrella program (see Figure 2.1). Under CAP, the federal government would continue to match on a dollar-for-dollar basis funds expended by provinces under existing categorical programs, including programs for blind, disabled, and aged persons. Federal cost sharing would also now be extended to existing provincial assistance programs for needy mothers and widows, programs that had developed over the past 50 years in all provinces but whose costs were not previously shared (see Figure 2.1). It would extend federal cost sharing as well to various welfare services, including day care, employment services (e.g., job search, employability enhancement, and training services), and health care. Federal policymakers explicitly recognized that CAP was essentially directing funds to provincially funded programs already in place though they "hoped" that provinces would use the additional funds to improve programs (Boychuk 1998, 46). Federal policymakers also strongly believed in flexibility as an end in itself, and the three substantive conditions of CAP are clearly reflective of this federal predisposition.

First was the needs-test requirement. Provinces had the latitude to define the categories of eligibility (age, disability, inability to find employment) and to determine whether recipients were genuinely unable to find employment. For applicants meeting these categorical eligibility criteria (e.g., job search tests), provinces would then apply a budgetary eligibility test based on provincially defined standards and maximum levels of

Figure 2.1 Federal Interventions in Social Assistance, 1950–2005

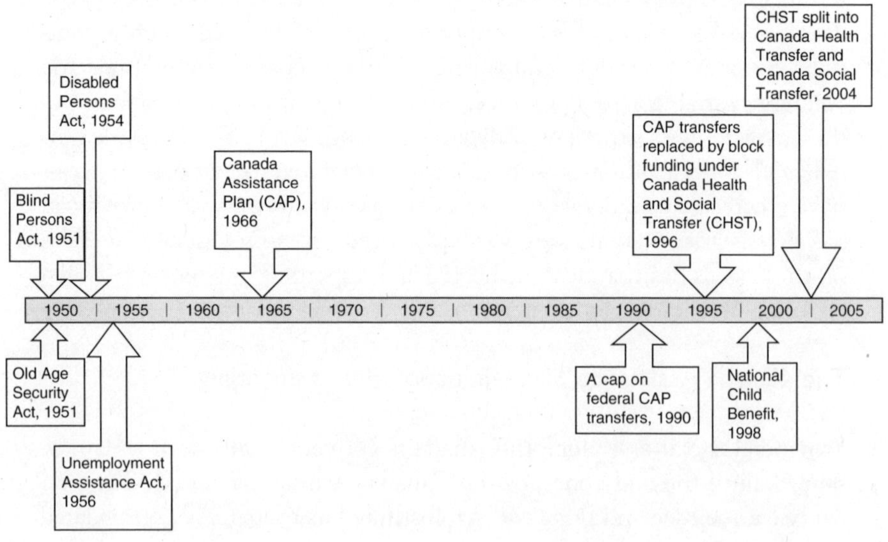

benefits. Both budgetary eligibility and the level of benefits to be provided had to be tested by applicant need—taking into account an individual applicant's basic budgetary *needs* and not only his or her *income* but also *other resources*, including assets or external support. If an applicant met both requirements, the province could not deny benefits on some other arbitrary grounds. Thus, provinces retained very wide latitude in determining the categories and broad circumstances of applicants to whom they provided assistance. On the other hand, this requirement clearly precluded federal cost sharing for broad-based, income-tested benefits targeted to people with low incomes (as eligible programs were required to incorporate an individual needs test rather than a simple income test) and benefits could not be at a flat rate (i.e., provided without consideration of individual needs and personal resources in addition to income). Thus, CAP was much stronger in outlining the expenditures that the federal government refused to share than the benefits provinces were required to provide.

Second, CAP required that, for work activity projects to be eligible for federal cost sharing, ". . . no person shall be denied assistance because he refuses or has refused to take part in a work activity project" (Canada Assistance Plan, RSC 1985, ch. C-1). This requirement precluded workfare programs from cost sharing. Various categories of applicants could be denied assistance effectively but they could not be required to work for benefits. Third, a provision prohibited residency requirements, ensuring that out-of-province applicants be treated the same as provincial residents. In summary, CAP reinforced provincial reliance on residual needs-tested programs (as opposed to broader-based, income-tested programs) while precluding workfare and residency requirements.

CAP was never intended by federal policymakers nor interpreted by provincial policymakers to imply any kind of right to assistance—the language of which was simply not an element in the central policy debates in this period. Nor, in terms of provincial practice, was social assistance provided on anything approximating an unconditional right or, in most cases, even at a reasonable level, with provinces differing widely in terms of conditionality and adequacy. For example, in the early 1990s under CAP, benefits to single employables in New Brunswick represented less than half the basic needs requirements (see Kneebone and White, in this volume). Rather, provinces differed significantly in the goals reflected in their social assistance systems—differences deeply rooted in the history and internal politics of each province (Boychuk 1998). Thus, distinct provincial systems were not simply the result of varying economic conditions or structure across provinces nor were they the outcome of differing technocratic prescriptions regarding means to achieve the same goals. Rather, the most important differences were about the goals of social assistance and, in turn, were rooted in the distinctive politics and political cultures of each province. Thus, social assistance provision in Canada, even under federal cost sharing, was best understood provincially—not as a national system but as a patchwork of unique provincial ones that embodied distinct purposes. In this rendering, the interaction between social assistance provision within individual provinces and federal cost sharing was complex and contingent.

CAP remained relatively unchanged from its inception until the early 1990s. The 1990 federal budget announced that the funds transferred to the three provinces not receiving federal equalization payments (Alberta, British Columbia, and Ontario) would be limited to a 5-per-cent annual increase for the following two fiscal years (see Figure 2.1). The caps were extended in the 1991 federal budget for an additional three years. The cap on CAP and its specific timing could be explained by the fact that Ontario (which had the highest rate of growth in CAP transfers in the mid- to late 1980s) was considering expensive plans for reform that the federal government was unwilling to share. Highlighting the divergent effects of federal cost sharing, Ontario's already generous social assistance program likely would have become even more generous relative to other provinces had CAP not been capped (Boychuk 1998, 48).

CAP would, of course, be subsequently dismantled with the federal announcement in 1995 of a shift to largely unconditional block funding under the Canada Health and Social Transfer (CHST), which came into effect in the 1996 fiscal year (see Figure 2.1). As part of a larger package of major federal budgetary restraint, the shift to CHST marked a significant reduction in federal transfers formerly falling under the rubric of Established Program Financing (EPF) and CAP. Moreover, in regard to the latter, there would no longer even be federal pretensions of ensuring any minimum standards of uniformity except for a provision against residency requirements (Boychuk 1998, 98–99). Major shifts in central indicators of social assistance provision across provinces, such as social assistance recipiency rates, are routinely attributed to these changes in federal policy.[1]

National trends, federal policy shifts, and the changing economic context

In fact, it is now conventional wisdom that this shift to block funding marked the main turning point in the politics of social assistance in

1 The CHST has since been replaced by the Canada Health Transfer and the Canada Social Transfer. See McIntosh (2004) and also Figure 2.1.

Canada. In the immediate term, the shift was seen as precipitating significant retrenchment in provincial social assistance programs:

> The intensity of retrenchment varied across the country . . . nevertheless, the direction of change was consistent across the country. The real value of benefits fell by large amounts. Caseloads dropped dramatically as eligibility conditions were tightened and beneficiaries came under increasing pressure to participate in employability programs and to move into employment. (Banting and Myles 2013a, 23)

This interpretation places significant weight on the importance of changes in federal policies in shaping related provincial policy responses: "Policy restructuring shrank programs that provided support to vulnerable Canadians, such as . . . social assistance" (Banting and Myles 2013a, 3). However, such assessments of the impacts of policy-related changes must be undertaken with consideration of the changing economic circumstances.

Cross-provincial social assistance trends and the changing economic context

Certainly, social assistance recipiency rates did decline dramatically from the early 1990s through the mid-2000s (see Figure 2.2).[2] However, employment rates underwent strong recovery in the same period. Over the period from 1990 to 2012, there is a strong inverse correlation between the median provincial social assistance recipiency rates and median provincial employment rates. Statistically speaking, variation in median provincial employment rates can account for just under 90 per cent of the variation in median social assistance recipiency rates over this period.

Figure 2.3 charts the actual provincial recipiency rate against the forecasted employment rate, which is based on the then-current employment rate and allows for a one-year lag for changes in the latter to have an effect. The resulting picture is striking—the overall pattern in actual median recipiency rates is largely determined by the median employment rate.

Presenting the linear trend lines for both actual recipiency rates and forecasted recipiency rates for specific time periods, Figure 2.4 suggests

2 Thanks to Ron Kneebone and Katherine White for graciously providing access to their very impressive data on provincial employment rates, recipiency rates, and benefit adequacy rates. Any errors in reporting or interpreting these data remain mine. Please see Kneebone and White (in this volume) for a description of these data.

Figure 2.2 Social Assistance Recipiency Rates and Employment Rates, 1990–2012, All Provinces (Median)

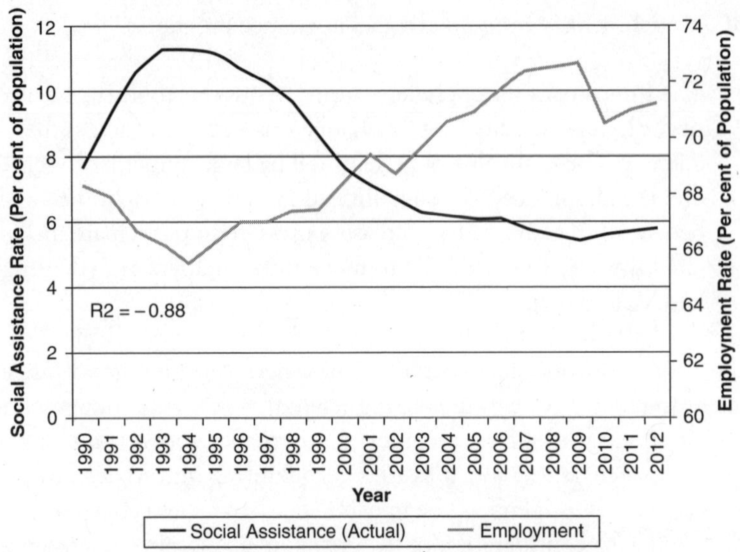

Source: Data on individual provincial employment rates and social assistance recipiency rates kindly provided by Kneebone and White (in this volume). Author's calculations.

Figure 2.3 Social Assistance Recipiency Rates, Actual and Forecasted, 1990–2012, All Provinces (Median)

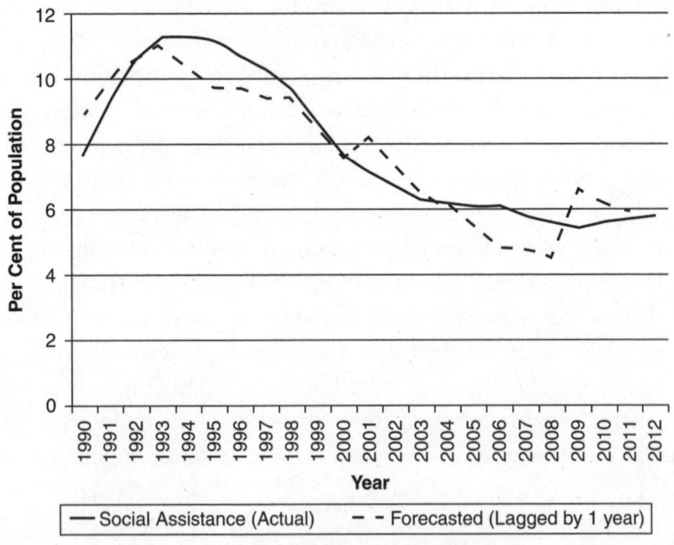

Source: Data on individual provincial employment rates and social assistance recipiency rates kindly provided by Kneebone and White (in this volume). Author's calculations.

some room for the effects of broad policy shifts over time. From 1995 to 2001, declines in actual recipiency rates were sharper than would be expected given changes in the employment rate, so this decline was potentially caused by policy changes. Conversely, from 2001 to 2008, declines in actual rates were less sharp than would be expected based on changes in the employment rate alone. In both periods, there is potential for policy effects to matter—albeit within a broader context in which the overall patterns are largely determined by changing economic conditions.

Do effects related to the shift from CAP to the CHST show up more clearly in provincial social assistance benefit levels than in the recipiency rates discussed above? Certainly, benefit adequacy (actual benefits as a proportion of basic necessity) is much more clearly dictated by policy than recipiency rates that reflect policies as they interact with changing economic conditions. There are three clear trends evident in Figure 2.5. First, median adequacy rates across provinces were increasing over the early 1990s. By 1994, however, they began to decline for each category. However,

Figure 2.4 Social Assistance Recipiency Rates, Actual and Forecasted, 1990–2012, All Provinces (Median, Linear Trend Lines)

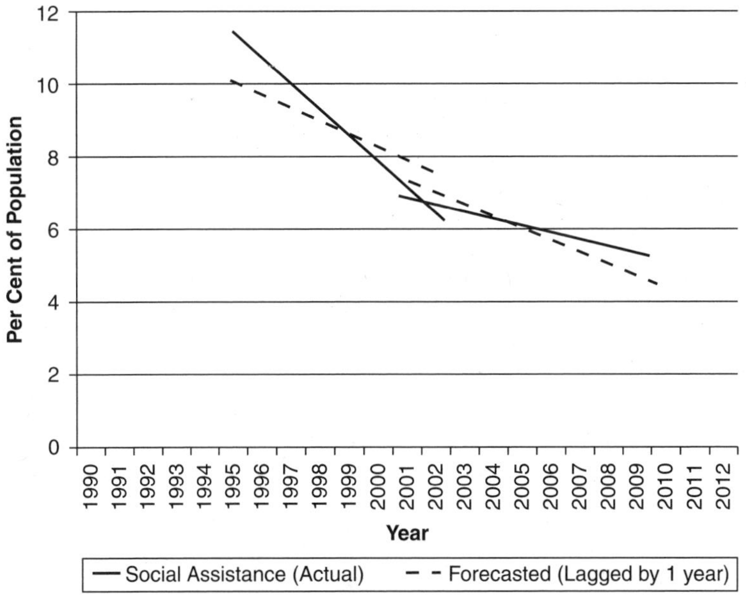

Source: Data on individual provincial employment rates and social assistance recipiency rates kindly provided by Kneebone and White (in this volume). Author's calculations.

Figure 2.5 Benefit Adequacy Index by Family Type, 1989–2011, All Provinces (Median)

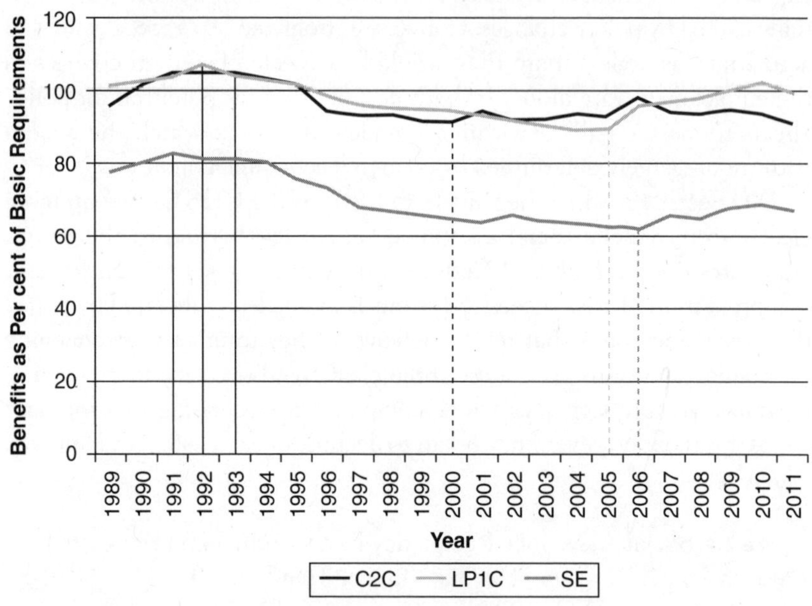

Source: Data on individual provincial employment rates, social assistance recipiency rates, and adequacy rates kindly provided by Kneebone and White. Author's calculations.
Note: Solid vertical lines indicate peak year. Dashed vertical lines indicate lowest year.
C2C = Couple, two children
LP1C = Lone parent, one child
SE = Single employable

the downward trend in benefits for each family type started gradually, for the most part, and 1995–96 did not appear as a major breakpoint with the exception of benefit adequacy levels for two-parent families, which declined significantly immediately after 1995. It is, of course, possible to argue that earlier declines in benefit adequacy might have been precipitated by the "cap on CAP," which limited the increase in total federal matching funds to the three provinces not receiving equalization payments (Alberta, Ontario, and British Columbia) to 5 per cent per year.[3] The decline that started in the early 1990s continued through 2000 for couples with children, and through 2005 and 2006 for single-parent families and single employables

3 I thank Peter Graefe for making this point.

respectively. After that point, benefit adequacy rates began to recover—most significantly for lone parents, to a somewhat lesser degree for single employables, and only marginally for couples with children.

Explaining trends in the 1990s

Important shifts in provincial social assistance provision clearly did occur in the mid-1990s; however, attributing them to the shift from CAP to the CHST understates the complexity of the relationship between federal policy and provincial social assistance. Most important, it overstates the significance of CAP conditions that, as argued earlier, were minimal. At the same time, the effects of matching cost sharing were complex and contingent. Certainly, for provinces considering social policy expansion, matching funding would have generated strong incentives to expand programs eligible for cost sharing (e.g., needs-tested programs) relative to those not eligible (e.g., income-tested programs). However, where provinces were governed by political parties ideologically inimical to social assistance, cost sharing most likely provided both little incentive for expansion and meagre protection against retrenchment. Similarly, as Jenson notes, "Building pan-Canadian social programs via conditional grants meant that the generosity of benefits depended less on the real needs of a province's population than on the fiscal capacity of its government; thus, regional inequalities and inequities were reproduced" (2013a, 49). Thus, overall, federal cost sharing likely had strongly divergent effects among provinces—increasing expansion in provinces where it was politically desirable and financially feasible but not having much effect in either prompting expansion or preventing rollbacks in provinces where social assistance was seen as public disutility (Boychuk 2006, 178). Thus, one might well expect less variation among provinces in the post-CAP period, other things being equal.

Other major shifts occurring at the same time are likely more powerful explanations of policy-related developments in provincial social assistance. First, the re-election of the Progressive Conservatives in Alberta under Ralph Klein in 1993 and the election of the Progressive Conservatives under Mike Harris in Ontario in 1995 were both striking examples of the major political shifts occurring in certain provinces. Both governments were stridently inimical to social assistance, and it simply strains credulity to presume that either government would have restrained itself from a program of radical retrenchment in the absence of changes to federal cost sharing for social assistance. Indeed, radical changes in Alberta took place before the dismantling of CAP. In turn, the resulting policy shifts in these provinces had important implications for the overall tenor of debates regarding social assistance in Canada. Radical retrenchment in both provinces raised the prospect of provincial offloading of social recipient caseloads onto other provinces, using means both passive (i.e., tightening eligibility and lowering benefits) and active (i.e., providing travel assistance to applicants to return to their former province of residence). This retrenchment likely had a significantly chilling effect on social assistance expansion in other provinces. The federal prohibition against provincial residency requirements undoubtedly exacerbated this chill—effectively removing waiting periods as a policy instrument for provinces that wished to maintain higher levels of benefits but were concerned about the political charge of becoming "welfare magnets" (Peterson and Rom 1990).

Second, the federal government had already embarked on a relatively radical retrenchment of unemployment insurance, which was seen by some as the deliberate offloading of erstwhile federal unemployment insurance beneficiaries onto provincial social assistance programs. Thus, provincial benefit reductions and eligibility tightening were in part a defensive response to this federal offloading of responsibility for the unemployed (see McIntosh and Boychuk 2000). This offloading—in the context of the federal government dismantling cost sharing while banning provincial residency requirements (thus continuing to subject provincial social assistance to cross-provincial competitive pressures)—combined with high unemployment and fiscal restraint placed tremendous pressures on provincial social assistance systems.

Each of these developments varied in its impact across provinces. The effects of federal matching and conditional cost sharing likely had divergent effects across provinces, ones relating to each province's political predisposition toward expanding social assistance as well as to its fiscal capacity to do so. The dismantling of federal cost sharing thus also would have different effects across provinces. Similarly, federal restructuring of unemployment insurance had widely differential effects across provinces due to both regional variations in actual federal policy (including minimum contribution requirements and maximum benefit periods) and regional variation in economic structure and context. Furthermore, the political dynamics generated by the possibility of offloading and of benefit-induced migration (outlined above) would have had varying effects across provinces. For example, although "welfare magnet" effects were felt powerfully in British Columbia because of its generous social assistance rates and proximity to Alberta, such effects likely mattered less in Newfoundland. Both the dismantling of federal cost sharing for social assistance as well as the federal restructuring of unemployment insurance (each having differential effects across provinces) would interact in a complex way both with each other as well as with existing provincial social assistance systems, which also varied considerably.

Explaining variation across provinces

The dismantling of CAP has been argued to have led to a new politics of social assistance in Canada in which ". . . the future of redistribution will be increasingly determined at the provincial level and will be shaped by differences in provincial politics" (Banting and Myles 2013b, 422). Such a shift was argued to be significant as "the difference between Canada's most and least redistributive provinces is strikingly large" and there is "little evidence of convergence in provincial redistributive regimes" (18; see also Haddow 2013). Jenson offers a highly consistent interpretation:

> The elimination of any conditionality allowed the provinces maximum autonomy of action and considerably reduced the federal government's influence over policy design. . . . The politics of redistribution in some key areas of income security, such as social assistance, have become therefore, more varied, responding more clearly to the political imperatives in each province. (Jenson 2013a, 56)

Of course, an alternative argument is that provincial diversity was significant previously under CAP and has not increased significantly as a result of changes in federal policy (Boychuk 1998). Has variation in social assistance provision across provinces increased in the wake of the federal policy changes of the 1990s and early twenty-first century?

Figure 2.6 charts the correlation between provincial employment rates and social assistance recipiency rates across all 10 provinces between 1989 and 2011.

Cross-provincial variation in recipiency rates over the late 1980s was less explained by variation in employment rates than in the period after the shift to the CHST. That is, before the shift from CAP, variation across provinces was not driven primarily by variation in employment rates. After the shift to the CHST, variation in employment rates provided a much stronger explanation of cross-provincial variation in recipiency rates. For example, in 2002, provincial variation in employment rates accounted for more than 80 per cent of provincial variation in social assistance recipiency rates, strongly suggesting that the variation observed in the early 2000s was the result of provincial economic differences.

Figure 2.6 Correlation of Employment Rates and Social Assistance Recipiency Rates by Year, 1989–2011, All Provinces

Source: Data on individual provincial employment rates and social assistance recipiency rates kindly provided by Kneebone and White (in this volume). Author's calculations.

In terms of benefit adequacy, only the category of single employables demonstrates a pattern suggestive of significant effects resulting from the federal policy shift. Over the post-CAP period, convergence among provinces in benefit adequacy for couples with two children, which had begun after 1992, continued through the late 1990s when provincial benefit adequacy rates began to diverge (although not to the levels evident in the early 1990s; see Figure 2.7). Provincial variation in benefit adequacy for lone parents was indeed increasing after 1995, but this trend appeared most clearly as part of a broader one that had begun much earlier. Neither trend appears closely related to the federal policy changes of the mid-1990s, and in neither case does 1995–96 mark a breakpoint. In contrast, variation among provinces in benefit adequacy for single employables, which had been dropping over the first half of the decade, rose dramatically after 1995 declining again only after 2000. Through the 2000s, variation in benefit adequacy for this category of recipient would wax and wane although, by 2010–11, it would reach levels lower than those of the early 1990s under CAP.

Figure 2.7 Provincial Variation in the Benefit Adequacy Index by Family Type, 1989–2011, All Provinces

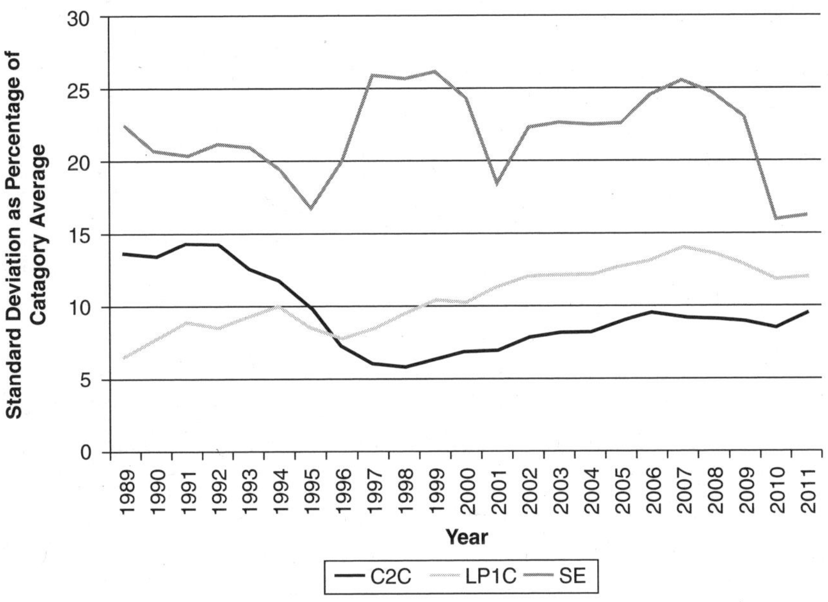

Source: See Figure 2.4. Author's calculations.
C2C = Couple, two children
LP1C = Lone parent, one child
SE = Single employable

Overall, differences among provinces in benefit adequacy were not shaped by the shift away from federal cost sharing in any clear manner across family types. The most plausible conclusion based on these data is that, to the extent that the dismantling of CAP had an effect on social assistance benefits rates, these effects differed significantly by family type. This highlights that the effects of cost sharing were complex, contingent, and variable—as well as pointing out the need to trace the effects of these shifts for specific family types within individual provinces.

A new cross-provincial consensus? "Activation" and the social investment perspective

Various observers have forcefully asserted the importance of shifts in the ideational context—especially the emergence of the social investment perspective developing out of an earlier focus on the idea of activation

(Green and Townsend 2013; Jenson 2013a). Jenson notes that the social investment perspective has "focused on the how of social policy interventions (human capital development and activation policies) and for whom (children, including pre-schoolers, and their parents)" (Jenson 2013b, 10). Most notably, "Social investment's calling card was that it is 'child-centred'" (Jenson 2013b, 7). Certainly, the perspective has been powerfully evident in policy debates regarding social policy in Canada (Jenson 2013a, 54–56).

The social investment perspective was clearly expressed, in the mid- to late 1990s, in the federal National Child Benefit (NCB)—an income-tested benefit for all families, including those in work, of the very type discouraged by federal cost sharing under CAP (see Figure 2.1). For families receiving social assistance, the federal government "urged provinces to offset the increase by reducing the child component of their social assistance benefits by the same amount" (Banting and Myles 2013a, 23). The intent, among other things, was to ensure that "low-wage workers with children would have less financial incentive to leave work for welfare" (23). Thus, the federal program was intended to have a direct effect in reducing provincial social assistance benefits and social assistance expenditures, although not the overall fiscal effort of provinces, as they were expected to reinvest these savings.

Notably, the federal government allowed provinces not to offset federal benefits (Boychuk 2013, 251; Jenson 2013a, 58). Initially, the only provinces that chose not to do so were New Brunswick and Newfoundland. One might have anticipated that these provinces would fall into line as the powerful logic of lowering the welfare wall became evident in other provinces and the approach generated more widespread buy-in. However, the reverse occurred. First, Manitoba implemented changes to allow NCB benefits to flow through directly to social assistance recipients from 2001 to 2003. Ontario partially followed suit in 2004 by allowing the flow-through of NCB increases with the full value of the NCB benefit to go directly to social assistance recipients in Ontario in 2008. The Ontario government apparently concluded after a decade of experience that the political disadvantages of the "clawback" outweighed the policy benefits of "lowering the welfare wall." Thus, after 2008, more than half of all social assistance beneficiaries in Canada lived in provinces that simply allowed the child benefits to flow through without offsets—presumably placing even greater pressure on the remaining provinces to follow suit and abandon offsets. The politics of the social investment perspective did not prove as robust as proponents thought—certainly, at least, not as they affected social assistance.

Are developments in benefit adequacy across different types of families consistent with an increased preference for providing benefits to families with children relative to those without? In terms of overall benefit adequacy by family type across provinces, Figure 2.5 does indeed reveal a growing gap over time between adequacy for families with children and for individuals without children. Although the gap in adequacy between benefits for a two-parent family and for single employables was no wider in 1996 than it was in 1990, after that point, the gap continued to grow before peaking in the mid-2000s and returning, at the end of the period, to levels comparable to those of the late 1990s. A very similar pattern emerges from an examination of the gap between benefit adequacy for lone-parent families and single employables although, here, growth in the gap persists through the end of the period. Thus, in an aggregate sense, the overall picture evident in Figure 2.5 is a sharpening of an implicit preference for families with children over the period, which is consistent with the social investment model informing the NCB.

However, this pattern is complicated by two other trends. Since 1998, cross-provincial differences in the adequacy rates for families with children (both two-parent and lone-parent families) have grown, suggesting increasing provincial variation within this overall broader trend (see Figure 2.7). Divergence among provinces in benefit adequacy rates for families with children is not what one would expect in light of a growing consensus around a social investment perspective. Second, median benefit adequacy rates across provinces for couples with children have been declining while they have been increasing for single employables (see Figure 2.5). The social investment perspective is not particularly powerful in explaining increasing benefit adequacy rates for single employables—especially given that benefit rates for the two-parent families remain inadequate to meet even basic needs except if the social investment perspective is seen primarily as an attempt to lower the welfare wall by lowering benefits to those on social assistance.

Thus, the lack of provincial consensus in regard to offsetting federal child benefits (which is key to lowering the welfare wall) is also reflected in the variation in provincial preferences for different family types, a variation implicit in the provinces' benefit rate structures. Both sets of evidence suggest significant cross-provincial differences in the adoption of a social investment perspective in the substance of policy.

Conclusion

Broad trends in social assistance policy and provision, as well as divergence from these trends, can only be fully understood by examining how various policy-related dynamics play out in specific provincial contexts.

Thus, rather than examining broad patterns in summary indicators and attributing them to changes in federal policy or shifts in policy ideas at the national level, a more challenging—but perhaps more fruitful—approach is to identify periods when a significant number of provinces veer away from the broader historical trajectory of development or, alternatively, to identify particular times when individual provinces diverge from broader cross-provincial trends. Moreover, in doing so, we must carefully attempt to isolate policy-related effects from economic effects.

The politics of social assistance were and remain unique to each province. The various dynamics related to the federal provision of matching conditional cost sharing and its dismantling, other federal policy shifts, and the politics of "social investment" have played out differently in each province. Thus, any national-level overview of social assistance in Canada can only be considered complete to the degree that such an overview is premised on a full appreciation of developments in the distinct provincial and territorial systems of which the Canadian "system" is comprised.

References

Banting, Keith, and John Myles. 2013a. "Introduction: Inequality and the Fading of Redistributive Politics." In *Inequality and the Fading of Redistributive Politics*, ed. Keith Banting and John Myles, 1–39. Vancouver: UBC Press.

Banting, Keith, and John Myles. 2013b. "Canadian Social Futures: Concluding Reflections." In *Inequality and the Fading of Redistributive Politics*, ed. Keith Banting and John Myles, 413–27. Vancouver: UBC Press.

Boychuk, Gerard W. 1998. *Patchworks of Purpose: The Development of Provincial Social Assistance Regimes in Canada*. Montréal: McGill-Queen's University Press.

Boychuk, Gerard W. 2006. "Slouching Toward the Bottom? Provincial Social Assistance Provision in Canada, 1980–2000." In *Racing to the Bottom? Provincial Interdependence in the Canadian Federation*, ed. Kathryn Harrison, 157–92. Vancouver: UBC Press.

Boychuk, Gerard W. 2013. "Territorial Politics and the New Politics of Redistribution." In *Inequality and the Fading of Redistributive Politics*, ed. Keith Banting and John Myles, 234–55. Vancouver: University of British Columbia Press.

Green, David A., and James Townsend. 2013. "Drivers of Increasing Market Income Inequality: Structural Change and Policy." In *Inequality and the Fading of Redistributive Politics*, ed. Keith Banting and John Myles, 65–92. Vancouver: UBC Press.

Haddow, Rodney. 2013. "Labour Market Income, Transfers, and Redistribution: National Themes and Provincial Variations." In *Inequality and the Fading of Redistributive Politics*, ed. Keith Banting and John Myles, 381–409. Vancouver: UBC Press.

Jenson, Jane. 2013a. "Historical Transformations of Canada's Social Architecture." In *Inequality and the Fading of Redistributive Politics*, ed. Keith Banting and John Myles, 43–64. Vancouver: UBC Press.

Jenson, Jane. 2013b. "Broadening the Frame: Extending the Social Investment Perspective in the Crisis." Paper presented at the Global Crisis and Changing Prospects for Social Policy Workshop, McMaster University, Hamilton, ON, September 27–28.

McIntosh, Tom. 2004. "Intergovernmental Relations, Social Policy and Federal Transfers after Romanow." *Canadian Public Administration / Administration publique du Canada* 47 (1): 27–51. http://dx.doi.org/10.1111/j.1754-7121.2004.tb01969.x.

McIntosh, Tom, and Gerard W. Boychuk. 2000. "Dis-Covered: EI, Social Assistance and the Growing Gap in Income Support for Unemployed Canadians." In *Federalism, Democracy and Labour Market Policy in Canada*, ed. Tom McIntosh, 65–158. Montréal: McGill-Queen's University Press.

Peterson, Paul, and Mark C. Rom. 1990. *Welfare Magnets: The Case for a New National Standard*. Washington, DC: Brookings Institution Press.

Rice, James J., and Michael J. Prince. 2013. *Changing Politics of Canadian Social Policy*. 2nd ed. Toronto: University of Toronto Press.

three

An Overview of Social Assistance Trends in Canada[1]

RONALD KNEEBONE AND KATHERINE WHITE[2]

Introduction

Our goal in this chapter is to provide a high-level overview of provincial social assistance programs in Canada. Our particular interest is to identify trends in social assistance use and social assistance policies. This is surprisingly challenging. It is challenging because the most basic of information—how many people are recipients of social assistance, how much do they receive in the form of income support, and how have each of these basic measures changed over time—is difficult to find. We comment on the implication of this difficulty in our concluding remarks.

In the next section, "The number of social assistance recipients," we discuss provincial data that show how social assistance use has changed over time and how it has varied with labour market conditions. We show that, since the early 1990s, the key driver of social assistance use has been the state of provincial labour markets. We then discuss, and offer some possible explanations for, the general lack of response in the social assistance rate to improvements in labour market conditions in the 1970s and 1980s.

"The social assistance rate and the business cycle" drills down below this broad overview to identify the characteristics of those receiving social assistance. We find evidence to suggest that, over the past two decades, there has been a significant change in the fraction of social assistance recipients who are identified as being single, a lone parent, or a member of a two-parent family. Changes have also occurred in the fraction of recipients identified as suffering a disability. Also in this section, we present data showing that the number of dependent children in families receiving social assistance benefits has fallen over time.

---

1 This paper was prepared for *Welfare Reform: The Future of Social Policy in Canada*, a conference held October 24–25, 2013 in Regina, Saskatchewan. We thank Margarita Wilkins for research assistance, Donna E. Wood for helpful comments, and the organizers of the conference for the opportunity to present our work.

2 The views expressed in this paper should in no way be attributed to the Alberta Treasury Board and Finance.

In "The characteristics of social assistance recipients," we turn to measures of social assistance incomes. Here, we rely on information gathered by the now-defunct National Council of Welfare (NCW) but recently published anew by the Caledon Institute of Social Policy (see Tweddle, Battle, and Torjman 2013). To gain perspective on the level of adequacy of social assistance incomes, we compare these incomes to a measure of the cost of meeting "basic needs." We also compare the payments made by provincial governments to those in need to the payments made by the federal government to low-income seniors, an arguably comparable group of citizens. Finally, in "Social assistance income," we complete our analysis by discussing social assistance income. We find that, across time, category of recipient, and province, it is exceptional for social assistance income to meet very basic needs. In addition, federal pensions given to poor seniors are universally much more generous than provincially provided social assistance incomes.

The number of social assistance recipients

How many people benefit from the receipt of an income support cheque from a provincial government? This seemingly innocent question must have a seemingly easy answer; surely provincial governments know the number of people to whom they write cheques and for what purpose. These same governments also ensure that the amount of these cheques reflects the size of the family unit to benefit from the receipt of this income. It should be, then, relatively straightforward to find information on the number of social assistance cases handled by provincial programs and the number of recipients or beneficiaries of social assistance income.[3]

Surprisingly, however, this information is difficult to obtain. In this section, we describe our efforts to put this information together and report on our findings.

In what follows, we rely on data we have previously published (see Kneebone and White 2014).[4] In that earlier research, we describe the difficulty of finding publicly available data on social assistance cases and beneficiaries by province. The earlier publication provides details on data

---

3 The number of recipients or beneficiaries refers to the total number of single individuals and heads of family units on social assistance, plus all their dependents (i.e., spouses, dependent children, and dependent adults). Data on caseloads, which we do not present here, report the number of family units receiving social assistance.

4 In the source cited, we compile data provided under the former Canada Assistance Plan (CAP) with those from provincial and territorial directors of income support as well as other publically available information such as the annual reports of provincial ministries and other government reporting.

sources and a table of data from fiscal year 1969 to 2012, showing the number of social assistance beneficiaries. We use those data here.

Our data spans a long period, so it is important, when evaluating the rise and fall in social assistance use, to account for a growing population. We define the *social assistance rate* as a fraction: the number of social assistance recipients compared to the population aged 0–64 years (Statistics Canada CANSIM database, Table 282–0001).

Social assistance is provided at the provincial level, and each province has its own unique set of policies and socio-economic conditions that impinge upon the social assistance rate. Still, it is useful to look at the Canadian average if only to gain insight into broad trends. Figure 3.1 aggregates social assistance use across provinces to show how the social assistance rate has changed over time in Canada.[5]

Figure 3.1 The Social Assistance Rate, Canada, 1969–2012

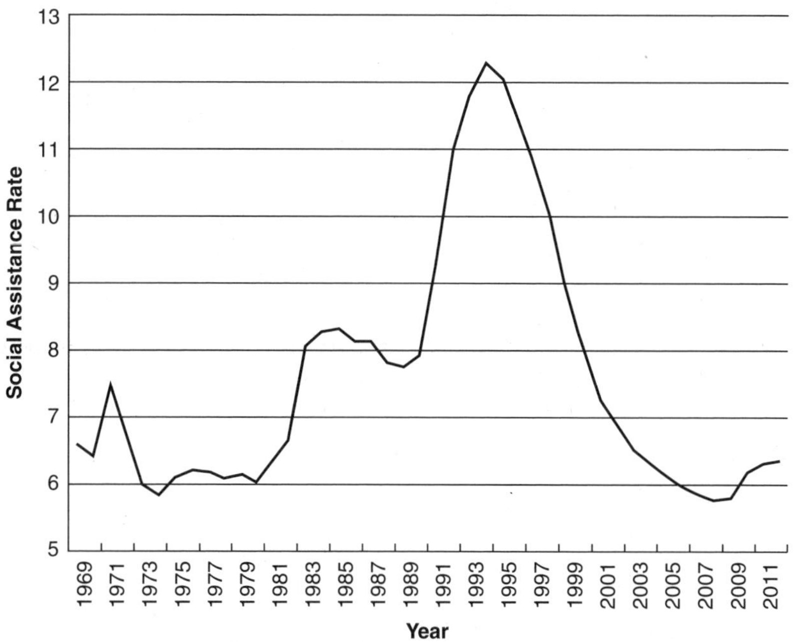

5 We define "Canada" as the sum of the 10 provinces. Only a limited amount of data on social assistance use is available for the territories, so we limit our attention to the 10 provinces. As described in Kneebone and White (2014), despite our best efforts, we could not find data on the number of social assistance recipients in PEI for fiscal years 2009–12. We recognize that the lack of PEI data for those years means that our data for Canada during that span are not quite accurate. We note, however, that for those years when data are available for all provinces, the number of recipients in PEI made up an average of only 0.4 per cent of all recipients in Canada.

The figure shows that the social assistance rate has exhibited considerable change over the period 1969–2012. Beginning and ending the period with similar values, the social assistance rate increased from 6 per cent to 8 per cent in the early 1980s but then increased quickly in the early 1990s. This increase was followed by a precipitous fall in the social assistance rate thereafter; it fell to half the percentage reached at its peak in just 14 years, between 1994 and 2008. Clearly, considerable change occurred in the determinants of the social assistance rate between 1981 and 2012.

In our earlier study, we present a similar graph for each of the 10 provinces. Rather than repeat those graphs here, we refer the reader to that earlier study (Kneebone and White 2014). The conclusion one comes to from looking at those graphs is that analysts seeking to explain movements in the social assistance rate must drill down to at least the level of the provinces.[6] Relying solely on national data will lead to very misleading conclusions because movements in the social assistance rate over time have varied widely across provinces. This variation will also be apparent in what we present in the next section, which relates changes in the social assistance rate to the state of the economy.

The social assistance rate and the business cycle

The social assistance rate and the drivers of that rate are of key significance to policymakers. The state of the economy—as measured by employment opportunities and rates of wage growth, in particular—is an obvious, though by no means the only explanation for the rise and fall in the social assistance rate.[7] The movements in the social assistance rate presented in Figure 3.1 therefore reflect, in part, the influence of the business cycle. In this

6 It would be even better to drill down to sub-provincial regions or cities. Our suspicion is that social assistance rates vary quite considerably across cities, by rural versus non-rural areas, and according to other regional considerations.

7 Kneebone and White (2009) report that between 18 and 30 per cent of the fall in the social assistance rate observed in Alberta, BC, and Ontario between 1994 and 2003 was due to changes in the state of the economy. Another 17 to 25 per cent was due to changes in the size of social assistance benefits and the rest—between one-half and two-thirds—was due to changes in administrative procedures introduced in those provinces during this period. US studies report a very wide range of estimates for the effect of the economy on social assistance use (e.g., Bell 2001). When one compares Canadian and US studies, it is important to note that the availability of welfare in the United States is restricted to a much narrower classification of recipients, namely, single parents. Canadian and US studies, then, measure the response to changes in the economy of two very different populations.

section, we illustrate in a fairly basic way how sensitive the social assistance rate is to the economic cycle in Canada and in each province.

The measure of the economic cycle we use is the ratio of total employment to the size of the working-age population (15–64 years); we call this the *employment ratio*.[8] The employment ratio has several advantages as a measure of labour market conditions. The employment ratio changes only if employment rises or falls relative to the size of the population. It is therefore an effective measure of employment prospects. An alternative measure that is often used—the unemployment rate—is problematic because the unemployment rate varies not only with employment but also with the size of the labour force. Because the size of the labour force is itself sensitive to perceptions of employment prospects, the unemployment rate can increase even though employment rises because more people choose to enter the labour force.

Although we stress the importance of recognizing that the unique characteristics of each province will ensure a different sensitivity of the social assistance rate to changes in its determinants, we nonetheless begin our discussion with Figure 3.2, which presents data describing Canada.

Figure 3.2 is a scatter plot of the social assistance rate and the employment ratio in Canada. Each point represents the size of the social assistance rate and the employment ratio in a particular year. The data run from fiscal year 1976 to fiscal year 2012.[9] Movements to the right in the figure denote an improvement in the employment ratio: an economic expansion during which a growing share of the working-age population is finding employment. Movements to the left identify an economic slowdown during which employment fell relative to the size of the working-age population. Upward movements identify an increase in the number of recipients of social assistance relative to the population aged 0–64 years while downward movements identify the opposite.

Economic conditions giving rise to an increase in the employment ratio and an increase in wages (we would normally expect these variables to

8 We use monthly provincial employment data from CANSIM Table 282–0081 covering the period from January 1976 to October 2012. The same source provides data on the population of those aged 15–64 years in each province. These monthly data are used to create observations by fiscal year from April 1 to March 31. As reported in our earlier study, data on the number of social assistance beneficiaries—particularly in the early years of our sample—are available only on a fiscal year basis. It is, therefore, valuable to use a measure of labour market conditions that can also be reported on a fiscal year basis. Unfortunately, employment data in this form are available only since January 1976, so we cannot make use of our data on social assistance beneficiaries available from fiscal year 1969–75.

9 In what follows, the period defined by reference to, for example, the year 2012, will be from April 1, 2011 to March 31, 2012.

Figure 3.2 The Employment Ratio and the Social Assistance Rate, Canada

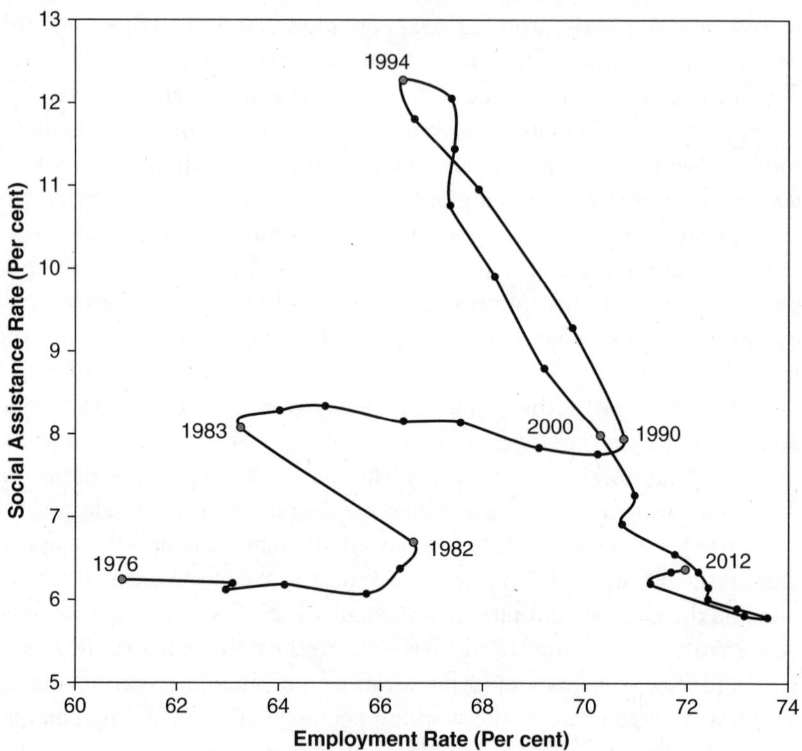

move together) would establish conditions likely to cause a fall in the social assistance rate. This expected negative relationship between economic conditions and the social assistance rate is observed by a downward slope to the line connecting annual observations of the employment ratio and the social assistance rate. It is important to note, however, that this relationship can be hidden by confounding influences. For example, a change to the rules determining eligibility for social assistance can be the cause of a change in the social assistance rate with no change in economic conditions. If that rule change caused it to become more difficult for claimants to become eligible for or to continue to receive social assistance, then we would expect the line connecting annual observations of the employment and the social assistance rate to shift up. Changes in other determinants of the social assistance rate will also cause a shift in the negative relationship between economic conditions and the social assistance rate.

The information in Figure 3.2 tells an interesting story. Twice during the period 1976–90, the Canadian economy experienced strong expansions—as measured by growth in the employment ratio—with virtually no reduction in the social assistance rate: once between 1976 and 1982 and again between 1983 and 1990. A strong contraction in 1982, however, resulted in a significant increase in the social assistance rate. During this 14-year period, then, the social assistance rate would ratchet upward during economic contractions but fail to fall during strong and prolonged expansions.

Starting in 1990, this pattern changed. An economic contraction between 1990 and 1994 resulted in a very large increase in the social assistance rate, from 8 per cent to over 12 per cent. This period was followed by a prolonged economic expansion that, by 2000, had returned the employment rate and the social assistance rate to their 1990 levels. The expected negative relationship between the social assistance rate and the employment rate therefore appeared not only during an economic contraction—as it had earlier in 1982–83—but also, for the first time, during the economic expansion that followed. Since 2000, the expected negative relationship has been maintained though in the last few years—2010 through 2012—the social assistance rate has increased very slightly even while the economy expanded.

A final fact that is noteworthy in the data presented in Figure 3.2 is that a social assistance rate of about 6 per cent was consistent with the relatively low employment ratio of 61 per cent in 1976 and with the relatively high employment ratio of nearly 74 per cent in 2008. This finding seems to suggest that there is, perhaps, a floor to the social assistance rate below which even the most robust labour market behaviour cannot push.

Even if the only determinant of the social assistance rate was the employment rate (which we do not claim to be true), we would expect different patterns from that observed for Canada to emerge from looking at these data by province. This is so because, as Kneebone and Gres (2013) have shown recently, business cycles differ in terms of timing, amplitude, and duration across Canadian provinces. It should not be surprising, then, that movements in the social assistance rate also vary by province.

Figure 3.3 looks at the relationship between the social assistance rate and the employment ratio in Ontario and Québec. Not surprising, given the size of Ontario in the Canadian economy (39 per cent of Canadian employment in 2012; Statistics Canada CANSIM database, Table 282–0001), the pattern for this province mimics that for Canada. That is, two strong expansions between 1976 and 1989 resulted in virtually no change in the social assistance rate in Ontario while the short and sharp recession of 1982–83 caused the rate to ratchet upward. After 1989, however, the negative relationship appeared in the form of a large increase in the social assistance rate during the 1990–94 contraction and a complete reversal of that increase during the following expansion to 2001. The negative relationship has remained in play since that time.[10] Interestingly, contrary to our comment with respect to Canada, in Ontario, the long-term trend has been for the social assistance rate to move upward even as the employment rate grows. The social assistance rate, which was less than 5 per cent in 1976, had increased by 2012 to nearly 8 per cent, despite a significant increase in the fraction of the working-age population that was employed. As we will see, Ontario is the *only* province for which it is true that the social assistance rate in 2012 is noticeably higher than it was in 1976. This fact, too, is worthy of the attention of those seeking to explain changes in the social assistance rate in Ontario.

Figure 3.3 The Employment Ratio and the Social Assistance Rate, Ontario and Québec

a. Ontario

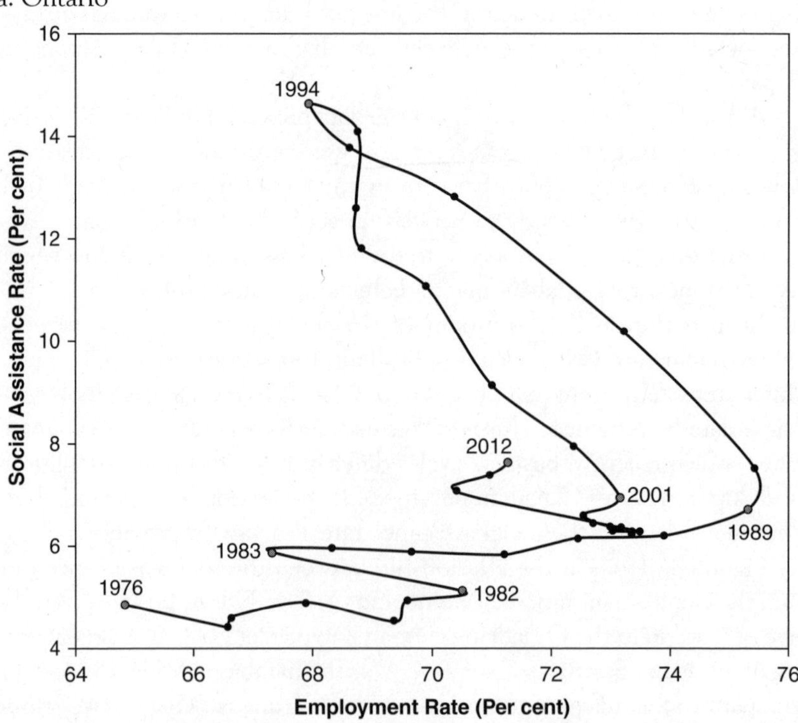

10 Though, as seen in the diagram for Canada, the last three years of the sample see the social assistance rate in Ontario increase even while the employment ratio increased.

b. Québec

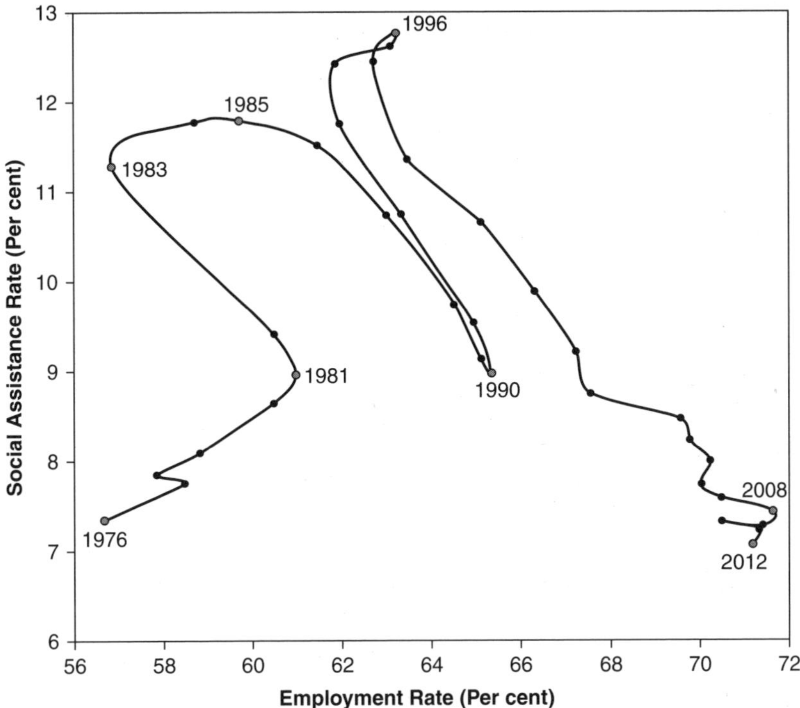

The pattern in Québec is somewhat different. An economic expansion from 1976 to 1981 was nonetheless associated with a steady rise in the social assistance rate. The 1981–83 recession lead to a further increase in the social assistance rate. Interestingly, though by 1983 the employment rate in Québec returned to its 1976 level, the social assistance rate increased from just over 7 per cent to over 11 per cent. After 1983, however, the negative relationship became established. The strong economic expansion from 1983 to 1990 saw the social assistance rate fall; the contraction that began in 1990 pushed the social assistance rate back up; and, finally, the strong expansion between 1996 and 2008 was witness to a steady fall in the social assistance rate. Similar to what we saw for Canada, in Québec, the social assistance rate in 1976 was almost identical to that in 2012 despite the strong trend of growth in the employment ratio. A social assistance rate of 7 per cent may, therefore, represent a floor level in Québec.

Figure 3.4 looks at the relationship between the social assistance rate and the employment rate in the four Atlantic Provinces. In Newfoundland

Figure 3.4 The Employment Ratio and the Social Assistance Rate, Atlantic Provinces

a. Newfoundland and Labrador

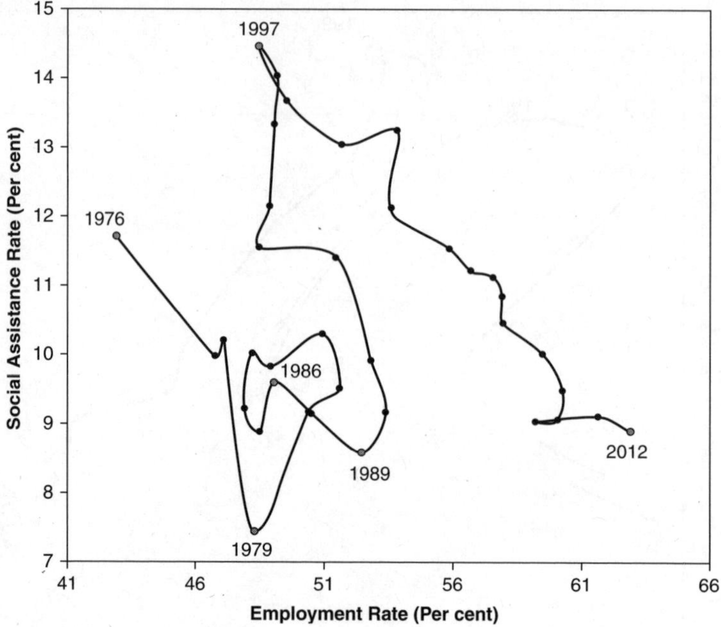

b. Prince Edward Island

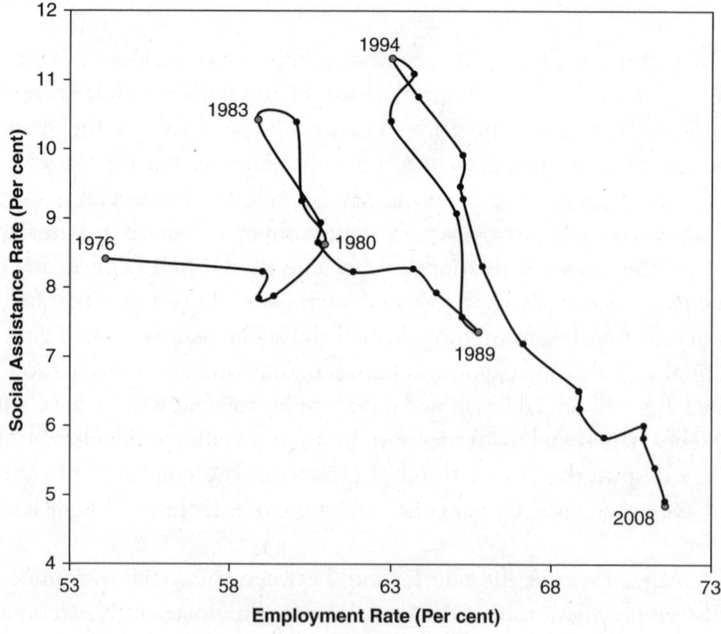

c. Nova Scotia

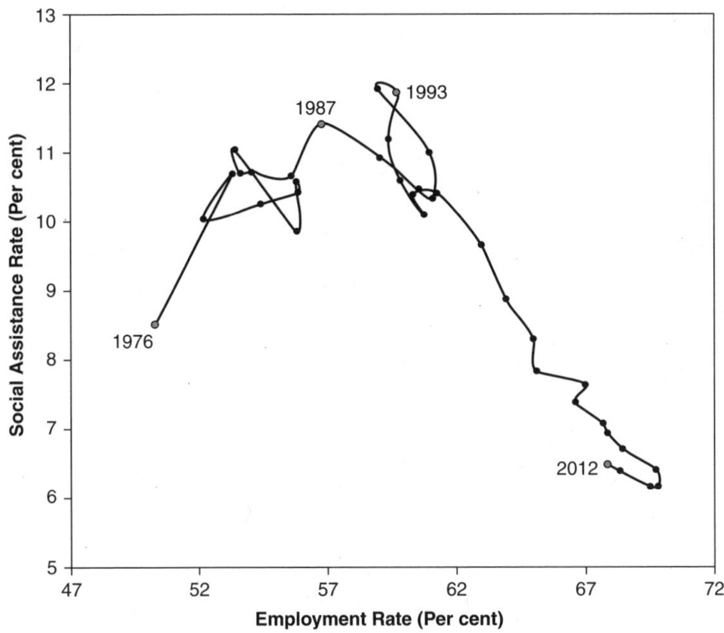

d. New Brunswick

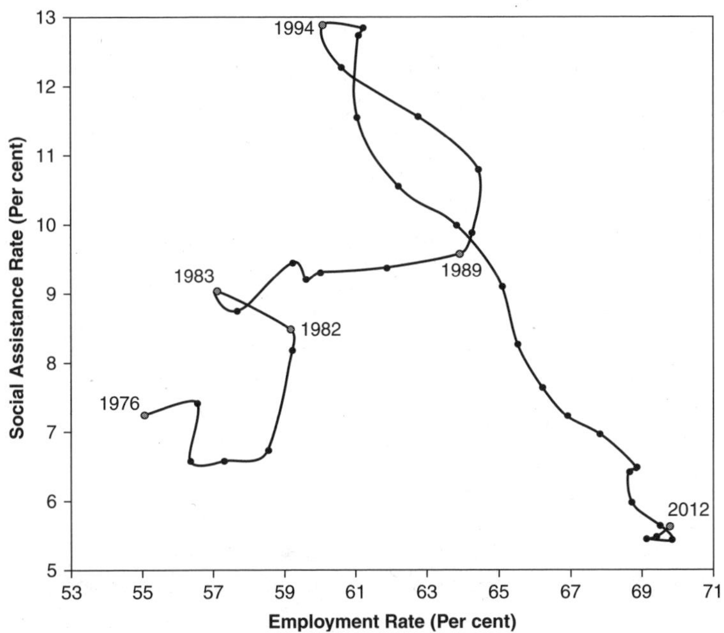

and Labrador, the negative relationship has been more or less consistently apparent throughout the period 1976–2012. The strength of the relationship is such that the rise in the social assistance rate when the province's economy was contracting during the period 1988–97 was completely reversed during the following expansion to 2012. A challenge for analysts is to perhaps explain the jumbled relationship during the period between 1979 and 1986.

In PEI, the negative relationship appears consistently after 1980, but, before that date, a strong labour market had no impact on the fairly high social assistance rate of over 8 per cent. Unlike Ontario and Québec's experience of the recession in the early 1980s, PEI's did not cause the social assistance rate to ratchet upward. Instead, this rate fell during expansion as quickly as it increased during recession. Between 1994 and 2008, the last year for which we have data for PEI, the social assistance rate more than halved during a period of robust employment growth. Strong employment growth since 1994 enabled the social assistance rate to establish a 30-year low in 2008.

The negative relationship between the social assistance rate and the employment rate appears in Nova Scotia only after 1989. Between 1976 and 1989, the social assistance rate increased noticeably despite—with the exception of 1982–83—a steadily growing economy. The recession that began in 1989 shot the social assistance rate upward to peak in 1994. By 1999, both the employment rate and the social assistance rate had returned to where they were at the beginning of the recession. Since that time, steady growth in the employment ratio has seen the social assistance rate fall so that, by 2012, it was at a 35-year low.

Finally, in New Brunswick, the negative relationship appears strongly after 1987, but, before that time, the trend was for the social assistance rate to increase along with the employment ratio. Analysts studying the history of social assistance in New Brunswick face the challenge of explaining this early pattern of expanding social assistance use even in the face of steady growth in employment. Consistent with the experience of the other Atlantic provinces, by 2012, the social assistance rate was well below its level in 1976.

Figure 3.5 looks at the relationship between the social assistance rate and the employment rate in the four Western provinces. It is important to note that the top percentage on the vertical axis, which measures the span of social assistance rates experienced over the period 1976–2012, is noticeably smaller for Manitoba, Saskatchewan, and Alberta than it is for other provinces. Indeed, in Alberta, this measurement reaches only 9 per cent. Of the Western provinces, only British Columbia has experienced social

Figure 3.5 The Employment Ratio and the Social Assistance Rate, Western Provinces

a. Manitoba

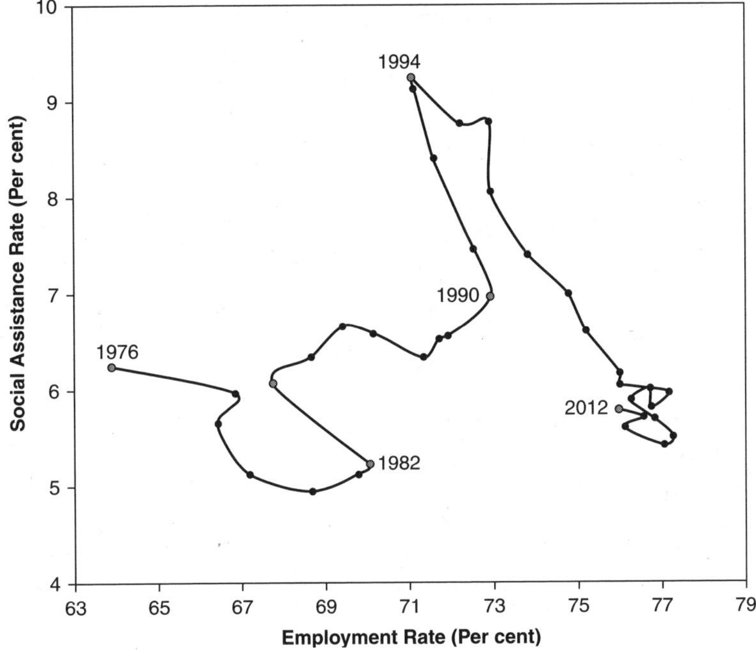

b. Saskatchewan

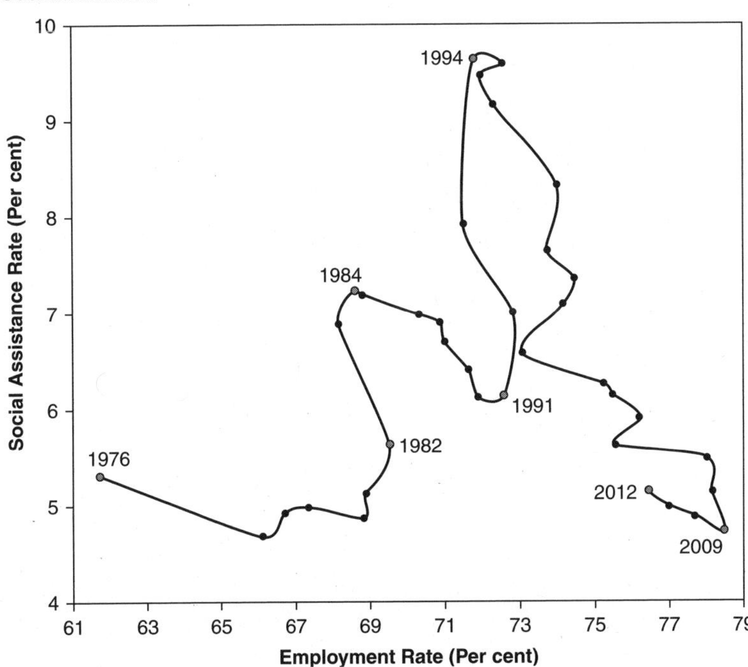

c. Alberta

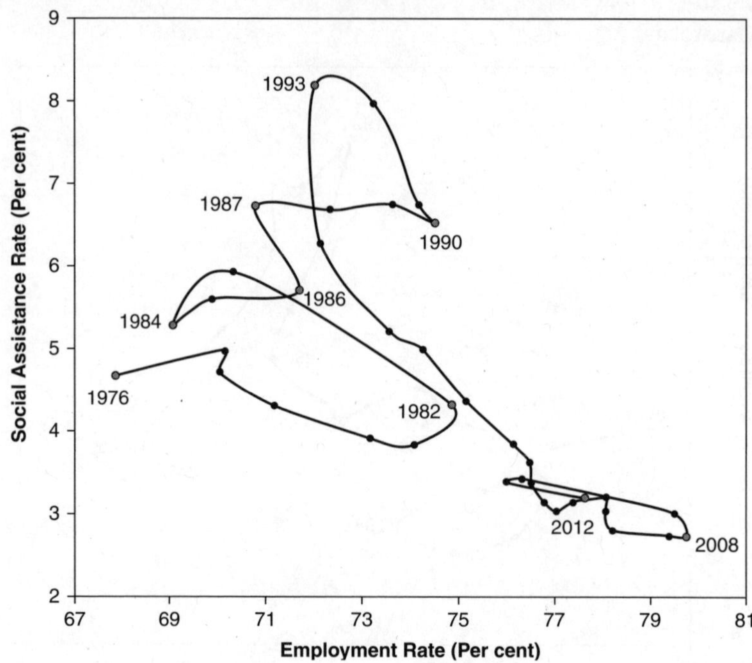

d. British Columbia

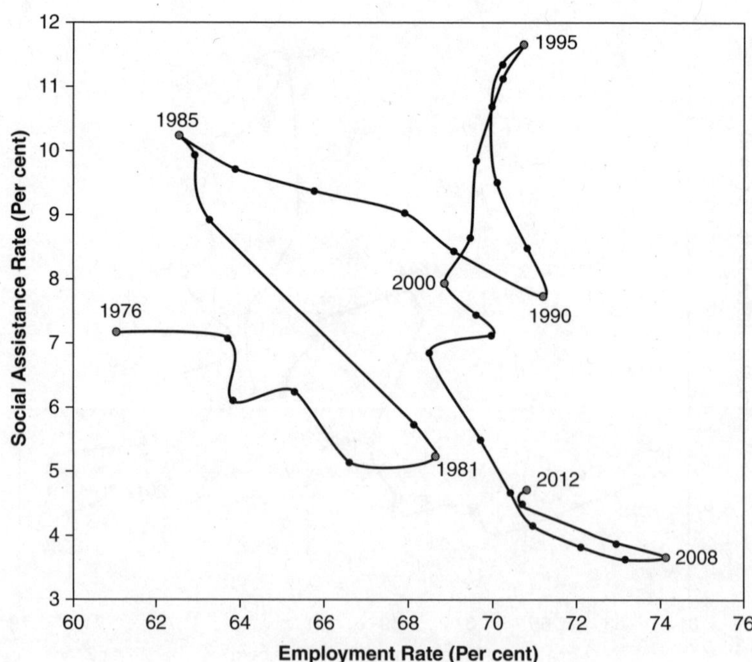

assistance rates exceeding 10 per cent, a level more commonly observed in central Canada and the Atlantic provinces.

The negative relationship between the social assistance rate and the employment rate is apparent in Manitoba between 1976 and 1983 and after 1990. Between 1983 and 1990, however, steady growth in the employment rate was associated with a steady rise in the social assistance rate. In the decade since 2002, neither the social assistance rate nor the employment rate has changed to any significant extent.

The movements in the figure for Saskatchewan are consistent with a negative relationship through the period 1976–2012. Strong employment growth between 1976 and 1980 saw a steady decline in the social assistance rate but recession in the early 1980s forced this rate upward. After 1984–85, employment growth saw the social assistance rate fall, though not to pre-recession levels. As we have seen quite often in these figures, the social assistance rate in Saskatchewan has fallen dramatically since 1994, and, by 2012, it was close to its 1976 level, suggesting, perhaps, a floor to the social assistance rate in Saskatchewan of about 4.5 to 5.5 per cent.

In Alberta the only notable instance of the social assistance rate and the employment rate not moving in opposite directions was during the period 1987–90, when strong economic growth had no impact on the social assistance rate. Other than during that period, slowdowns and speedups in the labour market have been associated with increases and decreases in the social assistance rate.

As in Alberta, in British Columbia, the negative relationship between the social assistance rate and the state of the labour market has been in clear evidence almost throughout the period 1976–2012. The notable exception was 1995–2005, during which the employment rate fell or showed no growth but the social assistance rate plummeted.

Generally speaking, the provincial data presented in Figures 3.3, 3.4, and 3.5 are consistent with the explanation that an expanding economy causes a fall in the social assistance rate and a contracting economy causes a rise. Periods during which this pattern fails to appear suggest that other influences on the social assistance rate were changing and were confounding this rate's negative relationship with the employment rate. We have avoided speculating very much about what those changes might have been because we believe they are likely specific to each province and so will be part of the discussion of the authors of other chapters in this volume. Still, we think some broad generalizations might be useful.

When we examine these data, there appear to be some additional broad economic and labour-market-specific factors at play, which may not be captured by changes in the employment ratio. Possibilities include changes in the generosity of social assistance payments and changes in the rules for social assistance eligibility.[11] In addition, other major transformational or longer-run changes in provincial economies may have affected the relationship of the labour market and social assistance rates during this period.

One possible influence is the large structural change that was taking place in the Canadian economy over that time, the movement from the traditionally high-wage, goods-producing sector to the often low-wage, service-producing sector. In Canada from 1976 to 2012, the proportion of goods-sector employment has declined from 35 per cent of employment to 22 per cent (Statistics Canada CANSIM database, Table 282–0008). Goods-sector employment is what is often thought of as "middle-class jobs." These are industries such as agriculture, mining, and manufacturing. This phenomenon is much more prevalent over the first half of the sample. From 1976 to 1994, the fraction of goods-sector employment fell from 35 per cent to 26 per cent; while over the second half of our sample, from 1995 to 2012, the ratio of goods-sector employment fell from 26 per cent to 22 per cent, a much lower rate of change. This may be a structural economic change that partially explains why the relationship between the social assistance rate and the employment rate shifted to the right during the 1980s. That is, during the first half of our sample, even though the employment ratio was growing, the social assistance rate did not fall because it was absorbing more and more people whose skills were no longer able to win them employment.

The employment ratio was also changing in its *composition* over the sample period. From 1976 to 1993, the proportion of full-time employment to total employment fell from 87.4 to 80.8 per cent. Since 1993, it has remained fairly steady, fluctuating between 80.6 and 81.9 per cent (Statistics Canada CANSIM database, Table 282–0087). This change meant that, even if one were employed, it was less likely each year that one's employment was full-time work, until about 1993. It is important to note that the benefits and security that often accompany full-time employment are not as prevalent in part-time employment. This structural change in the labour market, toward part-time employment, likely affected the relationship

11 Kneebone and White (2009) identify statistically significant influences of these factors on provincial social assistance rates. The approach they use is limited to periods starting after 1989 because data on social assistance income are available (from the National Council of Welfare) only after that date. This leaves open the question of the influence that these and other circumstances might have had on the social assistance rate prior to 1989.

between the employment ratio and the social assistance rate while this trend was in place. It helps to explain the unresponsiveness of the SA rate to improvements in the employment ratio over the first half of the sample.

Another structural change in the labour market that took place over our sample period is the change in the rate of participation of women in the paid labour force. In 1976, the proportion of females in the labour force was 37 per cent, but, by 2012, it was 48 per cent (Statistics Canada CANSIM database, Table 282–0008). Again, the bulk of the change occurred over the first half of our sample. In 1994, halfway through our sample, females made up 45 per cent of the labour force, so most of the increase in their participation rate came in the 1980s. Thus, during the early part of our sample, new employment opportunities were being filled by women who had not previously participated in the labour market—structural change that might have prevented the social assistance rate from falling despite rapid employment growth.

The characteristics of social assistance recipients

The characteristics of social assistance recipients are important to understand because public policies directed toward recipients depend on these characteristics. Whether a recipient is single or the head of a family of four; whether he or she is young or old, highly educated or not, skilled or unskilled, or living in an urban or a rural area; or whether he or she is disabled are all important considerations when it comes to deciding on the appropriate level of income support, the appropriate emphasis to be placed on retraining, and a host of other things. Unfortunately, information on these characteristics is not easily found. Fortunately, a few provincial governments do provide glimpses that allow some basic understanding of how the personal characteristics of those receiving income support has changed over time.

By family type

Data reporting the number of social assistance recipients in different family types is difficult to find. Only a few provinces report useful information over a sufficiently long period to enable us to identify trends. The government of British Columbia provides the most complete information.

Table 3.1 presents data on the number of social assistance recipients by five family types in British Columbia over the period 1995–2012. To be clear on the meaning of these data, the table shows, for example, that, in 1995, there were 63,056 individuals dependent upon social assistance

Table 3.1 Recipients of Social Assistance by Family Type, British Columbia, 1995–2012

	Number of Recipients						Recipients by Family Type				
	All Categories of Social Assistance						Percentage of Total				
	Single Men	Single Women	Couples	Two-Parent Families	Single-Parent Families	All Family Types	Single Men	Single Women	Couples	Two-Parent Families	Single-Parent Families
1995	89,869	43,704	17,737	63,056	153,021	367,387	24.5	11.9	4.8	17.2	41.7
1996	81,206	40,286	16,592	60,034	146,772	344,890	23.5	11.7	4.8	17.4	42.6
1997	73,734	38,386	15,591	49,134	128,128	304,973	24.2	12.6	5.1	16.1	42.0
1998	68,599	37,276	14,781	43,490	117,035	281,181	24.4	13.3	5.3	15.5	41.6
1999	64,476	36,560	14,202	38,637	109,315	263,190	24.5	13.9	5.4	14.7	41.5
2000	62,474	36,854	13,486	34,503	105,272	252,589	24.7	14.6	5.3	13.7	41.7
2001	62,230	37,593	13,279	31,886	99,833	244,821	25.4	15.4	5.4	13.0	40.8
2002	55,786	35,535	11,819	25,086	82,048	210,274	26.5	16.9	5.6	11.9	39.0
2003	48,073	32,673	10,089	17,521	62,022	170,378	28.2	19.2	5.9	10.3	36.4
2004	45,383	31,972	9,188	13,391	52,570	152,504	29.8	21.0	6.0	8.8	34.5
2005	44,032	31,512	8,556	10,721	45,313	140,134	31.4	22.5	6.1	7.7	32.3
2006	44,010	31,745	8,172	9,548	39,132	132,607	33.2	23.9	6.2	7.2	29.5
2007	46,960	33,313	8,016	9,526	37,333	135,148	34.7	24.6	5.9	7.0	27.6
2008	50,654	35,365	7,947	10,102	38,551	142,619	35.5	24.8	5.6	7.1	27.0
2009	59,637	38,930	8,797	13,241	44,239	164,844	36.2	23.6	5.3	8.0	26.8
2010	64,748	41,663	8,979	14,399	48,015	177,804	36.4	23.4	5.0	8.1	27.0
2011	66,219	43,292	8,847	14,409	49,085	181,852	36.4	23.8	4.9	7.9	27.0
2012	65,178	43,581	8,543	13,649	47,101	178,052	36.6	24.5	4.8	7.7	26.5

Source: British Columbia Ministry of Social Development and Social Innovation (2004, 2008).
Note: These are calendar-year data. These data include the number of recipients with disabilities.

living in families defined as having two parents. The individuals on assistance could include heads of these family units plus any of their dependents (i.e., spouses, dependent children, and dependent adults). The other family types have similar interpretations.

Noteworthy in this table is the dramatic fall in total number of recipients—particularly for those living as couples, in two-parent families, and in single-parent families. The measure of single-parent and two-parent families receiving social assistance has fallen dramatically not only in number but also as a percentage of all recipients. Consistent with this observation is the large decrease in the number of children living in families receiving social assistance, from 128,153 (34.9 per cent of all recipients) in 1995 to 36,007 (20.2 per cent of all recipients) in 2012. As a percentage of the total number of recipients, the share of singles—particularly single women—has increased over time. Over 60 per cent of all recipients of social assistance in BC are now single, up from 36 per cent in 1995. This increase is mainly a result of the falling share of families receiving assistance.

One possible explanation for the fall in the number of families receiving social assistance is the proliferation of direct childcare subsidies and grants over the post-1995 period aimed, in part, at supporting parental employment (see Beach and Friendly 2005). This form of provision could mean, essentially, that many low-income families would never need to collect social assistance as they would have access to means-tested childcare support outside of social assistance programs.

It is important to note that the data in the table indicate that most of the change in the number of recipients—both in total and by family type—occurred before the mid-2000s. Since that time, the shares of each family type, as fractions of the total, have remained more or less constant.

The government of Ontario provides similar data to these though the definitions of family types differ slightly from those used in BC. The length of the available time series is also shorter, making it difficult to identify trends. Table 3.2 presents those data.

If we restrict our attention to the period 2007–12, which is common to both tables, the information describing Ontario is not very different from that describing BC. That is, over that period, the share of social assistance beneficiaries by broad family types has not changed noticeably in either province. A significant difference in the two provinces is the smaller percentage of social assistance recipients who are single in Ontario (about 44 per cent) than in BC (about 60 per cent). The share of either single-parent or sole-support families is not very different in the two provinces. Differences in the other definitions of family type do not make any further

Table 3.2 Recipients of Social Assistance by Family Type, Ontario, 2007–2013

	Number of Recipients All Categories of Social Assistance				Recipients by Family Type (%)		
	Singles	Couples	Sole-Support Parents	All Family Types	Singles	Couples	Sole-Support Parents
2007	286,367	168,858	243,224	698,449	41.0	24.2	34.8
2008	296,579	172,668	244,151	713,397	41.6	24.2	34.2
2009	330,823	193,294	255,770	779,887	42.4	24.8	32.8
2010	357,167	209,360	270,318	836,845	42.7	25.0	32.3
2011	376,369	215,121	279,330	870,820	43.2	24.7	32.1
2012	389,291	219,484	283,903	892,677	43.6	24.6	31.8
2013	395,135	217,941	280,940	894,017	44.2	24.4	31.4

Source: Ontario Ministry of Community and Social Services.
Note: The data represent values reported in June of each year. These data include the number of recipients of assistance provided through Ontario Works (OW) and through the Ontario Disability Support Program (ODSP).

comparison possible.[12] From what we can find, Ontario does not report the number of children living in families receiving social assistance.

Finally, the government of Newfoundland and Labrador offers quite a long time series (1991–2012) of data reporting the number of families, by type, receiving social assistance. These data are reported in Table 3.3 below.

The data in Table 3.3 reports the number of families of various types receiving social assistance. So, for example, in 1991 there were 10,160 two-parent families receiving social assistance. The number of people in these 10,160 families is not known from these data because the number of children in families receiving social assistance (in either "two-parent families" or "lone-parent families") is reported separately. This reporting structure means it is only possible to calculate the number of single individuals receiving social assistance as a percentage of the total.

12 Reporting on social assistance beneficiaries by family type differs by province. In BC, the distinction between "couples" and "two-parent families" suggests that only the latter have children. In Ontario, "couples" presumably include families with and without children. Data from Québec (not reported) differ from those of both Ontario and BC by only reporting the number of adults in each family category; the number of children is reported separately but without reference to whether they live in single-parent or two-parent families.

Table 3.3 Families Receiving Social Assistance by Type, Newfoundland and Labrador, 1991–2012

	Singles	Couples	Two-Parent Families	Lone-Parent Families	Children (0–17)	Total Individuals	Singles as % of All Recipients
1991	18,650	3,970	10,160	9,900	35,735	93,025	20.0
1992	22,660	4,385	10,640	10,555	37,330	101,105	22.4
1993	24,235	4,650	10,440	10,480	36,330	101,760	23.8
1994	25,820	4,760	10,150	10,605	35,655	102,330	25.2
1995	26,495	5,115	10,325	10,615	35,655	104,065	25.5
1996	25,760	5,180	10,175	10,500	34,990	102,325	25.2
1997	23,360	5,025	9,370	10,165	32,820	95,485	24.5
1998	21,050	4,860	8,365	9,705	30,120	87,625	24.0
1999	20,075	4,650	7,215	9,225	27,235	80,560	24.9
2000	19,850	4,690	6,285	9,085	25,330	76,415	26.0
2001	19,000	4,605	5,525	8,485	22,980	70,885	26.8
2002	19,055	4,435	4,745	8,150	21,000	66,725	28.6
2003	19,725	4,425	4,370	8,175	20,235	65,875	29.9
2004	19,885	4,250	3,785	8,060	19,005	63,145	31.5
2005	20,000	4,170	3,210	7,765	17,500	60,140	33.3
2006	20,055	4,000	2,745	7,370	16,145	57,150	35.1
2007	19,620	3,755	2,230	6,900	14,655	53,220	36.9
2008	19,505	3,265	1,905	6,525	13,575	50,005	39.0
2009	20,180	3,160	1,830	6,455	13,415	50,075	40.3
2010	21,240	3,050	1,745	6,510	13,385	50,765	41.8
2011	21,395	2,940	1,540	6,270	12,720	49,090	43.6
2012	20,690	2,705	1,335	5,890	11,825	46,240	44.7

Source: Newfoundland and Labrador (2013).
Note: These are calendar-year data.

A remarkable finding from these data is the fall in the number of two-parent families and lone-parent families receiving social assistance. This decrease is also observed in British Columbia. Consistent with this observation is a dramatic fall in the number of children in families receiving social assistance: from a total of 35,735 in 1991 (38.4 per cent of all social assistance recipients) to 11,825 in 2012 (25.6 per cent of all recipients). As in British Columbia, the percentage of social assistance recipients who are single has increased dramatically since the early 1990s.

Persons with disabilities

Understanding the number of social assistance recipients who have disabilities is a key statistic as it informs the debate over the appropriate level of income support to provide. The fear that an overly generous level of income support might dampen work incentives is often behind recommendations to keep income support low. As impeding an individual's willingness to work is a far less serious concern when determining support levels for persons with disabilities, it would be useful to understand just how prevalent it is for persons with disabilities to be receiving social assistance.

To repeat a common refrain, the data on this issue are spotty. The government of British Columbia is the exception in that it reports data, reproduced in Table 3.4, on the number of persons with disabilities

Table 3.4 Recipients of Social Assistance, Persons with Disabilities, British Columbia and Alberta

	British Columbia		Alberta	
	Number	Percentage of All Social Assistance Recipients	Number	Percentage of All Social Assistance Recipients
1994	—	—	16,400	10.8
1995	26,708	7.3	17,100	13.4
1996	29,580	8.6	19,900	16.1
1997	33,913	11.1	21,500	19.7
1998	37,630	13.4	23,100	23.5
1999	41,219	15.7	24,700	26.1
2000	46,320	18.3	26,500	29.5
2001	52,883	21.6	28,200	33.2
2002	56,254	26.8	29,800	35.6
2003	59,641	35.0	30,900	35.0
2004	64,479	42.3	31,500	34.5
2005	68,691	49.0	32,000	36.2
2006	71,785	54.1	34,800	41.5
2007	75,818	56.1	36,100	42.9

Table 3.4 (Continued)

	British Columbia		Alberta	
	Number	Percentage of All Social Assistance Recipients	Number	Percentage of All Social Assistance Recipients
2008	79,873	56.0	37,000	42.8
2009	84,568	51.3	37,000	38.5
2010	88,822	50.0	40,000	35.3
2011	94,037	51.7	43,000	37.7
2012	99,133	55.7	45,000	41.9

Source: British Columbia Ministry of Social Development and Social Innovation (2004, 2008), as well as the annual reports of the Ministry of Community and Seniors Support and the Ministry of Seniors.
Note: The data for BC are calendar-year values. The data for Alberta are for the fiscal year ending in the year indicated.

receiving social assistance in that province since 1995. The number of recipients of income support provided by the government of Alberta's Assured Income for the Severely Handicapped (AISH) program is also available with some digging.[13] These data are also reported in Table 3.4.

Remarkable in this table is the dramatic growth in both provinces of the percentage of social assistance recipients who are persons with disabilities. Using administrative data provided by the government of Manitoba, Stevens, Simpson, and Frankel (2011) report a similar pattern in that province. Using monthly data from 1999 to 2008, they find that the caseload comprised of persons with a disability grew dramatically over the period, from 28 per cent to 50 per cent of the total.[14] The authors note that this change in the composition of social assistance recipients has very important implications for the appropriate design of the program and for appropriate levels of income support. In particular, they comment that this result raises serious questions about the effectiveness of policies aimed at

13 The number of AISH recipients is available for fiscal years 1994–2008 from the *Social Assistance Statistical Report*, 2004 and 2008. More recent data are more approximate as they rely on references in the annual reports of the Ministry of Community and Seniors Support and the Ministry of Seniors to the number of AISH recipients being "more than 37,000" in fiscal year 2009, "more than 40,000" in 2010, "approximately 43,000" in 2011, and "about 45,000" in 2012.

14 The authors note that a significant part of this increase is due to a reclassification of recipients from non-disabled to disabled status among social assistance recipients. One suspects that this recategorization is a possible explanation for the changes in Alberta and BC as well. As the authors of the Manitoba study suggest, this is an important area for future research.

reducing benefits as a way of reducing social assistance use. We would also comment that this evidence suggests it is appropriate to design an assistance program specifically for persons with disabilities and separate from that designed for persons without disabilities. The government of Alberta, having established its AISH program in 1978, is a leader in this regard.

Social assistance incomes

In this section, we turn to measures of social assistance incomes. Here, we rely on information published by the now-defunct National Council of Welfare (NCW) but recently re-released by the Caledon Institute of Social Policy. To gain perspective on the level of adequacy of social assistance incomes, we compare these incomes to a measure of the cost of meeting "basic needs," a measure relying upon the work of Sarlo (2001). Finally, we compare the payments made by provincial governments to those in need and the payments made by the federal government to low-income seniors, an arguably comparable group of citizens, although seniors are not expected to work.

The Caledon Institute provides data on the social assistance income paid, by each provincial government, to three family types: "Single Employable," "Lone Parent, One Child," and "Couple, Two Children." The published data are measured in real (inflation-adjusted) dollars and are available continuously from 1989 to 2012. At our request, the Caledon Institute provided us with these data measured in nominal (not inflation-adjusted) dollars.[15] If we want to gain perspective on the size of these incomes, it is useful to adjust them for some measure of the cost of living. Analysts will often deflate these data by using a consumer price index to remove the effects of inflation. Movements in the adjusted or real value of these incomes now show how the cost of living has risen or fallen relative to a base year.[16] Although this calculation is informative of the effects of inflation on social assistance incomes, the adjustment does not offer insight into how adequate the level of income is.

15 We thank Sherri Torjman, Anne Tweddle, and Ken Battle for providing these data.

16 How good a job the consumer price index does at this is a matter of debate. Movements in the CPI measure changes in the cost of purchasing a "basket" of goods that is imagined to represent the typical purchases of the average household in a specified jurisdiction. Those receiving social assistance are unlikely to consume a "basket" of goods similar to the CPI basket and so movements in the CPI may do a poor job of measuring the true change in the cost of living experienced by those people.

Another approach, which we adopt here, is to compare movements in social assistance incomes to a measure of the cost of meeting a certain standard of living. For this purpose, we use a measure of the cost of meeting "basic needs" as calculated by Sarlo (2001).

Sarlo's measure defines a basket of goods and services that includes shelter, food, clothing, personal hygiene needs, health care, transportation, and a telephone connection. The basket consciously excludes any goods or services that go beyond meeting very basic needs and is purposely designed to measure only the income required to ensure physical survival. This characteristic of Sarlo's measure makes it uncontroversial in the sense that no one would claim it defines a level of income support that is anything but minimal. We use the measure to show just how low the level is of income support provided to those receiving social assistance.[17]

Sarlo's measure of basic needs differs by province because the costs of items in the basket differ by location. The measure is determined for a base year (1997), and we then adjust according to the all-items consumer price index (CPI) for that province to show how the nominal cost of purchasing these basic needs has changed over time.[18] Sarlo provides his measure of basic needs for families of different sizes,[19] enabling us to report the measure appropriate for identifying the cost of meeting basic needs that matches the NCW and Caledon Institute data on the social assistance income received by a single employable person, a family of two parents and two children, and a family consisting of a lone parent and one child.

17 An alternative to using Sarlo's measure is to use the low-income cut-off (LICO) or the Market Basket Measure (MBM) published by Statistics Canada. We prefer to use Sarlo's measure for two reasons. First, Statistics Canada disavows the LICO as a measure of poverty. Second, the MBM is somewhat controversial in that it includes in its basket of "basic needs" items that some might judge to be superfluous to their personal concept of "basic." The measure developed by Sarlo is intentionally designed to be minimalist; *no one* would suggest that there is anything superfluous in his measure of basic needs. We therefore understand his measure to identify what is a bare minimum level of income needed to meet the basic needs of existence, not to flourish or to have the capacity to enjoy existence. A major drawback of the MBM, in addition to any controversy about what needs are "basic," is that the data are only available since 2002. As our interest is in identifying trends, we hesitate to forgo the opportunity to show how the degree of social assistance generosity changed during the 1990s.

18 Thus we cannot claim to escape completely the problem identified above of relying on a CPI designed to measure changes in the cost of living for an average household. One should note that this approach also assumes that the real (or inflation-adjusted) cost of meeting Sarlo's measure of basic needs has remained constant over time, which is unlikely to be true. It is, however, difficult to know in which direction the bias lies.

19 This approach is necessary because there are economies of scale to be enjoyed from living with others.

Figure 3.6 presents data for each province. The lines with markers identify the NCW and Caledon Institute data on the social assistance income received by three family types. The solid lines define the amount of income required to meet a definition of "basic needs" as calculated by Sarlo. Both series are measured in nominal dollars.

The information presented in Figure 3.6 offers some broad conclusions. The first is that the social assistance income received by singles is rarely sufficient to meet Sarlo's measure of basic needs. An exception is in Newfoundland and Labrador where, since 2002, the income support paid to singles has matched the cost of meeting basic needs. Saskatchewan and Québec come closer than other provinces to enabling singles to meet basic needs, but, generally speaking, the gap between income and the cost of meeting even minimal needs is quite substantial.

The social assistance income received by lone-parent families with one child typically does better though, again, it is important to emphasize we are comparing social assistance income to the cost of meeting the most basic of needs. Across the 10 provinces, 3 pay a social assistance income greater than the cost of meeting basic needs, 3 pay less, and 4 could be fairly described as providing an income just sufficient to meet the cost of purchasing basic needs. The government of Newfoundland and Labrador is notable for paying a level of income support in excess (by $4,300 in 2011) of the cost of meeting basic needs. But what is also notable is that the amount of social assistance paid in 2011 ($19,923) remains well below the level of income ($25,215 for those living in St. John's) defined by the Market Basket Measure (MBM) as being sufficient for a lone parent with one child to enjoy a "modest, basic standard of living."

A provincial comparison with respect to the social assistance income provided to a family of two parents and two children yields more variety than do those with respect to the first two family types. Newfoundland and Labrador, PEI, Québec, and Saskatchewan provide a level of income support that closely matches the cost of meeting basic needs, and these payments track these costs rather closely over time. The governments of Nova Scotia, New Brunswick, and British Columbia have provided income support consistently below the cost of meeting the basic needs of a family of this size. The support provided in BC is considerably below, by $4,000 in 2011. Once again, it is important to stress that the amount provided in social assistance ($22,005) was $4,000 short of the cost of meeting Sarlo's basic needs. It is a whopping $15,600 short of what was sufficient to meet the MBM measure for a family of four living in Vancouver ($37,663). The other provinces—Ontario, Manitoba, and Alberta—have a chequered history; the level of income support to this family type exceeded the cost

Figure 3.6 Social Assistance and Basic Needs by Family Type, Canadian Provinces, 1989–2012

a. Newfoundland and Labrador

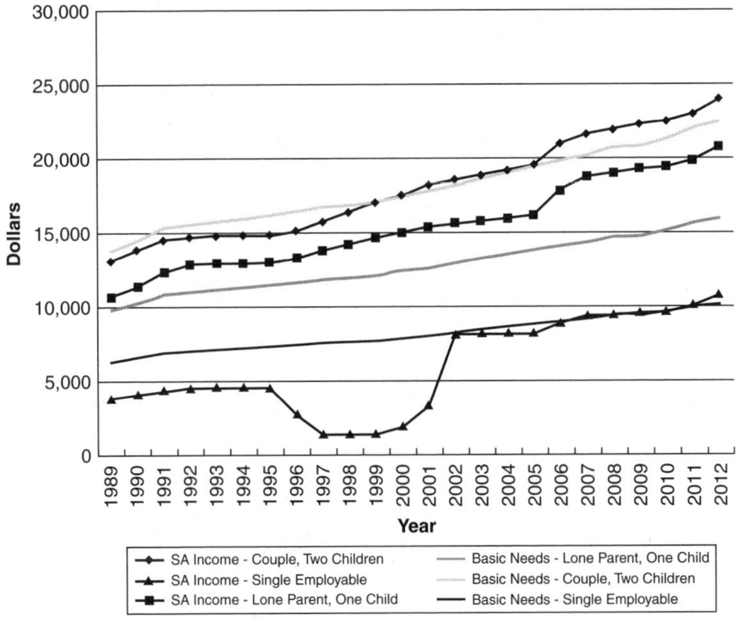

b. Prince Edward Island

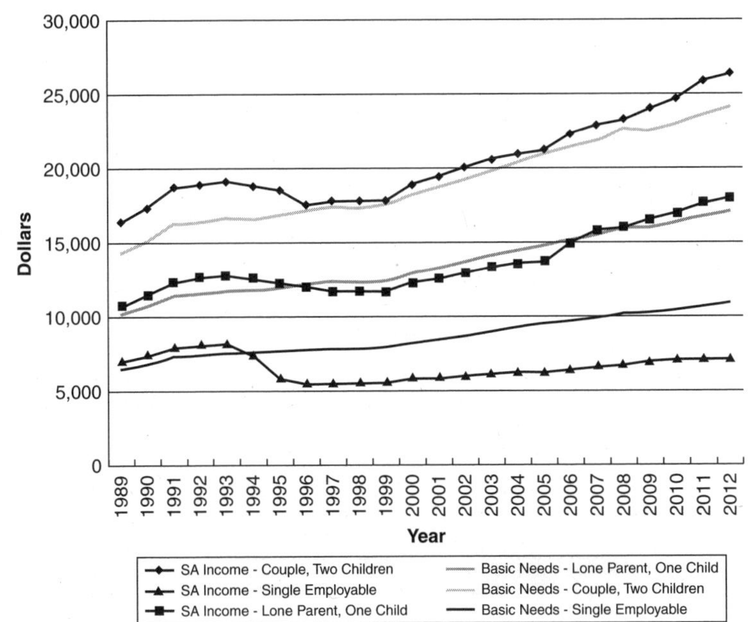

c. Nova Scotia

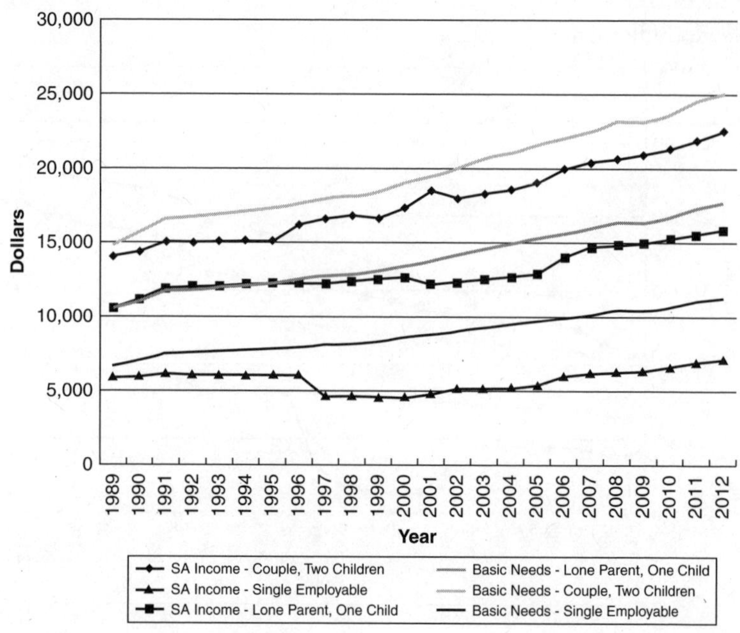

d. New Brunswick

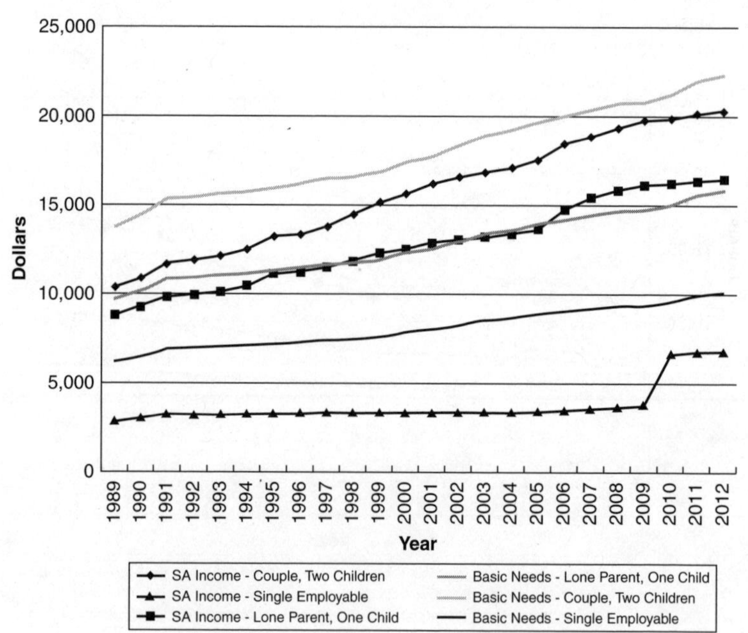

e. Québec

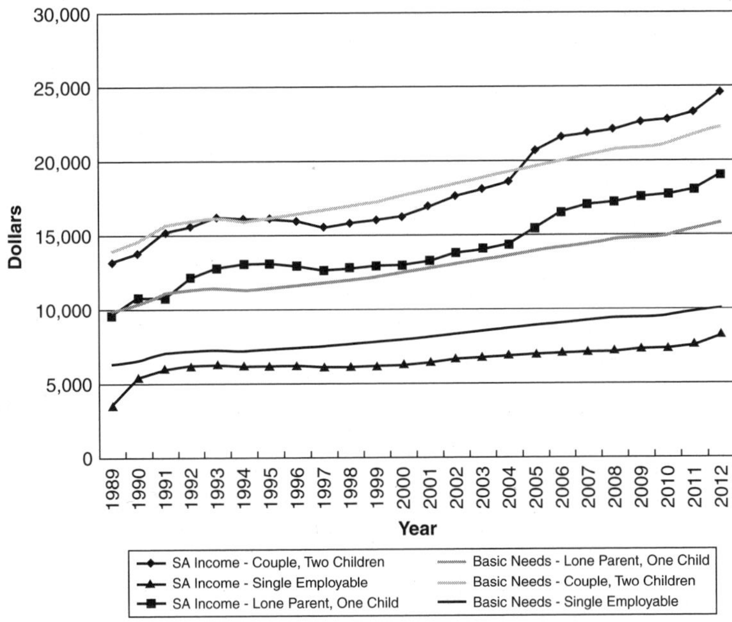

f. Ontario

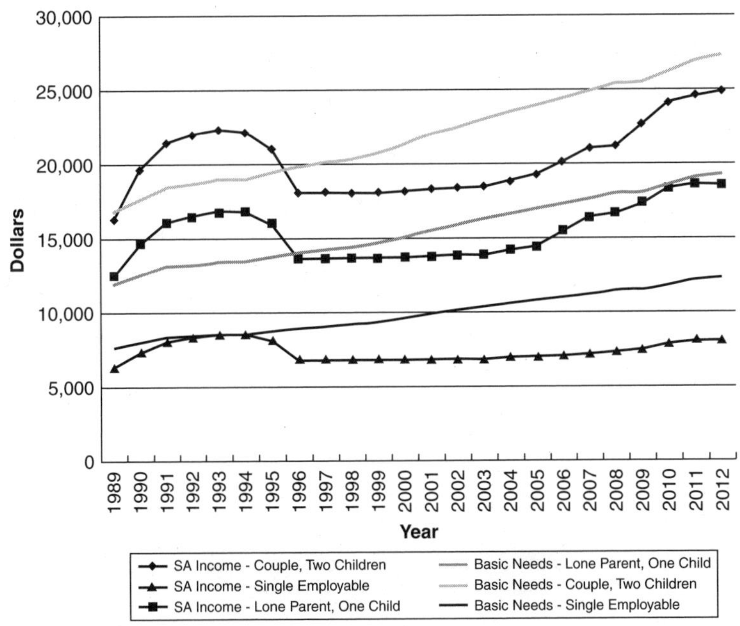

g. Manitoba

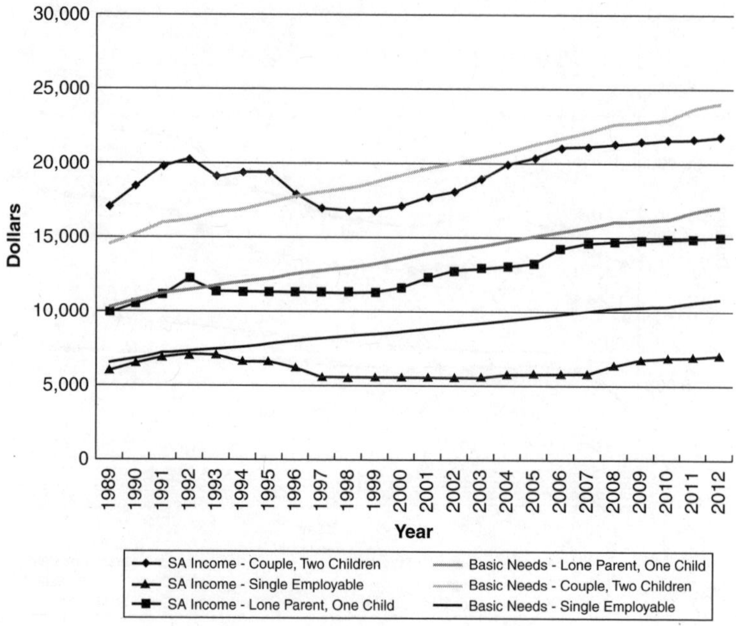

h. Saskatchewan

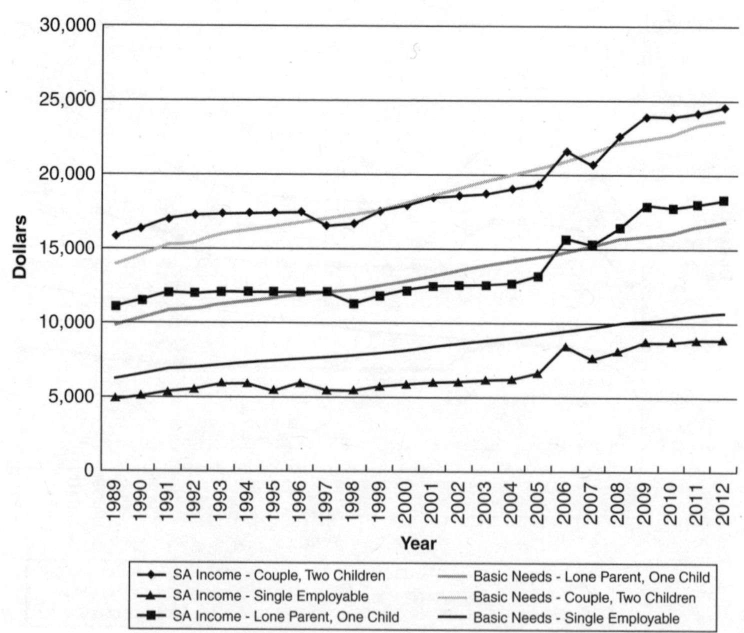

i. Alberta

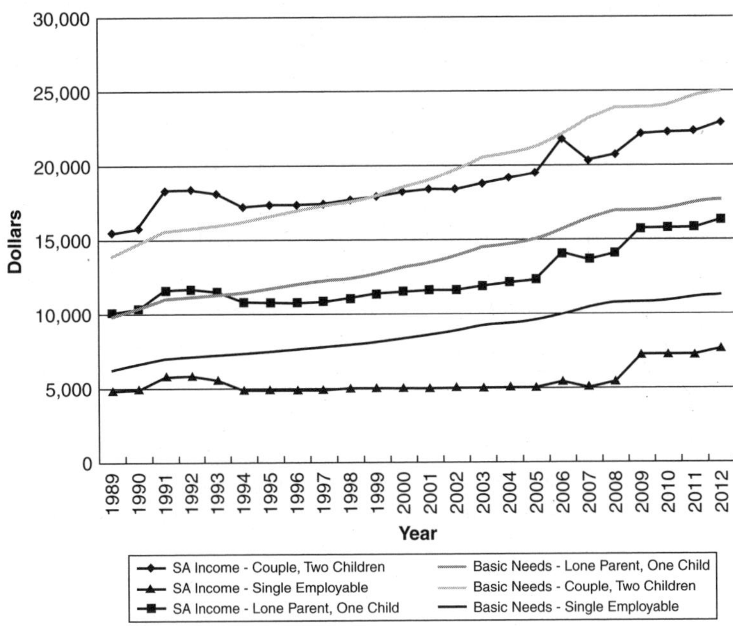

j. British Columbia

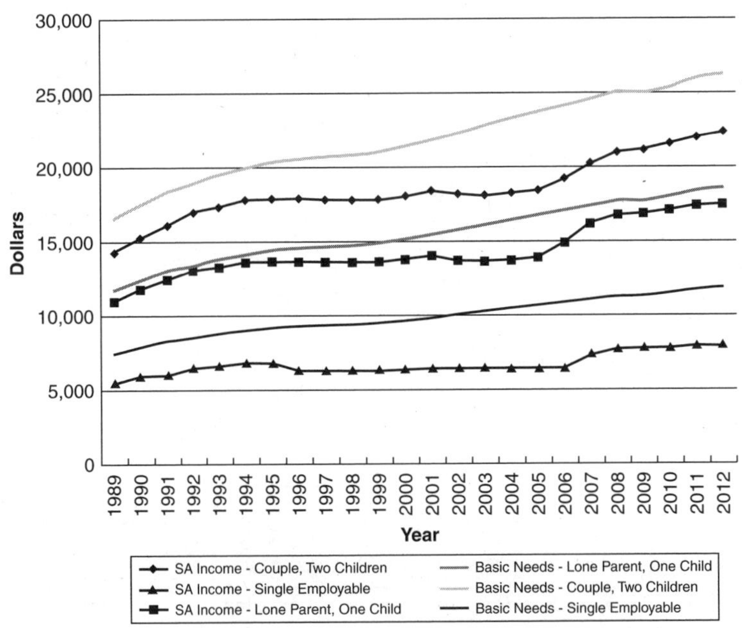

of meeting basic needs during the late 1980s and early 1990s but then dropped below by the mid-1990s. Ontario is notable for allowing income support to two-parent families with two children to fall well below the cost of meeting basic needs over the entire period of 1996–2012.

Another way of evaluating the adequacy of social assistance income paid by provincial governments is to compare it to the income provided by the federal government to poor seniors, those aged over 65 years with an insufficient work history to collect CPP benefits. Figure 3.7 shows, for each province, the sum of the amounts of Old Age Security (OAS) and Guaranteed Income Supplement (GIS) paid by the federal government to a poor, single senior. Also shown is the social assistance income provided by the provincial government to a single person and Sarlo's measure of the cost faced by a single person to meet basic needs.

In every province, the federal pension exceeds the cost of meeting Sarlo's measure of basic needs, and it also exceeds the amount of income identified by the MBM (not shown) as necessary to enjoy a modest, basic standard of living. The difference between social assistance income and

Figure 3.7 Social Assistance, Basic Needs, and the Federal Pension, Canadian Provinces, 1989–2012

a. Newfoundland and Labrador

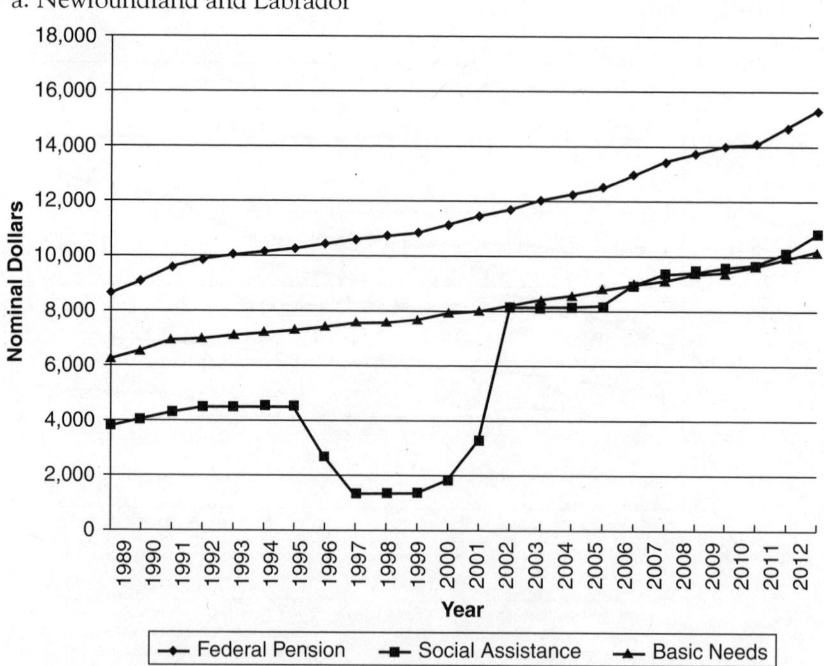

b. Prince Edward Island

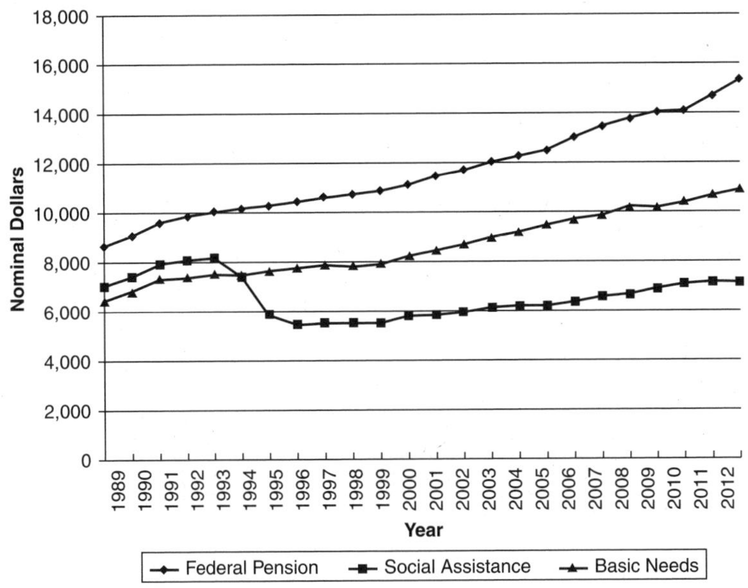

c. Nova Scotia

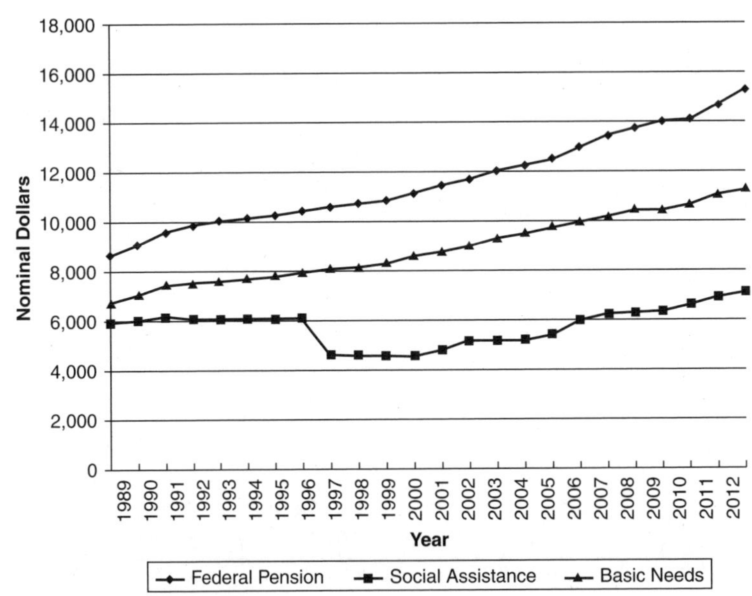

d. New Brunswick

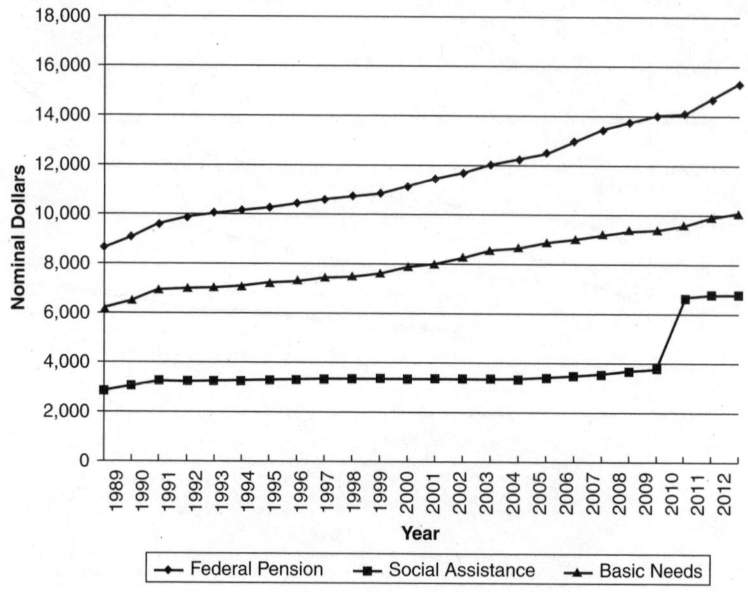

e. Québec

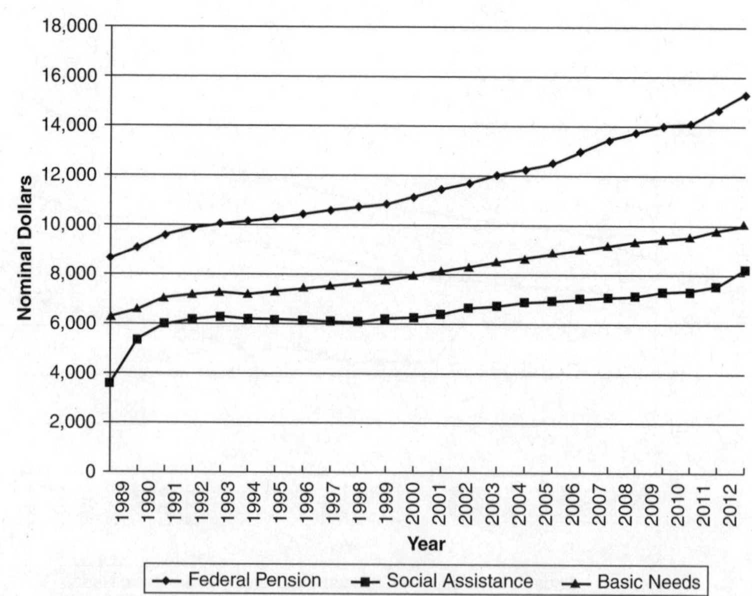

f. Ontario

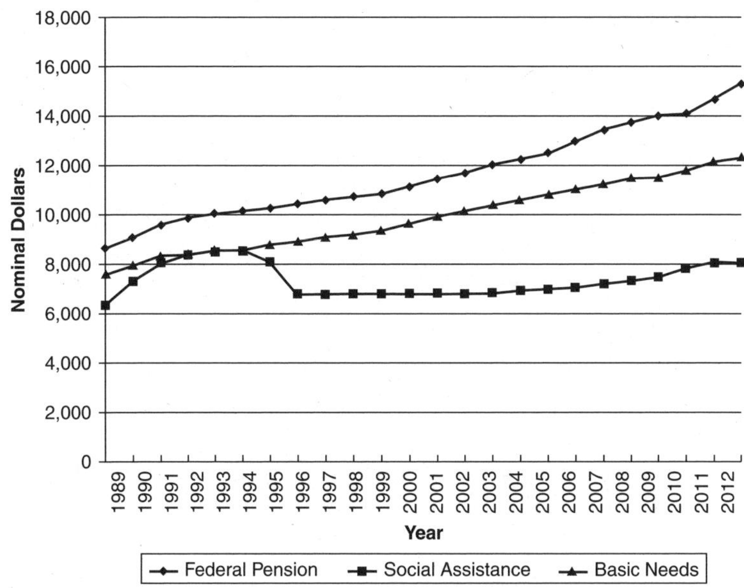

g. Manitoba

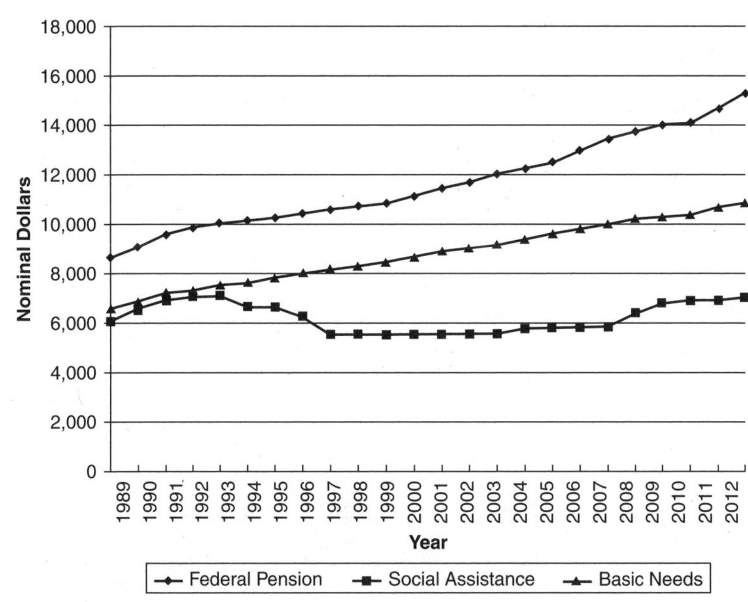

h. Saskatchewan

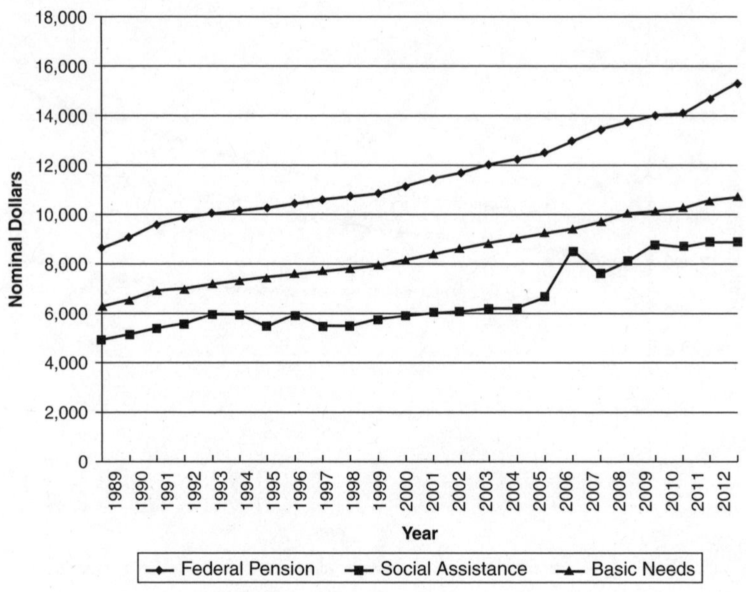

i. Alberta

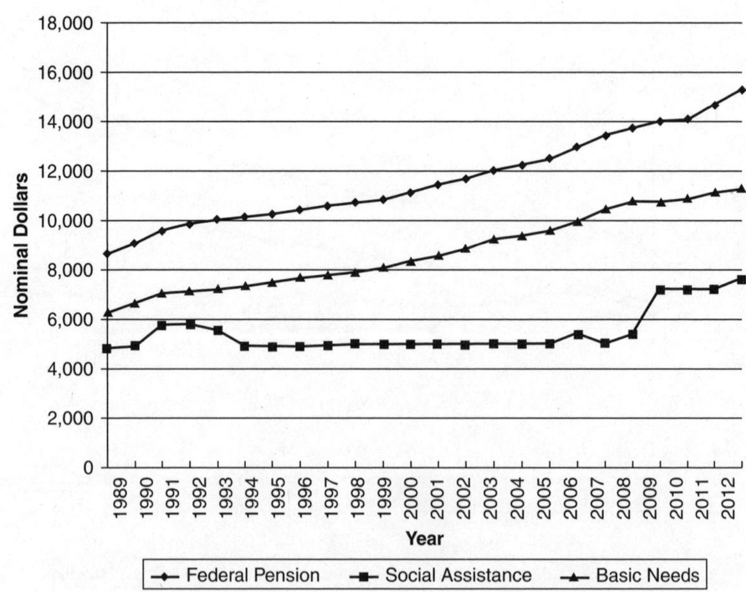

j. British Columbia

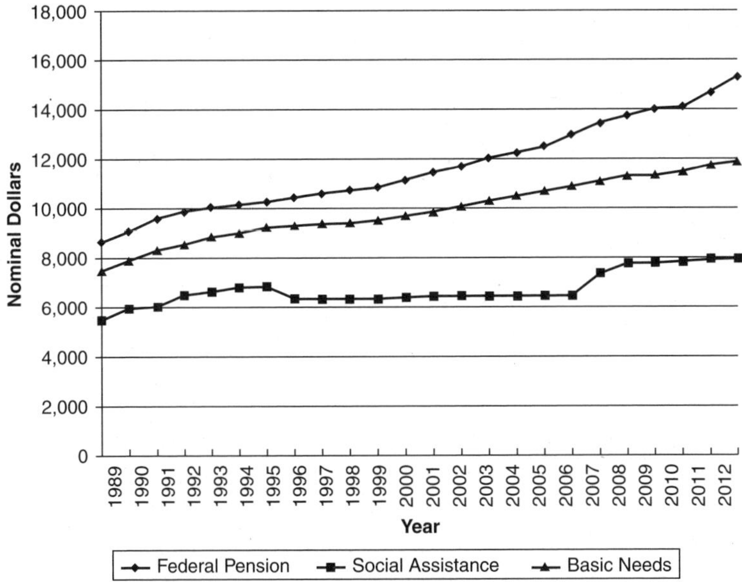

the cost of meeting basic needs as defined by Sarlo averaged about $4,000 in 2012, though it was less than that in Ontario and BC (about $3,000) and higher than that in Newfoundland and Labrador, New Brunswick, and Québec (about $5,000).[20] In every province, the federal pension also exceeds the amount of social assistance paid to a single person. In six provinces, the difference, as of 2011, was about $8,000. Newfoundland and Labrador, at about $5,000, paid an amount of social assistance nearest the amount of the federal pension provided to a poor senior.[21]

20 Note that we do not include the pension amounts that seniors receive from some provincial governments. Were this amount included in our calculations, the gap between the pension provided to a poor, single senior and the social assistance benefit paid to a single employable would be even larger than we show.

21 Of course, seniors do not necessarily need the same level of income as non-seniors to enjoy a similar standard of living. Seniors, for example, are no longer saving for retirement or raising children. On the other hand, private health-care costs likely increase with age. Hamilton (2001) suggests that, on balance, seniors can have significantly lower incomes than non-seniors yet maintain a similar standard of living. If this is so, the differences we have identified between pension incomes and social assistance incomes are even more striking. For a contrary view see MacDonald, Andrews, and Brown (2010) who derive a measure similar to Sarlo's measure of basic needs but specifically aimed at determining the basic living expenses of the elderly.

Overall, social assistance incomes appear to be inadequate to meet even the most meagre level of basic needs for many types of recipients, and they are particularly inadequate for families without children. Another measure of income adequacy, federal pensions, exceeded social assistance incomes in every case. This finding indicates that social assistance incomes in Canadian provinces are certainly not overly generous when compared to either measures of adequacy or other comparable programs.

Conclusion

The purpose of this chapter was to provide a high-level overview of the trends in provincial social assistance programs in Canada. Achieving this goal is surprisingly challenging. It is challenging because the most basic data—how many people receive social assistance and how much they receive in the form of income support—are difficult to find. As well as proving troubling for researchers, the difficulty in finding even basic information about those who receive social assistance is disturbing. Why? For one thing, developing solutions to important issues of public policy requires information. Effective public policies with respect to social assistance can only be established and maintained if there is high-quality, detailed information describing the characteristics of those affected by these policies, information describing how, in the past, those receiving social assistance have responded to events influencing their choices, and information revealing the successes and failures of past attempts to alleviate the problems that policies target. Without good information, we are left at the mercy of those advocating policy solutions based on unproven assertions, biased assessments of long-forgotten events, and the claims of ideologues. Good information and the careful, unbiased assessments and interpretations of that information are at the heart of good policymaking. It is discouraging, then, that it is so difficult to find even the most basic information about provincial social assistance programs.

In this chapter, we make use of data we published previously describing the number of social assistance beneficiaries by province since 1969. The benefit to examining a long time series is that we can comment on the history of social assistance use since 1976. The benefit is limited, however, because data on all of the variables researchers normally associate with determining social assistance use are only available for a much shorter period. Information on social assistance incomes, for example, is available only for the period 1989–2012, so researchers are unable to determine the influence of changes in incomes on social assistance use before 1989, a period during which we have shown the social assistance rate to have varied in ways suggestive of a very large influence being played by variables such as social assistance incomes. Frustratingly then, empirical researchers limit their attention to the years after 1989 even though, as we see in Figures 3.3, 3.4, and 3.5, doing so means ignoring a great deal of interesting variation of the sort that sharpens estimates of the size of influences on social assistance use.

Other information limitations include the general lack of data on the demographic characteristics of social assistance recipients. We have presented snippets of information that are suggestive of very important and very large changes in these characteristics, particularly in the direction of a growing fraction of social assistance beneficiaries being persons with disabilities. Unfortunately, these data are not generally available for all provinces and rarely for the long periods that enable trends to be identified. We applaud those provinces—particularly the provinces of British Columbia and Newfoundland and Labrador—that make available long time series of important data describing the characteristics of those receiving social assistance. These governments stand as impressive examples that we hope other governments will seek to emulate.

Areas for future research suggested by our writing of this chapter include examining the many puzzles we have uncovered in outlining the trends discussed. One major body of work would be econometrically decomposing the determinants of social assistance using the data provided in an attempt to uncover the relative magnitude of the impacts of socio-economic changes and administrative changes in social assistance. The impact of separate programs for those with disabilities is also suggested given their increasing share of all social assistance recipients.

References

Beach, Jane, and Martha Friendly. 2005. *Child Care Fee Subsidies in Canada*. Toronto: Childcare Resource and Research Unit, University of Toronto. http://www.childcarequality.ca/wdocs/QbD_FeeSubsidies_Canada.pdf.

Bell, Stephen. 2001. *Why Are Caseloads Falling?* Washington, DC: The Urban Institute.

British Columbia Ministry of Social Development and Social Innovation. 2004. *Social Assistance Statistical Report*. Victoria: Government Communications and Public Engagement.

British Columbia Ministry of Social Development and Social Innovation. 2008. *Social Assistance Statistical Report*. Victoria: Government Communications and Public Engagement.

Hamilton, Malcolm. 2001. "The Financial Circumstances of Elderly Canadians and the Implications for the Design of Canada's Retirement Income System." In *The State of Economics in Canada: Festschrift in Honour of David Slater*, ed. Patrick Grady and Andrew Sharpe, 225–53. Montréal: McGill-Queen's University Press.

Kneebone, Ronald, and Margarita Gres. 2013. *Trends, Peaks and Troughs: National and Regional Employment Cycles in Canada*. SPP Research Papers 6, no. 21. Calgary: The School of Public Policy, University of Calgary.

Kneebone, Ronald, and Katherine White. 2009. "Fiscal Retrenchment and Social Assistance in Canada." *Canadian Public Policy* 35 (1): 21–40. http://dx.doi.org/10.3138/cpp.35.1.21.

Kneebone, Ronald, and Katherine White. 2014. *The Rise and Fall of Social-Assistance Use in Canada, 1969–2012*. SPP Research Papers 7, no. 5. Calgary: The School of Public Policy, University of Calgary.

MacDonald, B.J., D. Andrews, and R.L. Brown. 2010. "The Cost of Basic Needs for the Canadian Elderly." *Canadian Journal on Aging / La revue canadienne du viellissement* 29 (1): 39–56.

Newfoundland and Labrador. 2013. *Newfoundland and Labrador: Income Support Assistance*. St. John's: Newfoundland and Labrador Statistics Agency. Last modified 26 August 2013. http://nl.communityaccounts.ca/table.asp?_=obfAjIydpaWrnbSTh5-FvKGts2iWlb7NqpODyp.znos_.

Sarlo, Christopher. 2001. *Measuring Poverty in Canada*. Critical Issues Bulletin. Vancouver: Fraser Institute.

Stevens, H., W. Simpson, and S. Frankel. 2011. "Explaining Declining Social Assistance Participation Rates: A Longitudinal Analysis of Manitoba Administrative and Population Data." *Canadian Public Policy* 37 (2): 163–81. http://dx.doi.org/10.3138/cpp.37.2.163.

Tweddle, Anne, Ken Battle, and Sherri Torjman. 2013. *Welfare in Canada 2012*. Ottawa: Caledon Institute of Social Policy.

four

Low-Income and Inequality Trends in Canada

BRIAN MURPHY, ANDREW HEISZ, AND XUELIN ZHANG

Introduction

There have been numerous recent efforts to understand and address the issues of income inequality and poverty in Canada. The House of Commons Standing Committee on Finance recently released the report *Income Inequality in Canada* (Canada 2013), and, a few years earlier, the House of Commons Standing Committee on Human Resources produced a report titled the *Federal Poverty Reduction Plan* (Canada 2010). In addition, between 2002 and 2010, six provinces produced plans for reducing poverty, and some, such as Ontario's, had specific measurable targets (Ontario 2010).

The economic well-being of Canadians is often characterized using poverty and inequality indicators. There is no commonly accepted definition of poverty in Canada, but, because low incomes are an important aspect of poverty, several different low-income rates have been used as a proxy for the incidence of poverty. These indicators help to mark broad trends in the well-being of Canadians, as well as to identify the groups of people and regions of the country that are potentially in need of some kind of income assistance (Murphy, Zhang, and Dionne 2012). They may also be useful for broadly indicating the combined outcomes of programs and policies. For example, several provinces, think tanks, and advocacy groups monitor these indicators to measure the progress of their anti-poverty strategies.

This chapter provides an overview of broad trends in low income and income inequality in Canada using Statistics Canada data. It explains the key measures, reports on basic trends, and draws on insights contributed by Statistics Canada researchers and others. The objective is to provide a background for the other chapters in the book by presenting the stylized facts on broad trends in low income and income inequality.

Definitions and measurement methods

The literature provides many different ways to examine low income and income inequality. Given the complexity of the questions related to low income and income inequality and the measures available, the best approach is to examine these questions from multiple perspectives and using multiple indicators.

There are three low-income rates produced by Statistics Canada, and each is identified according to the threshold used. The first is the well-known rate based on LICOs (low-income cut-offs). The LICO threshold represents the income at which Canadian households tended to spend 20 per cent more of their income on basic necessities (e.g., food, shelter, clothing) than did households in Canada on average. The LICO thresholds were last set in 1992, and 1976 through 2011 thresholds are developed by adjusting the 1992 thresholds for changes in the consumer price index (CPI). LICO thresholds are available for families of different sizes living in variously populated areas of residence. Because the thresholds are fixed (in real terms), LICO low-income rates tell us how population groups are doing in an absolute sense (whether they are falling below or above a fixed threshold).

The second low-income rate is the LIM (low-income measure). The LIM rate is defined as the share of the population whose household income falls below a threshold set at one-half of the median income in any given year. For the LIM, income is measured on an adult-equivalent basis, to adjust for family size and account for economies of scale enjoyed by larger households.[1] Because this threshold is based relative to a contemporary population, LIM rates tell us how population groups are doing relative to the overall population (e.g., whether their income is falling behind or catching up).

In this chapter, we report on low-income trends using both the LICO- and LIM-based indicators. Although Statistics Canada produces these statistics on before- and after-tax bases, in this chapter, we use after-tax measures exclusively (AT-LICO and AT-LIM, respectively). After-tax measures are preferable because after-tax income is a more complete representation of the disposable income available to the family.

The MBM (Market Basket Measure) is the third low-income rate produced by Statistics Canada. Developed by Employment and Social Development Canada (ESDC) and introduced in 2000, the MBM defines a low-income person as one who lives in a household whose income is insufficient to purchase a fixed basket of goods and services that have been

1 Adjusted household income is calculated by dividing the household income by the square-root of household size. Adjusted income is assigned to each household member, and then analysis takes place at the individual level.

deemed necessary to function in Canadian society. We will not be making reference to the MBM in this chapter because MBM-based low-income rates are only available since 2002 and also because the results from the LICO and LIM measures adequately capture the trends we wish to discuss. Additional analysis based on the MBM is available in Zhang (2010).

When measuring income inequality, we first use the well-known GINI coefficient. The GINI coefficient is a summary measure of inequality that is widely used and accepted. It is a number that ranges between 0 and 1 where 0 represents a situation of complete equality and 1 represents a situation of complete inequality. When discussing the GINI coefficient, we report statistics generated using after-tax income adjusted for adult equivalence. We use after-tax income for the reason mentioned above, and we use adult equivalized income as this renders incomes comparable across family sizes.

In examining income inequality, we also use various income concentration measures, which measure the concentration of income between particular quantiles of the income distribution. For example, we report the concentration of income "in the top 1 per cent" or "in the top percentile." Depending on the concentration indicator used, income may be measured on a before- or after-tax basis or in equivalized or non-equivalized forms, which we will clarify at the appropriate place in the text.

National trends in low income and inequality

Over the past 34 years, low-income individuals have accounted for as much as 16 per cent of the population and as little as 9 per cent depending on the time period and the low-income line used. In the short term, low-income tends to follow the unemployment rate under both LICO (the fixed standard) and LIM (the relative standard). For example, in Figure 4.1, when the unemployment rate rose from less than 8 per cent in 1981 to about 12 per cent in 1983, low-income rates increased one to two percentage points. Similarly, when the unemployment rate dropped from 12 per cent in 1983 to less than 8 per cent in 1989, low-income rates decreased between two to four percentage points. Likewise, between 2007 and 2009, when the unemployment rate jumped by two percentage points, low-income rates increased under both LICO and LIM.

LIM and LICO rates diverged in recent decades. Figure 4.1 shows that, from 1976 to the end of the 1980s, low-income incidences under LICO and LIM moved together, but post-1995, low-income incidence under LIM rose while incidence under LICO fell. Although the downward trend in low income under LICO is a natural reflection of the economic growth relative to a fixed standard, the upward trend in low income under LIM

Figure 4.1 Low-Income, Unemployment, and Inequality Indicators, 1976–2011

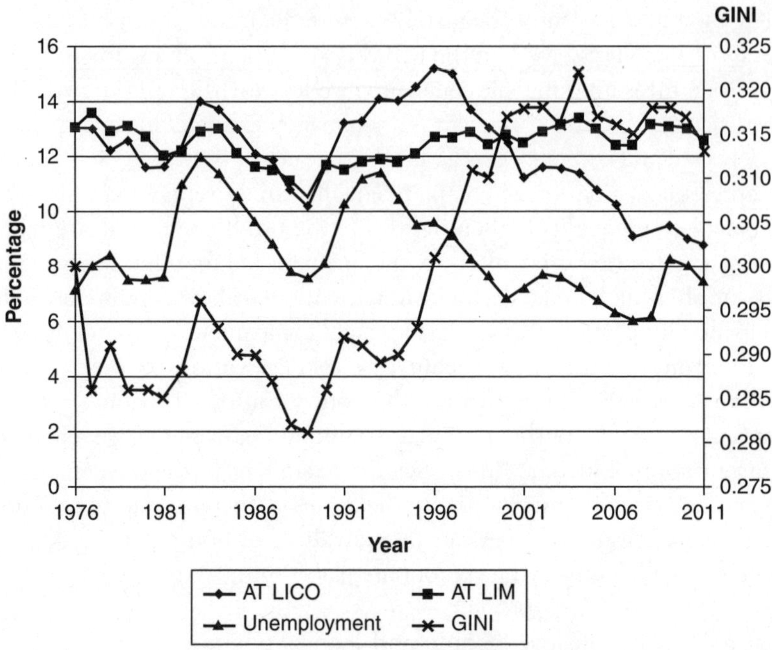

Source: For after-tax GINI coefficient, Statistics Canada CANSIM, *Table 202–0709: Gini Coefficients of Market, Total and After-Tax Income of Individuals*; for after-tax low-income rates, *Table 202–0802, Persons in Low Income Families Table 282–0002*; for unemployment rate *Labour Force Survey Estimates.*

reflects the fact that lower income families lost ground relative to those at the median.

Figure 4.1 also shows patterns of change in the GINI coefficient. It is important to note that income inequality and low income, though related, are not the same. Depending on how low income is measured, and depending on the nature of the changes in the income distribution, it is possible to have rising inequality at the same time as low-income rates are falling. As is now known (Heisz 2007; Saez and Veall 2007), income inequality measured by the GINI rose markedly over the late 1990s, from a level of about 0.290 across the 1976–95 period to nearly 0.320 after 2000. We compared the GINI to the low-income measures and found similarities in short-term trends in the GINI and LIM. For example, from 1983 to 1989, the GINI and the LIM both dropped, followed by increases during the 1990s and constant levels during the 2000s. Trends in the GINI are partly reflected

Figure 4.2 Percentage Change in Average Low-Income Incidence by Characteristics

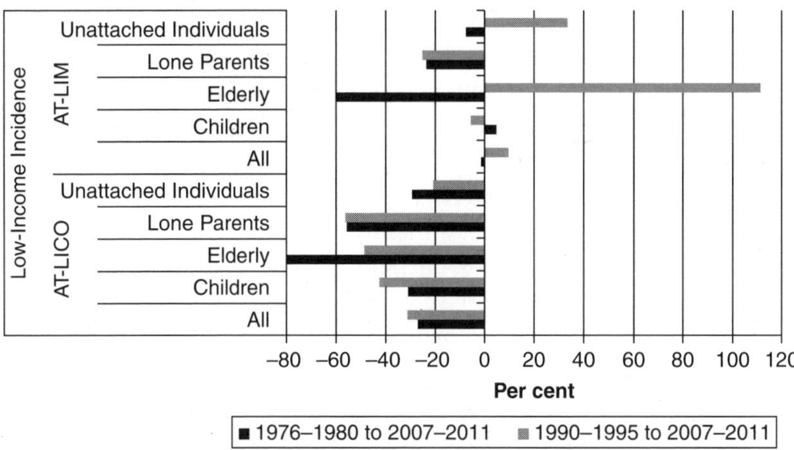

Source: Authors' caluculations based on Statistics Canada CANSIM, *Table 202–0802: Persons in Low Income Families, Annual.*

in the LIM because both measures respond to relative changes in income distribution, although the LIM mainly responds to changes in the bottom half of the income distribution.

Trends in low income for specific populations

Trends in low income across vulnerable groups, such as children, the elderly, or lone-parent families, and across individuals living in different parts of the country are important to our understanding of what groups may be in need of income assistance or other policy attention.[2] In this section, we discuss trends in low income across vulnerable groups and by province.

Children. Among those vulnerable to low income, children have drawn the most attention in industrialized countries.[3] Low income among children cannot be determined independently from the income rates of the adults with whom they live; hence, it is not surprising to see low income among Canadian children moving in a similar way as low income among the general population. However, under either LICO or LIM, low-income

2 The current chapter only highlights some groups of individuals. Please refer to Murphy, Zhang, and Dionne (2012) for other groups of individuals or more details.

3 Children are defined as those younger than 18 years old. For an early study, see Crossley and Curtis (2006).

incidence among Canadian children improved relative to that of the working-age population (aged between 18 and 64). During the 1980s and 1990s, the LICO rate for children was significantly higher than that for the working-age population, yet it fell to the same level as that for the working-age population in the 2000s. If we consider the LIM, low-income incidence among Canadian children was significantly higher than that for the working-age population between 1976 and 2011, but the gap has declined since 2000.

Lone-parent heads of families. Female lone parents in Canada have long been identified as a group with a high risk of falling into poverty. From 1976 to the mid-1990s, the low-income rate for persons in lone-parent families was routinely between 40 per cent and 50 per cent. However, low-income incidence for this group has generally declined since the mid-1990s. The drop in the LICO rate was particularly strong. By 2009, the incidence dropped more than half from its historical high, reached in the mid-1990s. Nevertheless, relative (LIM-based) low income has remained high for persons in lone-parent families, with low-income rates exceeding 30 per cent during the 2000s.

Elderly. There have also been dramatic trends in low income among the elderly in Canada.[4] From the 1970s to the mid-1990s, low-income incidence for the elderly followed a steep downward trend under both LICO and LIM. Under LICO, it fell from about 30 per cent to less than 10 per cent by 1995. Under LIM, it fell from above 30 per cent to a low of 4 per cent during the same period. Interestingly, the incidences under the two different thresholds have followed different paths since then. Under LICO, the low-income rate continued its downward trend and, by 2011, had reached an historic low of 5 per cent. But under LIM, it has increased, and, by 2011, the incidence had nearly tripled to 12 per cent. This increase provides us with an important signal that incomes for the elderly have fallen behind those of the general population.

Unattached late-middle-aged persons. Another group of interest are unattached persons in late middle age (from 45 to 64). Individuals in this group are generally not qualified for retirement benefits, and, unlike their younger counterparts, they may have fewer family supports to rely upon when they are in financial difficulty. There has been a remarkable improvement in low-income incidence for this group since 2000, particularly under the LIM threshold. At its historic high during the end of the 1990s, low income

4 Senior poverty in Canada has been examined by several authors (Milligan 2008; Osberg 2001; Veall 2008).

under LIM was around 45 per cent for this group. This incidence fell to about 35 per cent in more recent years, but, still, about one-third of this group fell under both the LICO and the LIM thresholds, and low income among this group was close to three times higher than incidence for individuals not belonging to this group.

Interprovincial trends

Studying low income across provinces has a direct bearing to the study of social assistance as the latter often falls under provincial jurisdiction. Here we will compare low-income rates across the provinces using movements in the national low-income rate as a reference.

LICO and LIM rates in the Atlantic provinces have improved steadily relative to Canada-wide rates over the 1976–2011 period. In the 1970s, their low-income rates under LICO were either higher or similar to Canadian levels. For example, incidence in Newfoundland and Labrador averaged 17.0 per cent between 1976 and 1980 while, over the same period, the Canadian average was just over 12.5 per cent. But in the past five years, the LICO rates of all Atlantic provinces fell below national levels. On the other hand, LIM rates were well above national levels during the 1970s and the 1980s. The province of Newfoundland and Labrador is again a typical example. In the 1970s, this province's incidence was almost twice as high as the national levels. But, during the last decade, low-income incidences in this and other Atlantic provinces approached the national level (about 13 per cent).

In Québec, low-income rates under both LICO and LIM improved relative to Canada-wide rates in the 2000s while, in Ontario, low-income rates steadily deteriorated relative to Canada-wide rates beginning in the mid-1980s. Under both LICO and LIM, low-income incidences in Québec have approached the Canadian levels from above while those in Ontario have approached the national levels from below.

In the Western provinces, low income in Alberta and Saskatchewan improved relative to the national low-income trend. Under both LICO and LIM, low-income rates in Alberta dropped well below the national level during the last two decades, and a clear downward trend formed since the mid-1990s. In Saskatchewan, low-income rates have dropped sharply since 2005. Low income in Manitoba, although still at or above the national levels in recent years, also improved relative to its levels in the late 1970s, when the provincial low-income rate was nearly five percentage points higher than the national level. A clear trend in British Columbia can be observed under both LICO and LIM: before the mid-1990s,

Figure 4.3 Percentage Change in Average Low-Income Incidence by Province

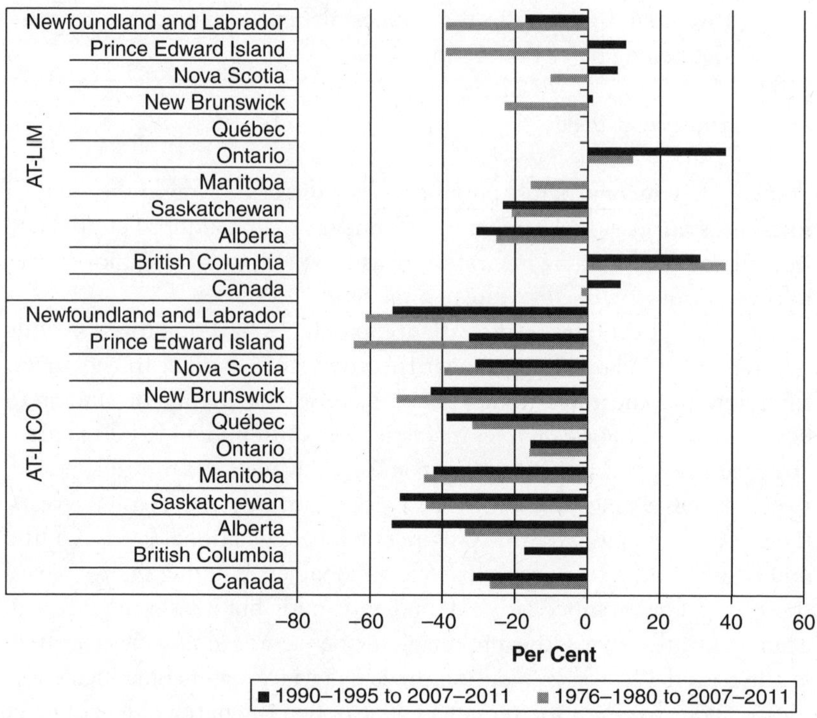

Source: Statistics Canada CANSIM, *Table 202–0802: Persons in Low Income Families*, with authors' calculations.[5]

provincial low-income incidences were similar to and sometimes below national levels, but, since the late 1990s, low income in this province has surpassed the national level.

Income inequality

Figure 4.4 shows the share of income held by the top 20 per cent (or top quintile) of income earners. The chart shows an increase in the concentration of income in the top quintile over the 1996 to 1999 period. Between

5 This change is calculated as the percentage change between the average low-income incidence from 1976 to 1980 and the average incidence between 2007 and 2011 or the percentage change between the average incidence from 1990 to 1994 and the average incidence between 2007 and 2011.

Figure 4.4 The Share of Income Held by the Top Quintile*

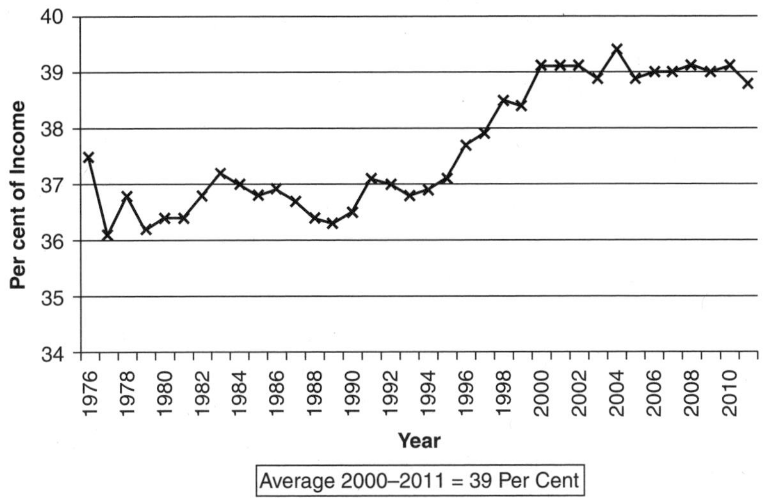

Source: Statistics Canada CANSIM, *Table 202–0707: Market, Total and After-Tax Income of Individuals*.
*Adult-equivalent-adjusted, after-tax family income.

2000 and 2011, the top 20 per cent of income earners earned 39.0 per cent of all income, up from 36.7 per cent measured between 1976 and 1995.

Inequality changes when certain parts of the income distribution grow at a different rate than others. Indeed, it is possible to have rising inequality when all parts of the income distribution are becoming better off in absolute terms. This has been the case in Canada over the period we are studying. Comparing 1989 (before the rise in income inequality) to 2011, we find that family income in the lowest quintile grew 8 per cent. In the highest quintile, it grew by 32 per cent. So, in Canada, it is the faster increase in income among high-income earners that has driven rising after-tax income inequality. The increase in inequality seen in Canada during this period was also seen in other countries (OECD 2011).

The widespread increase in inequality was also seen among the Canadian provinces. Statistics at the provincial level are somewhat more susceptible to higher sampling error due to smaller samples. To deal with this problem, we use data averaged over five years to reduce noise in the estimates, comparing the 1985–89 period to the 2007–11 period. We find that income inequality rose in each of the 10 provinces although some increases were small and statistically insignificant. Inequality increases were largest in Newfoundland and Labrador, Ontario, Alberta, and British Columbia.

The top one per cent

Figure 4.5 shows the share of total income received by the top one per cent of income earners. In this chart, income is measured on a pre-tax basis. When describing income at the top of the income distribution, economists commonly use measures reflecting income generated by the market (e.g., Veall 2012). We use this approach partly because it is the one used in comparative papers from the United States, which have used it because of data availability. Analysis of the data on a post-tax basis yields lower levels of concentration but does not affect the trends very much.

The share of income earned by the top one per cent has been increasing steadily over the period, except for during the time around the onsets of economic slowdowns when the income share of high-income earners tends to fall. It peaked at a 12 per cent income share in 2006 and 2007. The income threshold to enter the top one per cent was $209,600 in 2011. The concentration of income in the top one per cent fell between 2007 and 2011.

Figure 4.5 The Share of Income Held by the Top One Per Cent of Income Earners*

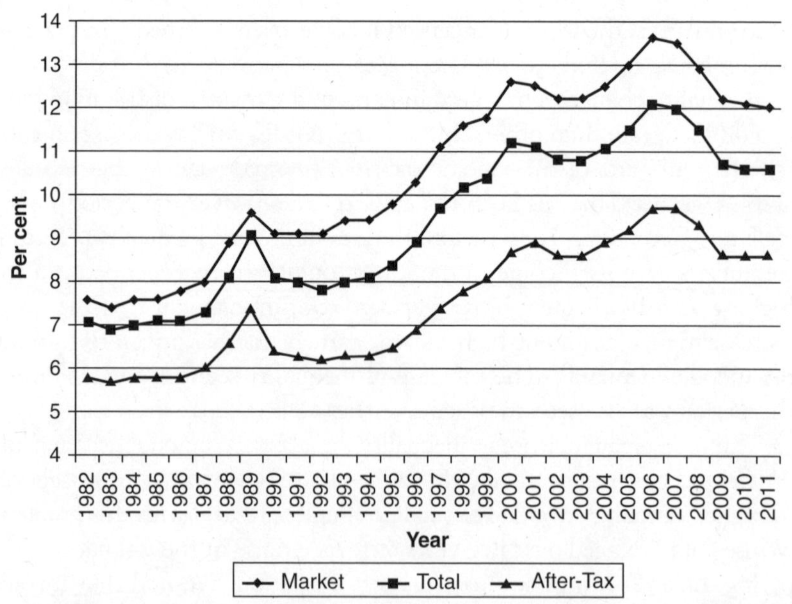

Source: Statistics Canada CANSIM, *Table 204–0001: High Income Trends of Tax Filers in Canada, Provinces, Territories and Census Metropolitan Areas.*
*Market, total (pre-tax), and after-tax income among individual tax filers.

The role of redistribution in income inequality trends

Broadly speaking, Canadian families receive their income from market sources, such as earnings or returns from investments, and from direct government transfers, such as employment insurance and social assistance, and they pay income taxes. It is well known that the government sector (through transfers and taxes) lowers income inequality.

One can demonstrate this effect of the government sector on income inequality by contrasting after-tax inequality to market-income inequality. The GINI measure of family market-income inequality, which mainly reflects differences in annual earnings, was 0.436 in 2011, compared to 0.388 in 1989 and 0.365 in 1979. Comparable figures for after-tax inequality were 0.313, 0.281, and 0.286. Hence, the level of inequality was lower and the increase was muted for after-tax income, after government transfers and taxes were factored in (e.g., the tax and transfer system reduced the GINI coefficient by nearly one-third in 2011).

The redistributive effect of the tax and transfer system has been studied many times over the past decade. The storyline that comes from these studies is that increases in market-income inequality that occurred during the 1980s' and 1990s' recessions were completely offset by a tax and transfer system that became more redistributive, such that there was no increase in after-tax income inequality up to 1995. During the second half of the 1990s, the tax and transfer system became somewhat less redistributive, and after-tax income inequality rose (Frenette, Green, and Milligan 2009; Heisz 2007).

However, the amount by which redistribution currently reduces inequality is not small by historical standards. Redistribution reduced market income inequality by about one-third in each of the 1970s, 1980s, and 2000s.

Importance of social assistance in low income and inequality

Later in the chapter, we list several factors that combine to influence the aggregate movements in income inequality and low income. Among these, institutional changes such as changes in policies related to social assistance might have played an important role. To gain some idea of the importance of social assistance to the distribution of income, we calculated low-income incidences and GINI coefficients for a hypothetical distribution of income assuming that income from social assistance did not exist. Of course, this exercise is a "thought experiment" and does not take into account any behavioural responses that would take place in reaction to the disappearance of a major social program such as social assistance. Thus, it does not tell us what low income or inequality would have been in the absence of social assistance; rather, it informs us about the relative importance of social assistance in reducing low income or inequality, all other things being equal.

Results are shown in Figure 4.6. The low-income rate based upon income not including social assistance measured at least six per cent higher than the rate based upon all income sources.[6] Likewise, the GINI coefficient was a minimum of three per cent higher for the entire 1976 to 2011 period. The importance of social assistance in the income composition of low-income individuals was higher in the 1990s, as indicated by the elevated differentials between low income and inequality with and without social assistance in that decade. In 1993 for example, the after-tax GINI coefficient was 0.289 (considering all income sources), but, if we exclude social assistance, it measures 0.316, a nine per cent difference. Similarly, in 1996, the low-income incidence under the after-tax LIM was 12.7 per cent while it was 16 per cent excluding social assistance, a 25 per cent difference.

Figure 4.6 Percentage Difference in After-Tax Income Distribution without Social Assistance

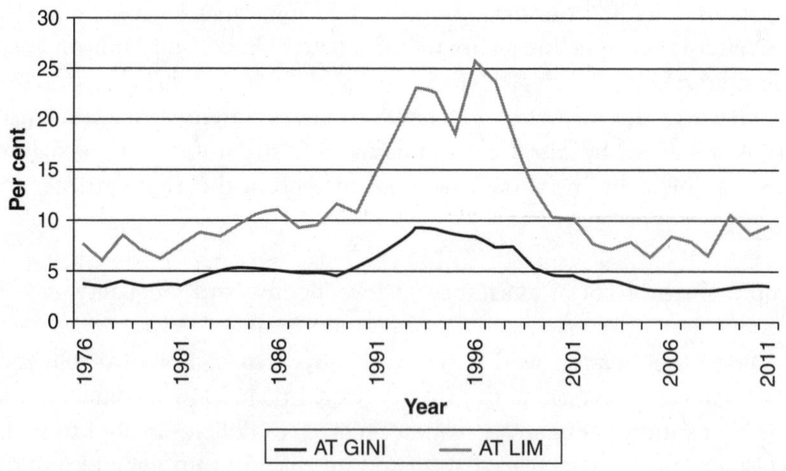

Source: Authors' calculations.
Note: The calculations are for adult-equivalent-adjusted, after-tax family income both with and without social assistance.

6 This thought experiment can be done only under the LIM methodology.

Income mobility

In recent decades, the study of low income has evolved from simply looking at cross-sectional incidences of low income to also looking at longitudinal or "dynamic" questions.[7] In longitudinal studies, the same respondents are followed for several years, with changes in their situations being recorded. In this way, researchers can see whether the low-income population remains fixed over time or if there is substantial mobility into and out of the low-income state.

Data for Canada indicate that there is quite a lot of change in the low-income population from one year to the next. For example, from the early 1990s (when these statistics began to be calculated) to 2008 about 40 per cent of low-income persons in one year had exited by the next.

Changes in the low-income rate reflect changes in the number of persons either entering or leaving low income. The low-income entry rate under both LICO and LIM has followed a downward trend from 1993–94 to 2009–10. Before the year 2000, the entry rate under LICO varied between four per cent and five per cent of the population. This rate dropped to the three per cent to four per cent range in the first five years thereafter, and, since 2004–05, the entry rate generally varied around the three-per-cent mark. In terms of the exit rate, there was a slight upward trend under LICO. In the 1990s, the low-income exit rate under LICO averaged close to 32 per cent, indicating that one-third of low-income individuals would escape low income each year, but, in the period after 2000, the average exit rate rose to 36 per cent. So the reduction in low income under LICO is a combination of lower entry rates and higher exit rates.

Likewise, a natural extension to the study of cross-sectional inequality is to ask these questions: "To what extent does a person's relative income change over time?" "How mobile is a person across the income distribution?" With longitudinal data, we can also describe how inequalities change over time. A forthcoming Statistics Canada study by Zhang, Chung, and Saani examines the income mobility of Canadians across the income distribution. It examines multiple indicators across a long period and finds, for example, that both the chances of moving up out of the bottom decile or moving down from the top decile have been decreasing over time. The results confirm the conclusion reached by other researchers—income mobility has declined in Canada. This finding is important as less income mobility for a given level of income inequality corresponds to less labour market opportunity and reduced equity (Beach 2006).

7 For an introduction to various measures of low-income dynamics, see Ren and Xu (2011).

One can also extend the time horizon and examine to what extent income rankings are transferred across generations. In these studies of intergenerational mobility, the income or earnings of parents are compared to the income or earnings of their children many years later. After adjusting for differences in incomes due to the life-cycle position of parents and children, one can see to what extent children inherit their parents' economic status. Thus, the results reflect the degree of equality of opportunity available in Canada, at least to the extent that the outcomes of Canadians are independent of their relative economic status as children. Several such studies over the past two decades have led to the conclusion that intergenerational mobility is higher in Canada compared to the United States (Corak and Heisz 1999). Additional research has shown a correlation between a country's income inequality and the level of intergenerational mobility, with more unequal societies being less mobile (Corak 2013).

Conclusion

In this chapter, we have focused on broad trends in low income and income inequality. Other studies have gone deeper into the compositional factors underlying these trends, such as changes in redistribution through taxes and transfers, changes in wage inequality and family structure, changes in the earnings of workers in particular occupations or industries, changes in the monetary returns afforded to education or experience (age), changes in the gender pay gap, and regional trends in Canada (Fortin et al. 2012). In addition, there is a large and growing economic literature on the causal drivers of changes in income distribution, such as the importance of the resource boom, of skill-biased technological change, and of other institutional factors: for example, minimum wages or unionization rates, the amount of offshoring and international trade, and the importance of changes in executive compensation (Canada 2013; Gordon and Dew-Becker 2008; OECD 2012).

Each of these potential drivers may have created advantages or disadvantages for some groups in the labour market, yielding higher relative wages for some and (if nothing else changed to offset the increase in wage inequality) leading to changes in the distribution of income. It is important to note that these factors may have affected different points in the income distribution. Factors found to influence earnings at the top one per cent may be different from those found to influence overall-earnings inequality or low-income rates. Each of these factors may be important; hence, a complex and interacting system of forces could underlie the trends described in this chapter.

The overview of low-income and income-inequality trends in Canada presented in this chapter has led to the following stylized facts.

- Recent trends in low income depend importantly on what low-income measure is used. Under the LICO, which compares income to a threshold that is fixed over time (an absolute measure of low income), the low-income rate has declined sharply since the mid-1990s. But under the LIM, a relative low-income measure, low income has risen. This difference reflects the fact that incomes have risen for those at the lower end of the income distribution, but not as fast as for those at the median.
- Since 1976, the elderly and persons living in lone-parent families experienced significant reductions in low-income incidence regardless of the low-income line used. In recent years, relative low-income rates have risen for unattached individuals and the elderly.
- Income inequality rose in Canada. A similar increase was seen in most OECD countries and occurred in most Canadian provinces. In Canada, the bulk of the increase was concentrated in the 1995–2000 period.
- Underlying the rise in income inequality is an increase in family market-income inequality. Income inequality is reduced through the tax and transfer system.
- Social assistance has played an important role in the reduction of low income and inequality.
- Income mobility is another important aspect of low income and inequality. For example, a significant fraction of low-income persons exit low income from one year to the next, and exit rates under LICO have risen.

References

Beach, Charles M. 2006. "How Has Earnings Mobility Changed in Canada?" In *Dimensions of Inequality in Canada*, ed. David A. Green and Jonathan Kesselman, 101–26. Vancouver: UBC Press.

Canada. Parliament. House of Commons. Standing Committee on Finance. 2013. *Income Inequality in Canada: An Overview*. 2nd sess., 41st Parliament. http://www.parl.gc.ca/HousePublications/Publication.aspx?DocId=6380060&Language=E&Mode=1&Parl=41&Ses=2.

Canada. Parliament. House of Commons. Standing Committee on Human Resources, Skills, and Social Development and the Status of Persons with Disabilities. 2010. *Federal Poverty Reduction Plan: Working in Partnership Towards Reducing Poverty in Canada*. 3rd sess., 40th Parliament. http://www.parl.gc.ca/HousePublications/Publication.aspx?DocId=4770921.

Corak, Miles. 2013. "Income Inequality, Equality of Opportunity, and Intergenerational Mobility." *Economic Journal* 27 (3): 79–102.

Corak, Miles, and Andrew Heisz. 1999. "The Intergenerational Earnings and Income Mobility of Canadian Men, Evidence from Longitudinal Income Tax Data." *Journal of Human Resources* 34 (3): 504–33. http://dx.doi.org/10.2307/146378.

Crossley, Thomas, and Lori Curtis. 2006. "Child Poverty in Canada." *Review of Income and Wealth* 52 (2): 237–60. http://dx.doi.org/10.1111/j.1475-4991.2006.00186.x.

Fortin, Nicole, David A. Green, Thomas Lemieux, Kevin Milligan, and W. Craig Riddell. 2012. "Canadian Inequality: Recent Developments and Policy Options." *Canadian Public Policy* 38 (2): 121–45. http://dx.doi.org/10.3138/cpp.38.2.121.

Frenette, Marc, David A. Green, and Kevin Milligan. 2009. "Taxes, Transfers, and Canadian Income Inequality." *Canadian Public Policy* 35 (4): 389–411.

Gordon, Robert J., and Ian Dew-Becker. 2008. *Controversies about the Rise of American Inequality: A Survey*. NBER Working Paper No. 13982. Cambridge, MA: National Bureau of Economic Research. http://www.nber.org/papers/w13982.

Heisz, Andrew. 2007. *Income Inequality and Redistribution in Canada: 1976 to 2004*. Analytic Studies Branch Research Paper Series No. 298. Ottawa: Statistics Canada.

Milligan, Kevin. 2008. "The Evolution of Elderly Poverty in Canada." *Canadian Public Policy* 34 (4): S79–S94. http://dx.doi.org/10.3138/cpp.34.4.S79.

Murphy, Brian, X. Zhang, and C. Dionne. 2012. *Low Income in Canada: A Multi-Line and Multi-Index Perspective*. Income Research Paper Series No. 75F0002M–001. Ottawa: Statistics Canada.

OECD (Organisation for Economic Cooperation and Development). 2011. *Divided We Stand: Why Inequality Keeps Rising*. Paris: OECD Publishing. http://www.oecd-ilibrary.org/social-issues-migration-health/the-causes-of-growing-inequality-in-oecd-countries-9789264119536-en.

OECD (Organisation for Economic Cooperation and Development). 2012. "Inequality in Labour Income: What Are Its Drivers and How Can It Be Reduced?" *OECD Economics Department Policy Notes* 8. http://www.oecd.org/tax/public-finance/49417273.pdf.

Ontario. Cabinet Committee on Poverty Reduction. 2010. *Breaking the Cycle: Ontario's Poverty Reduction Strategy*. Toronto: Queen's Printer for Ontario.

Osberg, Lars. 2001. "Poverty among Senior Citizens: A Canadian Success Story." In *The State of Economics in Canada: Festschrift in Honour of David Slater*, ed. P. Grady and A. Sharpe, 151–81. Ottawa: Centre for the Study of Living Standards and John Deutsch Institute.

Ren, Zhe, and Kuan Xu. 2011. *Low-Income Dynamics and Determinants under Different Thresholds: New Findings for Canada in 2000 and Beyond*. Income Research Paper Series No. 75F0002M– 003. Ottawa: Statistics Canada.

Saez, Emmanuel, and Michael R. Veall. 2007. "The Evolution of Top Incomes in Canada." In *Top Incomes over the Twentieth Century: A Contrast between Continental European and English-Speaking Countries*, ed. A.B. Atkinson and T. Piketty, 226–308. New York: Oxford University Press.

Veall, Michael R. 2008. "Canadian Seniors and the Low Income Measure." *Canadian Public Policy* 34 (4): S47–S58. http://dx.doi.org/10.3138/cpp.34.4.S47.

Veall, Michael R. 2012. "Top Income Shares in Canada: Recent Trends and Policy Implications." *Canadian Journal of Economics / Revue canadienne d'économique* 45 (4): 1247–72. http://dx.doi.org/10.1111/j.1540-5982.2012.01744.x.

Zhang, Xuelin. 2010. *Low Income Measurement in Canada: What Do Different Lines and Indexes Tell Us?* Income Research Paper Series No. 75F0002M–003. Ottawa: Statistics Canada.

Zhang, Xuelin, Jackson Chung, and Habib Saani. Forthcoming. *Evolution of Income Mobility in Canada, 1982 to 2010*. Ottawa: Statistics Canada.

PART II

The State of Social Assistance in the Provinces

five
Social Assistance in Ontario

PETER GRAEFE

Introduction

As Ontario is Canada's most populous province, its initiatives in social assistance have drawn a fair degree of interest, even if these initiatives have never been terribly innovative. Its history has been marked by an emphasis on "less eligibility" and on distinctions of the "deserving" and "undeserving." The latest major reforms to the program, dating from 1997,[1] remain in this tradition: rates below subsistence for those deemed without disability and a slightly less meagre set of benefits for those with a disability. Although the recent Commission for the Review of Social Assistance in Ontario noted problems such as the inadequacy of rates, the increasing weight of people with disabilities in the caseload, and a poorly functioning labour market and training program, there is little reason to expect other than incremental changes to the system.

This chapter develops the points made above by providing a brief history of the development of social assistance in Ontario, a description of the institutional features of the current program and of caseload trends, and then some thoughts on the future trajectory of social assistance.

The origins and evolution of Ontario's welfare

The beginnings of social assistance in Ontario were municipally based, in the tradition of indoor relief organized through "Houses of Industry" and "Houses of Refuge." These houses received some government support through the late nineteenth century, albeit with allocations based on a patchwork of decisions, forcing the early provincial welfare bureaucracy to develop more standardized formulae. However, in developing funding formulae, they worked hard to ensure it did not displace charitable and municipal support (Splane 1965).

1 There have been a number of changes since 1997, but the main enabling legislation, program architecture, and announced goals and objectives date from the 1997 reform.

As Palmer and Heroux (2012) argue, from its origins, the right to assistance in Ontario has always been qualified by the question of *less eligibility*, as well as the assumption that assistance is truly a last resort, after the labour market and the family have failed in supporting individuals. The emphasis on work has led to struggles over time, with periods of unemployment (and thus higher expense) tending to give rise to more stringent work tests (e.g., at the Toronto House of Industry, those seeking a bed for the night or outdoor relief would chop wood and, when a more rigorous test of deservedness was instituted, break stone). Protests by the poor and the unemployed pushed back the other way.

The first major provincial foray into social assistance was the adoption of a mother's allowance in the 1920s. The main advocates for this allowance were middle-class social reformers, mostly white women, supported by church and charity leaders, judges, and medical professionals seeking to reinforce "respectable motherhood" and reduce the costs of foster care (Little 1998).

The 1930s' depression pushed the province to more decisive action, given the wide variations in municipal relief and the financial difficulties of municipalities faced with heavy relief rolls. In 1932, the Conservative government appointed the Advisory Committee on Direct Relief, better known as the Campbell Committee, whose report "provided the first rationale for the standardization of welfare policy and practice at the provincial level" and set the benchmark for social assistance rates for the next dozen years (Struthers 1994, 85).

With mother's allowances in the 1920s, as with relief in the 1930s and 1940s, attempts at setting a rate that reflected real housing and food costs fell short. For instance, what the Campbell Committee recommended as rate "ceilings" were soon shown to be inadequate in providing enough to eat (Struthers 1994, Ch. 3). Similarly, the rates for the mother's allowance were consistently set below the cost of living (Little 1998, Ch. 2). This lack of adequacy reflected both successive governments' unwillingness to shoulder the expense of guaranteeing a living at or above subsistence levels and popular support for work ethic and the related principle of less eligibility. Employers also opposed the development of minimum liveable incomes for fear that they would bid up the price of labour.

In the early post–World War II period, social work professionals started pushing the province toward a more centralized and institutionalized system but were largely stymied by a Conservative government caucus that translated the fears of rural and small-town Ontario. The Conservative government's main push on social assistance was to deny responsibility for providing aid. The Ontario Conservatives instead insisted that the federal government should assist able-bodied men, because of its constitutional responsibility for unemployment insurance (Struthers 1994).

This overall picture is consistent with the idea that Ontario's history is not one of measured reform but of conservative social governance. In his comparative study, Gerard Boychuk (1998, 62–64) classified Ontario in the conservative category for the 1930–90 period. He underlines several persistent features extending into the 1970s and 1980s, including the emphasis on less eligibility and the work test, stingy benefits for single employables, and better rates for categories deemed "deserving," albeit only if they comply with expected behaviour. For instance, even in the 1980s, mothers receiving assistance under the Ontario Family Benefits Act (1967) were discouraged from taking full-time work and faced a loss of benefits should they contravene the "man in the house" rule.

Employability and "workfare"

As in most provinces, social assistance was revisited in Ontario in the 1980s; the push was toward "employability" and more active labour market policies. These themes were central to the Social Assistance Review Committee and its landmark 1988 *Transitions* report. The report struck a compromise between the idea of workfare, which was being experimented with in the United States, and the idea of expanding social rights (to include the right to adequate benefits, to childcare, to transportation, and to training, for example). *Transitions* advocated aiding social assistance recipients to participate fully through "opportunity planning": moving into the workforce or, when that was not realistic, developing new skills and participating in community activity. The focus on the labour market was not to discipline recipients but instead to include them through trying to realize the right to work along with other social rights (Graefe 2002).

Less visible in the framing of the report was another project for social assistance, namely dismantling the system from within. The idea was to extend existing social assistance benefits (such as money for dependent children or housing allowances or health benefits or those related to disability) to all similarly situated low-income earners. Thus, to receive these benefits, people would no longer have to qualify for social assistance, while the income received from social assistance would shrink (as an increasing share of what is currently social assistance would be delivered through a range of income-tested transfers and services). The end result would be a modest guaranteed annual income, with the resources of the welfare bureaucracy turned toward providing quality training and job placement. This vision has been carried forward by *Transitions* research director John

Stapleton and continues to inform social assistance discussions to this day, as we will see below (Stapleton 2004).

In responding to the *Transitions* report, the Peterson Liberal government was limited by a lack of bureaucratic capacity to roll out "opportunity planning" on any scale. Although the province had experimented with employability programs in the early 1980s, these were small-scale pilots with muted results. As a result, the government's first actions favoured benefit enhancement.

The NDP government elected in 1990 at first continued in this direction, enhancing benefits and striking an advisory committee to change problematic rules, with the effect of expanding eligibility and increasing benefits for people caught in certain rule traps. The cost of providing higher benefits to a caseload that was swollen by the recession was further compounded by the federal government's unilateral decision in 1990 to stop cost sharing new social assistance expenditures above 5 per cent per year (on this "cap on CAP," see Boychuk, in this volume). The government changed course and proposed reforms to enhance labour market discipline, on the one hand, while bringing in a child benefit as a means of making it easier for recipients to negotiate the "welfare wall." In the face of the federal government's unwillingness to move forward with the child benefit, this plan was stillborn. When the federal child benefit was launched in 1998, Ontario had moved on to other things.

Employability would therefore arrive not in the empowering language of "transitions" but instead from a Conservative party that had made popular electoral promises to tighten up what its members portrayed as an overly generous and fraud-ridden system. The Conservatives immediately reduced rates by 20 per cent, enhanced verification and surveillance, and applied a stricter "spouse-in-the-house" rule to disentitle some single mothers. It then merged the Family Benefits Act and the General Welfare Assistance Act into the Social Assistance Reform Act, which created Ontario Works (OW) and the Ontario Disability Support Program (ODSP) in 1997–98.

This legislation has marked Ontario's social assistance system for the past 15 years, a system that will be described further in this chapter. The changes were controversial. They were seen as the introduction of workfare and were resisted, a resistance that included concerted efforts by the community sector to oppose taking on large number of OW placements. In practice, OW was less a "workfare" program (one in which participants work to receive welfare) than a "work-first" program (one that pushes recipients to look for work actively and take the first available job); the investment was in encouraging a job search instead of in creating places for recipients to work in exchange for their cheque.

The current Liberal administration, elected in 2003, has skirted around social assistance, both to avoid an anti-welfare backlash that could benefit the Conservatives and to maintain a strategy of using low-wage, private, service-sector jobs to soak up excess labour supply. In 2003–04, it reviewed employment assistance programs for OW recipients and suggested adopting a less punitive and more facilitative approach. This review resulted in 2005 in a reduction of the tax-back rate on employment income to 50 per cent (from 75 to 100 per cent) and in the extension of drug and dental benefits to recipients leaving welfare.

Following the 2005 changes, social assistance fell off the radar and was replaced in 2007 with the idea of a provincial poverty reduction strategy (PRS). From the very beginning, the government wished to avoid addressing social assistance, and, though anti-poverty organizations did bring social assistance rates into the frame of the government's consultations, the province's first five-year strategy promised only a further review of welfare (see Hudson and Graefe 2011). This review was drawn out to ensure it did not interfere with the 2011 election. First, the government appointed a Social Assistance Review Advisory Council to propose the terms of reference for a review; this council again took up the idea of replacing social assistance with a new income security architecture that would extend existing social assistance benefits to all low-income Ontarians (Ontario Ministry of Community and Social Services 2010). Then the government appointed a Commission for the Review of Social Assistance that would not report until October 2012 (Lankin and Sheikh 2012).

The review's wide-ranging report included recommendations to collapse OW and ODSP into a single program and to reorient front-line staff toward helping recipients develop "Pathway to Employment Plans." Although the report noted that rates should be raised by $100, the general stance on benefits was that significant movement on adequacy would undermine fairness and incentives in comparison to minimum-wage work, and thus that the better course was to extend disability, drug, dental, child, and health benefits to all low-income Ontarians (Lankin and Sheikh 2012).

The government's first response came with the 2013 budget, which increased asset limits from $606 to $2,500 for singles (and to $5,000 for couples), enabled OW and ODSP recipients to earn $200 per month before facing a clawback, and established a Partnership Council on Employment Opportunities for People with Disabilities (Ontario 2013, ch. 1, s. B). The budget also included a top-up of $14 per month for single adults without children, as well as a lot of language pledging to undertake larger parts of the report (such as developing a consistent method for determining rates or encouraging employers and service delivery partners to improve employment services).

Major institutional features of the social assistance architecture

The basic program structure for social assistance in Ontario is a dual one. On one side, there is Ontario Works (OW) as a last resort income program for adults while, on the other, there is the Ontario Disability Support Program (ODSP) for adults with disabilities. Given this dual structure, our discussion of the basic architecture below will take each separately.

Program aims and structure

According to the Ontario Works Act, 1997, the purpose of OW is fourfold: to "recognize individual responsibility and promote self-reliance through employment," to "provide temporary financial assistance to those most in need while they satisfy obligations to become and stay employed," to "effectively serve people needing assistance," and to be "accountable to the taxpayers of Ontario." In announced intent, OW is focused on putting people in work, providing assistance in a temporary and cost-effective manner. In practice, however, employment seems much less central, both in terms of directives, which primarily emphasize controlling eligibility, and casework, which, again, focuses on monitoring eligibility (Pennisi 2014). Thus, the real aim of the program appears to be limiting cost by stringently managing access to benefits.

The Ontario Disability Support Program Act, 1997, takes a slightly different tack. It sets out the purposes of "providing income and employment supports to eligible persons with disabilities"; "recognizing that government, communities, families and individuals share responsibility for providing such supports"; "effectively serving persons with disabilities who need assistance"; and being "accountable to the taxpayers of Ontario." As with OW, there is recognition of taxpayer responsibility and the need to support employment, but the idea of providing income support is more central, and ideas of individual responsibility and self-reliance are tempered by the act's recognition of government, community, and family responsibility.

The major component of both programs is income support. Table 5.1 sets out current rates, as of February 2014. In historical terms, social assistance benefits in Ontario peaked in real terms in the early 1990s, before being cut by 20 per cent in 1995 (and frozen in the case of disability benefits, representing about a 15 per cent erosion due to inflation). They were then held constant until the change of government in 2003, having had

Table 5.1 Social Assistance Rates in Ontario, February 2014

	Ontario Works	Ontario Disability Support Program
Single	$626 ($250 basic needs, $376 shelter)	$1,086 ($607 basic needs, $479 shelter)
Single Parent, One Child	$1,041 ($344 basic needs, $596 shelter, $101 Ontario Child Benefit)	$1,604 ($750 basic needs, $753 shelter, $101 Ontario Child Benefit)
Two Adults	$1,054 ($458 basic needs, $596 shelter)	

Note: Material in parentheses shows the various allowances and benefits that comprise the total. Welfare incomes for recipients with children have fared better, particularly in response to investments in child benefits and the McGuinty government's decision to flow through incremental National Child Benefit increases to social assistance recipients, even if this was contrary to the design of the benefit. Indeed, nearly 40 per cent of total income for families composed of single parents with one child is delivered through child benefits and tax credits. This emphasis on supporting low-income children might help to explain why single employables' incomes reached just 41 per cent of the low-income cut-off (LICO) in 2009, versus the incomes of singles with disabilities or of single-parent, one-child families, which reached 70 per cent and 77 per cent of the LICO, respectively (National Council of Welfare 2010).

their value eroded by inflation. Since 2003, they have been increased just marginally below the rate of inflation. Single employables on OW receive less in straight dollar terms ($626, a bit more than 36 per cent of full-time minimum wage) in late 2013 than they did in 1993 ($663, 65 per cent of minimum wage). Had that rate increased with inflation, it would be $944 today (Stapleton 2013a).

Under OW, there are mandatory supplemental benefits such as the "community start-up and maintenance" benefit (in 2009, $799 for singles and $1,500 for a family, every two years), a special diet allowance (to deal with the additional costs of food for people with health concerns, up to $250 per month), employment-related expenses (up to $250 per month), eye exams (every 24 months), health benefits, and diabetic supplies, as well as dental and vision care for dependent children. Other supplemental benefits available by discretion of the service manager include monies for funerals and burials, prosthetics, vision and dental care for adults, and moving expenses. In the 2012 budget, the provincial government announced that it was ending the community start-up benefit and capping discretionary benefits, thereby putting pressure on municipal budgets (Ontario Ministry of Community and Social Services 2008).

Under ODSP, caseworkers can provide employment supports ranging from job readiness and job coaching through to transportation assistance, assistive devices, tools and clothing, and specialized computer training. These supports are only offered where they are not available through other channels or sources in government. ODSP recipients also receive prescription drug coverage, basic dental coverage, and the range of discretionary benefits found under OW (Ontario Ministry of Community and Social Services 2008).

Eligibility

OW is available to Canadian citizens, permanent residents, refugee claimants, and convention refugees living in Ontario. Access is based largely on financial eligibility, which is determined with an assets test. Until recently, the asset limit was one month's benefits (e.g., $572 for a single person in 2008, $989 for a couple) plus $500 dollars for eligible dependents. The 2013 budget raised this to $2,500 for a single, following the advice of the Commission for the Review of Social Assistance and the Commission on the Reform of Ontario's Public Services. Primary residences, primary vehicles valued at less than $10,000, locked-in registered retirement savings plans (RRSPs), and prepaid funerals are excluded from the calculation. Applicants with earned income must ensure that this is less than the potential OW entitlement, and this income is clawed back at 100 per cent for the first three months and 50 per cent thereafter. Again, the 2013 provincial budget now protects the first $200 in earned income from this clawback.

Eligibility determination remains controversial. To determine legal status and benefit eligibility, caseworkers can request documents including social insurance and health insurance cards, birth certificates, monthly bank statements, pay stubs, records of employment, vehicle registration forms, forms related to sponsorship, legal documents related to separation or divorce, support orders, and evidence of shelter costs (Herd, Mitchell, and Lightman 2005; Ontario Auditor General 2009). Some researchers treat this process as "disentitlement by design" (Herd and Mitchell 2003), saying that new administrative practices deter applications by requiring applicants to undertake significant amounts of work to prove and maintain eligibility (see Pennisi 2014). The Ontario Auditor General (2009, 260–61), by contrast, criticizes caseworkers for being insufficiently systematic in collecting and verifying data at the application stage and subsequently.

All OW recipients must sign a participation agreement committing them to take part in employability activities such as basic education and literacy, independent or assisted job searches, or volunteer or paid job placements. These are meant to be based on a skill assessment by the caseworker and renewed every three months, but, in practice, there is lax commitment to systematic casework in labour market preparation and placement (Ontario Auditor General 2009, 267–68). Pennisi's thesis about the meaning of "Works" in Ontario Works highlights that there are no standard employability assessment tools, that the emphasis on determining and rechecking eligibility monopolizes the caseworkers' time and creates a misalignment between their purported role of supporting people into work and their actual role of policing those people.

Eligibility for ODSP follows a more complex process. In cases of immediate need, applicants are directed to apply for OW while their disability status is adjudicated; otherwise, their financial eligibility is determined through an income-and-asset test. Here, the thresholds are $5,000 for singles, $7,500 if there is a spouse, and an additional $500 for each eligible dependent. Principal residences, primary vehicles, locked-in RRSPs and trust funds less than $100,000 are excluded when determining the limit, but bank accounts and cashable RRSPs are included. On the income side, 50 per cent of the applicant's total income must be less than the ODSP entitlement (Ontario Auditor General 2009, 224). Following the financial test, applicants must complete a disability-determination package, including a "health status and activities of daily living index report" completed by a physician. These forms are reviewed by an adjudicator who determines whether the applicant meets the test for disability.

Service delivery

Administratively, OW is delivered by municipal governments, district service boards, and First Nations, which follow very specific provincial regulations and directives. Where municipalities have experimented is in tying OW work requirements to local labour market development processes (Marquardt 2007). They also have some limited flexibility in allocating discretionary benefits. Consistent with the long tradition of municipal contribution, OW had municipalities paying 20 per cent of benefit costs plus 50 per cent of administration costs, although the share of benefit costs will fall to zero within a decade with provincial cost uploading (Ontario Ministry of Community and Social Services 2010). Beyond setting the rules, the province oversees statistical and data management functions. Since 2006, the funding model also has the province negotiating with municipalities on employment targets such as caseload exits to employment, length of time between leaving OW and returning, savings from caseload exits, and time to exit OW with earnings (Pennisi 2014, 92). Meanwhile, ODSP is delivered provincially. Although municipalities originally footed 10 per cent of the bill, this cost was uploaded to the province in 2011 (Ontario Ministry of Community and Social Services 2010).

This situation presents several barriers to reforming the system in the direction of an integrated program. First, it would require uploading or downloading financial and administrative responsibility, depending on whether the integrated program would be placed in the municipalities or with the province. Already, the distinction between the municipally directed employability services for social assistance recipients and the provincial training programs delivered through Employment Ontario offices prevents an easy replication of Québec's experiment in integrating employment services under one roof. Second, because provincial ODSP and municipal OW staff members are represented by different unions and have different collective agreements, unions resist most proposed changes; an example of this resistance is the Ontario Public Service Employees Union's campaign against the recent proposal of the Commission for the Review of Social Assistance in Ontario to merge ODSP and OW.

The nature and evolution of caseload

The current caseload points in a couple of directions and can explain why the recent commission on social assistance paid so much attention to the disability side of social assistance. As Table 5.2 indicates, total caseload, measured in terms of average monthly cases, fell from 633,800 in 1995–96 to 388,600 in 2001, before creeping steadily back up to 562,600 in 2012–13. If we take population growth into account, this measurement reflects a move from 12.4 per cent of the population receiving social assistance in 1993 to a low of 5.4 per cent in 2004, followed by a rise after the 2008 crisis to 6.5 per cent in 2012 (see Stapleton 2009, 2). This aggregate performance nevertheless masks two separate trajectories.

In OW, one observes the expected movement across the business cycle, dropping from 461,700 in 1995–96, bottoming out at 191,700 in 2004–05, rising up to 260,800 in 2011–12, and now seeming to level off. Within OW, the impact of the shift to expecting single mothers to pursue employment once their youngest is above two years of age can be seen in the drop from 195,200 at the end of the 1990s' recession to 71,000 in 2004–05, only 36 per cent of the earlier total, and even with the post-2008 recession, OW-supported sole-parent families peaked at 40 per cent of the 1995–96 level in 2011–12. The drop in terms of couples is similar: from 72,600 in

Table 5.2 Social Assistance Caseload, Ontario Works and ODSP, Average Monthly Cases, Fiscal Years 1995–96 to 2012–13

	Ontario Works				ODSP				
Fiscal Year	Singles	Couples	Sole-Support Parents	Total OW	Singles	Couples	Sole-Support Parents	Total ODSP	Total
1995–96	193,800	72,600	195,200	460,700	131,300	32,300	8,000	172,100	633,800
1996–97	150,800	65,400	172,000	395,100	135,600	34,800	9,300	179,700	577,800
1997–98	145,200	57,500	155,600	352,300	139,700	35,600	10,200	185,500	547,800
1998–99	123,000	45,700	141,700	310,500	142,500	35,500	11,100	189,400	499,900
1999–2000	105,600	36,500	117,100	252,400	142,900	35,000	11,500	159,500	452,000
2000–01	91,700	28,700	95,200	215,600	145,000	34,400	12,500	191,900	407,500
2001–02	87,900	25,100	82,600	196,600	145,500	33,200	13,300	192,000	388,600
2002–03	98,000	25,600	75,600	195,100	145,000	32,200	14,000	194,100	389,900
2003–04	95,000	24,300	72,800	192,100	153,300	31,900	14,900	200,100	392,200
2004–05	97,900	22,900	71,000	191,700	158,500	31,600	15,800	205,900	397,600
2005–06	104,000	22,500	71,900	198,400	168,900	31,600	16,600	212,000	410,400
2006–07	105,500	21,600	71,100	199,200	171,900	32,000	17,800	221,700	421,000
2007–08	105,400	20,300	69,200	194,900	182,500	33,600	19,600	135,700	430,600
2008–09	112,000	21,400	68,700	200,200	191,700	34,800	11,000	247,500	449,7000
2009–10	137,700	25,300	73,600	237,600	202,200	36,800	12,500	151,500	499,100
2010–11	147,300	27,500	76,500	251,300	213,500	38,600	24,100	276,200	527,500
2011–12	154,800	27,500	78,100	260,800	224,100	40,100	25,400	289,700	550,400
2012–13	155,200	27,100	77,600	259,800	234,700	41,500	26,600	302,700	562,600

Source: Ontario Ministry of Community and Social Services. Data compiled at author's request.
Note: A case refers to a single individual or a family unit on social assistance (e.g., a family on social assistance is counted as one case).

1995–96 to 20,300 in 2007–08 and only back to 27,800 during the recession. The situation for singles, who did not see as noticeable a change in work expectations with the introduction of OW, still witnessed a reduction of more than 50 per cent from its peak in 1995–96 to its early 2000s' trough, although the recession pushed these numbers back up to over 75 per cent of the mid-1990s' peak.

In contrast, ODSP numbers have grown every year since 1995, from being 37 per cent of the OW caseload in 1995–96 to being 116 per cent in 2012–13, and, presumably, the future will see a higher percentage should economic growth erode the OW numbers. The ODSP caseload was 302,700 in the last complete year for which we have data, a growth of roughly 75 per cent from the caseload number of 172,100 in 1995–96. The driver in terms of numbers has been singles (up 100,000), although the largest percentage increase came from the tripling of sole-support parents covered (from 8,000 to 26,600).

The reasons for the ODSP increase require more study. John Stapleton (2013b) raises several possible drivers, including an aging population, advances in medicine and medical care, lower rates of standard employment (and thus lower access to work-based disability benefits), greater acceptance and diagnosis of mental illness, and this list was compiled "without even scratching the surface of program rules and rate differentials between ODSP and Ontario Works" (para. 9).

In the context of ODSP being the driver of social assistance cost pressures, it is understandable that disability advocates are wary of the Commission for the Review of Social Assistance's recommendation to merge OW and ODSP. Having previously been hived off as "deserving," ODSP recipients fear they will face a softer version of the treatment given single mothers: a reduction of the benefits differential and the use of employment expectations to police recipients.

Conclusion: Possible paths of reform

What does the future hold for social assistance in Ontario? The recent Commission for the Review of Social Assistance heard almost unanimous agreement that the current system needs a radical overhaul, be it in terms of changing a punitive, rules-bound culture or of providing real transitions to employment. There was even a fairly high degree of consensus around the need to improve adequacy, especially for singles.

Given the importance of the principle of "less eligibility" in the history of social assistance in Ontario, significantly increased benefits are unlikely. The space for such change is constrained by the long-term trajectory of Ontario as a low-wage economy, a trajectory that has been reinforced by deindustrialization in the early twenty-first century. In a period during which the percentage of workers at the minimum wage doubled (from 4.3 per cent in 2003 to 9 per cent in 2011) and another 18 per cent were making between $10.25 and $14.25 an hour (Block 2013), campaigns to raise assistance rates confront the horizontal hostilities of the working poor.

When we turn to formal politics, all parties show signs of holding to the lesson of the mid-1990s: there are no votes in investing in social assistance, and, indeed, such an investment brings with it a strong chance of losing votes. The post-2003 Liberal government has consistently avoided addressing social assistance directly, favouring instead the discussion of poverty, and especially child poverty and in-work poverty. Even after the report of the Commission on social assistance, the consultation documents for the government's second poverty strategy suggested that action on social assistance would wait until well into the second five-year plan.

The provincial NDP, who in the past called for enhanced adequacy, have been content to push for cost-of-living increases for ODSP recipients and a $200 earned-income exemption for OW recipients in budgetary negotiations with the minority Liberal government. The Conservatives, by contrast, released a white paper on welfare in 2013, which emphasized policing fraud, experimenting with food stamps, and cutting benefits for long-term recipients while providing better transitions to employment and merging the OW and ODSP systems (Ontario PC Caucus 2013).

Future changes in social assistance are therefore not likely to take the form of enhanced adequacy. The most likely driver in a province such as Ontario will be a desire to rein in the costs of ODSP. There may eventually be pressure on the federal government to develop a system of disability pensions to pull those with disabilities out of social assistance. Of course, another possible response to disability system costs is the reduction of disability benefits relative to straight social assistance, or of increasing eligibility requirements.

The deck thus appears stacked in favour of incremental changes to the status quo. The next most likely alternative is another form of incrementalism, one building off the example of child benefits and starting to extend other social assistance benefits (housing, health, and dental) to all low-income Ontarians. This reform would involve a slow build toward something approximating a stingy guaranteed annual income. It would do little to improve living standards for social assistance recipients, but it might aid them in navigating the employability cliff, and it would remove larger shares of their income from the discretion of welfare bureaucrats. That said, given the size of the low-wage labour force in Ontario, such a strategy is costly, and the willingness of the middle class to subsidize poverty wages is not immediately apparent in contemporary Ontario, where all parties campaign on cutting taxes.

References

Block, Sheila. 2013. *Who Is Working for Minimum Wage in Ontario?* Toronto: Wellesley Institute.

Boychuk, Gerard. 1998. *Patchworks of Purpose: The Development of Provincial Social Assistance Regimes in Canada*. Montréal: McGill-Queen's University Press.

Graefe, Peter. 2002. "Striking a New Balance: Neoliberalism, the Provinces and Intergovernmental Relations in Canada, 1985–2002." PhD diss., Université de Montréal.

Herd, Dean, and Andrew Mitchell. 2003. "Cutting Caseloads by Design: The Impact of the New Service Delivery Model for Ontario Works." *Canadian Review of Social Policy* 51: 114–20.

Herd, Dean, Andrew Mitchell, and Ernie Lightman. 2005. "Rituals of Degradation: Administration as Policy in the Ontario Works Programme." *Social Policy and Administration* 39 (1): 65–79. http://dx.doi.org/10.1111/j.1467-9515.2005.00425.x.

Hudson, Carol-Anne, and Peter Graefe. 2011. "The Toronto Origins of Ontario's 2008 Poverty Reduction Strategy: Mobilizing Multiple Channels for Progressive Social Policy Change." *Canadian Review of Social Policy* 65–66: 1–15.

Lankin, Frances, and Munir A. Sheikh. 2012. *Brighter Prospects: Transforming Social Assistance in Ontario*. Report of the Commission for the Review of Social Assistance to the Minister of Community and Social Services. Toronto: Ontario Ministry of Community and Social Services.

Little, Margaret Jane Hillyard. 1998. *"No Car, No Radio, No Liquor Permit": The Moral Regulation of Single Mothers in Ontario, 1920–1997*. Toronto: Oxford University Press.

Marquardt, Richard. 2007. "The Progressive Potential of Municipal Social Policy: A Case Study of the Struggle over Welfare Reform in Ottawa During the Common Sense Revolution." PhD diss., Carleton University.

National Council of Welfare. 2010. *Welfare Incomes 2009*. Ottawa: National Council of Welfare.

Ontario. 2013. *Ontario Budget*. Toronto. Accessed October 22, 2013. http://www.fin.gov.on.ca/en/budget/ontariobudgets/2013/ch1b.html#ch1b_12.

Ontario Auditor General. 2009. *2009 Annual Report*. Toronto: Queen's Printer for Ontario.

Ontario Ministry of Community and Social Services. 2008. *Social Assistance Policy Directives*. Toronto: Ontario Ministry of Community and Social Services. Accessed February 10, 2014. http://www.mcss.gov.on.ca/en/mcss/programs/social/directives/.

Ontario Ministry of Community and Social Services. Social Assistance Review Advisory Council. 2010. *Recommendations for an Ontario Income Security Review*. Toronto: Ontario Ministry of Community and Social Services.

Ontario PC Caucus. 2013. *Pathways to Prosperity: Welfare to Work*. Toronto: PC Caucus.

Palmer, Bryan D., and Gaetan Heroux. 2012. "'Cracking the Stone': The Long History of Capitalist Crisis and Toronto's Dispossessed, 1830–1930." *Labour / Le travail* 69: 9–34.

Pennisi, Sarah. 2014. "'Everybody Needs to Be Doing Something': Exploring the Contradictions in Ontario Works and the Normative Expectations Behind the Work of Becoming Eligible, Employable and Employed." PhD diss., McMaster University.

Splane, Richard. 1965. *Social Welfare in Ontario 1791–1893*. Toronto: University of Toronto Press.

Stapleton, John. 2004. *Transitions Revisited: Implementing the Vision*. Ottawa: Caledon Institute of Social Policy.

Stapleton, John. 2009. *The Silence of the Lines: Poverty Reduction Strategies and the Crash of 2008*. Ottawa: Canadian Centre for Policy Alternatives.

Stapleton, John. 2013a. "A Ball Player, a Cop, a Janitor, and a Welfare Recipient." *The Broadbent Blog*, January 16. http://www.broadbentinstitute.ca/en/blog/john-stapleton-ball-player-cop-janitor-and-welfare-recipient.

Stapleton, John. 2013b. "More Thoughts on Ontario Social Assistance Caseloads." *The Broadbent Blog*, April 16. http://openpolicyontario.com/more-thoughts-on-ontario-social-assistance-caseloads/.

Struthers, James. 1994. *The Limits of Affluence: Welfare in Ontario, 1920–1970*. Toronto: University of Toronto Press.

six
Québec: The Ambivalent Politics of Social Solidarity

ALAIN NOËL[1]

In contemporary Québec, social assistance is cast in the language of social solidarity. Managed by the Ministry of Work, Employment, and Social Solidarity, the "last-resort" financial assistance programs create two tracks: a Social Assistance Program for persons who could be employed and a Social Solidarity Program for people with a severely limited capacity for employment. By contrast, in Ontario these same two tracks are named Ontario Works and Ontario Disability Support, and they are run by the Ministry of Community and Social Services. The structure is similar, but the aims seem somehow more local and pragmatic, less encompassing, ambitious, or engaging.

One should not, of course, make too much of labelling. Still, Québec's social assistance programs stand among the most generous in an ungenerous country. In *Welfare in Canada 2012*, the Caledon Institute of Social Policy estimates the adequacy of provincial welfare incomes for various types of households by comparing these incomes to the Market Basket Measure (MBM), a low-income threshold. For a lone parent with a two-year-old child, for instance, Québec welfare incomes amounted in 2012 to 84.9 per cent of the MBM. Only Newfoundland and Labrador (87.5 per cent) offered more. For a single employable person, the level fell far below the MBM, at 52.0 per cent, but Québec again ranked near the top, behind Newfoundland and Labrador (64.3 per cent) and Saskatchewan (55.1 per cent). For a single person with a disability, Québec came second to Ontario (respectively 75.6 per cent and 79.8 per cent), if we leave aside the effects of Alberta's Assured Income for the Severely Handicapped, which raised a subset of persons, but not all those with a disability, above the MBM. Finally, for a couple with two children, Québec's welfare incomes were at 77.7 per cent of the MBM, just behind Prince Edward Island's at 78.6 per cent (Tweddle, Battle, and Torjman 2013, 51–54).

1 I am grateful to Léa Maude Gobeille Paré for her work as a research assistant, to Guy Fréchet for his help with social assistance caseload data, and to the editors and Gabriel Arsenault for comments on an earlier version. I also wish to acknowledge the financial support of the Fonds de recherche du Québec—Société et culture (Actions concertées—Programme de recherche sur la pauvreté et l'exclusion sociale).

The Québec government was also the first, in 2002, to adopt a law against poverty and social exclusion. This law was followed by two poverty action plans, in 2004 and 2010, and by the creation in 2005 of two autonomous institutions, one to advise the government on issues related to poverty, the Comité consultatif de lutte contre la pauvreté et l'exclusion (CCLP), and the other to produce data and studies to measure progress, the Centre d'étude sur la pauvreté et l'exclusion (CEPE). This institutionalized commitment, which inspired other provincial governments in the following years, emerged from a broad civil society mobilization. Afterward, a strong network of community organizations remained vigilant, monitoring developments and implementation. Québec, indeed, has a broad and dense associative sector, which includes solid advocates for the poor that are able to connect with more mainstream associations and are always determined to remind governments of the imperatives of solidarity.

The language of social solidarity, then, is not simply a form of branding. It reflects a genuine commitment to redistribution, one anchored in a politics where people on social assistance and the poor have a voice. Québec's politics of social solidarity, however, remains ambivalent, as can be seen from the social assistance adequacy rates presented above, which are not all that distant from those of other provinces and which reveal as well a huge income gap between households with and without children. Social assistance remains social assistance, a measure of last resort that governments prove reluctant to use as an instrument to fight poverty.

To understand Québec's ambivalent politics of social solidarity, we must situate social assistance in a broader political and policy framework. The first section briefly considers the historical origins of social assistance programs. The chapter then turns to the main institutional features of current programs and underlines the close connection, not unique to Québec, between income support and activation mechanisms. The following section looks at policy outcomes, focusing on a declining caseload, mixed results with respect to poverty, and innovative governance instruments. The last section points to the coming years, as Québec confronts slow economic growth and budgetary constraints. In Québec, social assistance does express values of social solidarity, but these values do interact with other imperatives to create an ambivalent politics of social solidarity.

From charity to social aid, to income security, and to social solidarity

In the first half of the twentieth century, Québec's social assistance policies remained residual, fragmented, and ungenerous. The key legislation was the 1921 Public Charities Act, which guaranteed public funding to the private, mostly religious, and municipal institutions that offered aid to the poor (Boychuk 1998, 27). The underlying principle was charity, and assistance was understood as a private matter, at least in principle. The financial support offered by the state concerned primarily indigents in the care of charitable institutions (Morel 2002, 33). Some organizations experimented with workhouses, where those able to work lived and worked in exchange for help (Morel 2002, 32). This English poor law model, however, with its stringent, almost penal, conditions to enforce the work ethic never exercised in Québec the influence it had elsewhere in Canada. The state and private charities simply offered little to those who were able to work (Vaillancourt 1988, 241).

In the years following the Great Depression, new programs were introduced to meet the needs of additional categories of the population, often in response to developments elsewhere in Canada. The main breakthrough in this respect was the 1937 allowance for needy mothers, a purely provincial program. Means tested, restrictive, stigmatizing, paternalist, and stingy, this program had all the hallmarks of traditional social assistance (Vaillancourt 1988, 277–98). At the same time, the new allowance went beyond the logic of charity by creating something like an entitlement for a large category of the population. "This is not public assistance legislation, nor a kind of charity . . . it is the granting of a right," stated the minister of labour (quoted in Morel 2002, 39). Other categorical measures were introduced in the 1950s, as Québec took advantage of federal shared-cost programs, for the blind, the old, the handicapped, and the unemployed (Vaillancourt 1988, 288). The general thrust of these programs, however, remained residual and fragmented.

In the beginning of the 1960s, this haphazard assemblage of programs was increasingly challenged as incoherent and inadequate. Committed to modernizing the Québec state, the new Liberal government of Jean Lesage mandated a study group, chaired by judge J.-Émile Boucher, to review existing social assistance programs. Released in June 1963, the Boucher report concluded that private charity was no longer sufficient. "Only the State," the report pointed out, "possesses capacities proportionate to the task at hand" (author's translation; Boucher, Bélanger, and Morin 1963, 120). Social assistance should no longer be a matter of circumstances, categories of difficulties, or charity: "any person in need has a right to assistance from the state, whatever the proximate or distant cause of this need" (118).

The Boucher report contributed significantly to the broader Canadian discussion on social assistance that led to the adoption of the Canada Assistance Plan in 1966 (Haddow 1993, 39). More important, it laid the foundations for the 1969 Social Aid Act, the law that established social assistance as a right for all in Québec. This reform was facilitated by the expanded financial contribution that came with the Canada Assistance Plan, but it was not the simple manifestation of a common trend. Indeed, the new federal framework left provincial governments free to define financial need and organize social assistance categories as they wished (Boychuk 1998, 46–47). In Ontario, for instance, the Canada Assistance Plan contributed to end an old tradition of mandatory work requirements, but it did not alter long-established distinctions between employable and less employable persons (Boychuk 1998, 63–64). Québec's new social assistance regime, on the contrary, eliminated all existing categories and affirmed a general right to a minimum income. This choice brought major improvements for employable persons, except for those below 30, who still received less (Fugère and Lanctôt 1985, 40).

In the early 1980s, however, unemployment increased, especially among youth, leading to an important rise and a significant transformation in the social assistance caseload. In March 1971, one year after the modern social assistance program was put in place, "able to work" recipients counted for little more than a third of the total (37 per cent), whereas those deemed "unable to work" represented roughly two-thirds (63 per cent). By 1987, these proportions had been reversed, with those "able to work" now counting for almost three-quarters of the total, or 73 per cent (Québec Ministère de la Main-d'œuvre 1993, 19–20). Confronted with a new type of recipient, often young, single, and employable, and with rising costs, the Liberal government of Robert Bourassa introduced in 1989 a major reform, which abolished the distinction for those below 30 but created two distinct tracks: the more generous Financial Support Program for those who could not be expected to work and the Work and Employment Incentive Program, which assigned applicants different types of status, for those who could participate in several new training and insertion programs. A new measure was also added to supplement the income of working parents. A complex arrangement of categories, measures, and rates thus replaced the simple, more or less universal regime introduced during the Quiet Revolution; primarily, the motives for this change were to control costs and reinforce work incentives. The government also initiated home visits to check living arrangements, and it stopped indexing benefits for persons able to work (Gow, Noël, and Villeneuve 1995; Québec Ministère de la Sécurité du revenu 1996, 20).

This evolution toward a more differentiated and conditional regime was strongly contested by social rights organizations as stigmatizing, inefficient, and unfair, and it did not even prevent a further increase in the number of employable recipients (Ulysse and Lesemann 2004, 50). When the Parti Québécois took power in 1994, it mandated a study group to review the whole program. This group, co-chaired by psychologist Camil Bouchard and economist Pierre Fortin, ended up producing two conflicting reports, from which the government made choices to design its own project (Noël 1996). Adopted in 1998, this last reform renamed and modified the programs but kept the basic distinction between a social welfare track, for persons with a "severely limited capacity for employment," and an employment assistance one, for those able to work. In many ways, this reform completed the transition initiated by the Liberals. In the process, the idea of income security was abandoned, giving way to an explicitly dual configuration that distinguished employment and social solidarity programs. The 1998 reform brought improvements, however, to training and employment programs (Ulysse and Lesemann 2004, 76).

Other modifications and adjustments followed. The general structure of Québec's social assistance was nevertheless established away from the principles of charity or income security and in line with the contrasting objectives of employment and social solidarity.

Employment and social solidarity

Québec's current social assistance framework was given its final shape with the Individual and Family Assistance Act adopted in 2005. It includes a Social Assistance Program, for those who could work, and a somewhat more generous Social Solidarity Program for persons with "severely limited capacity for employment." For recipients under 25, there is also a voluntary Youth Alternative Program, which offers an additional youth allowance in exchange for participation in a coaching and training program.

In December 2013, there were 210,772 adults in the Social Assistance Program. Of this number, 113,496 (63 per cent) had no employment limitations, and 77,276 (37 per cent) faced temporary constraints related to health, age, pregnancy, young children, or a handicap. Among adults in this Social Assistance Program, 10 per cent were below 25, 17 per cent headed single-parent households, and 27 per cent were born outside Canada. In parallel, the Social Solidarity Program reached 136,189 adults. Of these, 78 per cent had mental or physical health problems, and 22 per cent faced other types of difficulties. These persons were largely born in Canada (92 per cent), lived alone (85 per cent), were older (67 per cent above 45), and had been social assistance recipients for 10 years or more (77 per cent). The two programs clearly reached different clienteles. At the end of 2013, there were also 7,624 participants in the Youth Alternative Program (Québec MESS 2014).

In 2013, the basic allowance for a single person receiving social assistance was $604 per month, with a supplement of $129 offered to those facing temporary limitations related to health or to a personal situation. Added to the other transfers that a person on social assistance could receive, these monthly benefits amounted to a welfare income of $8,444 per year, equivalent to 49 per cent of the Montréal MBM low-income threshold. The Social Solidarity Program offered $918 a month, for an annual welfare income of $12,260, which was equivalent to 71 per cent of the MBM threshold (Québec CEPE 2014, 31, 34). The difference between the two programs was, of course, intended, but it had increased over the years because benefits for those able to work were not indexed to inflation between 1994 and 2004 and only partially indexed between 2004 and 2008 (Tweddle, Battle, and Torjman 2013, 23).

Families fared better, given transfers targeted at children. A single parent with a three-year-old child, for instance, obtained $19,455, or 80 per cent of the MBM threshold. A couple with two children received $26,140, equivalent to 76 per cent of the low-income threshold (Québec CEPE 2014, 37, 43).

In all cases, voluntary participation in a training or insertion program could improve income. Registering in the Youth Alternative Program, for instance, gave a young adult $76 more per month, plus reimbursement for day care or transportation costs. Participants in one of Emploi-Québec's training and insertion programs received an additional $45 per week, plus reimbursement for incurred costs (Québec MESS 2011a).

Created in the wake of the devolution of federal labour market programs that came with the 1997 Canada-Québec Labour Market Development Agreement, Emploi-Québec pooled together federal and provincial staff and resources to offer undifferentiated training and insertion programs to all the unemployed, whether they received social assistance, employment insurance benefits, or no financial support at all. At first, the integration of different programs, personnel, and clienteles proved difficult. There were tensions, in particular, between the top-down, control-oriented management of social assistance and the more concerted and cooperative practices of conventional labour market programs (Saint-Martin 2001). Soon, however, Emploi-Québec became coherent and effective, and able to achieve its aims.

Between April 1, 2012, and March 31, 2013, 281,484 adults participated in a training or insertion program managed by Emploi-Québec. Of these, 88,292 received social assistance benefits (31 per cent). The rest were admissible to employment insurance (170,029 or 60 per cent) or did not get any benefits (60,915 or 20 per cent; Québec MESS 2013b).[2]

Emploi-Québec is an organization without parallel elsewhere in Canada. Though it remains under the authority of the Minister of Work, Employment and Social Solidarity, this agency is governed in consultation with the Commission des partenaires du marché du travail, a multipartite body that includes representatives from business, labour, education, and community and governmental organizations. A similar consultative structure is reproduced in Québec's 17 regions and in 30 sector-based committees, as well as in special advisory committees dealing with the preoccupations of persons with disabilities, immigrants, young adults, women, persons with a judicial background, and workers aged 45 and over (Québec CPMT 2007). Work integration programs are thus designed to encompass all sectors of society, regardless of a person's relationship to employment insurance or social assistance. In every region, this integrated logic is implemented by a local employment centre, where seamless services are provided to all job seekers (Ulysse and Lesemann 2004, 77–86).

The Canada-Québec Labour Market Development Agreement transferred the management of programs to the Québec government on the condition that federal funds be reserved to persons admissible under employment insurance rules. To extend services to adults on social assistance or without benefits, Québec had to use its own funds. Over the years, these additional contributions grew significantly, to reach 37 per cent of the total budget by 2008–09 (Noël 2012, 433). Québec thus chose to invest in the training and work integration of persons receiving social assistance. And it worked. Rigorous program evaluations demonstrated that Emploi-Québec's training and employment measures made the most difference for social assistance recipients, people who were less likely to find a job otherwise. The cost of these measures was soon recuperated in lowered expenditures and increased government revenues (Noël 2012, 434–35).

Acknowledging the results of these evaluations, the federal government agreed in 2008 to sign new, complementary bilateral agreements with all the provinces. These Labour Market Agreements (LMAs) extended additional federal funding for persons not admissible under EI rules. The Québec model became, for a short while, the Canadian model (Noël 2012, 435).

In the 2013 budget, however, the Harper government announced that it would not renew these agreements. Ottawa proposed instead a Canada

2 The sum of the three categories surpasses the total, and the percentages do not add up because the first two groups overlap.

Job Grant, focused on the perceived demand for skilled workers. Provincial governments resisted for a while, but they consented in the end to the principle of a new program focused on skills and tied to contributions from employers and provincial governments (Curry 2014). The Québec government, however, obtained a distinct agreement, which in effect renewed the existing arrangement. The Québec model, acknowledged Federal Employment Minister Jason Kenney, already involved employers in defining and funding training programs; there was thus no need to change it (Curry and Séguin 2014). This integrated and concerted model had become, once again, unique to Québec.

Québec's social assistance regime is thus closely tied to its inclusive and concerted governance of training and work integration programs. For persons on social assistance, this approach creates genuine bridges toward employment. But it also contributes to maintain a tension, or some ambivalence, between the objectives of social solidarity and those of employment.

Successes and failures in combating poverty and social exclusion

The creation of Emploi-Québec in 1998 was not an isolated phenomenon. It was an element of a broad renewal of Québec's social policies that corresponded to what European welfare state scholars have identified as a turn toward social investment. As is explained in this book's introduction, this new perspective focused both on the need to invest in human capital from an early age and on the promotion of labour market integration, for women and the long-term unemployed in particular (Hemerijck 2013). Québec's reforms of the late 1990s were not cast explicitly in this language of social investment, but they conformed to the new approach. They included an ambitious family policy that introduced universal, largely public, low-cost day-care services, as well as generous family allowances and a new parental insurance plan; a host of labour market policies designed to facilitate labour market integration and reinforce work incentives; improved labour and minimum wage standards; and the 2002 law against poverty and social exclusion, which placed poverty on the public agenda, gave an institutionalized voice to the poor, and led to the abolition of penalties in social assistance (Noël 2013, 266–70).

The results were spectacular: the number of subsidized day-care places exploded, family incomes improved, and the rate of employment of women aged between 25 and 44 rose above the Canadian average. Between 1997 and 2008, inequality did not rise in Québec while it did in other Canadian provinces, and the prevalence of poverty also diminished, especially among children (Noël 2013).

This evolution contributed to a remarkable decrease in the social assistance caseload. In March 1996, 813,249 persons received social assistance benefits (including children). By March 2013, this number was down to 463,777. Between these two points in time, the social assistance rate—the ratio of social assistance recipients to the total population aged 0 to 64—went from 11.5 per cent to 6.9 per cent, the lowest percentage in 35 years. And this downward trend continued in 2013, to reach a rate of 6.7 per cent by December (Québec MESS 2013a, 2014).

As Ronald Kneebone and Katherine White explain in their contribution to this volume, much of this evolution can be associated with an improved employment situation. Some residual differences remain, however, leaving Québec with more solid results than Ontario. One should also note that the presence of families with children in social assistance decreased faster than that of single persons or childless couples (Morin et al. 2010, 221). As Figure 6.1 indicates, the number of single parents

Figure 6.1 Adults Receiving Social Assistance Benefits, by Household Type, Québec, March 1996–March 2013

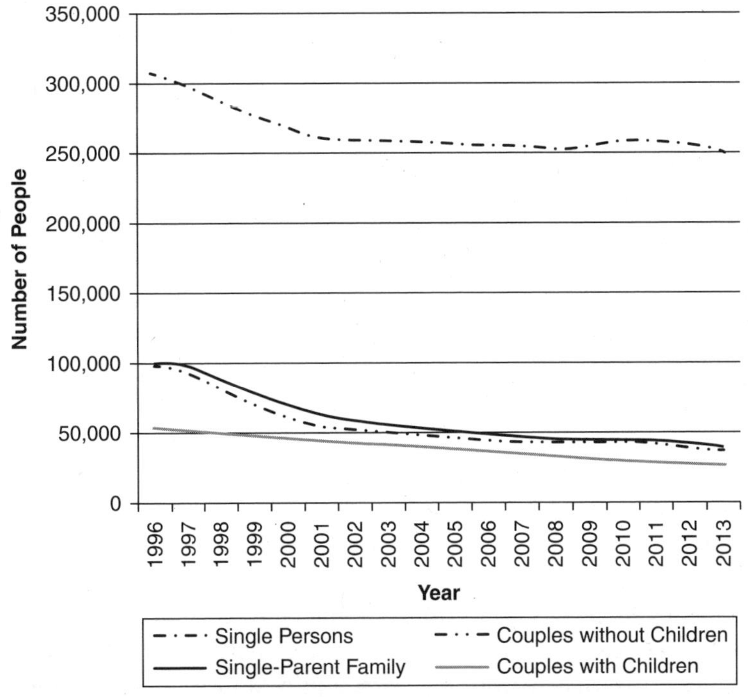

Source: Ministry of Work, Employment and Social Solidarity.

receiving social assistance decreased by 60 per cent between 1996 and 2013, compared to a more modest reduction of 18 per cent for single adults.

This contrasted evolution was possibly experienced in other provinces as well, as Kneebone and White find with imperfect data. Whatever the case, this simple observation runs counter to the common idea that an excess of generosity creates welfare dependency. In the past 15 years, those most likely to leave social assistance were precisely the adults who received the most generous support (Morin et al. 2010, 222–23). This evolution may be attributed to better transfers, as well, in favour of low-income working families. It remains that enhanced welfare incomes did not prevent an exit from social assistance.

The situation was quite different for able-to-work, childless persons. In 2013, a single employable adult obtained a welfare income equivalent to 49 per cent of the low-income threshold, compared to 76 per cent for a couple with children and 80 per cent for a single parent. The difficult living conditions of social assistance became particularly harsh for these persons, who had to survive with half the resources recognized by governments as necessary to live decently.

The consultative committee created in the wake of the law against poverty and social exclusion recommended to raise social assistance benefits for single employable persons to 80 per cent of the low-income threshold in 2009 (Québec CCLP 2009). The government's initial response was that this objective was already obtained for persons with children or with severe employment limitations but would be too costly and would reduce work incentives exceedingly if applied to adults who were able to work and childless (Québec MESS 2011b). In October 2013, the government of Pauline Marois acknowledged that such a response was not sufficient and introduced a modest benefits improvement of $50 per month over three years. This increment, however, hardly reduced what remained a major gap in welfare incomes (Québec MESS 2013a).

Social rights and community groups representing persons living in situations of poverty are well established in Québec, and they are recognized and financed by the government (Ulysse and Lesemann 2004, 174–77). There is, notably, a strong group articulating the demands of social assistance recipients, the Front commun des personnes assistées sociales du Québec, as well as a vocal organization concerned with housing, the Front d'action populaire en réaménagement urbain (FRAPRU). The Fédération des femmes du Québec also constitutes an important voice for women in situations of poverty, along, of course, with the Collectif pour un Québec sans pauvreté. This capacity for mobilization proved instrumental in bringing about the 2002 law against poverty and social exclusion, which started as a genuine initiative from below (Noël 2002). It also contributed to the law's implementation in the following years and to the development of institutionalized participation mechanisms, such as the Comité consultatif de lutte contre la pauvreté et l'exclusion, a respected and relatively effective consultative mechanism. This type of formal participation mechanism, designed to include persons living in situations of poverty, remains unique in Canada, and it has few equivalents in Europe (Larocque 2011, 890, 895).

When the news came out in March 2013 that the Minister of Employment and Social Solidarity, Agnès Maltais, had introduced adjustments to the definition of employment "limitations" that would reduce the social assistance benefits of some households, broad opposition arose, on the ground that she was jeopardizing the living conditions of the worst off (Porter 2013; Chouinard 2013). These adjustments were maintained, but the debate they provoked led to the later introduction of the improvement in social assistance benefits mentioned above. A new government had, once again, tested the commitment and public clout of organizations representing persons living in situations of poverty to find that social rights and the idea of a minimum income remained well entrenched in Québec.

The limits of social investment

Through family policy and labour market programs, the Québec government succeeded in moving persons from social assistance to the labour market. Over the years, however, social assistance benefits were not well protected against inflation. In real terms, they declined, leaving many households poorer. This result may well be inherent to the social investment approach pursued by the government. Focused on the family, on activation, and on labour market integration, this strategy had indeed little to offer to those who could not work or remained without jobs (Cantillon 2014).

In the coming years, Québec faces demographic aging, slow economic growth, and genuine budgetary constraints (Godbout et al. 2014). This context is tailor made for retrenchment or for what Paul Pierson (1998) once called "permanent austerity." At the same time, there will also be pressures to meet a growing demand for labour in a tighter job market. Social and labour market policies will therefore remain critical, and so will Québec's capacity for solidarity and concerted action. To bring satisfactory results, however, family policy and activation programs will not be enough. These social investment policies will have to be matched by an effective commitment to redistribute and support the poor in a context where markets increasingly foster inequality.

Conclusion

Québec's social assistance programs evolved significantly over the last century, going from a residual and indirect approach associated with religion and public charity in the 1920s to the affirmation of a social right in the 1960s and later to the contemporary focus on employment and social solidarity. In the process, a regime of minimum income protection was put in place, which guaranteed a basic income to all, abandoned the use of penalties for inappropriate behaviour, and made training and labour market programs available to all, but voluntary. This regime moved along with the broader structure of social protection, which transformed transfers, services, and labour market programs.

Social assistance also came to reflect the concerted manner in which social policies are constructed and implemented in Québec, with a dense and mobilized network of associations and groups defending individual and collective rights and with institutionalized participation structures to bring in the voices of all stakeholders, including persons living in situations of poverty. In the twenty-first century, this structure was completed by a law against poverty and social exclusion, which acted as a safeguard to affirm and protect the rights of the poorest and which reinforced the scope of existing participation instruments.

Québec social assistance protects persons living in situations of poverty better than before, and more generously than in most Canadian provinces, and it has succeeded in significantly reducing the number of households in need of income support. This protection, however, remains very uneven, and it leaves many persons (single, employable adults in particular) far below an income level sufficient to cover basic needs.

This uneven situation points to the ambivalent politics of social solidarity in Québec, a politics torn between a broadly shared support for redistribution and poverty reduction on the one hand, and the ever-present concerns for work incentives and budgetary constraints on the other. In this respect, Québec is far from unique. Everywhere, this opposition between social solidarity and market imperatives defines the politics of social assistance. In the end, one should keep in mind that, in any country, the constitution of a minimum income protection framework "provides the foundation of social citizenship rights" (Bahle, Hubl, and Pfeifer 2011, 2). As a project, the welfare state only makes sense if the real living conditions of the most vulnerable remain acceptable.

References

Bahle, Thomas, Vanessa Hubl, and Michaela Pfeifer. 2011. *The Last Safety Net: A Handbook of Minimum Income Protection in Europe*. Bristol, UK: Policy Press. http://dx.doi.org/10.1332/policypress/9781847427250.001.0001.

Boucher, J.-Émile, Marcel Bélanger, and Claude Morin. 1963. *Rapport du Comité d'étude sur l'assistance publique*. Québec: Conseil exécutif.

Boychuk, Gerard William. 1998. *Patchworks of Purpose: The Development of Provincial Social Assistance Regimes in Canada*. Montréal: McGill-Queen's University Press.

Cantillon, Bea. 2014. "Beyond Social Investment. Which Concepts and Values for Social Policy-Making in Europe?" In *Reconciling Work and Poverty Reduction: How Successful Are European Welfare States?* ed. Bea Cantillon and Frank Vandenbroucke, 286–318. Oxford: Oxford University Press.

Chouinard, Marie-Andrée. 2013. "Critiques sévères contre la ministre Maltais." *Le Devoir*, March 29. http://www.ledevoir.com/politique/quebec/374542/critiques-severes-contre-la-ministre-maltais.

Curry, Bill. 2014. "Ottawa, Provinces Reach Deal on Canada Job Grant." *Globe and Mail*, February 28. http://www.theglobeandmail.com/news/politics/ottawa-reaches-agreement-in-principle-on-job-grant-with-provinces-except-quebec/article17160343/.

Curry, Bill, and Rhéal Séguin. 2014. "Ottawa Gives Québec Special Deal Instead of Job Grant." *Globe and Mail*, March 4. http://www.theglobeandmail.com/news/politics/ottawa-gives-quebec-special-deal-instead-of-job-grant/article17295658/.

Fugère, Denis, and Pierre Lanctôt. 1985. *Méthodologie de détermination des seuils de revenu minimum au Québec*. Québec: Ministère de la Main-d'œuvre et de la Sécurité du revenu.

Godbout, Luc, Suzie St-Cerny, Matthieu Arseneau, Ngoc Ha Dao, and Pierre Fortin. 2014. *La soutenabilité budgétaire des finances publiques du gouvernement du Québec*. Sherbrooke, QC: Chaire de recherche en fiscalité et en finances publiques de l'Université de Sherbrooke.

Gow, James Iain, Alain Noël, and Patrick Villeneuve. 1995. "Les contrôles à l'aide sociale: L'expérience québécoise des visites à domicile." *Canadian Public Policy* 21 (1): 31–52. http://dx.doi.org/10.2307/3552042.

Haddow, Rodney S. 1993. *Poverty Reform in Canada, 1958–1978: State and Class Influences on Policy Making*. Montréal: McGill-Queen's University Press.

Hemerijck, Anton. 2013. *Changing Welfare States*. Oxford: Oxford University Press.

Larocque, Florence. 2011. "The Impact of Institutionalization, Politicization and Mobilization on the Direct Participation of Citizens Experiencing Poverty." *Canadian Journal of Political Science* 44 (4): 883–902. http://dx.doi.org/10.1017/S0008423911000795.

Morel, Sylvie. 2002. *The Insertion Model or the Workfare Model? The Transformation of Social Assistance within Québec and Canada*. Ottawa: Status of Women Canada.

Morin, Alexandre, Fritz-Herbert Remarais, Francis Crépeau, and Aline Lechaume. 2010. "L'assistance sociale de 1996 à 2008: Avancées et défis." In *Portrait social du Québec; Données et analyses*, ed. Sylvie Rheault, 213–30. Québec: Institut de la statistique du Québec.

Noël, Alain. 1996. "La contrepartie dans l'aide sociale au Québec." *Revue Francaise des Affaires Sociales* 50: 99–122.

Noël, Alain. 2002. *A Law Against Poverty: Québec's New Approach to Combating Poverty and Social Exclusion*. Ottawa: Canadian Policy Research Networks.

Noël, Alain. 2012. "Asymmetry at Work: Québec's Distinct Implementation of Programs for the Unemployed." In *Making EI Work: Research from the Mowat Centre Employment Insurance Task Force*, ed. Keith Banting and Jon Medow, 421–48. Montréal: McGill-Queen's University Press.

Noël, Alain. 2013. "Québec's New Politics of Redistribution." In *Inequality and the Fading of Redistributive Politics*, ed. Keith Banting and John Myles, 256–82. Vancouver: UBC Press.

Pierson, Paul. 1998. "Irresistible Forces, Immovable Objects: Post-Industrial Welfare States Confront Permanent Austerity." *Journal of European Public Policy* 5 (4): 539–60. http://dx.doi.org/10.1080/135017698800000011.

Porter, Isabelle. 2013. "Aide sociale: Les critiques fusent de toutes parts." *Le Devoir*, March 5. http://www.ledevoir.com/politique/quebec/372472/aide-sociale-les-critiques-fusent-de-toutes-parts.

Québec CCLP (Comité consultatif de lutte contre la pauvreté et l'exclusion sociale). 2009. *Individual and Family Income Improvement Targets: On Optimal Means for Achieving Them, and on Baseline Financial Support*. Québec: CCLP.

Québec CEPE (Centre d'étude sur la pauvreté et l'exclusion). 2014. *La pauvreté, les inégalités et l'exclusion sociale au Québec: État de situation 2013*. Québec: CEPE.

Québec CPMT (Commission des partenaires du marché du travail). 2007. *Commission des partenaires du marché du travail: A Provincial Forum Devoted to Employment and Workforce Qualification*. Québec: Ministère de l'Emploi et de la Solidarité sociale.

Québec MESS (Ministère de l'Emploi et de la Solidarité sociale). 2011a. *Allocation d'aide à l'emploi (AAE)*. Québec: Ministère de l'Emploi et de la Solidarité sociale. http://www.mess.gouv.qc.ca/regles-normatives/d-ressources/11-revenus-gains-avantages/11.03.02.html.

Québec MESS (Ministère de l'Emploi et de la Solidarité sociale). 2011b. *Améliorer la situation économique des personnes: Un engagement continu. Rapport de la ministre de l'Emploi et de la Solidarité sociale en vertu de l'article 60 de la Loi visant à lutter contre la pauvreté et l'exclusion sociale*. Québec: Ministère de l'Emploi et de la Solidarité sociale.

Québec MESS (Ministère de l'Emploi et de la Solidarité sociale). 2013a. *La Solidarité: Une richesse pour le Québec; Agir auprès des personnes, soutenir ceux qui aident, préparer l'avenir*. Québec: Ministère de l'Emploi et de la Solidarité sociale.

Québec MESS (Ministère de l'Emploi et de la Solidarité sociale). 2013b. *Rapport statistique sur les individus, entreprises et organismes participant aux interventions des services publics d'emploi; Année 2012–2013*. Québec: Direction de la statistique et de l'information de gestion, Ministère de l'Emploi et de la Solidarité sociale.

Québec MESS (Ministère de l'Emploi et de la Solidarité sociale). 2014. *Rapport statistique sur la clientèle des programmes d'aide sociale: Décembre 2013*. Québec: Ministère de l'Emploi et de la Solidarité sociale.

Québec Ministère de la Main-d'œuvre, de la Sécurité du revenu et de la Formation professionnelle. Direction des politiques et des programmes de sécurité du revenu. 1993. *Au cœur de la sécurité du revenu; l'aide de dernier recours au Québec: Origine, objectifs, fonctionnement*. Québec: MMSRFP.

Québec Ministère de la Sécurité du revenu. 1996. *Fiscalité et financement des services publics: Oser choisir ensemble. Le coût et l'efficacité du régime de sécurité du revenue*. Québec: Ministère de la sécurité du revenu.

Saint-Martin, Denis. 2001. "Guichet unique et reconfiguration des réseaux de politiques publiques: Le cas d'Emploi-Québec." *Politique et Sociétés* 20 (2-3): 117–39. http://dx.doi.org/10.7202/040277ar.

Tweddle, Anne, Ken Battle, and Sherri Torjman. 2013. *Welfare in Canada 2012.* Ottawa: Caledon Institute of Social Policy.

Ulysse, Pierre-Joseph, and Frédéric Lesemann. 2004. *Citoyenneté et pauvreté: Politiques, pratiques et stratégies d'insertion en emploi et de lutte contre la pauvreté.* Montréal: Presses de l'Université du Québec.

Vaillancourt, Yves. 1988. *L'évolution des politiques sociales au Québec, 1940–1960.* Montréal: Presses de l'Université de Montréal.

seven
Social Assistance in British Columbia

JANE PULKINGHAM

Introduction

Over the course of the past 30 years, successive governments in British Columbia (BC) actively experimented with social assistance programming. Using Boychuk's (1998) fivefold typology[1] of social assistance regime development in twentieth-century Canada, BC can be described as a "conservative" welfare regime for much of the previous century. In the 1990s and the early years of the current millennium, however, the province experimented with "market performance" and "market/family enforcement" welfare regimes. In addition to changes in program architecture, the welfare caseload itself has changed considerably, which is evident in the double movement associated with the "incredible shrinking" welfare caseload and the simultaneous dramatic rise in disability assistance. As this chapter will map out, the associated medicalization of social assistance in BC is a process that began in the mid-1990s but continues apace in the current millennium with dramatic effect on the caseload, access to welfare, and contemporary welfare regime development in the province.

A recent history of social assistance in British Columbia

Across many welfare regimes, the distinction between the employable and the unemployable is central, but approached in distinctive ways. Conservative regimes emphasize hierarchical status distinctions between "deserving" unemployable persons exempt from reliance on the market or family and "undeserving" employable recipients subject to coercive and stigmatizing measures designed to limit welfare use. The limiting of welfare use is accomplished in a variety of ways, for example, by establishing very different levels of income support for employable and unemployable categories, with much less generous levels of support for the former. In contrast to the conservative regime, the market performance model defines

1 The identified regimes are residual, conservative, market performance, market/family enforcement, and redistributive.

a broader cross-section of the potential recipient population as employable, circumscribing more narrowly who is deemed to be unemployable. However, rather than maintain a purely coercive approach to enforcing reliance on supports other than welfare, as is the case with the conservative regime, the market performance model provides positive inducements for individuals to leave welfare as well as to engage in labour market participation. Incentives include generous earnings exemptions, transportation and childcare subsidies for those entering the labour market or participating in training in preparation for labour market entry, and the removal of barriers to exiting welfare through in-kind health benefits for recipients who participate in the labour market (Boychuk 1998).

In the early 1990s, the NDP government in BC embraced a market performance model of welfare delivery, signalling an end to the long-prevailing conservative regime (Boychuk 1998). It accomplished this transition by reforming, but not abandoning, the administration of and the legislation associated with the existing Guaranteed Available Income for Need (GAIN) program, which was initially implemented in 1979 by the governing Social Credit Party. By the mid-1990s, however, political support for a market performance approach quickly waned. Rising welfare caseloads, economic recession, years of declining federal transfer payments to the province,[2] and rising provincial deficits and debt created an environment that played into a strong anti-welfare sentiment. In 1996, a newly re-elected NDP government quickly moved to dissolve the GAIN Act and implement the BC Benefits Act. In doing so, the NDP government ushered in another welfare regime, this time one designed to "get tough" on welfare by disincentivizing individuals from leaving the market or the family in favour of social assistance (Boychuk 1998). With BC Benefits, the province firmly established social assistance as a "'payer of last resort' where a person may come when between jobs and after having exhausted all other sources of income" (British Columbia Ministry of Social Services 1995). As with the market performance model, the market/family enforcement model is informed by a work-first agenda intended "to make work a better deal than welfare" (British Columbia Ministry of Social Development and Economic Security 1999, 5). It does this not by improving working conditions or creating positive incentives to work but by eroding welfare supports and reinforcing privatized familial support

2 Transfer declines started with the cap on the Canada Assistance Plan (CAP) imposed by the federal government in 1990 and accelerated under the Canada Health and Social Transfer (CHST) established in 1996 to replace the CAP.

obligations, thus making it more difficult and risky for individuals to leave an abusive job situation or family support system.

In keeping with these sets of principles, BC Benefits put in place a three-month residency requirement, eliminated hardship grants for those who quit their jobs "without cause" or were fired from their jobs, reduced allowable asset levels, and cut benefits for employable singles and couples without dependents. The flat-rate earnings exemption[3] was eliminated for all designations except those classified as disabled. Single parents continued to be designated as employable unless they were eligible for disability benefits, but fewer were exempt from work-search obligations because this exemption was now extended only to those with a youngest child under 7 years of age (down from 12 years).

In common with residual regimes, a market/family enforcement regime seeks to ensure that everyone who can participate in the market or can depend on the family will not turn to the state. However, the main disincentive to turning to welfare is not low welfare benefit rates or restrictive eligibility criteria per se but "high levels of deliberate and active stigmatization applied against all recipients" (Boychuk 1998, 19). In this vein, government rhetoric concerning welfare at the time BC Benefits was introduced played heavily on the issue of "welfare dependency." Correspondingly, BC Benefits created a new set of social assistance beneficiary designations that had the effect of identifying problem groups within the program, in particular youth, and imposing more onerous obligations on these applicants requiring them to rely on family and the labour market.

In 2001, a more fiscally and ideologically conservative Liberal government assumed power and soon implemented a new program of welfare administration called BC Employment and Assistance (BCEA). The shift from BC Benefits to BCEA in 2002 was heralded as "strategic . . . redefining British Columbia's income assistance system through new guiding principles," including those of "personal responsibility," "active participation," and "accountability for results" (British Columbia Ministry of Human Resources 2002, 1). Yet rather than engineering a new welfare regime per se, the changes more firmly entrenched the principles of the market/family enforcement regime first introduced through BC Benefits.

The adoption of BCEA nevertheless involved several significant changes designed to reduce the welfare caseload. As happened with BC Benefits, BCEA entailed a "reinvention" of the constituent programs and

3 Earnings exemptions consisted of a flat-rate amount ($100), and recipients could retain 25 per cent of earnings above this threshold.

welfare beneficiary designations. Initially divided into two main programs, Temporary Assistance and Continuous Assistance, welfare beneficiaries were placed into designations that identified their employability obligations and the basis for their exemption from them. As part of the government's broader low-wage strategy that included a new $6-per-hour "training wage" for new labour force entrants ($2 lower than the existing minimum wage), implementation of BCEA also involved cuts to welfare benefits affecting all recipient designations, even those with dependent children and those receiving disability benefits. BC became the only Canadian province to eliminate earnings exemptions entirely for non-disability welfare recipients, and asset exemptions for those applying for assistance were cut to the lowest level in the country (National Council of Welfare 2008). Eligibility rules were further tightened, more stringent employment plans enforced, a three-week work-search wait period was introduced requiring employable applicants to demonstrate engagement in active work search before they could receive benefits, and employability screens and client employability profiles had to be completed. In addition, a two-year independence test was introduced, designed to deny assistance to people who were deemed to have insufficient attachment to the labour market, a policy affecting youth and people with marginal formal employment records in particular.[4]

With this round of welfare reforms, single parents, who already were deemed employable under BC Benefits but excused from the requirement if their youngest child was younger than seven years of age, were now required to seek work when their youngest child reached three years. The child support income exemption was eliminated and, as a result, single parents were no longer able to keep a portion of child support income even though the ministry required recipients to have a family maintenance order in place. This round of reforms also brought in the highly punitive and unprecedented (in Canada) "two-in-five" time-limit rule that limited "employable" welfare recipients without children to two years of support during any five-year period. For parents with dependent children, once their youngest child reached three years of age, this rule was applied but with modifications; rather than be cut off welfare if they exceeded the two-year time limit, parents faced a cut in benefits (by $100 per month for single parents and $200 per month for couples).

Many of the reforms introduced through BCEA were designed to discourage people from applying for assistance—and to deny assistance

---

4 Applicants subject to the test are required to demonstrate that they have worked for 840 hours or earned at least $7,000 in each of the two preceding years (British Columbia Ministry of Social Development and Social Innovation 2004).

altogether (Wallace, Klein, and Reitsma-Street 2006). A key element in this strategy is the way that service delivery and application processes were changed through the adoption of "alternative service delivery models": application processes became more complicated and difficult, requiring applicants to first direct their enquiries through a 1-866 telephone line rather than receive in-person assistance, even for those showing up at a welfare office for the first time; applicants were also required to complete an online orientation; the number of welfare offices was reduced as were ministry staff; the operating budget of the ministry was cut by 30 per cent over three years; claimants were no longer assigned a dedicated caseworker, but were handled by a revolving team of workers often unfamiliar with their cases; and appeal procedures were even more limited than they had been under BC Benefits.

The structure of social assistance in British Columbia today

Today, BCEA consists of two main programs, Temporary Assistance (TA) and Disability Assistance (DA).[5] Legislative authority for the programs is provided through the Employment and Assistance Act and the Employment and Assistance for Persons with Disabilities Act and companion regulations. TA and DA applicants must meet eligibility requirements, including BC residency, citizenship, and income and asset tests, as well as completing a five- or three-week work-search requirement (for new applicants and former recipients, respectively) before being able to apply for full assistance. Those applying for temporary assistance cannot be full-time students and are subject to a two-year financial independence test to "promote self-reliance and decrease the likelihood of dependence on income assistance" (British Columbia Ministry of Social Development and Social Innovation 2013a).

Eligibility for disability assistance is established through a daily living activities assessment, requiring the applicant to submit a 28-page form that includes a physician report (completed by a physician registered and licensed to practice in BC) as well as an assessor's report (completed by a prescribed professional such as a medical practitioner, registered psychologist, registered nurse, or social worker). These applicants are exempt from the two-year independence test and the full-time student restriction. In addition to differences in the eligibility criteria, temporary and disability

5 There is also a third residual program, "Hardship," for those who are ineligible for Temporary or Disability Assistance, and a fourth program, "Child in the Home of a Relative," which, as of March 31, 2010, has stopped accepting new applications.

assistance are distinguished from one another regarding mandatory work-search obligations and support-allowance quantum. Disability assistance is delivered through the beneficiary designation "Persons with Disabilities" (PWD). Though it is no longer subject to automatic regular review,[6] PWD is not a permanent designation and can be rescinded by the ministry.

Temporary assistance is subdivided into four assistance designations: "Expected to Work" (ETW), "Expected to Work–Medical Condition" (ETW-MC), "Temporarily Excused" (TE), and "Persons with Persistent Multiple Barriers" (PPMB). These four designations are distinguished from one another in relation to whether recipients are required to engage in mandatory work-search activities or are temporarily exempt. ETW cases are required to engage in mandatory work-search activities as spelled out in their Employment Plan, but those in the other three designations are temporarily exempt. ETW-MC recipients are exempt for a period of six months, PPMB recipients are exempt for a period of two years,[7] and TE recipients are exempt for as long as they hold a TE designation. Most TE cases are single parents with a child under three years of age. Once the youngest child is three, parents are considered to have employment-related obligations and move into the ETW designation unless assessed otherwise.

Although the BCEA legislation initially implemented in 2002 remains in place today, in the intervening years, key aspects of the program architecture have changed. One of the more notable changes concerns the time-limit rule. When faced with the prospect of cutting off thousands of welfare recipients who had reached their maximum allowable time (2003–04), the government established "exemptions" to this rule (e.g., Employment Plan compliance; Klein and Pulkingham 2008). At the same time, a corollary development was the establishment of the temporary assistance designation ETW-MC, which, together with the PPMB designation, became an important mechanism by which to exempt eligible assistance recipients temporarily from employment obligations as well as the time-limit rule.

In 2012, as part of the newly elected premier's "Families First Agenda," the government removed time limits from the legislation altogether (British Columbia 2012) while also reversing and reinforcing other strategic provisions. For example, the flat-rate earnings exemption is once again available to all claimants of temporary assistance. At the same time,

6 Initially the PWD designation was subject to review once every five years. This requirement was removed in 2007.

7 Only those recipients who have been on assistance for at least 12 of the past 15 months and are unable to achieve financial independence are eligible to be assessed for PPMB designation.

the earnings exemption for those who receive disability assistance is now significantly higher and available to a limited number of PWD recipients as an "Annualized Earnings Exemption" (AEE).[8] Allowable personal asset thresholds are also higher. Companion initiatives accompanying BCEA legislative changes include abolition of the provincial training wage and increases to the minimum wage (to $10.25 per hour). In early 2015, as a response to advocacy efforts on the part of anti-poverty organizations, the government announced it will increase the earnings exemptions from $200 to $400 for TA families with children, and it will end the child support clawback. Other changes, such as lengthening work-search requirements from three to five weeks for new applicants, are more restrictive. According to the government, it has "expanded the application and intensity of work search requirements" to "help families avoid the cycle of income assistance dependence . . ." (British Columbia 2012, 6).

BCEA benefit rates

BCEA benefits (see Table 7.1) consist of a monthly support and shelter allowance and additional program benefits, including general and health supplements, most of which require separate application. The support allowance is a fixed rate for each family type, but the temporary and disability assistance rates differ. For example, the monthly support allowance for a single person receiving temporary assistance is $235; for a single person receiving disability assistance, it is $531.42. For parents (couples or single), the value of the support allowance does not increase with the number of dependent children: the support allowance for a single parent receiving temporary assistance is a flat-rate $375.58 compared to $672.08 for a single parent receiving disability assistance. In addition, parents with dependent children also receive the federal Canada Child Tax Benefit (CCTB), the National Child Benefit Supplement (NCBS), and, for those with children under six years of age, the Universal Child Care Benefit (UCCB). An individual with a PPMB designation receives a monthly earnings exemption and a monthly support allowance each of which respectively is higher than that given to those with any other temporary assistance designation, though not as high as that received by PWD recipients. For example, the monthly

8 The ministry limits the availability of the AEE: in 2013, it was available by invitation only to a very small group of PWD recipients. For 2014, it was extended to those who, at minimum, had a PWD designation for the previous 12 months, had received assistance for the previous 2 consecutive months, had earned more than $500 in one of the preceding 12 months, or had applied by the annual January 2014 deadline (British Columbia Ministry of Social Development and Social Innovation 2014).

Table 7.1 British Columbia Social Assistance Rates, Earnings Exemptions and Liquid Asset Exemption Levels, 2013 (Persons under 65 years of age)

	Single Person Employable (ETW)	Single Person with Disabilities (PWD)	Lone Parent, Employable; One Child under 6 Years (ETW)	Lone Parent with Disabilities (PWD); One Child under 6 Years
Monthly Support Allowance	$235.00[1]	$531.42	$375.581	$672.08
Monthly Maximum Shelter Allowance[2]	$375.00	$375.00	$570.00	$570.00
Total Monthly Welfare Income[3]	$660.46	$956.88	$1,469.74	$1,752.90
Additional Program Benefits (annual)[4]	$35.00	$35.00	$180.00	$180.00
Monthly Maximum Earnings Exemptions	$200.00	$800.00 (or $9,600.00 annually)	$200.00	$800.00 (or $9,600.00 annually)
Liquid Asset Exemption Levels	$2,000.00	$5,000.00	$4,000.00	$10,000.00

Source: British Columbia Ministry of Social Development and Social Innovation (2007a, 2007b, 2012, 2013b, 2013c); Canada Revenue Agency (2011a, 2011b).

[1] PPMB recipients receive $48 more per month.

[2] The maximum allowance is $820 for a seven-person household.

[3] This includes support and shelter allowances; the GST/HST/BC Low-Income Climate Action Tax Credit; and, for lone parents, the federal Canada Child Tax Benefit ($117.08), National Child Benefit Supplement ($181.41), and Universal Child Care Benefit ($100).

[4] Additional benefits include the annual Christmas Supplement and the annual School Start-up Supplement for a child aged 5–11.

earnings exemption for a PPMB recipient is $500 compared to $200 for all those with other temporary assistance designations; it is $800 for those regarded as disabled (PWD recipients). Unlike the PWD recipient, those on temporary assistance must "use or lose" their monthly earnings exemption in the month the earnings accrue; exemptions cannot be accrued cumulatively over the course of the year. The monthly shelter allowance is the same for TA and DA recipients, starting at $375 for a one-person household and rising to a maximum of $820 for a seven-person household.

Monthly support and shelter allowance benefits for those on social assistance are not inflation indexed and are not regularly reviewed. On the two occasions since 1996 when new program architecture has been introduced, benefits were cut; a few years later, there was a selective and partial reversal of these cuts. For example, implementation of BC Benefits in 1996 entailed cuts of 8 to 10 per cent in benefits for employable recipients without dependents. In 2000, the government reversed some of the previous cuts by increasing the total value of support and shelter allowances by 2 per cent for all recipient groups, adding the final dollar amount to the support allowance component (Goldberg and Long 2001).

In 2002, with the implementation of BCEA, the government cut both the support and shelter allowances for certain recipients and family types. For example, monthly support allowance for single parents dropped by $51. At the same time, the monthly shelter allowance for households with three persons or more was reduced by an amount ranging from $55 to $75, depending on family size (Long and Goldberg 2002). Five years later (in 2007), all recipient groups received an increase to their monthly benefits ranging from a low of approximately 3 to 5 per cent for couples with no children to a high of approximately 20 per cent for singles and for PPMB-designated couples with children (British Columbia Ministry of Social Development and Social Innovation 2008). This was the first time employable singles had received an increase to support allowances since the early 1990s. Welfare rates have not been raised since 2007.

Welfare benefits have much less purchasing power than they did 20 years ago but not just because of direct benefit cuts. Successive governments have relied heavily on the less visible but more corrosive effect of allowing inflationary pressures to erode the value of benefits, a strategy of "social policy by stealth" (Battle 1990). The devaluation of benefits is a problem for all welfare recipients but is more pronounced for singles receiving temporary or disability assistance who do not have children. The slide in the value of welfare benefits over time means that, today, the total welfare incomes of singles (ETW and PWD) are worth just two-thirds of their respective peak values, reached in 1994. In 2013 dollars, the CPI-adjusted value of the 1994 total annual welfare income for a single employable person is $12,209 (compared to the 2013 actual of $7,923) and $17,119 for a single person with a disability (compared to the 2013 actual of $11,483). As these figures show, the relative value of disability assistance for singles today is less than the comparable income of employable singles in 1994 ($12,209). Meanwhile, the welfare income of employable single parents is worth approximately three-quarters of its 1994 value. In 2013 dollars, the CPI-adjusted value of the 1994 total annual welfare income for an employable lone parent with one child under 6 years is $24,478 compared to the

2013 actual of $21,035.[9] The decline is slightly less pronounced for single parents because their total welfare income includes the inflation-indexed federal child benefit payments.

The nature and evolution of the caseload in British Columbia

Today, the welfare caseload in BC is very different than it was 20 years ago (see also Kneebone and White, in this volume). A combination of factors drives the welfare caseload changes observed, including the welfare policy reforms themselves, changes in the economy that affect the need for individuals and families to turn to social assistance for support in the first place, demographic shifts in the single-parent population, and rising rates of disability in the general population. One of the striking changes is the decline in the overall size of the caseload. In 2012, the total number of adults and children ("clients") supported by BCEA represented 3.9 per cent of the BC population, down from 9.7 per cent in 1995 (British Columbia Ministry of Social Development and Social Innovation 2013d, 2; see also Kneebone and White, in this volume). Other differences include the dramatic transformation in who receives support, based on beneficiary designation, and the demographic make-up of the caseload in terms of family type.

Social assistance in BC today is no longer a system that largely supports those deemed to be temporarily unemployed and "expected to work"; it is one that supports those deemed to have a recognized disability, medical condition, or other health-related barrier to employment and who are exempt, or temporarily exempt, from mandatory work-search requirements. The trend toward a medicalized system of income support began almost two decades ago and unfolded in the context of declining welfare rolls and changes to social assistance eligibility. After peaking in the mid-1990s in the wake of the 1990–92 recession, the total welfare caseload in BC declined significantly over a 10-year period, bottoming out in 2006 (97,197) at less than half its former size (214,859 in 1995; see Figure 7.1). Although the total caseload started to climb again in 2006 before the recession of 2008–09, and at an accelerated pace during the recession, it levelled off once again in 2012 (at 134,402), remaining well below its 1995 peak.

9 The 2013 CPI-adjusted figures are based on the author's calculation using the *BC CPI Annual Averages* retrieved on February 13, 2014 at http://www.bcstats.gov.bc.ca/Files/115a55c8-2e68-495d-96ea-2a7b79a6bae7/ConsumerPriceIndexAnnualAverages.csv.

Figure 7.1 BC Employment and Assistance Cases by Program, 1990–2012

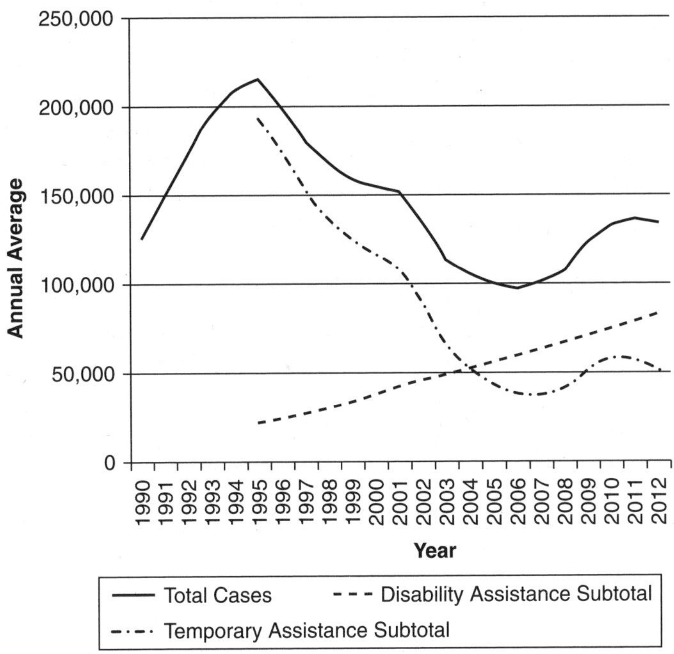

Source: British Columbia Ministry of Social Development and Social Innovation (2013d).

The reduction in the overall welfare caseload since the mid-1990s is dramatic, but the changes to temporary assistance and disability assistance caseloads respectively are even more striking. As Figure 7.1 shows, the reduction in the temporary assistance caseload (almost fourfold, from 192,693 in 1995 to 51,197 in 2012) is much more pronounced than for the caseload as whole. At the same time, an equally dramatic but opposite trend occurred for the disability assistance caseload: it increased fourfold from 22,167 to 83,205. As a result of these two different trends, commencing in 2004 disability assistance cases outnumbered temporary assistance cases for the first time, and continue to do so by a wide margin. Today, disability assistance cases currently make up the majority (62 per cent) of the total welfare caseload compared to just one-tenth in 1995.

The medicalizing trend is also evident if we look at when and how the different designations within the temporary assistance caseload evolved. In 1995, the temporary assistance welfare caseload (then comprised of those on "Basic Income Assistance") consisted overwhelmingly of cases designated as "employable" (174,937 out of a total of 192, 693 or 90 per cent) rather than temporarily excused from employment obligations. Since then, the proportion of TA recipients who were deemed employable fell dramatically, from 90 to 54 per cent. Also, TA recipients temporarily excused from employment obligations because of a medical condition (ETW-MC or PPMB cases) did not exist as such in 1995, but, combined, they made up 24 per cent of the caseload in 2012. Because most BCEA clients receive disability assistance or are ETW-MC or PPMB cases, only 24 per cent of the program's total caseload is in a beneficiary category that expects recipients to work and subjects them to work-search requirements.

The demographic profile of the welfare caseload has also shifted during this period (see Figure 7.2). Singles continue to make up the majority of cases but now constitute an even larger portion of the total welfare caseload

Figure 7.2 BCEA Total Cases by Family Type, 1995–2012

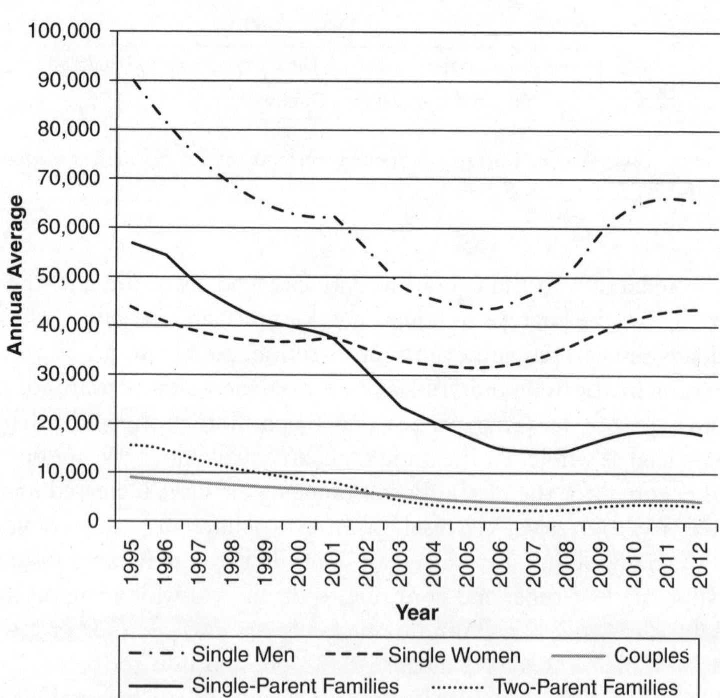

Source: British Columbia Ministry of Social Development and Social Innovation (2013d).

(81 per cent in 2012 compared to 62 per cent in 1995) while other family types, specifically single- and two-parent families, have fallen from just over one-third to less than one-fifth of the caseload. Single men remain the largest group of welfare recipients (48.5 per cent), a reality that has become more accentuated over time. Nevertheless, in proportionate terms, the share of the welfare caseload occupied by single women changed more than it did for single men. Single women now make up one-third (32.4 per cent) of total welfare cases today, up from one-fifth, and, in surpassing single parents receiving assistance, they now constitute the second-largest group of cases. Unlike all other family types, however, their numbers in aggregate have changed little over the period considered because the drop in the number of single women in the temporary assistance caseload was much smaller than that for any other family type, and this drop was entirely offset by an increase in the number of single women in the disability assistance caseload.

Meanwhile, the number of single parents receiving assistance, most of whom are women, has declined dramatically overall (from 26.5 to 13.4 per cent), driven entirely by reductions in the number of single parents receiving temporary assistance. They are, however, now much more likely to receive disability assistance; between 1995 and 2012, the number of single parents in receipt of disability assistance grew almost fivefold, a rate of growth that is much more dramatic than that observed for other family types (see Table 7.2).

Table 7.2 British Columbia Disability Assistance Caseload by Family Type and Change in Annual Average Caseload, 1995 and 2012 (Cases)

	1995 Number (%)	2012 Number (%)	1995–2012 % Change in Number of Cases
Single Men	10,844 (48.9)	41,718 (50.1)	284.7
Single Women	8,287 (37.4)	31,251 (37.6)	277.1
Couples	1,511 (6.8)	3,219 (3.9)	113.0
Two-Parent Families	604 (2.7)	1,734 (2.1)	187.1
Single-Parent Families	922 (4.2)	5,283 (6.3)	473.0
Total	22,167 (100)	83,205 (100)	275.4

Source: British Columbia Ministry of Social Development and Social Innovation (2013d).

The future evolution of social assistance in British Columbia

Over the past 20 years, access to social assistance has become increasingly medicalized in BC, and, going forward, this trend will likely continue. The Families First Agenda and a more recent initiative, Increasing Accessibility for People with Disabilities (British Columbia 2013), signal that the government is sharpening distinctions between those eligible for temporary assistance and disability assistance, and, in so doing, it is reinscribing old divisions between the "deserving" and "undeserving" poor. Within this environment, the market/family enforcement welfare regime appears to be evolving into a version of the conservative model.

On the one hand, reintroduction of the flat-rate earnings exemption for those on temporary assistance who are subject to mandatory work-search requirements will assist these individuals in establishing and maintaining some degree of labour force attachment, if only to defray a portion of the costs associated with finding and keeping a job. The enhanced earnings exemption provision for PWD recipients, who are not required to engage in mandatory work-search activities, will do likewise, but it also has the potential to improve significantly the standard of living of PWD recipients who are able to secure employment and make use of the maximum annual earnings exemption.

On the other hand, other initiatives make it more onerous for non-disability applicants to qualify for support in the first place, as a way to redouble efforts to shrink the temporary assistance caseload. In addition, the government has made it clear that, for the foreseeable future, welfare rates (in particular welfare rates for the non-disabled) will not be increased, thus continuing to make it very hard for those who do qualify for social assistance to survive on the benefits received. The scenario of stagnating welfare rates is especially troublesome for single TA recipients, whose welfare incomes fall well below even the most parsimonious of poverty lines advocated by the Fraser Institute. Families with children are also penalized by low welfare rates and by the prospect of little to no change on this front. Most of the BCEA-supported children (two-thirds) are in families who receive temporary assistance, and, for these children, the time their families must subsist on poverty-level welfare rates constitutes a large portion of their childhood and critical developmental years.

Meanwhile, the province is moving ahead with several initiatives that are directed at improving supports for people living with disabilities—a reform driven by "a vision of becoming the most progressive region for people living with disabilities in Canada" (British Columbia 2013).

In addition to the enhanced BCEA provisions for disability assistance recipients introduced in 2012, the premier is on record as saying that disability welfare rates should be increased when the fiscal climate allows (Harrington 2013). The province also initiated a consultation on increasing accessibility for people with disabilities, which led to the release of the *Disability Consultation Report: Moving Together Toward an Accessible B.C.* (British Columbia 2014a) and the action plan *Accessibility 2024: Making B.C. the Most Progressive Province in Canada for People with Disabilities by 2024* (British Columbia 2014b).

Current initiatives appear to be moving the province away from the more punitive elements of a market/family enforcement model. The shift may indicate that the province is once again embracing a conservative welfare regime, one in which the basis for deserving status and protection from mandatory employability requirements is narrowly drawn and, in this instance, medicalized, while the numbers qualifying for this form of support grows. However, this is not a simple back-to-the-future scenario. Rather, this shift is happening when all social assistance recipients, those on temporary and disability assistance alike, are considerably worse off financially than they were 20 years ago, and the financial advantage to securing disability assistance today is relative only to the situation of temporary assistance contemporaries. Today, the province may support many more people through the Disability Assistance Program, but the level of financial support provided is considerably less than it used to be—and is even less than the amount of support previously provided to those in receipt of non-disability assistance (the "undeserving" employable). Another interesting development is that, in directing its attention to questions of employment accessibility for those living with a disability, BC's conservative welfare regime "in the making" is re-envisioning the employable-unemployable divide among those recognized as living with and without disabilities,[10] even while it continues to reinforce the deserving-undeserving distinction between these two groups.

10 The *2013/14 Annual Service Report Plan* for the BC Ministry of Social Development and Social Innovation indicates that, in 2013–14, 15.6 per cent of "Persons with Disabilities" cases declared earnings, up from 14.2 per cent in 2012–13. This relatively large increase from the previous year is attributed to the changes introduced in 2012 to increase the earnings exemption and to introduce an annualized exemption (11.2 per cent of PWD cases declared earnings in 2002–03, the baseline year). The report does not provide information on earnings exemptions for other BCEA cases.

References

Battle, Ken [Grattan Gray, pseud.]. 1990. "Social Policy by Stealth." *Policy Options* 11 (2): 17–29.

Boychuk, Gerard. 1998. *Patchworks of Purpose: The Development of Provincial Social Assistance Regimes in Canada*. Montréal: McGill-Queen's University Press.

British Columbia. 2012. *Families First Agenda for British Columbia*. Victoria: Government of British Columbia. http://www.familiesfirstbc.ca/.

British Columbia. 2013. *Increasing Accessibility for People with Disabilities*. Victoria: Government of British Columbia.

British Columbia. 2014a. *Disability Consultation Report: Moving Together Toward an Accessible* B.C. Victoria: Ministry of Social Development and Social Innovation.

British Columbia. 2014b. *Accessibility 2024: Making B.C. the Most Progressive Province in Canada for People with Disabilities by 2024*. Victoria: Government of British Columbia.

British Columbia Ministry of Human Resources. 2002. *Service Plan Summary 2002/03–2004/05*. Victoria: Government of British Columbia. http://www.sdsi.gov.bc.ca/ministry/sp/docs/2002-03_summary.pdf.

British Columbia Ministry of Social Development and Economic Security. 1999. *BC Benefits: The First Three Years*. Victoria: Government of British Columbia.

British Columbia Ministry of Social Development and Social Innovation. 2004. "Two-Year Independence Test." *Ministry Quick Links*. Victoria: Government of British Columbia. http://www.hsd.gov.bc.ca/factsheets/2004/2year_independ.htm.

British Columbia Ministry of Social Development and Social Innovation. 2007a. *BC Employment and Assistance Rate Tables: Income Assistance*. Victoria: Government of British Columbia. http://www.eia.gov.bc.ca/mhr/ia.htm.

British Columbia Ministry of Social Development and Social Innovation. 2007b. *BC Employment and Assistance Rate Tables: Disability Assistance*. Victoria: Government of British Columbia. http://www.eia.gov.bc.ca/mhr/da.htm.

British Columbia Ministry of Social Development and Social Innovation. 2008. *Increases to Income Assistance Rate Tables*. Victoria: Government of British Columbia. http://www.sdsi.gov.bc.ca/factsheets/2007/increase_table.htm.

British Columbia Ministry of Social Development and Social Innovation. 2012. *BC Employment and Assistance Rate Tables: Assets*. Victoria: Government of British Columbia. http://www.eia.gov.bc.ca/mhr/assets.htm.

British Columbia Ministry of Social Development and Social Innovation. 2013a. "Two-Year Financial Independence: Overview." *Online Resources: Verification and Eligibility*. Victoria: Government of British Columbia. http://www.gov.bc.ca/meia/online_resource/verification_and_eligibility/two_year/.

British Columbia Ministry of Social Development and Social Innovation. 2013b. *Online Resource Home: Table of Contents*. Victoria: Government of British Columbia. http://www.hsd.gov.bc.ca/olr/online_resource_toc.pdf.

British Columbia Ministry of Social Development and Social Innovation. 2013c. *BC Employment and Assistance Rate Tables: General Supplements*. Victoria: Government of British Columbia. Last modified August 1, 2013. http://www.eia.gov.bc.ca/mhr/gs.htm.

British Columbia Ministry of Social Development and Social Innovation. 2013d. *BC Employment and Assistance: Summary Report 2013*. Victoria: Government of British Columbia. http://www.sd.gov.bc.ca/research/archive/13/08-jul2013.pdf.

British Columbia Ministry of Social Development and Social Innovation. 2014. *Annualized Earnings Exemption 2014*. Victoria: Government of British Columbia. http://www.sdsi.gov.bc.ca/pwd/aee/index.html.

British Columbia Ministry of Social Services. 1995. "Program Overview—Program Philosophy and Values: Section 2.1.1." *Income Assistance Manual*. Victoria: Government of British Columbia.

Canada Revenue Agency. 2011a. *Canada Child Tax Benefit (CCTB) Online Calculator*. Base Year Period July 2012 to June 2013. Ottawa: Government of Canada. http://www.cra-arc.gc.ca/bnfts/clcltr/cctb_clcltr-eng.html.

Canada Revenue Agency. 2011b. *GST/HST and Related Provincial Programs Online Calculator*. Base Year Period July 2012 to June 2013. Ottawa: Government of Canada. http://www.cra-arc.gc.ca/bnfts/clcltr/gstc_clcltr-eng.html.

Goldberg, Michael, and Andrea Long. 2001. *Falling Behind: A Comparison of Living Costs and Income Assistance Rates (BC Benefits) in British Columbia*. Vancouver: SPARC of BC.

Harrington, Molly. 2013. Presentation to First Call BC Child and Youth Advocacy Coalition, Vancouver, BC, November 13.

Klein, Seth, and Jane Pulkingham. 2008. *Living on Welfare in BC: Experiences of Longer-Term "Expected to Work" Recipients*. Vancouver: Canadian Centre for Policy Alternative, BC Office and Raise the Rates.

Long, Andrea, and Michael Goldberg. 2002. *Falling Further Behind: A Comparison of Living Costs and Employment and Assistance Rates in British Columbia*. Vancouver: SPARC of BC.

National Council of Welfare. 2008. *Welfare Incomes, 2006 and 2007*. Ottawa: National Council of Welfare.

Wallace, Bruce, Seth Klein, and Marge Reitsma-Street. 2006. *Denied Assistance: Closing the Front Door on Welfare in BC*. Vancouver: Canadian Centre for Policy Alternatives.

eight
Social Assistance in Alberta

DONNA E. WOOD[1]

Introduction

Alberta became a province in 1905. This meant that the provincial government also assumed constitutional responsibility for the well-being of its citizens, including "relief for the poor." Building upon the English poor laws—transposed to all English-speaking provinces to prevent the burden of indigent people from falling on the state—attitudes toward relief in Alberta have been shaped by three key factors. In its formative years, the Alberta mind-set reflected the influence of American immigrants, whose form of "moral conservatism" placed more emphasis on individual as opposed to collective responsibility. This emphasis resulted in Alberta's early political leaders being especially adverse to socialist messages. With the left marginalized, a consensus developed around conservative values, resulting in stable governments and a strong, executive-based approach to governing. Since 1935, Alberta has had only 11 premiers, and—until 2015 when the Alberta NDP assumed power—the Progressive Conservatives had been in charge for 44 years. Ever since oil was discovered in 1947, the presence of unreliable natural resource revenues has produced a "boom and bust" economic characteristic marked by expansionary spending and then restraint (Wiseman 2007).

All of these factors have significantly affected the generosity and nature of Alberta's last-resort welfare programming. As this chapter will demonstrate, the provincial government readily accepts responsibility for the "deserving poor"—people who are considered as poor through no fault of their own—but provides only marginal support for the "undeserving poor"—for fear of encouraging idleness. This approach to welfare has been consistent in Alberta for almost 100 years. Today, there are two separate and distinct programs that provide financial assistance to Albertans in need: Alberta Works Income Support (AW-IS) and Assured Income for the Severely Handicapped (AISH). In 2013, the programs collectively cost

1 The author would like to thank the Albertans who agreed to be interviewed for this paper, and those who provided comments on earlier drafts.

over $1.7 billion, representing 80,212 cases and over 115,000 Albertans receiving income support benefits each month.

To explore the premise that Alberta's approach to welfare distinguishes between the "deserving" and "undeserving" poor, the chapter starts by reviewing historical developments, including changes in caseloads. The major institutional features of the current architecture are considered next, including subprogram categories, financial eligibility criteria, benefit levels, service delivery arrangements, and client characteristics. The chapter concludes by looking at the future evolution of income support programming in Alberta, and at some of the challenges ahead.

A brief history of social assistance in Alberta

Reflecting government's desire to help the "deserving" poor, Alberta developed a mother's allowance program in 1919, an old age pension in 1929, and a blind person's pension in 1938. The rest of those in need were left to municipal relief (Reichwein 2002). During the Great Depression of the 1930s, many Albertans experienced extreme hardship. Although the Social Credit government elected in 1935 disliked the idea of "socialism," by the late 1950s, it had started to introduce many reforms, including a needs-based Social Allowance (SA) program in 1961. Alberta civil servants were significantly involved in the federal-provincial discussions that shaped the development of the shared-cost Canada Assistance Plan (CAP; Splane 1985). CAP allowed Alberta to modernize its categorical programs into a consolidated and integrated needs-based approach, while still retaining distinctions between "employable" and "unemployable" benefit recipients. In 1970, the province started to provide employment support services to help "employables" access the labour market.

When the Progressive Conservatives under Peter Lougheed assumed power in 1971, they promised additional improvements in social programs. In 1975, all last-resort income support programs were consolidated under provincial control as responsibility for "employables" was transferred from municipalities. In 1979, the Assured Income for the Severely Handicapped program, or AISH, was introduced with its own separate legislation, providing a flat-rate benefit equivalent to that given to Alberta seniors and one higher than SA rates. AISH was the first program in the country designed for the permanently disabled. It was unique as there were no asset limits. It was also a move back to categorical programming, a direction further reinforced in 1983 with the introduction of a separate Widows' Pension (WP) program. During this period, the range of benefits for all income support programs expanded, and benefit levels were increased through periodic and routine adjustments (Reichwein 2002). The primary focus of the three programs was on safeguarding client rights and on ensuring that basic necessities were provided to those in need. When work expectations started to be placed on single parents, employment services and day-care supports were expanded (Wood 1988).

By the early 1980s, the Alberta unemployment rate had increased dramatically to over 11 per cent, resulting in very large increases to SA caseloads. Internal reforms—including a rebranding of the Social Allowance program, which became the Supports for Independence (SFI) program, and a new focus on client responsibilities over client rights—had little impact on reducing caseloads or program costs. When another recession hit in the early 1990s and Ralph Klein became premier, he pledged to reduce Alberta's debt and deficit. Welfare reform was one of the province's flagship deficit-elimination initiatives and included a new administrative culture (applications deferred, fraud and eligibility checks), benefit reductions (a decline of 19 per cent for single employables and of 13 per cent for single parents), and new work projects (Faid 2009).

The impact on SFI caseloads was dramatic. Between March 1993 and March 1994, caseloads dropped from 94,087 to 62,394; by 1997, they were down to 36,210. A variety of factors beyond welfare reform also contributed to the drop in caseloads. Federal and provincial employment services were integrated and streamlined. Supports outside the welfare system were expanded through the National Child Benefit, extended health benefits for children, and the Alberta Family Employment Tax Credit. The economy improved. However, the loss of key aspects of Alberta's last-resort social-safety net directly affected related programs and services. By 1996, demands on the Edmonton food bank had reached their peak (Goldberg and Green 2009). Homelessness and child welfare referrals increased significantly (Gaetz 2010; Kinjerski and Hebert 2000).

During this period AISH and Widows' Pension benefits were frozen, not reduced. However, program recipients were not shielded from the impact of inflation, which, by 2003, had reduced the real purchasing power of the AISH stipend by over 20 per cent (Kneebone 2005). In 1998, a $100,000 assets limit was introduced to AISH, as politicians became concerned over "millionaires" on the program.

By the late 1990s, Alberta municipalities had started to raise concerns about poverty in their communities, and, in 2001, an MLA committee consulted on and reviewed all provincial programs for low-income Albertans. Thirty-two recommendations were made, but only minor changes resulted. Although reintegration of the SFI, AISH, and WP programs was recommended, government decided only to phase out the small Widows' Pension program. AISH was kept separate as a result of lobbying from the disability community, keen to avoid the "welfare culture" within the more general social assistance program (Faid 2009). In 2004, a different MLA committee—influenced by community boards responsible for support services for persons with developmental disabilities—reviewed AISH and recommended benefit increases, a capacity to add supplementary personal and child benefits to the flat-rate benefit, increased earnings exemptions, and a process to review benefit levels regularly. All of these recommendations were accepted by government and implemented. The new capacity within AISH to provide variable benefits reinforced the distinction in Alberta between the "deserving" and "undeserving" poor.

In 2003 the Income and Employment Supports Act was passed to replace the Social Development Act. With a buoyant economy, by then the SFI caseload had dropped below 30,000. The general social assistance program was relabelled Alberta Works–Income Support, or AW-IS, and included as one component of a larger array of services alongside employment and training services, health benefits, and child support services. After 2005–06, statistics on those dependent on government last-resort social assistance benefits were no longer even identified in departmental annual reports. One informant suggested that "we pretend that welfare doesn't exist in Alberta anymore."

But certainly, AISH has not disappeared; instead, it has grown larger and more visible. The almost doubling of AISH caseloads from 2000 to 2014 is not surprising given the aging of the population and that better benefits draw people from AW-IS onto AISH. By 2010, AISH benefit levels had returned to that available to Alberta seniors (Kneebone and Grynishak 2011). In 2012, the AISH living allowance was further increased, from $1,188 to $1,588, making it the highest in Canada and reflecting a campaign commitment made during the Alberta leadership race by the winner, Alison Redford. In Alberta today the "deserving" poor are relatively well taken care of.

The same cannot be said for those who are dependent on AW-IS benefits, or for others who can be considered part of the "undeserving" poor. Benefits remained almost completely stagnant between 1993 and 2008, a period of 15 years. Despite a 45-per-cent increase in AW-IS payments for single persons in 2008, food bank usage in March 2012 was 50 per cent higher than before the start of the recession (Alberta Food Bank Network Association 2012). There has, however, been concerted action to combat homelessness through a 10-year plan, which was announced in 2007 and led by the Calgary Homeless Foundation and the Alberta Secretariat for Action on Homelessness. Consequently, Alberta is now considered a leader in Canada, having developed a comprehensive plan with targets, benchmarks, and a rigorous evaluation process (Gaetz 2010).

The 2012 budget also increased AW-IS benefits by a further 5 per cent, put more money into fighting homelessness, and promised to eliminate child poverty in 5 years and reduce poverty for everyone in 10 years through the development of an Alberta Social Policy Framework (Kleiss 2012). Consultations were held in the summer of 2012, and a broad framework was adopted by the government in February 2013. In June 2013, a provincial consultation strategy to identify how to eliminate child poverty in 5 years and reduce poverty for everyone in 10 years was launched with a discussion paper, and engagement continued to October 2013. A public engagement report was released in November 2014 (Alberta Human Services 2014).

Nature and evolution of the caseload

Figure 8.1 presents a picture of the ups and downs of social assistance and AISH caseloads since 1970, as described previously. This 40-year picture—all under Progressive Conservative Party of Alberta rule—provides several interesting insights.

During the expansionary "rights" phase that lasted up to 1990, income support caseloads grew slowly until 1981, reflecting Alberta's low unemployment rate and buoyant economy. The economic downturn of the early 1980s had a major impact, with social assistance caseloads more than doubling from 1980–81 to 1990–91, even though, by 1990, the Alberta unemployment rate had eased to 6.9 per cent from an earlier high of more than 11 per cent. AISH caseloads also increased each year over this period, albeit at a much slower pace.

The welfare reforms starting in 1993 that included an emphasis on deferral, fraud and eligibility checks, benefit reductions, and new work projects had a huge impact, as did an improved economy and alternatives outside of the welfare system. By 2001, social assistance caseloads had fallen by almost two-thirds to an annual average of about 27,000 cases per month. For most of this period, AISH caseloads remained steady—even rising slightly—despite increased client eligibility scrutiny and the introduction of assets testing.

By 2001, the AISH caseload actually exceeded the social assistance caseload, which, until 2008, remained low, reflecting the booming Alberta economy. The economic downturn that started that year and an increase in the Alberta unemployment rate to 6.6 per cent in 2009 resulted in rising Alberta Works–Income Support caseload counts, which peaked at an

Figure 8.1 Alberta Income Support Caseloads, 1969–70 to 2011–12

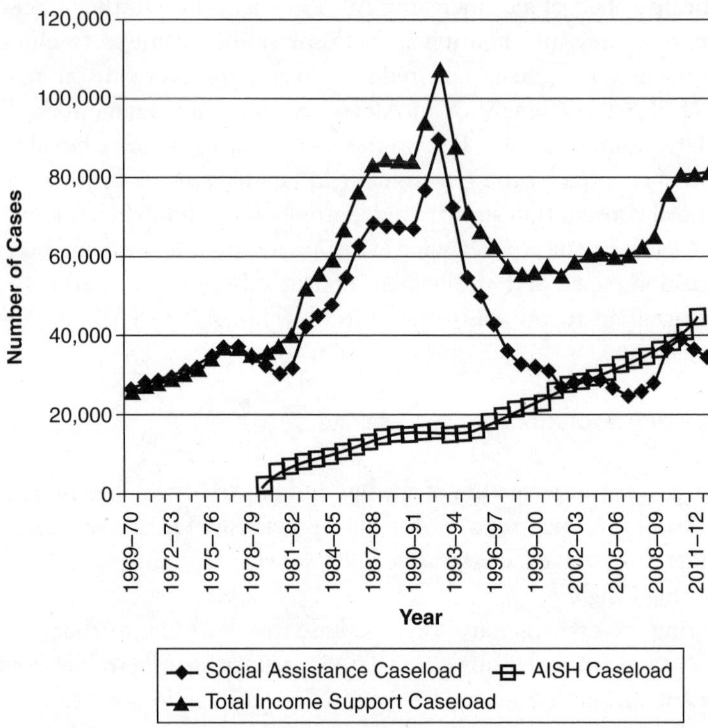

Note: Numbers are caseload not recipient counts. "Social assistance" in this chart refers to Social Allowance, Supports for Independence, and Alberta Works–Income Support (Expected to Work and Barriers to Full Employment) programs. The data have been compiled primarily through a review of departmental annual reports going back to 1969–70. The Alberta Office of Official Statistics releases Alberta Works–Income Support caseload data monthly; however, these data only go back to 2005–06. AISH statistics are available only on request.

annual average of 39,388 in 2010–11. The dramatic story over this period, however, is the steady rise of the AISH caseload, which has almost doubled from 28,586 cases in 2001–02 to approximately 46,000 cases in 2013. This outcome is not surprising given that the AISH review in 2004 clearly privileged support for persons with disabilities, thereby drawing people from AW-IS into the AISH program. It also reflects an aging population and the overall growth in the Alberta population, as more people move into the province.

These caseload changes have also resulted in changes to the social assistance rate—that is the number of income support beneficiaries measured as a fraction of the population aged 0 to 64 years. In 1969, Alberta's rate was estimated at 5.0 per cent. It peaked in 1993 (just before the welfare reforms) at around 8.0 per cent. Since 2000, the rate in Alberta has averaged about 3 per cent, the lowest in Canada (Kneebone and White 2014).

Alberta's social assistance architecture in 2013

Program structure and client types

To qualify for either AW-IS or AISH, applicants are assessed on the basis of their ability to work and their financial need. Once they are deemed eligible through an employability assessment, they are then slotted into different program streams.

1) Alberta Works–Income Support is subdivided into

- Expected to Work (ETW)—people who are looking for work, working but not earning enough, or temporarily unable to work in the short term.
- Barriers to Full Employment (BFE)—people who cannot work due to chronic mental or physical health problems or because of multiple barriers to employment.
- Learners—people who need academic upgrading or training so that they can get a job.

2) Assured Income for the Severely Handicapped

- Adults with a severe handicap that substantially limits their ability to earn a living may qualify for AISH. The disability must be permanent and must be the main factor limiting their ability to earn a living. Other factors such as age or level of education are not considered in determining eligibility. There must be no training, rehabilitation, or medical treatment available that would help the person to work enough to earn a livelihood. Applicants undergo a medical assessment by a physician, but the eligibility decision is taken by a civil servant called an AISH administrator.

Reviewing Alberta's AISH medical eligibility criteria against those of Ontario and British Columbia, Kneebone and Grynishak (2011) concluded that the AISH criteria are more strict and onerous, as they emphasize the permanence of the disability.

Eligibility, benefits, and services

Determining financial eligibility includes an assessment of income and assets. There are different criteria dependent upon the program stream that an individual is slotted into. This assignment also determines the core and supplementary benefits available, as well as how an individual will receive services. Table 8.1 summarizes the key features of AW-IS and AISH in 2013 for a single person. There are different levels for families. The table also provides some information on caseloads and client characteristics.

Assets are the resources that an individual is expected to use to support himself or herself. The cash assets noted for AW-IS are the level below which an individual may be deemed eligible for income support. In general, a house of any value, vehicles with up to $10,000 in equity, and $5,000 per adult in RRSPs, RESPs (registered education savings plans), or children's assets are exempt. AISH allows assets of up to $100,000. Assets exemption limits in AISH are the most generous and become less generous the closer a recipient is to the labour market.

An individual may be receiving other *income* (including employment income) and still qualify for government assistance. For both AW-IS and AISH, the applicant's current income is reviewed against predefined categories of needs, and the program funds the gap. Some types of income are deducted dollar for dollar from income support benefits while other income is considered as partially or fully exempt. Each program has detailed rules regarding income. AISH has the most generous income exemptions compared to AW-IS; spousal income exemptions are also available in AISH that are not available to AW-IS clients.

Core benefits are meant to cover food, clothing, household needs, personal needs, laundry, telephone, transportation, and shelter. Since welfare reform in 1993, Alberta's social assistance benefits have not kept up with the cost of living and are well below what is considered as adequate to meet basic needs. In 2012, Alberta's annual benefit of $7,649 for single employable adults was the lowest in the country, representing 39 per cent of the low-income cut-off (LICO) and 45.2 per cent of the Market Basket Measure (MBM) in Calgary (Tweddle, Battle, and Torjman 2013). Alberta's ranking was not always so low; in 1986, Alberta's annual benefits for single employables, at $11,246, were 53 per cent higher than those in British Columbia, Ontario, or Québec (Boessenkool 1997). The province that provided the most generous benefits for single employables in 2012 was Newfoundland and Labrador, at 65.2 per cent of the LICO and 64.3 per cent of the MBM.

Table 8.1 Key Features of Alberta's Income Support Programs, 2013

Program	Alberta Works			Assured Income for the Severely Handicapped
Program Feature	AW–Expected to Work	AW–Barriers to Full Employment	AW–Learners	
Cash Asset Exemption	$627	$1,462	$11,694	$100,000
Income Exemptions (single person)	$230 plus 25%	$230 plus 25%	Considers projected income	50% between $800 and $1,500 to a maximum of $1,150
Core Benefits (single person)	$627/month	$731/month	$847/month	$1,588/month
Supplementary Benefits	Core health plus supplementary	Core health plus supplementary	Core health, learning, plus supplementary	Core health plus extensive supplementary
Access	53 Alberta Works centres across province	53 Alberta Works centres; then centralized administration	53 Alberta Works centres; then centralized administration	28 AISH offices across province
Monitoring	Monthly reporting card	Monthly reporting card	Monthly reporting card	Monthly, quarterly, or annually as appropriate
Average Monthly Caseload	16,775	17,459	Not available	45,977
Client Characteristics	64% single; 30% single parents; 6% couples	64% single; 30% single parents; 6% couples	No information	46% physical disability; 32% mental illness disorder; 22% cognitive disorder. 88% of clients have assets less than $3,000 89% single

Source: Alberta Human Services (2013a, 2013b, 2013c, 2013d).

In contrast, AISH benefits have maintained relative parity with the federal and provincial benefits available to Alberta seniors. Total annual AISH benefits in 2012 were calculated at $18,228 (Tweddle, Battle, and Torjman 2013), representing 93 per cent of the low-income cut-off and 107.8 per cent of the MBM. This is the highest benefit level in the country. AISH recipients receive more than twice the level of monthly benefits than those paid to Alberta Works–Barriers to Full Employment recipients ($1,588 vs. $731). The differences in characteristics between the two groups are marginal, as all have chronic mental or physical health problems or multiple barriers to employment.

Supplementary benefits for AW-IS recipients are based on demonstrated need and can include child care, transportation to day programs, children's school expenses, special transportation, and utility deposit. Each program has an extensive list, and most have a defined rate. The cost of tuition, books, and supplies is covered, for example, in the Learners program.

Until 2004, supplementary benefits were not available in AISH. Today, they are available in defined circumstances if clients have non-exempt assets of $3,000 or less. Even employment and training supports can be provided, despite the fact that, to qualify for AISH in the first place, applicants must demonstrate that there is no training, rehabilitation, or medical treatment available that would help them to work enough to earn a livelihood.

Health benefits for all three groups include basic dental care, eye exams, prescriptions, essential diabetic supplies, and emergency ambulance services. Some health supports such as special diet and medical surgical supplies can be added as a supplementary benefit.

Applicants for AW-IS access services through 53 Alberta Works centres managed by Alberta Human Services (AHS). In one location, a broad spectrum of employment, welfare, and workplace services are available. Eligibility is assessed through a personal interview with a government employee, and people are slotted into the defined subprograms. People in the Barriers to Employment and Learners subprograms have their benefits administered through Alberta Supports, a website and large central call centre. All clients must complete and send in a reporting card every month declaring income and changes to their circumstances.

Responsibility for AISH was transferred to Alberta Human Services in 2012; previously, it was managed by the Seniors Ministry through 28 offices across Alberta. AISH administrators—in consultation with the AISH client—decide the most appropriate reporting period (monthly, quarterly, or annually). A combined AISH and AW-IS appeal panel handles reviews for those dissatisfied with program decisions. One informant noted that many AW-IS recipients are high need, and community agencies routinely advocate for them to get into the AISH program. Currently, there is a huge demand on this program, and processing applications is very challenging.

The Alberta Office of Official Statistics provides a monthly release on the caseloads of the Alberta Works Expected to Work and Barriers to Full Employment subprograms, but not on those of the Learners subprogram or AISH. Until 2015, when the Caledon Institute of Social Policy took the initiative to assemble and publish provincial social assistance statistics, the only information publicly available on AISH client characteristics was from a 2008 report compiled by the directors of income assistance in all provinces (Federal-Provincial-Territorial (FTP) Directors of Income Support 2010).

In conclusion, Alberta has continued to operate provincial income support programs in the traditional fashion, which sees reasonable support and assistance provided to the "deserving" poor but not to the "undeserving" poor. Although there is some public reporting available on Alberta Works' clients, very little contemporary information beyond annual reports is available on AISH. Indeed, scant research or analysis is made public on these programs, despite their $1.7 billion-price tag.

The future evolution of social assistance in the province

Until Alison Redford became premier in 2011, the established policy of the governing Progressive Conservatives was that the best social policy for Alberta was for everyone to get a job. Community organizations fundamentally disagreed with this direction, especially because Alberta traditionally has had the lowest minimum-wage rates in the country. Over the years, many had tried unsuccessfully to focus the attention of the Alberta government on the unmet needs of low-income earners and of those who continued to be dependent on AW-IS and AISH benefits.

In 2010–11 community efforts started to take hold politically. The municipal-based Inter-City Forum on Social Policy came together with Public Interest Alberta to create Action to End Poverty in Alberta as a way for municipal leaders to pressure the provincial government for improved social policies. This initiative built on work by the Alberta College of Social Workers, the Parkland Institute of the University of Alberta, the Edmonton Social Planning Council, and Vibrant Communities Calgary. In 2010, these groups began a concerted campaign highlighting problems with inequality and social disparity in Alberta.

This campaign bore fruit when Alison Redford assumed the premier's job in 2011 and directed the development of an Alberta Social Policy Framework and a poverty reduction strategy. With her resignation in 2014, community advocates became pessimistic about whether concrete results would emerge from these initiatives, as the 2015 Alberta government budgets made no financial commitments to support this new era of social policy. In fact, there were cutbacks and increased privatization, affecting seniors and persons with disabilities in particular. The fall of the price of oil in 2014 has constrained public finances even further. However, a change that may develop roots involves partnerships with municipalities and the community, as well as a commitment to increased transparency and accountability. The demonstrated success of the partnership approach to homelessness and the municipal-led action on poverty reduction may result in a new way of doing business in the province.

Certainly, there are challenges ahead, especially financial ones. Over the past 15 years, health care has every time trumped social assistance and other areas of social policy in competition for scarce public resources. Although conversations moderated by government may have started now to mention the kinds of social programs Albertans want, there do not seem to be similar conversations underway on how these can be paid for. Just as the Alberta population crosses the four million mark and other Canadians continue to move to the province, Albertans have not yet had a discussion about how additional resources—including potentially introducing a provincial sales tax and eliminating the flat tax—might be acquired to support citizen demands for adequate social programs. It is evident that there are a variety of conflicting views on this subject (Love 2013; Public Interest Alberta 2013; Simpson 2013).[2]

Budget pressures will escalate as AISH caseloads continue to grow because benefit levels are committed to be adjusted upwards along with inflation. AISH is an expensive program that provides support to those who qualify until they turn 65 or die (the cut-off age will be 67, once federal changes are implemented starting in April 2023). A variety of challenges face AISH. Drawing a line between the "deserving" and "undeserving" poor is very difficult. For people with barriers to full employment on AW-IS, the financial and security reward for qualifying for AISH is substantial. Alberta's program rules, which treat people in relatively similar circumstances so differently, seem unfair. In their 2011 study examining income support benefits for persons with disabilities in Alberta, British Columbia, and Ontario, Kneebone and Grynishak (2011) note the differences in the levels of base support provided by these provinces, with Ontario at $1,053 per month, British Columbia at $906 per month, and Alberta at $1,188 per month. With the dramatic increase in Alberta of

2 The spring 2015 provincial budget signalled a start to this conversation.

$400 more per month in 2012, which took this support from $1,188 to $1,588 per month, the differential is even greater. Whether higher AISH benefits will draw persons with disabilities to Alberta from other provinces is another issue to be faced.

Almost certainly there will be changes to program administration and delivery, with potentially all programs moving toward a single point of entry, and benefit processing and administration done from a centralized call centre as opposed to local offices. Folding the AISH program into the same department as AW-IS and having it be part of a department concerned with disability and children's issues—as opposed to one with an economic development and employment orientation—may assist with overall coordination and help break down the silos that often occur in government administration.

Conclusion

This chapter illustrates that, over the past 40 years, there have been dramatic changes in the support provided to the "undeserving" poor in Alberta. Changes in name—from Social Allowance to Supports for Independence to Alberta Works–Income Support—reflect dramatic changes to the underlying purpose, philosophy, and value base of this program. For a brief period after CAP, income support in Alberta was relatively generous and based on client rights; today, last-resort social assistance as part of Alberta Works seems to have almost disappeared. The financial benefits that are available have declined dramatically. Alberta not only has the lowest level of benefits in the country for single employables but also the lowest proportion of the population dependent upon government income support. Community-run food banks and homelessness appear to be the face of welfare in Alberta today, not any provincial government program.

On the other hand, support for the "deserving" poor through AISH has continued to improve. The purpose of AISH has remained consistent since it was established in 1979 as a program to enhance the living conditions of Albertans with severe disabilities. Certainly, the changes following the AISH review in 2004—adding personal benefits and committing to regular increases in benefit levels—supported this purpose. The importance of AISH as a flagship Alberta government program was further reinforced in 2012 through dramatic benefit increases.

Until 2014 and the resignation of Alison Redford as premier, Alberta appeared to be undergoing a social policy renaissance, with commitments made to eliminate child poverty in 5 years and reduce poverty for everyone within 10 years. Consultations have been done but no results announced. With the election of an NDP government in 2015 and the end of the Progressive Conservative era, improvements to both Alberta Works-Income Support and AISH are much more likely. Certainly, any changes made to either program will make a dramatic difference to the over 115,000 vulnerable Albertans who rely on these programs to provide for their basic needs every month.

References

Alberta Food Bank Network Association. 2012. *HungerCount 2012 Alberta Provincial Report*. Accessed October 2, 2013. http://www.foodbankscanada.ca/getmedia/a608c612-d270-4847-bbab-e9fcb55e96a2/HungerCount-report-2012-AB-final.pdf.aspx?ext=.pdf.

Alberta Human Services. 2013a. *Financial Benefits Summary*. Edmonton: Government of Alberta. Accessed September 23, 2013. http://humanservices.alberta.ca/AWonline/documents/EMP0433.pdf.

Alberta Human Services. 2013b. *Albert Works: Income Support Program for Expected to Work (ETW) and Barriers to Full Employment (BFE)*. Edmonton: Government of Alberta.

Alberta Human Services. 2013c. *Employment Income: AISH*. Edmonton: Government of Alberta. Accessed September 23, 2013. http://humanservices.alberta.ca/documents/aish-tipsheet-employment-income.pdf.

Alberta Human Services. 2013d. *Personal Benefits: AISH*. Edmonton: Government of Alberta. Accessed September 23, 2013. http://humanservices.alberta.ca/documents/aish-tipsheet-personal-benefits.pdf.

Alberta Human Services. 2014. *Summing Up: What Albertans Said about Poverty Reduction*. Edmonton: Government of Alberta. Accessed March 2, 2015. http://povertyreduction.alberta.ca/Document/Poverty_Reduction_Summing_Report.

Boessenkool, Ken. 1997. *Alberta Welfare Reforms a Model for Other Provinces*. Toronto: C.D. Howe Institute. http://www.cdhowe.org/pdf/kbkool.pdf.

Faid, Peter. 2009. *Poverty Reduction Policies and Programs: Extending the Alberta Advantage*. Social Development Report Series. Kanata, ON: Canadian Council on Social Development. http://www.ccsd.ca/images/research/SocialReports/PDF/AB_Report_FINAL.pdf.

Federal-Provincial-Territorial (FTP) Directors of Income Support. 2010. *Social Assistance Statistical Report: 2008*. Ottawa: Human Resources and Skills Development. http://publications.gc.ca/collections/collection_2011/rhdcc-hrsdc/HS25-2-2008-eng.pdf.

Gaetz, Stephen. 2010. "The Struggle to End Homelessness in Canada: How We Created the Crisis and How We Can End It." *Open Health Services and Policy Journal* 3 (1): 21–26. http://www.homelesshub.ca/sites/default/files/rjhmnzr4.pdf.

Goldberg, Michael, and David A. Green. 2009. *Understanding the Link between Welfare Policy and the Use of Food Banks*. Ottawa: Canadian Centre for Policy Alternatives. http://www.policyalternatives.ca/sites/default/files/uploads/publications/National_Office_Pubs/2009/Link_Between_Welfare_Policy_and_Food_Banks.pdf.

Kinjerski, Val, and Margot Hebert. 2000. "Child Welfare Growth in Alberta, Connecting the Dots." Paper prepared for Alberta Ministry of Children's Services and presented at the Alberta College of Social Workers Conference, August 31.

Kleiss, Karen. 2012. "Redford's Vow to End Poverty Portends Major Shift in Social Services." *Edmonton Journal*, April 25. Accessed July 25, 2013. http://pialberta.org/content/redfords-vow-end-poverty-portends-major-shift-social-services.

Kneebone, Ronald D. 2005. *Assured Income for the Severely Handicapped: The Decline in Financial Benefits Since 1993*. Institute for Advanced Research Policy Brief No. 0501. Calgary: IAPR, University of Calgary. http://www.ucalgary.ca/iaprfiles/policybriefs/iapr-pb-0501.pdf.

Kneebone, Ronald, and Oksana Grynishak. 2011. *Income Support for Persons with Disabilities*. SPP Research Paper 4 No. 11. http://policyschool.ucalgary.ca/sites/default/files/research/disabilitiessept_0.pdf.

Kneebone, Ronald, and Katherine White. 2014. *The Rise and Fall of Social Assistance Use in Canada, 1969–2012*. SPP Research Papers 7 No. 5. http://policyschool.ucalgary.ca/?q=content/rise-and-fall-social-assistance-use-canada-1969-2012.

Love, Rod. 2013. "Why Western Canadians Say No to Sales Tax: That Horse Has Died." *Globe and Mail*, September 31. Accessed October 1, 2013. http://www.theglobeandmail.com/globe-debate/why-western-canadians-say-no-to-sales-tax-that-horse-has-died/article14602891/.

Public Interest Alberta. 2013. *Redford Government Targets Seniors*. Edmonton: Public Interest Alberta. Accessed October 1, 2013. http://pialberta.org/sites/default/files/Documents/Redford%20targets%20seniors_June28_2013.pdf.

Reichwein, Baldwin. 2002. *Benchmarks in Alberta's Public Welfare Services: History Rooted in Benevolence, Harshness, Punitiveness and Stinginess*. Edmonton: Alberta College of Social Workers. http://www.canadiansocialresearch.net/Alberta_welfare_history.pdf.

Simpson, Jeffery. 2013. "A Sales Tax Makes Sense—Just Not to Albertans." *Globe and Mail*, September 28. http://www.theglobeandmail.com/globe-debate/a-sales-tax-makes-sense-just-not-to-albertans/article14570850.

Splane, Richard. 1985. "Social Welfare Development in Alberta: The Federal-Provincial Interplay." In *Canadian Social Welfare Policy, Federal and Provincial Dimensions*, ed. Jacqueline S. Ismael, 173–87. Montréal: McGill-Queen's University Press.

Tweddle, Anne, Ken Battle, and Sherri Torjman. 2013. *Welfare in Canada 2012*. Ottawa: Caledon Institute of Social Policy. http://www.caledoninst.org/Publications/PDF/1031ENG.pdf.

Wiseman, Nelson. 2007. *In Search of Canadian Political Culture*. Vancouver: UBC Press.

Wood, Donna E. 1988. "Strategies to Reduce Social Allowance Caseloads in Alberta." Master's thesis, University of Alberta.

nine
Saskatchewan: Development, Reform, and Retrenchment

RICK AUGUST

Introduction

Saskatchewan is a relatively new political jurisdiction, having been created as a province in 1905 from the Northwest Territories. During the twentieth century, it progressed from an agriculturally based economy to a more developed, though still thinly populated, province with an increasingly diversified economy. Over the course of this development, changing economic and social circumstances created pressures for greater income protection for citizens. These were answered in part by the emergence of a social assistance system, created with the intention of preventing destitution and, for some parts of its history, of reducing or eliminating poverty.

From its roots, however, in Depression-era relief, Saskatchewan's social assistance has been sporadically controversial, the debate being marked by differing viewpoints on two competing dynamics in welfare policy—financial security and work incentives. This chapter will briefly outline the current structure and legal basis of Saskatchewan's social assistance programs, review their developmental history, and discuss more recent reform processes aimed at reducing work disincentives and encouraging labour market attachment among low-income citizens.

I will argue that incremental reforms in recent decades have begun to address the shortcomings in Canada's social assistance model and reduce the tensions between income security and work incentives. These measures, in Saskatchewan, have involved the development of strategic alternatives to elements of social assistance policy. It will be argued, however, that this strategic reform process has stalled and, in some respects, been reversed, with the result that Saskatchewan's lowest-income citizens remain deterred by public policy from sharing in the growing economic prosperity of the province.

Historical background

Saskatchewan was one of the last landmasses in North America settled for agriculture and development beginning in the late nineteenth century.

The province was first envisioned as an agriculture-based economy, with a strong emphasis on wheat (Saskatchewan 1937). The province was promoted enthusiastically as such to potential immigrants and settlers by the federal government (see, for example, Kitto 1919). The population would, in fact, increase 10-fold to 921,000 between 1901 and 1931 (Smith 1997).

In part because it was an economic monoculture, however, Saskatchewan was hit particularly hard by the Great Depression that began in 1929, and its effect was exacerbated by severe and prolonged drought (Saskatchewan 1937). At the start of the Depression, social protection still relied mainly on family, church, and the local community, and these local resources were soon overwhelmed (Lawton 1969). A "relief" system emerged in the early 1930s as a temporary structure of public works employment, cash, and in-kind transfers, jointly funded by municipal, provincial, and federal governments—the first involvement of the provincial and federal governments in funding basic income support (Saskatchewan 1937). This relief system would serve a significant portion of the province's population through the Depression years (see Figure 9.1).

Depression relief acted as a prototype for social assistance. After 1934, the temporary relief structure resolved into a more permanent one, with

Figure 9.1 City and Town Relief, 1930–36

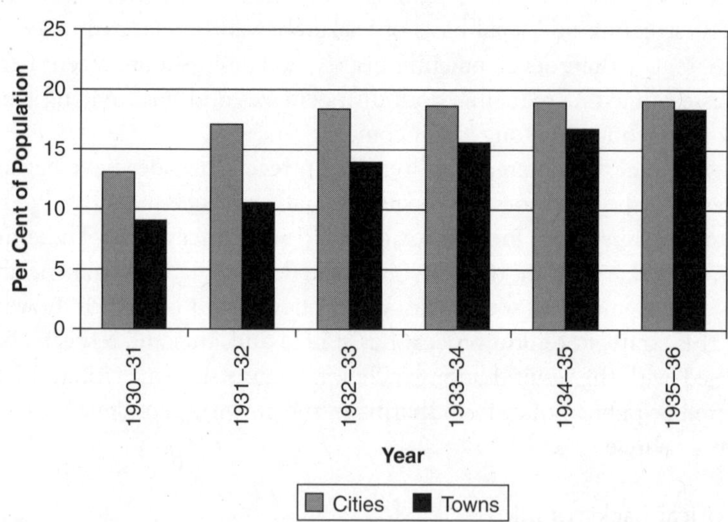

Source: Saskatchewan (1937, 410).

Note: Data are for 8 cities and 15 representative towns; the "representative towns" are not identified in the source.

municipalities assuming responsibility for basic income support under a cost-sharing arrangement with the province (Saskatchewan 1937). The province gradually assumed a larger fiscal role in municipal income assistance and, by virtue of that, also assumed a larger policy-setting role. The Department of Social Welfare was formed in 1944, and more formal guidelines were laid out for the municipal administration of a program then referred to as "Social Aid." By 1959, local residency requirements had effectively been eliminated (Lawton 1969). Rate guidelines served to further unify local social aid into a quasi-provincial program, while parallel provincial structures were developed to serve those groups, such as off-reserve Indians, that municipalities viewed as outside their jurisdiction (Saskatchewan Legislative Assembly 1973).

This was effectively the basic income support structure Saskatchewan carried into the era of national social policy reform that spanned the mid-1960s to the early 1970s. Some of the national programs developed in that period—e.g., public pensions, unemployment insurance—were the product of structural thinking about social security. Others, such as health care and social assistance, were arguably more ideologically driven. Most relevant to social assistance was the establishment of the Canada Assistance Plan (CAP) in 1966 (see Boychuk, in this volume). At the same time as social security reforms such as the Canada Pension Plan were intended to reduce specific social risks, social assistance was seen as the residual, last-resort income source that would, it was hoped, effectively eliminate poverty.

While these national developments occurred, Saskatchewan launched a Social Aid Review in 1965, in part in expectation of the Canada Assistance Plan. The review resulted in new provincial legislation and the implementation of the Saskatchewan Assistance Plan (SAP) in 1966, designed for consistency with CAP. It centralized administrative authority with the province and relieved municipalities of almost all financial responsibility for social assistance (Saskatchewan Legislative Assembly 1973).

The reform that created the Saskatchewan Assistance Plan was strongly oriented toward entitlement, as a 1966 government pamphlet illustrates:

> The Saskatchewan Assistance Plan is founded on a belief in the worth and dignity of the individual and the recognition that:
>
> - Members of society are dependent upon one another, and
> - The welfare of each individual is essential to the total welfare of the community.
>
> Inherent in this belief is the right of every individual, regardless of race, creed, residence or citizenship, to financial assistance when his need can be demonstrated and the conviction that no

individual should have to meet a test of moral worthiness in order to receive assistance.

> Every individual receiving assistance should have the right to plan his own life as he chooses even though he has lost his financial independence. This means he should have the right to decide such things as:
>
> - How he shall spend his financial assistance (except if he fails to use it to provide the necessities of life for himself and his dependents),
> - Where he shall live,
> - What services he shall accept.
>
> Also inherent in the belief are:
>
> - A respect for the privateness of the circumstances of every individual applying for or receiving assistance,
> - His right to appeal any decisions concerning his application for assistance which he thinks are unjust,
> - His right and obligation to take as much responsibility as he can in seeking a solution to his financial problems,
> - Recognition that counseling and other services should be offered to help the recipient toward greater self-dependence and to prevent his situation becoming worse. (Quoted in Zarski 1979, Appendix A1)

There are several apparent contradictions in this statement of principles; chief among them is the right to assistance without moral justification set against an obligation to pursue all alternatives to social assistance. This author's direct observation of the operation of the program in following decades suggests that its balance, in practice, was strongly toward entitlement rather than obligation.[1]

Social assistance caseload trends

There are data limitations in examining dependency levels before and after the implementation of SAP. In addition to Social Aid, the new program absorbed some small categorical schemes such as mothers' allowance, but discrete beneficiary counts for the various programs are unavailable from

1 This entitlement focus was probably intentional, given statements of the time. In retrospect, however, it may have been inevitable because entitlements are notably easier to codify and operationalize than behavioural expectations. Similar principles to those used in SAP are set forth in the framework of the *de facto* parent program, the Canada Assistance Plan, suggesting that, to a greater or lesser extent, all provincial, territorial, and on-reserve social assistance programs began their new post-CAP lives as entitlement-leaning programs.

Figure 9.2 Saskatchewan Basic Assistance Cases, 1964–74

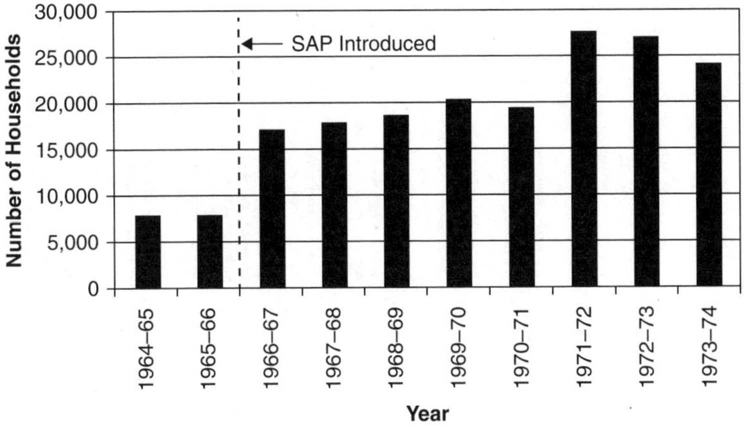

Source: Data are taken from the annual reports of the Saskatchewan Ministry of Social Services (and of the earlier departments charged with responsibility for social assistance).

published sources. The time series represented in Figure 9.2 is a best-effort reconstruction from ministry annual reports.

Dependency rates appear to have increased substantially in the years immediately following implementation of SAP. Raw caseloads increased rather sharply at a time when Saskatchewan's population was actually declining (Statistics Canada 2011). Externalities such as rising divorce rates, increasing single parenthood, international oil crises, and the labour market impacts of nascent globalization were still largely in the future.

Social assistance caseloads can be strongly influenced by several intrinsic or contextual factors, including the demographic effect of rate changes (as rate changes move entry points up or, less often, down the income distribution), administrative culture, and political and cultural messaging (August 2012). As we have seen, SAP was presented to the public as an answer to poverty and a right of citizenship to be exercised on perceived need. Inflation-adjusted assistance rates were rising rapidly year over year.[2] A strong argument can be made that rising dependency in SAP's early years was a result of policy choice more than of any objective change in the circumstances of low-income citizens.

2 Based on 1966 and 1979 SAP rate cards for a two-parent, two-child family (from Zarski 1979) supplemented by a scan of available rental rates for two-bedroom apartments in *The Leader-Post* (Regina) on July 16, 1979, rates for this family type appear to have risen an average of 18 per cent per year between 1966 and 1979, compared to an average CPI increase (for Canada—provincial CPI is not available for this period) of 4.6 per cent.

Figure 9.3 Saskatchewan Social Assistance Cases, 1974–2012

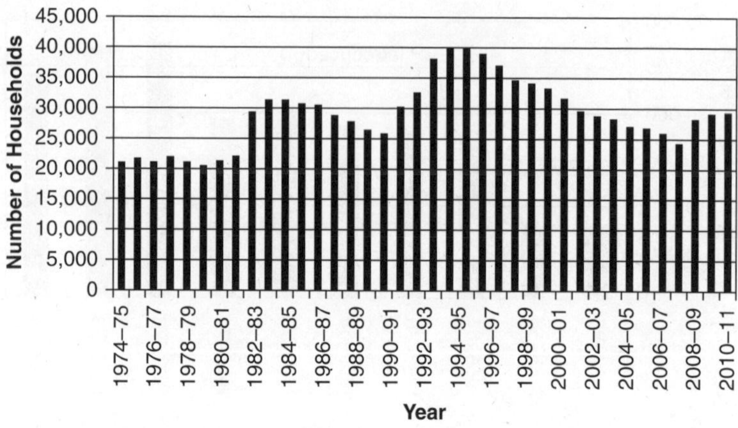

Source: Data are taken from the annual reports of the Saskatchewan Ministry of Social Services (and of the earlier departments charged with responsibility for social assistance).
Note: Includes the Saskatchewan Assistance Program (SAP), Transitional Employment Allowance (TEA), and Saskatchewan Assured Income for Disability (SAID).

External factors are less easy to discount when rising social assistance case numbers are considered in the 1980s and early 1990s (see Figure 9.3). According to Statistics Canada, national CPI inflation averaged 11.1 per cent per year between 1979 and 1982, before levelling off at a still-painful 4.6 per cent for the rest of the decade (Statistics Canada CANSIM database, Table 326–0021). The proportion of single-parent families in the province increased by about 40 per cent between 1976 and 1991 (Statistics Canada 2011). Saskatchewan unemployment, which had averaged 4.1 per cent between 1976 and 1981, averaged 7.1 per cent between 1982 and 1993 (Statistics Canada CANSIM database, Table 282–0086). Within Saskatchewan's lowest-income quintile of families with children and employment income, real market income had declined by 46 per cent over the decade ending in 1994 (August 2003). It should hardly be surprising, then, that, although provincial welfare policy varied quite widely over this period, case numbers continued to trend up toward peak levels of about 40,000 households in the mid-1990s.[3]

---

3 According to a report by the Federal-Provincial-Territorial (FPT) Directors of Income Support (2010) Saskatchewan's peak modern-era dependency appears to be 40,400 cases representing 82,100 persons in March 1996, while the lowest number since that time was about 27,500 cases (47,100 persons) in March 2006.

Child and family poverty rates were much in the news in the mid-1990s, as dependency costs put increased pressure on government finances. Governments were becoming more sensitized to arguments that the disincentives of social assistance meant that such benefit programs, once entered into, were often very difficult to leave for employment, particularly for parents (see, for example, Torjman and Battle 1993). These circumstances helped set the stage for a process of national and provincial structural reforms that would significantly affect social assistance.

Structure and benefits

The core social assistance program is called the Saskatchewan Assistance Plan or SAP. This program is enabled by the Saskatchewan Assistance Act of 1966 and governed by the Saskatchewan Assistance Regulations. SAP is a needs-tested program, with benefits determined by a budget-deficit system. Deemed available resources are compared to rate standards for given household structures, and the difference paid as a benefit.[4]

The basic benefit structure is relatively simple by the standards of such programs. Benefits are aimed at adult needs and overall household needs, such as shelter. A flat-rate amount is payable to cover food, clothing, travel, and personal and household items. Beyond single-parent supplements, no child benefits are paid, as this element of the rate structure was replaced by the National Child Benefit Supplement. Shelter benefit rates vary by family size and location. Basic utilities—electricity, natural gas, telephone—are usually paid at actual cost. There are some limited variations in rates based on assessed employability and disability. Regulations provide for several exemptions for earned income and other resources and for special-need benefits in certain circumstances defined in the regulations. The Saskatchewan Assistance Plan is administered by the provincial Ministry of Social Services.

The ministry also administers two parallel categorical social assistance programs, the Transitional Employment Allowance program (TEA), for short-term assistance to employable adults, and the Saskatchewan Assured Income for Disability Program (SAID), aimed at individuals with significant and long-term disabilities. Both of these programs are also enabled by the Saskatchewan Assistance Act and governed by separate regulations under that act.

4 Rates for various social services income support programs are available from the ministry website at www.socialservices.gov.sk.ca/.

The same ministry also offers two income transfer programs that are independent of social assistance but strategically linked to it. One is the Saskatchewan Employment Supplement, an income-tested earnings supplement aimed at low-income parents. The other is the Saskatchewan Rental Housing Supplement, which offers subsidy to low-income renters whose accommodations meet basic-quality standards. These programs, too, are fiscally enabled by the Saskatchewan Assistance Act and governed by separate regulations under that act.

The three social assistance programs (SAP, TEA, and SAID) are considered last-resort programs, with benefits intended to provide minimal adequacy for basic needs. However, disposable incomes of social assistance beneficiaries cannot be accurately understood without considering concurrent eligibility for other programs, federal or provincial. Adult recipients without children, for example, may also qualify for the federal Goods and Services Rebate, the Working Income Tax Benefit, and Saskatchewan's Low-Income Tax Credit. In addition to these adult-oriented benefits, social assistance recipients with children are also eligible for significant monthly benefits from the Canada Child Tax Benefit and may qualify for the Saskatchewan Employment Supplement and the Saskatchewan Rental Housing Supplement.[5]

Income-tested transfer programs to lower-income citizens have expanded considerably in Canada and Saskatchewan in recent decades. One reason for this development is that income-tested benefits have a less negative effect on work incentives than does needs-tested social assistance (August 2005). Figures 9.4 and 9.5 illustrate the relative balance of needs and income-tested benefits for two household types. Figure 9.4 shows the aggregated needs-tested and income-tested benefits available to a typical single individual in Saskatchewan.

As this figure shows, a single individual (assumed here to be non-disabled and employable) is eligible for just under $9,000 per year in total government support for basic personal needs. This compares to an after-tax income from full-time, minimum-wage employment of approximately $16,500. Social assistance support ends at about $12,000 of annual gross earnings, while support from income-tested programs extends to about $42,000.

5 The programs noted here are major, broad-based programs available based on need or income. There are numerous other potential benefits available depending on an applicant's circumstances: for example, special needs social assistance, disability benefits, social housing and childcare subsidies. Low-income children may also be eligible for Family Health Benefits, which is a cost-avoidance program rather than a cash benefit.

Figure 9.4 Benefits for a Single Person, July 2012

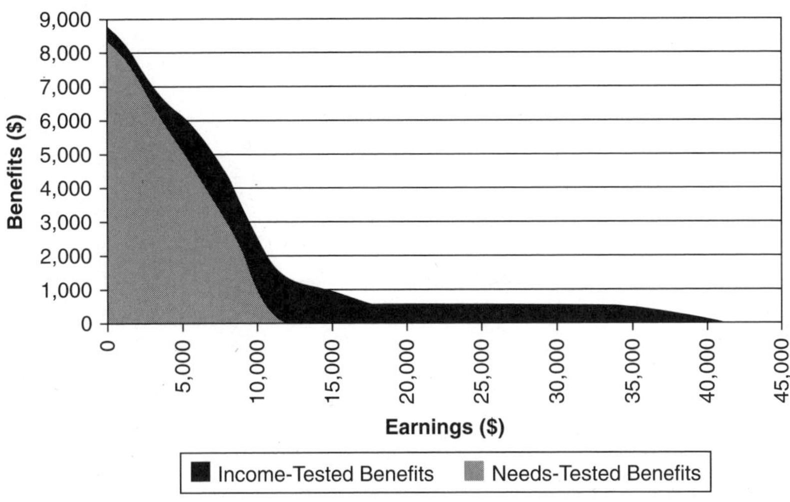

Source: Data from the author's tax-benefit model.

Figure 9.5 Benefits for a Single Parent, Two Children, July 2012

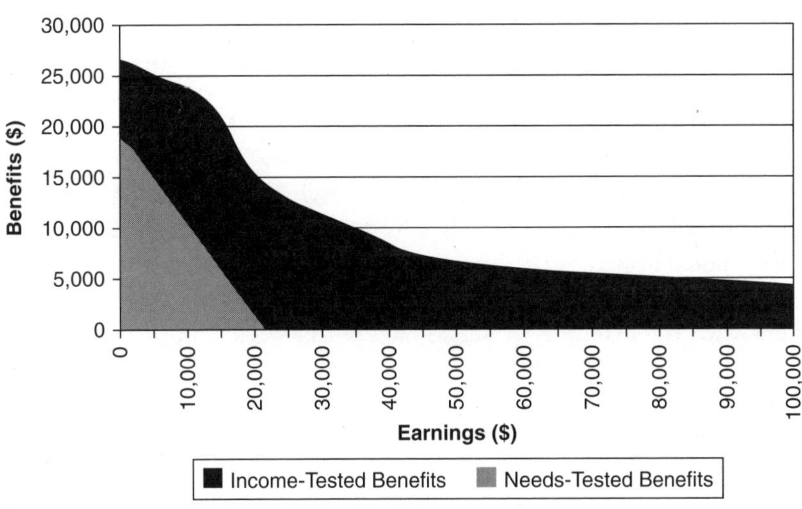

Source: Data from the author's tax-benefit model.

The situation for low-income parents is different because this group is eligible for more income-tested benefits than are singles. Figure 9.5 shows aggregate needs- and income-tested benefits for a typical single parent with two young children.

As can be seen, the impact of non-welfare benefit programs on families with children is very substantial, with social assistance taking, in the overall scheme of benefits, a relatively minor role.

Strategic reform

The caseload and cost pressures of the mid-1990s, present to various degrees across the country, led to the National Child Benefit initiative, a cooperative (at least in its early stages) exercise of the federal government, provinces, and territories.[6] Saskatchewan was an active proponent of the National Child Benefit and related reforms, in part because of its own developing strategic social policy agenda and its history of past reform attempts. In 1974, in anticipation of a federal cost-sharing agreement (which did not in fact come to be), Saskatchewan launched the Family Income Plan (FIP). This was an income-tested child benefit program, with benefits originally equivalent to social assistance child benefits. Its intent was to support low-income working parents with labour market attachment outside the welfare system.[7]

The program was initially popular, with family enrollment at one point exceeding social assistance. However, because it was less fully cost shared than SAP, and thus more expensive to the province, Saskatchewan's focus gradually shifted over time back to social assistance. FIP, which had a peak enrolment of 23,000 families in March 1976, had fewer than 1,500 in March 1996, according to ministry annual reports. The program naturally was challenged on a regular basis in budget reviews, but it was successfully defended over the years as a kernel of the "right thing to do."

The Saskatchewan government was faced with crushing debt in the early 1990s. In part pushed by fiscal imperative, Saskatchewan began to revisit active social programming strategies.[8] Bilateral cost-sharing discussions with the federal government were unsuccessful, but the province's internal analysis gave Saskatchewan an agenda to carry forward, when opportunity allowed, through the National Child Benefit initiative. The National Child Benefit Supplement (NCBS) became, in effect, the "new FIP," a substitute for social assistance benefits for children. Lower welfare

6 For a detailed study of the National Child Benefit process, see Warriner 2005.

7 This was an early Canadian example of using child benefits as a labour market attachment device, but the idea was an old one. The Research Committee of the League for Social Reconstruction, for example, proposed a similar approach in 1935 and noted several international precedents, some of which well predated World War I.

8 Active versus passive social program models are discussed and contrasted in OECD (1988), August (2003), and more recently in Daigneault (2015).

benefits that resulted from the transfer of basic child benefits to the federal government meant significantly lower earnings levels needed for parents to leave welfare through work, and greater competitive equity between parents and non-parents in the labour market.[9]

Because the federal government was assuming the full cost of children's basic social assistance, Saskatchewan had a resource pool available for further employment support programs for low-income parents. Initially, this support included a transitional Saskatchewan Child Benefit that was phased out with the maturation of the NCBS. A permanent Saskatchewan Employment Supplement (SES) program and an income-tested Family Health Benefit for children were created, and FIP "retired with honour." The policy transition in family benefits was branded as "Building Independence" (BI). BI was later expanded to include the Transitional Employment Allowance and other programs, and the Saskatchewan Rental Housing Supplement (SRHS) was added to the program suite in 2005.

This last program merits some note in that it provides portable subsidies (i.e., directed to renters, not landlords), it subsidizes market rents, and it has a quality component. Housing support is problematic for social assistance because it subsidizes both adequate and poor housing alike. In Saskatchewan, the migration of deeply marginalized households from reserves to urban areas has resulted in inner-city slums (and slumlords) largely sustained by the welfare system. The SRHS link between subsidy and quality was designed to break this pattern and empower low-income renters in the private rental market.

Strategic reform stalls

By the time the SRHS was launched, however, momentum had already turned against the province's employment-based anti-poverty strategy. In the early years of the National Child Benefit and Building Independence, social policy reform appeared to produce political capital for the government, which invited its administration to propose further reforms. A change in leadership in the ruling New Democratic Party in 2001, however, increased the influence of the province's welfare lobby. The Ministry

9 Although Saskatchewan held to the original NCB plan in this regard, several provinces succumbed to lobbying efforts to retain or restore provincial child benefits that should have been displaced by the NCBS. This move, in effect, restored the welfare wall the NCB initiative was intended to combat, particularly for single parents. For a discussion of the welfare wall concept, see Torjman and Battle (1993). For a discussion of welfare escape thresholds and employment potential, see August (2012).

of Social Services had made plans to extend the employment benefits of Building Independence to singles by imposing real work testing and deploying an effective employment transitions service, but it was unable to gain political support. Plans to reform the welfare service culture and streamline benefit delivery systems were similarly stopped in their tracks when, after a change of government in 2007, strategic policy was replaced by an interest group–based populist philosophy. Since that time, the social assistance system has been built up once again through a series of rate increases, and a passive welfare-based disability policy adopted with the creation of the SAID program in 2009.[10]

The Saskatchewan structural reforms from 1998 to 2005 were aimed at reducing social assistance utilization and poverty by encouraging work among low-income citizens. On the face of it, assistance caseloads did, in fact, decline by some 20 per cent between 1998 and 2004, and the Saskatchewan government, not surprisingly, claimed strategic effect (Saskatchewan Community Resources 2007). Attributing causality is challenging, however, given changing economic circumstances and concurrent National Child Benefit reform, which itself, according to subsequent evaluation, had a net positive impact on labour force participation (Federal-Provincial-Territorial (FPT) Ministers Responsible for Social Services 2005). In fact, social assistance dependency declined in the same period in provinces with less aggressive strategic programs. However, an empirical study for the United States National Bureau of Economic Research (Milligan and Stabile 2004) did conclude that the NCB had a greater labour market effect in provinces such as Saskatchewan, which consciously acted to improve work incentives.

On-reserve social assistance

It merits note that the province's strategic reforms did not reach the approximately 75,000 reserve residents under the jurisdiction of federally funded Aboriginal Affairs and Northern Development Canada programs. This system is an often-overlooked part of Saskatchewan's income security landscape, through which band-administered social assistance is provided to residents on the province's Indian reserves (see Papillon, in this volume). Though on-reserve assistance generally follows provincial rates and operational policies, there has been little attempt, until recently, to

10 For a discussion of passive disability policy in Canada and its consequences, see August (2009). For an overview of an international perspective, see OECD (2003).

match provincial strategic changes (see Aboriginal Affairs and Northern Development Canada 2012, 2013).

Although reserve households on social assistance do benefit from programs such as the National Child Benefit Supplement (and, to a lesser degree, NCB reinvestments), traditional welfare on reserves remains unchanged and strategically unchallenged. On-reserve dependency is currently over 47 per cent, more than six times overall provincial levels.[11]

Although many Saskatchewan reserves have no real economies other than federal subsidy, there are notable exceptions, and, one hopes, there will be more economic opportunity in future for this segment of the Saskatchewan population. An unreformed social assistance system will deter reserve residents from accessing economic opportunity, if and when present.[12] The federal government has recently embraced a more active social policy and the reduction of on-reserve poverty through employment (Aboriginal Affairs and Northern Development Canada 2013). However, it chooses to influence rather than direct band social policy. As a result, a strategic gap has opened between income support programs under band administration and provincial programs and policies.

Conclusion

Saskatchewan, like the rest of Canada's provinces and territories, entered the mid-1990s with a distinctly passive income security system, dominated at the provincial level by a traditional, needs-tested social assistance program. For Saskatchewan, the National Child Benefit initiative provided the fiscal and policy leverage that enabled the province to begin to move toward a more active social policy based on a partnership approach between citizen and state.

Some progress was made toward this goal. Signature programs such as the Saskatchewan Employment Supplement and the Saskatchewan Rental Housing Supplement remain, although these employment support programs are unpromoted and underused.[13] On the other hand, social assistance rates

11 Based on preliminary caseload and dependency statistics for March 31, 2012, obtained in private correspondence with Saskatchewan Region staff of Aboriginal Affairs Canada.

12 For a description of an anti-poverty strategy for Saskatchewan based on employment and human resource development, see August (2006).

13 The employment supplement had a case count of 5,985 at the end of 2011–12, on a declining trend. The rental supplement's case count was 8,868. The latter count, while small, is up at least 16 per cent from the previous year. These counts represent 20 per cent and 30 per cent, respectively, of the social assistance case total.

have been increased significantly in recent years, and some have even been indexed. The relatively new disability income program, modelled as it is on Alberta's, can expect, by virtue of its design and philosophy, to see a steady caseload increase, one not necessarily related to the actual incidence of severe disability or to better economic outcomes for people with disabilities.[14] The evidence points to a government that has, consciously or not, decided to rebuild a passive income support system in Saskatchewan.

At the time of writing, about 9 per cent of the province's population is economically dependent on one form or another of social assistance.[15] Compared to the recipients of the 1990s, today's include fewer single parents, more single males, more people assessed as having disabilities (though often by questionable criteria), and more Aboriginal people. Although numbers in the provincial system declined for 20 years, they have been trending upward since 2009, while dependency rates on reserves remain, by any reasonable measure, unacceptably high. The reader is encouraged to consider the human cost and the cost to the provincial economy and to communities that these figures represent. No one knows for sure what proportion of dependent households could potentially become part of the economic mainstream under the right policy and program conditions and in the presence of economic opportunity. Previous reforms can be thought of as having released the self-motivated poor—particularly single parents—from welfare dependency by lowering barriers and increasing in-work supports. The remaining dependent population has, in general, more significant barriers to overcome—attitudinal, emotional, and motivational issues; disability impacts; literacy and numeracy deficiencies; and a lack of job skills and workforce experience.

Saskatchewan's economy has high demand for skilled workers but also significant entry-level labour demand. The latter is the kind of labour demand now met by teenagers and new immigrants seeking "starter jobs" in the Canadian market, and also the most likely path for social assistance recipients into the workforce. I would argue that it is the responsibility of governments to help economically marginalized citizens compete for starter places in the labour force, from which they can build more prosperous and

---

14 For a critique of Alberta's Assured Income for the Severely Handicapped (AISH) program, see August (2009). For AISH caseload trends, see Wood, in this volume.

15 This is an estimate based on total persons covered by the Saskatchewan Assistance Plan, the Transitional Employment Allowance, the Saskatchewan Assured Income for Disability Program, and federally funded band-delivered welfare on reserves. Statistics sufficient for a more precise analysis are not currently published.

fulfilling lives. To fail to do so is to waste the social and economic potential of a significant proportion of Saskatchewan's population, and to consign those people to continued poverty.

Canadian lawmakers have been slow to learn from international experience, particularly in social policy. European countries, especially, went farther and faster with passive postwar entitlement programming. As the OECD has observed, in several contexts, these policies have largely failed both national economies and low-income citizens. This author would argue that, in Canada in general and in Saskatchewan in particular, deficient or misguided policy helps sustain a disadvantaged and economically unproductive underclass of citizens. The cost to the economy and to public finances and the concurrent waste of human potential are difficult to quantify, but the economic exclusion of nearly 1 in 10 citizens cannot and should not be ignored.

Author Richard Gwyn has referred perceptively to welfare dependency as "state-induced, and subsidized poverty" (1996, 153). Social assistance was created in an attempt to manage certain social risks in a market economy. As I have argued elsewhere (August 2012), Canadian and international experience demonstrate that welfare is a policy tool that has failed both low-income citizens and the societies they live in. Small steps have been taken, in Saskatchewan and in other Canadian jurisdictions, to move forward from social assistance to a better social policy model. A great deal more needs to be done to create the policy and program structure that will open up the opportunities of a buoyant Saskatchewan economy to its least advantaged citizens.

References

Aboriginal Affairs and Northern Development Canada. 2012. *National Social Programs Manual*. Ottawa: Government of Canada.

Aboriginal Affairs and Northern Development Canada. 2013. *Improving Income Assistance*. Ottawa: Government of Canada. http://www.aadnc-aandc.gc.ca/eng/1369768013912/1369768043942.

August, Rick. 2003. *The Development of Active Social Policy in Saskatchewan* (unpublished draft).

August, Rick. 2005. "Income Security." In *Encyclopedia of Saskatchewan*, 478–79. Regina: Canadian Plains Research Centre. http://esask.uregina.ca/entry/income_security.html.

August, Rick. 2006. *Strategies for Achieving Equity and Prosperity in Saskatchewan*. Ottawa: Caledon Institute of Social Policy.

August, Rick. 2009. *Paved with Good Intentions: The Failure of Passive Disability Policy in Canada*. Ottawa: Caledon Institute of Social Policy.

August, Rick. 2012. *Taming Two Dragons: Poverty, Welfare, and the Future of Income Support*. Winnipeg: Frontier Centre for Public Policy.

Daigneault, Pierre-Marc. 2015. "Ideas and Welfare Reform in Saskatchewan: Entitlement, Workfare or Activation?" *Canadian Journal of Political Science / Revue canadienne de science politique*. (Published online, ahead of print, April.) http://dx.doi.org/10.1017/s0008423915000098.

Federal-Provincial-Territorial (FPT) Directors of Income Support. 2010. *Social Assistance Statistical Report: 2007*. Ottawa: Human Resources and Skills Development Canada. http://publications.gc.ca/collections/collection_2010/rhdcc-hrsdc/HS25-2-2007-eng.pdf.

Federal-Provincial-Territorial (FPT) Ministers Responsible for Social Services. 2005. *Evaluation of the National Child Benefit Initiative: Synthesis Report*. Ottawa: National Child Benefit. http://www.nationalchildbenefit.ca/eng/pdf/eval_ncb.pdf.

Gwyn, Richard. 1996. *Nationalism without Walls: The Unbearable Lightness of Being Canadian*. Toronto: McClelland and Stewart.

Kitto, F.H. 1919. *The Province of Saskatchewan, Canada: Its Development and Opportunities*. Ottawa: Department of the Interior.

Lawton, Alma. 1969. "Urban Relief in Saskatchewan During the Years of the Depression, 1930–1939." MA thesis, University of Saskatchewan.

League for Social Reconstruction. Research Committee. 1935. *Social Planning for Canada*. Toronto: Thomas Nelson and Sons.

Milligan, Keith, and Mark Stabile. 2004. *The Integration of Child Tax Credits and Welfare: Evidence from the National Child Benefit Program*. National Bureau of Economic Research Working Paper No. 10968. Cambridge, MA: NBER.

OECD (Organisation for Economic Cooperation and Development). 1988. *The Future of Social Protection*. OECD Social Policy Studies No. 6. Paris: OECD.

OECD (Organisation for Economic Cooperation and Development). 2003. *Disability Programmes in Need of Reform*. OECD Policy Brief. Paris: OECD.

Saskatchewan. 1937. *A Submission by the Government of Saskatchewan to the Royal Commission on Dominion-Provincial Relations*. Regina: T.H. McConica, King's Printer.

Saskatchewan Community Resources. 2007. *Saskatchewan's Long-Term Social Assistance Caseload*. Regina: Government of Saskatchewan.

Saskatchewan Legislative Assembly. 1973. *Final Report of the Special Committee on Welfare*. Regina: Government of Saskatchewan.

Smith, David. 1997. "Saskatchewan Perspectives." In *Saskatchewan and Aboriginal Peoples in the 21st Century: Social, Economic and Political Changes and Challenges*, 4–36. Regina: Federation of Saskatchewan Indian Nations.

Statistics Canada. 2011. *Visual Census*. Ottawa: Statistics Canada. http://www12.statcan.gc.ca/census-recensement/2011/dp-pd/vc-rv/index.cfm?Lang=eng.

Torjman, Sherri, and Ken Battle. 1993. *Breaking Down the Welfare Wall*. Ottawa: Caledon Institute of Social Policy.

Warriner, Bill. 2005. *Canadian Social Policy Renewal and the National Child Benefit*. Regina: Saskatchewan Institute of Public Policy.

Zarski, Dorothy. 1979. *An Evaluation of the Saskatchewan Assistance Plan*. Regina: Saskatchewan Department of Social Services.

ten
Social Assistance in Manitoba

WAYNE SIMPSON

Introduction

Manitoba's location in the middle of the Canadian federation is often viewed as indicative of its position on the economic and political spectrum: a province firmly rooted in the middle in terms of its economic performance and public policy development that has withstood financial turbulence and partisan strife (Thomas and Brown 2010). The province endured the recent recession well and returned to a growth path that tracks the Canadian average while the four-term NDP government has offered a cautious, centrist approach that, until recently, has produced little controversy and steady support. This rather bland image belies Manitoba's central historical role in Canada's economic and social development as a cornerstone of the grain trade and in the development of the West.

This contrast between Manitoba's past and present is also a feature of its social assistance (SA) programs. Though Manitoba's recent SA programming has evolved in a fashion typical of other Canadian jurisdictions, the province has a rich tradition in the development of Canada's income support network. In this chapter, we look at the development of SA programming in Manitoba, including its foray into the social experimentation of offering a guaranteed annual income. We then assess current features of the SA program and the evolution of its caseload. We conclude with some thoughts on the future of SA in the province.

Manitoba's experience: From social allowance to income assistance

The BNA Act delegated poor relief to the provinces and left public assistance, initially, to municipalities. The City of Winnipeg passed its first relief appropriation in 1874, while other Manitoba municipalities provided discretionary support. As the relief burden grew, however, provincial support and direction were required to sustain assistance levels. Indeed, Manitoba took the lead in providing mothers' allowances in 1916 and adopting a budget assessment system (Manitoba Task Force on Social Assistance 1983, 4–6). The province also established the Manitoba

Public Welfare Commission in 1917 and its Department of Public Welfare in 1927, although most recipients other than mothers remained under municipal discretion.

The Great Depression, which bankrupted many municipalities providing relief, led to the Manitoba Social Assistance Act of 1949. A precursor of future interjurisdictional funding arrangements, the act allowed municipalities to apply to the province to share relief costs. In 1956, the act was amended to allow for federal reimbursement of relief costs for unemployed employables as provided in the new Canada Unemployment Assistance Act. The Social Allowance Act of 1959 repealed the SA Act and clarified eligibility criteria for all provincial assistance. This act remained in force until 1996, when it was replaced by the Employment and Income Assistance Act that, among other features, substituted the term "income assistance" for "social allowance."[1]

The Canada Assistance Plan (CAP) imposed considerable uniformity and minimum standards across provinces but respected provincial authority for programming and administration. Unlike most provinces, Manitoba continued its practice of sharing responsibility for SA with the municipalities. Municipalities would provide short-term and emergency assistance at locally determined rates, typically relatively modest benefits to recipients deemed employable, while the province would support long-term and unemployable recipients, including mothers (Manitoba Task Force on Social Assistance 1983, 7–9). This strong categorization of recipients as eligible for municipal or provincial assistance on the basis of employability led Boychuk (1998, 59–60) to characterize Manitoba's regime as "conservative." It was not until 1972 that Manitoba required municipalities to institute by-laws regulating SA, but program design and delivery remained firmly in municipal hands such that benefits, eligibility, and administrative practices varied widely. Some municipalities denied assistance on the basis of past employment, imposed job search and work requirements or strict asset exemptions, treated assistance as a repayable debt, or provided benefits in the stigmatizing form of vouchers (Boychuk 1998, 65–67). Brandon, for example, exempted only 50 per cent of the federal Child Tax Credit in determining social allowance eligibility (National Council of Welfare 1987, 35).

After many calls for a unified welfare system, the government moved toward province-wide standards with the passage of the Municipal Assistance Regulation in 1992. The regulation retained municipal responsibility for households headed by an employable person but established

1 See Manitoba Laws, The Social Allowances Amendment and Consequential Amendments Act, http://web2.gov.mb.ca/laws/statutes/1996/c04196e.php.

minimum rates and a standard definition of income for needs testing (National Council of Welfare 1997, 70–71). Thus, Winnipeg used federal cost sharing under CAP to sustain more generous food supplements for children. Concomitantly, however, the federal government terminated welfare payments to treaty Indians leaving their reserve, which imposed considerable hardship on Winnipeg and compelled a sharp drop in benefits for single employables and families with children.

The replacement of cost sharing under CAP with block funding for health, postsecondary education, and social services under the Canada Health and Social Transfer (CHST) in the federal austerity budget of 1995 may have been directed at spending patterns in Ontario and other "have" provinces, but its impact was no less serious for less prosperous provinces such as Manitoba. Indeed, the introduction of the CHST coincided with welfare reform in Manitoba designed to cut welfare costs. Between 1994 and 1996, the Manitoba government cut supplemental health benefits, shelter allowances, special needs allocations, and special benefits to students while opening a welfare "snitch line" (National Council of Welfare 1997, 74). The focus of assistance would now be to help Manitobans achieve independence from welfare through employment whenever possible; initiatives included mandatory personalized training and employability plans for new welfare applicants.

Subsequent budgeting for welfare spending has been less controversial, although separation of block funding for health with the creation of the Canada Social Transfer for education and social services and assistance in 2004 left the provincial government in a similarly difficult financial quandary. The province finally assumed responsibility for the administration of income assistance in the City of Winnipeg in 1998, but it was not until 2004—with the passing of the Employment and Income Assistance Amendment Act (One-Tier Assistance for Rural and Northern Manitoba)—that the two-tier system of SA administration was finally eliminated entirely.[2]

The Manitoba SA experiment

A discussion of Manitoba's experience with SA would be incomplete without reference to the grand social experiment on a negative income tax,

2 See Manitoba Laws, The Employment and Income Assistance Amendment Act (One-Tier Assistance for Rural and Northern Manitoba), http://web2.gov.mb.ca/laws/statutes/2004/c00204e.php. The Association of Manitoba Municipalities requested provincial administration of all income assistance in 1999 because many municipalities were poorly trained to administer the program and had experienced difficulties with clients (Association of Manitoba Municipalities 2004).

or guaranteed annual income, conducted during the 1970s. The negative income tax concept was remarkable in its simplicity: assign all households an income support level, or income guarantee, based on family composition, pay up to that level when no income was earned, and establish a rate at which the income support would decline, or a "negative" income tax rate, that would apply to earnings. Income support at the poverty level would eradicate poverty, while a suitable tax rate would provide some work incentive. Although appealing and garnering support across the political spectrum, the idea raised concerns about administrative issues, such as whether the tax system could deliver income support efficiently, and economic questions, particularly about the work disincentives associated with this type of plan.

The 1968 review from the Economic Council of Canada identified widespread poverty among Canadians, prompting several government reports recommending some form of universal, needs-tested income support program. In particular, the Special Senate Committee on Poverty (1971) proposal for a national guaranteed annual income based on the principles of a negative income tax received Canada-wide attention and support. At this point, Premier Schreyer committed his administration to the idea of a demonstration project for a guaranteed annual income and submitted a successful proposal for funding to the Department of National Health and Welfare in 1973 (Hum and Simpson 1991). Of note is that Premier Schreyer went on record as viewing the guaranteed annual income as a replacement for provincially designed SA programs.

What emerged from the negotiations was not a modest demonstration project, however, but a more ambitious and rigorous social experiment along the lines of the US trials already in progress (Hum and Simpson 1993). Low-income families were randomly selected and assigned to a guaranteed annual income plan or a control group (no plan) in Winnipeg, Dauphin, and several small rural communities. The Winnipeg site involved a "dispersed" or limited sample of families enrolled in one of seven plans (combinations of income guarantees and tax rates) and a control group, while the Dauphin "saturation" site provided a single plan to every resident.[3] The Winnipeg site constituted a classic negative income tax experiment comparable to its US counterparts, while the Dauphin site provided a unique demonstration project for a universal guaranteed annual income plan. Although planned

3 Each plan consisted of an income guarantee, varying by family composition, and a negative tax rate. To illustrate: for a family of four in 1975, the guarantee for Dauphin's saturation site was $3,800 with a tax rate of 50 per cent while Winnipeg programs combined guarantees of $3,800, $4,800, and $5,800 with tax rates of 35 per cent, 50 per cent, and 75 per cent. Variability in plan generosity and comparison with the control group formed the basis for analysis of labour supply response, or work disincentives, and other issues.

research on the impact of the experiment was eliminated, the data were collected, eventually digitized and archived, and analyzed for the Winnipeg sample. Hum and Simpson (1993, S287) concluded that the Winnipeg results conformed to published US research indicating that "adverse effects, such as work response, are smaller than would have been expected without experimentation." More recently, Forget (2011) found favourable population health outcomes arising from the Dauphin experiment.

The Manitoba Basic Annual Income Experiment, or Mincome, did not counter declining interest in social security reform at the end of the 1970s. It would be a mistake, however, to think that the concept of a guaranteed annual income died on the research table. Several refundable tax credit programs have been introduced by the federal government, including the GST tax credit and the National Child Benefit, which reflect the design of a negative income tax at a modest and targeted level delivered through the income tax system (Hum and Simpson 2001). Indeed, any administrative obstacles associated with Mincome and the delivery of a guaranteed annual income through the income tax system would appear to have receded with the increasing technical sophistication of the Canada Revenue Agency and the increasing participation of low-income tax filers. Moreover, the claw-back of such benefit programs as Old Age Security or Employment Insurance constitutes a negative income tax designed for specific groups of recipients, and the Guaranteed Income Supplement represents an archetypical guaranteed annual income for seniors. Calls continue for some form of a universal guaranteed annual income, presumably to replace current SA and other income support programs. The idea was present in the 1985 report of the Royal Commission on the Economic Union and Development Prospects of Canada (the Macdonald Commission) and, more recently, in less prominent proposals by the Yukon Legislative Assembly and the Green Party of Canada. In addition, the guaranteed annual income or negative income tax provides a useful framework for understanding and assessing existing income support policies such as the provincial SA programs now in place.

Institutional features of current SA in Manitoba

Provincial responsibility for SA programming, administration, and data collection has generated an assortment of distinctive features across the federation that will be difficult to explain and assess. Though Manitoba is generally seen to be a province in the middle of the spectrum on most political and economic issues, its SA experience has been viewed as conservative because of its long adherence to a two-tiered system that devolved SA programming and delivery to its municipalities. Municipalities are no longer responsible for any aspect of SA administration, however, permitting an assessment of a unitary provincial system that doubtless retains some idiosyncratic features.

The Manitoba Employment and Income Assistance (EIA) program is a universal program of income support in the sense that it is open to all residents of Manitoba based on a needs test. The test compares individual or family income to a basic needs budget set by the program and adjusted annually, which constitutes the income guarantee in the vernacular of a guaranteed annual income. This basic needs budget differs according to family composition, age, and disability status and is more generous for persons with a disability and parents, as shown in the second column of Table 10.1. An important change in the guarantee for parents has been the gradual restoration between 2001 and 2004 of the National Child Benefit Supplement, which was deducted from provincial SA when the federal

Table 10.1 Manitoba Employment and Income Assistance Budget by Family Type, 2012, and Total Welfare Incomes in Manitoba Relative to the Low-Income Cut-Off and the Market Basket Measure, 2009

Family Type	Monthly Manitoba EIA Allowance, 2012	Total (Federal and Manitoba) Welfare Income as % of LICO, 2009	Total Welfare Income as % of MBM, 2009
Single Employables	$565	37	49
Single Parents	$678	66	83
Couples with Children	$833 + children's allowance	62	78
Persons with a Disability	$781	51	68

Source: For the second column (monthly allowances), see Manitoba (2012). For the third and fourth columns, see Table 4 and 5 of National Council of Welfare (2010).
Notes: (i) For the second column, the monthly allowance for shelter, food, clothing, household supplies, and personal needs may be supplemented to include utility costs not included in rent, a northern allowance, funds for special dietary needs, and disability living costs where applicable. RentAid is now included in the assistance levels, which are tax free. The general assistance category principally includes single persons and couples with children. The children's allowance depends on the age and number of children in the family. For example, the monthly children's allowance for two adults with a child between 7 and 11 years of age is $93, and a second child 6 or younger adds $135.
(ii) For the third and fourth columns, total welfare income includes SA but also additional provincial and federal benefits.

government introduced it in 1998. All other recent improvements in the guarantee are limited to the discretion of the Manitoba government and, because formal indexation of benefits to inflation was abandoned in 1993, may not have kept pace with inflation or other provincial programs.

The earnings exemption reflects the rate of benefit reduction or the "negative tax" in a guaranteed annual income scheme. Those with work expectations, including single parents and those in the general assistance category, are permitted to keep the first $200 of net monthly earnings and 30 per cent of any additional earnings. This implies a tax rate of 0 on the first $200 of earnings, followed by a tax rate of 70 per cent on additional earnings until EIA entitlement is exhausted. The discontinuity at $200 may discourage some work beyond this point, but the 70 per cent tax represents a significant improvement since 2000 in both the initial earnings exemption (the earnings on which the tax rate is zero) and the tax rate for earnings above the initial exemption.[4] As the name of the program implies, there is emphasis on linking income assistance to employment, and this link is supported by a variety of recently introduced incentives, including an allowance to assist job seekers and a one-time bonus for those leaving EIA. The effect of these enhanced work incentive benefits may have been limited by retention of the exit level of earnings at 135 per cent of the basic needs budget, leading to higher income loss at the exit point, which may discourage employment and exit from the program (Stevens, Simpson, and Frankel 2011).

Even though people with disabilities might not have work expectations, they are encouraged to take advantage of the employment services available under EIA on a voluntarily basis. Qualification for disability status requires a disability assessment report from a doctor or nurse practitioner that indicates one or more physical, psychological, or intellectual impairments expected to last more than 90 days. Clients may also complete a self-report describing their functional difficulties and the community disability services they are receiving. The reports are provided to an EIA Disability Assessment Panel of three people (in Winnipeg and Selkirk). The panel assesses the applicant and makes a recommendation to the director of the regional EIA office or his or her designate, who decides whether to grant disability case status. Disability cases are typically time limited and reviewed at the expiry date.

4 The so-called welfare wall reflected effective tax rates on SA around 100 per cent in older provincial schemes, including the Manitoba program before 2000, which presented a serious deterrent to leaving SA. An alternative to the current scheme would be a uniform tax rate in the range of 55–60 per cent that could provide stronger work incentives without increasing SA expenditures.

The implementation of an integrated service delivery model in 2004 allocated all SA cases in Winnipeg to community area offices, based on the participants' address. Caseworkers who had not previously managed disability cases were given that responsibility and provided with training regarding disability-related issues, which may have increased referrals to the Winnipeg EIA Disability Assessment Panel. Moreover, the decisions in 2006 to allow nurse practitioners to complete the Disability Assessment Report and to enroll Canada Pension Plan Disability participants automatically in the disability category broadened eligibility conditions and allowed for expansion of disability recipients on provincial SA.

Manitoba SA benefits

Figures 10.1 and 10.2 show how total welfare incomes in constant 2009 dollars have evolved since 1986 for Manitoba, its neighbouring provinces of Ontario and Saskatchewan, and the rest of Canada outside Manitoba (including Ontario and Saskatchewan) for two of the four standard groups

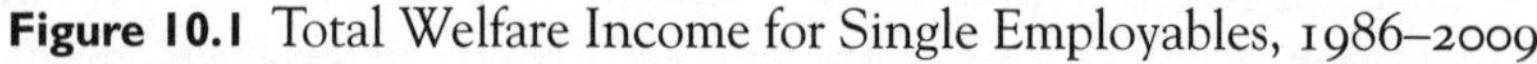

Figure 10.1 Total Welfare Income for Single Employables, 1986–2009

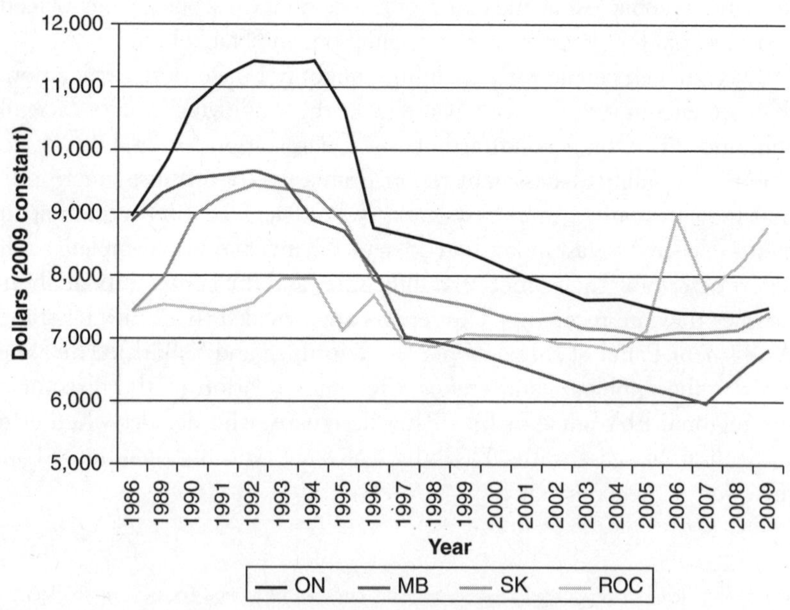

Source: Table 8, National Council of Welfare (2010).
Note: Provinces are indicated with official abbreviations. ROC stands for the rest of Canada, excluding Manitoba.

Figure 10.2 Total Welfare Income for Couples with Two Children, 1986–2009

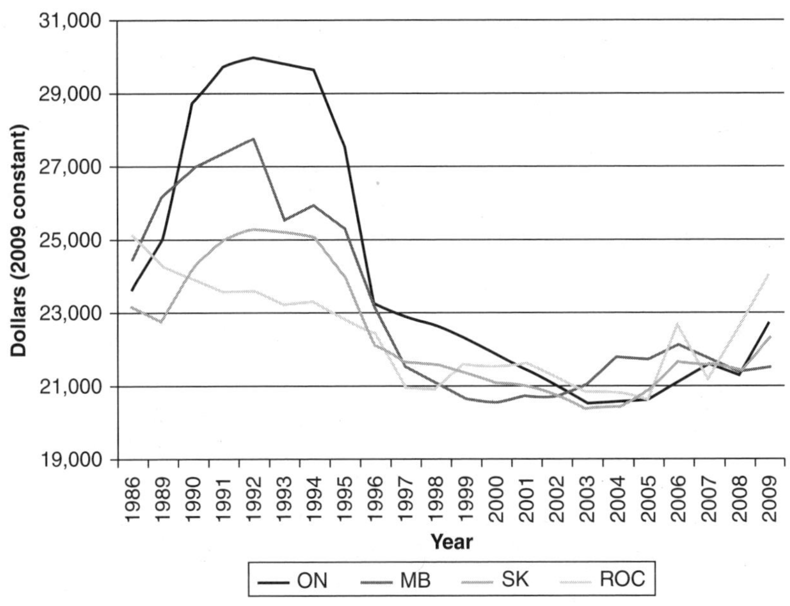

Source: Table 8, National Council of Welfare (2010).
Note: Provinces are indicated with official abbreviations. ROC stands for the rest of Canada, excluding Manitoba.

of recipients: single employables and couples with two children.[5] For each category of recipient, Ontario had more generous benefits in the 1990s, and the differences between benefits in Manitoba, Saskatchewan, and the rest of Canada (ROC) were much smaller. Benefits clearly decline sharply in the 1990s although the decline begins before the introduction of the CHST (see also Boychuk, in this volume). For single employables, the decline in Manitoba's benefits is greater than for the ROC or Saskatchewan, although this pattern is also apparent for couples with children. The decline in benefits for lone parents and persons with disabilities (not shown) is less pronounced, which is consistent with Manitoba's tradition of protecting those more "deserving," although the benefit levels remain below those in Ontario, Saskatchewan, and the rest of Canada.[6]

5 The rest of Canada incomes are weighted according to provincial population in 1999.
6 The graphs for lone parents and persons with disabilities are not shown but are available from the author upon request.

How generous are Manitoba's SA benefits today? The main source of information on SA incomes has been the National Council of Welfare, which was eliminated in the 2012 federal budget. The council's final annual report provides estimates of what amounts to the income guarantee for specified family types for each provincial SA program for 2009 (National Council of Welfare 2010). I treat these as estimates because any comparison of SA benefits across provinces must recognize the complex set of additional benefit entitlements beyond the basic (minimum) payment. Moreover, it is important to note that the generosity and work incentives of each provincial plan should consider the rates of earnings exemptions, or negative income taxes, as well as the income guarantees to those without earnings. Thus, a program with a higher income guarantee might be less generous to the average SA recipient if it is coupled with a lower earnings exemption (higher tax) rate. Although the National Council of Welfare has considered earnings exemptions separately, these are not reflected in the total welfare income figures.[7]

Figures 10.3 and 10.4 compare basic SA levels, total provincial benefits, and total (provincial and federal) welfare benefits for single employables

Figure 10.3 Assistance Rates for Single Employables in Manitoba Compared to Those in Ontario, Saskatchewan, and the Rest of Canada, 2009

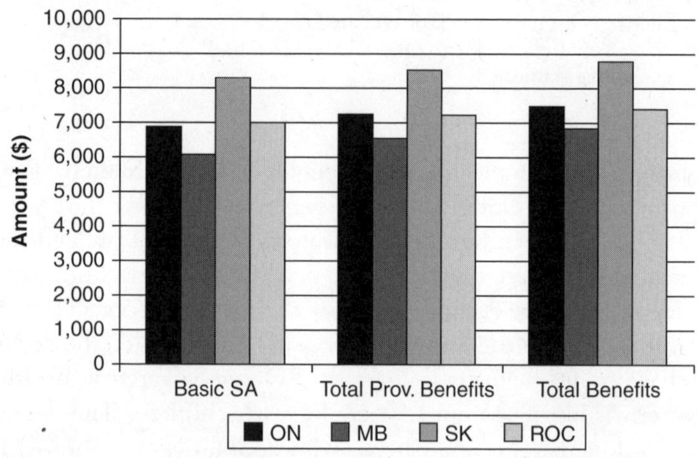

Source: National Council of Welfare (2010).
Notes: Rates are in 2009 dollars; the rest of Canada (ROC) measurement is the population-weighted average of assistance rates for all provinces except Manitoba; SA refers to social assistance; Prov. refers to provincial.

7 National Council of Welfare (2010, Table 3) provides the most recent comparison of provincial earnings exemption regimes.

Figure 10.4 Assistance Rates for a Couple with Two Children in Manitoba Compared to Those in Ontario, Saskatchewan, and the Rest of Canada, 2009

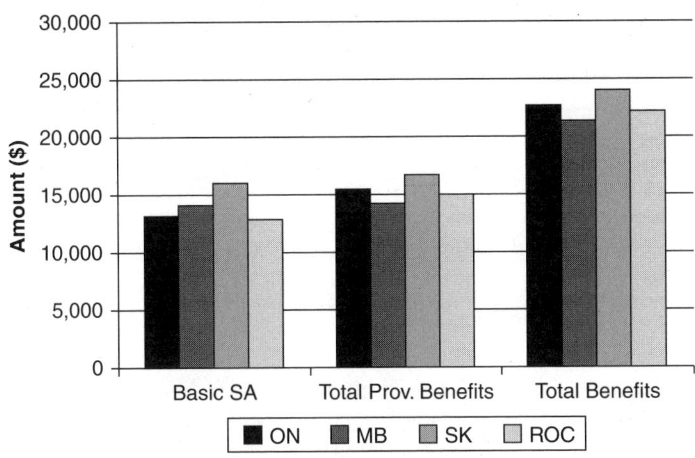

Source: National Council of Welfare (2010).
Notes: Rates are in 2009 dollars; the rest of Canada (ROC) measurement is the population-weighted average of assistance rates for all provinces except Manitoba; SA refers to social assistance; Prov. refers to provincial.

and couples with children. Again, comparisons are made between rates in Manitoba, in Manitoba's neighbouring provinces of Ontario and Saskatchewan, and in all other provinces except Manitoba (the ROC). Note that the rates for the ROC constitute a population-weighted average. Figure 10.3 illustrates that Manitoba's benefit levels clearly lie below those of the ROC, Ontario, and Saskatchewan for single employables. What is more surprising—especially in view of Boychuk's (1998, 66–67) assessment of Manitoba's regime as one favouring the deserving poor in the past—is that Manitoba's levels are also clearly below the ROC, Ontario, and Saskatchewan levels for single parents with one child and for persons with a disability (not shown).[8] Figure 10.4 shows that it is only for couples with two children that Manitoba's benefits are comparable to those received in other jurisdictions, perhaps reflecting the fact that not all provinces had restored the National Child Benefit Supplement in 2009.

Assessment of the generosity of the income guarantee of an SA program is often placed in the context of a poverty standard. Although Canada has

8 The graphs for lone parents and persons with disabilities are not shown but are available from the author upon request.

no official poverty standard, the low-income cut-off (LICO) calculated by Statistics Canada is often used. As shown in the third column of Table 10.1, Manitoba's total welfare incomes lie well below the LICO, especially for single employables and persons with disabilities, and are generally lower than incomes in all other Canadian provinces. Stevens (2009) argues, however, that the LICO does not reflect the lower living costs for the poor in Manitoba, especially in Winnipeg, relative to these costs in other major Canadian cities and that a better measure, the Market Basket Measure (MBM), should be used. As the final column of Table 10.1 shows, Manitoba fares much better under this measure. In relative terms, these figures are better than those of the Atlantic provinces and similar to those of all other provinces.

The evolution of the Manitoba caseload

Despite experiencing some data challenges, researchers can safely say that there has been a fairly substantial decline across Canada in SA participation rates (namely, in the SA caseload per capita for the adult population 17 to 64) since the mid-1990s (see Kneebone and White, in this volume). Kneebone and White (2009) argue that, facing fiscal challenges, several provinces introduced tighter eligibility rules and administrative procedures, which, along with improving employment and earnings prospects, caused SA participation to fall until to 2003. Using an alternative administrative database, the longitudinal file of tax records from 1992 to 2000, Finnie, Irvine, and Sceviour (2005) determined that the decline involved both falling rates of entry into SA for all family types and rising rates of exit from SA for lone parents and families with children. Administrative data from the provinces to 2007 confirm the continuation of the downward trend in SA caseloads and participation (Federal-Provincial-Territorial (FPT) Directors of Income Support 2010), but the impact of the sharp recession in 2008 and its aftermath awaits further data dissemination and analysis.

Caseload comparisons over time for Manitoba involve the additional complication that the province did not assume responsibility for municipal cases in Winnipeg until 1999 and in rural and northern municipalities until 2004. The provincial caseload fell fairly steadily after the Winnipeg amalgamation in 2000 from 33,200 to 31,500 in 2007, a decline of 5.1 per cent that emulates the national trend (Federal-Provincial-Territorial (FPT) Directors of Income Support 2010).[9] However, Manitoba

9 Total recipients also declined by 5.3 per cent (from 60,900 to 57,700). Manitoba's population grew from 1.15 to 1.19 million during this period, so that the SA participation rate fell by 8.5 per cent.

Entrepreneurship, Training, and Trade (2012, 50) reported increases in the average monthly caseload to 32,800 in 2010, 34,100 in 2011, and 35,400 in 2012, which reversed the decade-long decline. An important development in the composition of the caseload is the growing importance of disability cases (see Kneebone and White; Prince, in this volume). As of March 2007, the dominant reason for income support was disability (57 per cent) rather than being a sole-support parent (27 per cent), or unemployment (16 per cent). The major reason for the dominance of disability cases was their longevity; most long-term recipients were disability cases (Federal-Provincial-Territorial (FPT) Directors of Income Support 2010, 76–78). Moreover, the recent increase in the Manitoba caseload has also seen an even larger increase in disability cases—to 20,400 or 58 per cent of the total caseload in 2012 (Manitoba 2012, 50).

In a recent paper, Stevens, Simpson, and Frankel (2011) analyze caseload evolution in Manitoba using a monthly administrative data file of SA recipients between 1999 and 2008. The SA participation rate in Manitoba fell fairly steadily from 5.5 per cent to 4.4 per cent (Stevens, Simpson, and Frankel 2011, Figure 2B). The decline is entirely attributable to the falling rate of entry into SA during the period, as the rate of continuation on SA actually rose by 2 per cent during the same period from 94.6 per cent to 96.6 per cent. In other words, the SA participation rate in Manitoba would have fallen more sharply if remaining SA recipients were not more likely to continue on SA (or, equivalently, less likely to exit SA).

Our analysis examined the factors associated with falling entry and rising continuation rates from 1999 to 2008. We attributed about 40 per cent of the decline in entry rates to an aging population with higher rates of postsecondary educational attainment. Other economic, program, and sociodemographic factors, such as those analyzed by Kneebone and White (2009), were not statistically significant determinants of the entry pattern during this period. For continuation rates, the longitudinal administrative microdata permit detailed analysis of the factors that affect behaviour. Declines in Manitoba's unemployment rate, real SA benefits, and average caseload per caseworker, as well as an increase in the real minimum wage rate, all exerted downward pressure on the continuation rate during this period, but these pressures were overwhelmed by a dramatic increase in the disability caseload (from 28.6 per cent to 51.9 per cent of all cases) and a sharp increase in the duration of SA spells (from 54 to 71 months). Other demographic and program factors—including the doubling of the liquid asset exemption in 2007, progressive enhancements to the work incentive program, and the termination of specialized disability caseloads in 2004—appeared to have had little effect on the continuation rate.

The most striking difference between our results and previous evidence for Canada and the United States was the rise in SA continuation rates associated with rising disability conversion rates and assistance spell duration. Our subsequent analysis of the Manitoba data suggests that disability conversion is sensitive to changes in the incentives and administrative procedures of the Employment and Income Assistance program, which generally encouraged disability conversion during the period. As real benefits fell, the decline was greater for those without disabilities, raising both the benefits gap between persons with and without disabilities and the incentive for disability conversion. In addition, the termination of specialized disability caseloads appears to have increased conversions to official disability status, perhaps by expanding the scope for service providers who support such conversions. Conversely, program changes to emphasize the functional assessment of disabilities by medical review panels reduced conversions, perhaps by increasing requirements for a disability classification and providing more consistent application of the criteria for disability status, while rising service provider caseloads also reduced conversion rates, perhaps by limiting the capacity of staff to document disability cases. As well, increases in the initial earnings exemption and in the retention rate for earnings above the initial exemption (i.e., declining tax rates on benefits) provided work incentives that appear to have reduced conversion to disability case status. In short, the overall effect of program changes seems to have enhanced the successful negotiation of disability status.[10] Further analysis of the changes in the status of SA program participants in Manitoba and other provinces may yield important insights for future policy initiatives.

Conclusion

The SA experience in Manitoba blends conservative and progressive ingredients. The conservative side includes a long adherence to a two-tiered system of program benefits and administration that limited benefits to those deemed employable. It also reflects benefit levels that lag behind those of most provinces on most scales, despite the presence of a fourth-term NDP government that one would have expected to be sympathetic to poverty reduction. Yet the province has also been a trailblazer in certain areas, including in the granting of mothers' allowances to combat child poverty. Manitoba was also the host during the 1970s of the only large-scale social experiment on the provision of a guaranteed annual income in Canada.

10 One caveat is that program impacts are based on weak identifying assumptions associated with the timing of program changes.

This experiment was a precursor to the design or redesign of many modern income-tested support programs, including SA, that provide a basic level of benefits, which are taxed, or clawed back, as income rises.

The Manitoba SA caseload has declined significantly in recent years in concert with provincial trends elsewhere. This decline reflects a determined provincial effort to reduce welfare dependence as federal financial support dwindled. The evidence suggests that SA program features, including benefit levels and effective tax rates but also administrative provisions, have played some role in this decline, but economic and demographic factors are also at play. If the diminished caseload can be classified as a success, it still leaves policymakers with important concerns. In particular, the remaining caseload in Manitoba, and likely elsewhere, is dominated by longer-term recipients who are more likely to be classified as disabled. Policy to encourage work by limiting benefits and offering tax incentives and other provisions that encourage job placement may be less effective, if not entirely inappropriate, for the salient group no longer able to work.

References

Association of Manitoba Municipalities. 2004. "Presentation by the AMM to the Legislative Standing Committee on Bill 8: The Employment and Income Assistance Amendment Act." February 18, Winnipeg.

Boychuk, Gerard William. 1998. *Patchworks of Purpose: The Development of Provincial Social Assistance Regimes in Canada*. Montréal: McGill-Queen's University Press.

Canada. Parliament. Senate. Senate Special Committee on Poverty. 1971. *Poverty in Canada*. 3d sess., 28th Parliament.

Federal-Provincial-Territorial (FPT) Directors of Income Support. 2010. *Social Assistance Statistical Report: 2007*. Ottawa: Human Resources and Skills Development Canada. http://publications.gc.ca/collections/collection_2010/rhdcc-hrsdc/HS25-2-2007-eng.pdf.

Finnie, Ross, Ian Irvine, and Roger Sceviour. 2005. *Summary of Social Assistance Use in Canada: National and Provincial Trends in Incidence, Entry and Exit*. Analytical Studies Branch Research Paper Series. Ottawa: Statistics Canada.

Forget, Evelyn. 2011. "The Town with No Poverty: The Health Effects of a Canadian Guaranteed Annual Income Field Experiment." *Canadian Public Policy* 37 (3): 283–305. http://dx.doi.org/10.1353/cpp.2011.0036.

Hum, Derek, and Wayne Simpson. 1991. *Income Maintenance, Work Effort, and the Canadian Mincome Experiment*. A study prepared for the Economic Council of Canada, Supply and Services Canada. Ottawa: Canadian Communications Group.

Hum, Derek, and Wayne Simpson. 1993. "Economic Response to a Guaranteed Annual Income: Experience from Canada and the United States." *Journal of Labor Economics* 11 (1.2): S263–96. http://dx.doi.org/10.1086/298335.

Hum, Derek, and Wayne Simpson. 2001. "A Guaranteed Annual Income? From Mincome to the Millenium." *Policy Options / Option politiques* 22: 78–82.

Kneebone, Ronald, and Kathleen White. 2009. "Fiscal Retrenchment and Social Assistance in Canada." *Canadian Public Policy* 35 (1): 21–40. http://dx.doi.org/10.3138/cpp.35.1.21.

Manitoba. 2012. *Employment and Income Assistance (EIA)*. Winnipeg: Government of Manitoba.

Manitoba Entrepreneurship, Training, and Trade (METT). 2012. *Annual Report 2011–12*. Winnipeg: METT. http://www.gov.mb.ca/jec/pdfs/11_12_ett_ar.pdf.

Manitoba Task Force on Social Assistance. 1983. *Report of the Manitoba Task Force on Social Assistance*. Winnipeg: Manitoba Task Force on Social Assistance.

National Council of Welfare. 1987. *Welfare in Canada: The Tangled Safety Net*. Ottawa: Government of Canada.

National Council of Welfare. 1997. *Another Look at Welfare Reform*. Ottawa: Minister of Public Works and Government Services.

National Council of Welfare. 2010. *Welfare Incomes 2009*. Ottawa: Government of Canada.

Stevens, Harvey. 2009. "Poverty Statistics Misleading." *Winnipeg Free Press*, December 5.

Stevens, Harvey, Wayne Simpson, and Sid Frankel. 2011. "Explaining Declining Social Assistance Participation Rates: A Longitudinal Analysis of Manitoba Administrative and Population Data." *Canadian Public Policy* 37 (2): 163–81. http://dx.doi.org/10.3138/cpp.37.2.163.

Thomas, P., and C. Brown. 2010. *Manitoba Politics and Government: Issues, Institutions, Traditions*. Winnipeg: University of Manitoba Press.

eleven

Social Assistance in New Brunswick: Origins, Developments, and the Current Situation

LUC THÉRIAULT AND HÉLÈNE LEBRETON[1]

Introduction

New Brunswick is home to 751,170 citizens and is the second-most populated province on the Atlantic coast after Nova Scotia. New Brunswick's residents are older relative to those in the rest of Canada. The population's median age of 43.7 years is the second highest in the country (Statistics Canada 2013). The prevalence of disability among the working-aged population (15 to 64 years old) is also the second highest in the country. One in eight or 12.2 per cent of New Brunswickers in this age category self-report that their daily activities are limited due to a long-term health condition (Statistics Canada CANSIM database, Table 115–0001).

The proportion of New Brunswick's 2011 population in low income, as defined by the low-income cut-off after tax, is lower than the Atlantic Canadian average for most common household types. The National Household Survey estimates an overall low-income rate of 5.8 per cent (6.1 per cent in Atlantic Canada), of 17.9 per cent for unattached individuals (20.2 per cent in Atlantic Canada), and 13.2 per cent for persons in single-parent families (17.6 per cent in Atlantic Canada) (Statistics Canada CANSIM database, Table 202–0804).

In the 10-year period between 2005 and 2014, annual employment rates[2] varied between 56.7 per cent in 2012 and 59.1 per cent in 2008 (Statistics Canada CANSIM database, Table 282–0002). Over this same 10-year period, monthly employment rates follow a seasonal trend with summer peaks between 59.1 per cent (August 2014) and 62.1 per cent

1 The views expressed in this chapter are those of the authors and do not necessarily reflect those of their employers.

2 The employment rate is calculated as the ratio of those who are employed compared to the general population of working age (15 to 64 years) regardless of whether they are working or looking for work. This calculation is a more relevant economic indicator of those on income support, as they are included in the denominator.

(June 2007) and winter lows between 53.9 per cent (March 2012) and 56.7 per cent (January 2008) (Statistics Canada CANSIM database, Table 282–0001). Seasonal trends in the number of employed New Brunswickers appear to be inversely related to seasonal trends in the number of households on income support. Most of the time, the number of households on income support increases as seasonal employment levels decrease and vice versa (see Figure 11.1).

New Brunswick's social assistance programs mitigate the risks of unemployment and poverty for vulnerable segments of the population. In this chapter, we start by briefly outlining the historical development of social assistance in New Brunswick from the late eighteenth century to present policy reforms. This section references the historical development pertaining to the federal welfare state as well as more recent provincial poverty reduction strategies. The current architecture of the income support system in New Brunswick is then presented and includes descriptions of complementary programs offering health and childcare benefits to low-income earners who are not in receipt of monthly income transfers. A discussion of the nature of the social assistance caseload and of recent trends precedes the conclusion.

Origins and recent developments in social assistance

The historical evolution of social assistance in New Brunswick has been well documented by Ysabel Provencher (2004). She highlights that private charity was the policy vehicle used to address poverty in the province's formative years. In early 1784, many poor families arrived in Saint John from famine-ridden Ireland, and this immigration might have been one of the impetuses for the New Brunswick Poor Law of 1786. Inspired by the exclusionary and stigmatizing English poor law tradition, it distinguished between "deserving" poor (orphans, widows, elderly, and disabled) and "undeserving" poor (unemployed able-bodied individuals who might receive a form of help tied to work-related measures). This ideological perspective has had a prolonged influence on how the poor were treated in the province.

Provencher (2004) explains that, under the New Brunswick Poor Law, each parish had "officers of the poor" (generally local businessmen) who were in charge of managing public relief funds. These officers could force any undeserving poor person to work in exchange for the assistance he or she received. The undeserving poor were "sold" at an annual auction. A poor person was "bought" by providing him or her with room and board for one year, although the individual whose care was auctioned off might still receive some financial support from the parish or municipal authorities. In the 1860s, the first almshouses were created in New Brunswick's English-speaking counties, and these were complemented by workhouses where the undeserving poor were "corrected" or rehabilitated through work. Around the same period in French-speaking counties, religious communities fostered orphanages, hospitals, and sanatoriums for similar rehabilitative purposes.

Private charity remained the key form of assistance in the province until the 1930s, when the dire economic conditions experienced during the Great Depression triggered a timid entry of the provincial and federal governments into providing relief for the population in need.

Development in New Brunswick (1960–2010)

The New Brunswick context evolved within the federal funding formulas in a unique way. In the early 1960s, a quiet revolution of sorts took place, one epitomized by the election of Louis J. Robichaud and his Liberal government. The recommendations of the Byrne Commission, established by Robichaud in 1962, formed the basis of the *Equal Opportunity* program of reforms. These reforms would modernize the structure of the provincial state apparatus, which, until then, was still organized around a decentralized county structure. This restructuring made province-wide coordinated initiatives in economic and social development possible, which ensured more uniform access to public services. County governments were abolished and the provincial taxation system was reformed.[3] In 1967, the jurisdiction for the provision of social assistance in New Brunswick was transferred from the municipality or parish to province. This change in funding mechanism enabled the poor law tradition to make way for a more modern public administration approach to social assistance.

In the late 1970s, the Department of Social Services revised the income maintenance programs according to distinct case types based upon disability, marital status, and earning potential (New Brunswick Department of Social Services 1978, 1980). Disabled persons were able to access higher monthly transfers while non-disabled clients were encouraged to obtain wages to complement their lower monthly benefits. In the 1980s,

3 The county taxation system was based on property taxes primarily. This created and reproduced spatial inequality as wealthier counties were able to raise more taxes and offer better services while disadvantaged counties experienced many needs but had few resources at their disposal.

programming continued to be designed along the lines of providing various amounts of monthly transfers to supplement or replace earned income according to disability, marital status, and potential for financial self-sufficiency. Program designs at this stage attempted to leverage the financial self-sufficiency of clients by altering the amount of passively transferred income according to distinct client groups.

In the early 1990s, New Brunswick shared the effects of an important recessionary period with the rest of the industrialized world. New Brunswick adopted the emerging neoliberal economic agenda, which sought to reform welfare using a "mutual obligation" approach in which the mediation of the risks related to unemployment is shared between the individual and the state. This new politics lent a more important role to the free-market economy as a mediator of economic opportunities for citizens. New welfare programming in New Brunswick sought to "activate" clients on income support so that they would seek any available labour market opportunity over the free time and money offered by a passively designed system. In response to these emerging policy reforms, the contributions of educational and labour market factors to the problem of welfare dependency were studied. Two national demonstration projects were thus implemented in New Brunswick in 1992.

NB Works (1992–98) provided "employment based counselling," education, training, and work experience to 2,898 family households with parents who had not yet completed high school. The case management process that developed as a result served as the basis for the approach to service delivery in New Brunswick (New Brunswick Department of Human Resources Development 1997). The Self-Sufficiency Project was an experiment aimed at assessing whether the provision of time-limited cash incentives is effective in breaking the cycle of dependency on social assistance (see Foley, in this volume).

A department focused solely on income support was created by the Liberal government of Frank McKenna in 1994–95. This spawned important investments in the technological and bureaucratic infrastructures of income support service delivery, which streamlined outdated work processes and enabled new service delivery principles (New Brunswick Department of Human Resources Development 1997). Employees were aligned by a common intervention strategy, embodied in the automated work processes and case management functions of a new computer system. The "NB Case" system, still in use today, aimed at enabling employees to spend less time on paperwork and more time counselling clients on how to be independent from the system (New Brunswick Office of the Auditor General 1998). Program design has evolved to leverage client self-sufficiency by engaging clients in interviews to identify and address each individual's specific barriers to employment.

Poverty reduction strategy

In 2009, the government of New Brunswick underwent a public engagement exercise around the question of poverty. The final consultation forum, held in November 2009, sought consensus from 50 participants from four areas of civic life: government, business, private citizens, and third-sector organizations that advocate for vulnerable populations. The forum agreed to initiate a massive overhaul of the social assistance system and adopted the first-ever poverty reduction plan for the province, *Overcoming Poverty Together: The New Brunswick Social and Economic Inclusion Plan* (New Brunswick 2009). The plan fostered immediate and important changes in New Brunswick's social assistance policy landscape. In January 2010, one of the three income support programs was eliminated. The now-defunct Interim Assistance Program (IAP) was designed to offer "financial assistance to individuals and families, who were in need, yet were expected to attain self-reliance in a relatively short period of time" (New Brunswick Department of Social Development 2011). Low monthly benefits combined with high wage exemption amounts were intended to keep clients engaged in labour force participation. Peak participation in the IAP occurred around 1993 94 when a little over 1,500 households were participating. By January 2010, the slightly more than 1,000 households that remained under this category of assistance were transferred to the current Transitional Assistance Program (TAP). All IAP clients received monthly rate increases with their transfer to the TAP.

Poverty reduction initiatives were further developed over the course of the next three years. Effective October 1, 2013, the schedule of basic unit rates was simplified and the benefit clawback rates due to earnings were reduced. A key structural barrier to employment was addressed when wage exemption policies became more generous and rewarding. As benefit clawback rates were reduced, additional efforts to obtain earnings from the labour market resulted in additional income to the household.

Rate increases were also instituted as part of the reform initiated by the poverty reduction plan. An additional 7 per cent rate increase was applied to most households over the course of six months: a 4 per cent increase in October 2013 and a 3 per cent increase in April 2014.

Changes to the Household Income Policy (HIP) were also introduced at this time. The HIP determines the number of members within the same household who must contribute to meeting the basic needs of the shared living arrangement. Shelter deductions for persons with disabilities living with their parents were reduced, increasing the amount of income support received by these clients.

Current system architecture

Overall, approximately 30,800 New Brunswick households benefit from at least one part of the spectrum of income support, ranging from the regular supplementation of monthly income to subsidies for health benefits and daycare services. The public social assistance system supports unemployed individuals needing regular income from transfers (80 per cent of clients) as well as the working poor (20 per cent). For the four out of five clients who receive regular monthly income assistance, two basic rate programs prescribe monthly income support amounts: the Transitional Assistance Program (TAP) and the Extended Benefits Program (EBP).

EBP targets higher monthly benefits to those who are certified by the Medical Advisory Board as blind, deaf, or otherwise disabled. One quarter (25 per cent) of income-receiving households are granted assistance under the Extended Benefits Program. Most (90 per cent) of EBP households are comprised of single persons.

The Transitional Assistance Program (TAP) provides monthly income support to those with less severe health issues as well as to qualifying families and single persons who are not able to access wages from the labour market for other reasons. Though this program does not limit the time clients spend on income support, activation measures in the form of extra training for extra benefits are available to those with close ties to the labour market. Over 95 per cent of qualifying families with dependent children are granted monthly assistance under the TAP. Single persons comprise 41 per cent of households in this program.

Social assistance rate schedules found in regulation 95–61 under the Family Income Security Act provide the "basic unit rates" for both TAP and EBP programs and are used in the determination of intake eligibility for monthly income support. Rates are scheduled according to household size and the presence of a medically certified disability (see Table 11.1). Simply speaking, a household qualifies for monthly income support if the combined income of all household members amounts to less than the monthly assistance rate that applies to them in the regulations. The Household Income Policy (HIP) is implicitly reflected in the rate schedule. In the determination of needs, monthly income support rates are related to household size, which considers all household members, regardless of

Table 11.1 New Brunswick Social Assistance Monthly Rates, April 2014

Household Type	EBP	TAP
1 person—employable	$663	$537
1 person—designated	$663	$576
1 adult, 1 child under 19 years	$974	$887
2 adults	$994	$903
3 persons	$1,030	$938
4 persons	$1,092	$995
5 persons	$1,154	$1,052
6 persons	$1,216	$1,109
7 persons	$1,278	$1,166
8 persons	$1,340	$1,223

Note: Rates are prescribed in the regulation for households of up to 13 persons.

whether they are related by blood, adoption, or marriage. Children are counted as part of the household unit, regardless of age and parentage. The number of children and adults informs the need side of the equation. On the resource side of the eligibility equation, the earned income from all household members is considered, even the income of working-aged dependents.

The "income supplement" is added to the monthly transfers of households with dependent-aged children. An additional $84 is added in the warmer months between May and October while $120 is added to the monthly cheque from November to April. The "disability supplement" adds $100.00 to the monthly cheque of a certified disabled person in the EBP program. Both the income and disability supplements were recently enhanced in government efforts to further reduce poverty.

Selected tax benefits such as the Harmonized Sales Tax Credit (HST), the Working Income Tax Benefit (WITB), and all child tax benefits are exempted from consideration in calculating eligibility for income support in New Brunswick.

Considering income available from all exempted sources, a single person on income support has access to approximately $709 per month if he or she is relatively healthy, and a single disabled person sees $326 more due to additional supplements and differences in the monthly rate of assistance. Households with dependent children are able to benefit from additional federal and provincial transfers. For example, the average Child Tax Benefit cheque to a New Brunswick single parent with one child on income assistance in 2013 is between $325 and $425 per month (Canada Revenue Agency 2012). The extra $100 depends on whether the child is less than six years old (see Table 11.2).

Consideration of household assets depends upon the household's disability status and size. Non-disabled clients or applicants are considered eligible if they have liquid assets up to $1,000 for a single-person household and up to $2,000 per household encompassing more than one person. Households

Table 11.2 Monthly Incomes of Hypothetical Reference Families on Social Assistance in NB

Components of Income	Single Employable	Single Disabled	Single Parent, One Child, Aged 2 Years	Two Parents, Two Children, Aged 10 and 15 Years
Flat-Earnings Exemption	$150.00	$250.00	$200.00	$200.00
SA Basic Unit Rate as of April 2014	$537.00	$663.00	$887.00	$995.00
SA Monthly Income Supplement	$0.00	$0.00	$102.00	$102.00
SA Disability Supplement	$0.00	$100.00	$0.00	$0.00
HST Rebate	$22.08	$22.08	$55.75	$67.33
NB Child Tax Benefit (NB CTB)	$0.00	$0.00	$20.83	$41.66
NB Working Income Supplement (NB WIS)	$0.00	$0.00	$0.00	$0.00
Canadian Child Tax Benefit (CCTB)	$0.00	$0.00	$119.42	$238.83
National Child Benefit Supplement (NCBS)	$0.00	$0.00	$185.08	$348.75
Universal Child Care Benefit (UCCB)	$0.00	$0.00	$100.00	$0.00
Total—Available Monthly Income	$709.08	$1,035.08	$1,670.08	$1,993.58

Note: Flat-earnings exemptions are used here as hypothetical examples. Clients who work for amounts higher than the monthly flat exemption receive 30 per cent of their earned monthly income above the flat exemption amount.

including a certified disabled person are eligible for a liquid asset exemption of $10,000. To support the attachment to the labour force of vulnerable citizens near social-assistance-level incomes, access to subsidies for chronic health conditions and childcare are made available beyond the income support system.

Health benefits

Under related poverty-reduction initiatives, health benefits typically only available to social assistance households are now automatically extended for up to three years after a client has exited the system for reasons of employment; and a new vision and dental insurance program (Healthy Smiles, Clear Vision) for low-income New Brunswick children under the age of 19 was implemented in September 2012. These important investments extend the scope of social assistance to low-income workers in the population and shape support options for vulnerable households. Programs that offer benefits to low-income earners working just above income-support-level incomes mediate the effect of the "welfare wall" as they stretch available supports beyond the social assistance system (Torjman and Battle 1993).

Day care

Daycare service eligibility is determined according to the rules of the province's Day Care Assistance Program and is independent of the social assistance rate schedule. Subsidies are paid directly to the daycare centre, and the client is responsible for paying any difference in the cost. Anyone with an annual net family income under $29,000 (not including child tax benefits or HST refunds) qualifies for the maximum subsidy; partial subsidies are awarded for annual family incomes between $29,000 and $54,000. The subsidy is highest for infants under the age of two years, at $28.50 per day. Preschool care for those over two years old may be subsidized up to $24.50 per day, and subsidies for after-school care are up to $12.75 per day. Investments in childcare spaces were made in recent years. As a result of poverty reduction initiatives, the number of spaces in the province increased by 3,802 to 22,587 between March 2010 and February 2013.

Interfaces with the employment insurance (EI) system

Income from other transfer programs can factor into the determination of who is eligible for social assistance, so the larger context of available social transfers influences trends in provincial income replacement and subsidy programs. The interface between the federal EI system and provincial social assistance is an important example. New legislation enacted in January 2013 by the Canadian government clarifies what constitutes a suitable and reasonable job search for EI recipients (Service Canada 2013), which sets up activation measures that may provide provisions for the termination of EI benefits according to citizens' compliance to these participation policies. The interface between social assistance and EI may change depending upon how these measures are enacted on the ground. A further influx of income support cases may occur in the future, if fewer people are able to obtain or maintain federal unemployment benefits. The interface with the EI system will be interesting to monitor in the near future, as laid-off workers from the oilfields of Alberta return to New Brunswick.

The nature and evolution of the SA caseload

The lowest number of cases on income support on record for any given month since the early 1980s was experienced in December 2008, when 22,727 New Brunswick households comprised of 38,201 individuals were obtaining monthly income benefits (see Figure 11.1). The number of New Brunswick households receiving a regular monthly cheque then underwent 40 months of almost steady increases until April 2012, when the number of households grew by 11.6 per cent to 25,372 and the number of individuals within these households increased by 8.0 per cent to 41,269 individuals. That the number of households increased more rapidly than the number of individuals over this time suggests that smaller households were being absorbed into the system.

In the 1990s, the income support caseload in New Brunswick reacted to the recessionary period around 1991–92 by showing year-over-year increases in the average monthly number of cases of between 5 and 9 per cent from 1990 to 1992. Activation measures put in place by the development of a new service delivery model enabled more active policy interventions in the post-1996 period. These new directions in service delivery quelled the potential increases in the number of income support cases that threatened to emerge in response to a decrease in the number of employed New Brunswickers in 2001 (see Figure 11.1).

The impact of the rate increase given to former IAP recipients due to their transfer to the TAP in January 2010, as well as decreases in levels of employment in the province, may have contributed to the year-over-year average increases in the monthly caseload of 5.5 per cent in 2010–11 and 2.2 per cent in 2011–12. Between December 2009 and April 2012, typical

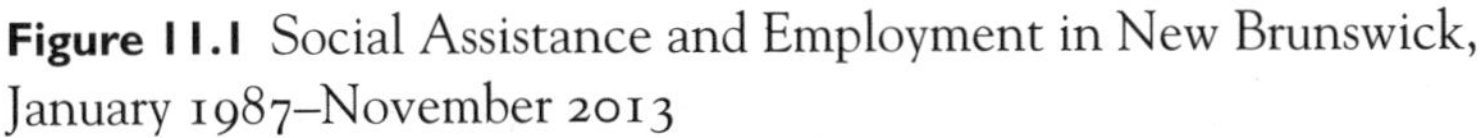

Figure 11.1 Social Assistance and Employment in New Brunswick, January 1987–November 2013

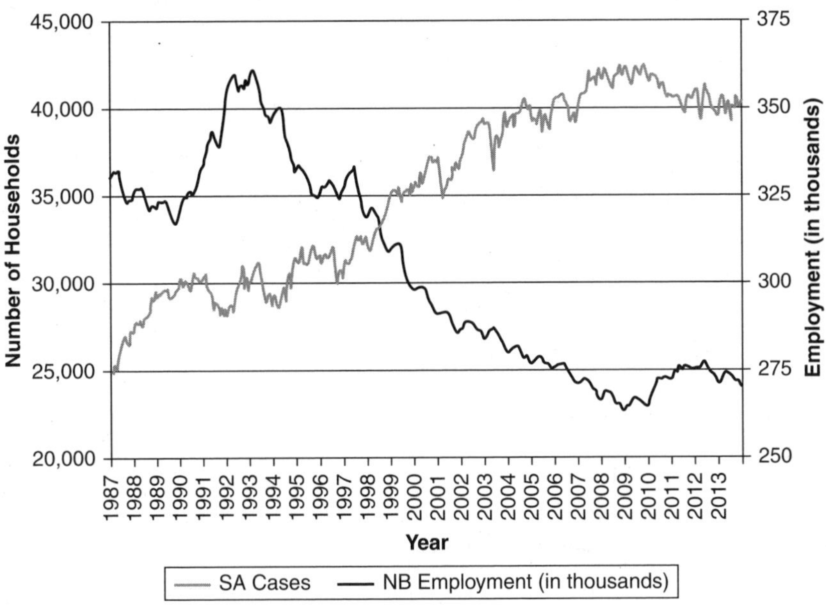

Source: New Brunswick Department of Social Development; Statistics Canada CANSIM (database), *Table 282–0001: Labour Force Survey Estimates (LFS), by Sex and Detailed Age Group, Unadjusted for Seasonality, Monthly (Persons Unless Otherwise Noted).*

summer lows and winter highs were replaced by almost constant month-over-month increases in the number of households receiving income support. Seasonal trends reappeared after April 2012, and, by November 2013, 24,093 households involving 38,560 children, youth, and adults were in receipt of a monthly cheque for income support.

Single persons, disabled or not, are the largest group of clients on income support: they represented almost two-thirds of welfare cases (65.3 per cent) by November 2013. This growth is fuelled by an increase in the number of medically disabled cases, who are mostly single persons.

The share of the overall caseload attributable to certified disabled persons reached a high of 26.2 per cent by November 2008, when the number of households on social assistance was at a record low. Their share stood at 25.5 per cent as of November 2013.

Future evolution and challenges

The New Brunswick caseload has declined significantly since the early 1990s and seems to be relatively stable around the 25,000 household mark. The composition of that caseload keeps evolving, with the proportion of single beneficiaries, disabled or not, on the rise during the last decade. The success of the policy levers being used will depend considerably upon the segment of the social assistance clientele concerned. Though some activation measures may be more appropriate for able-bodied, childless adults, the same measures may have different effects on other client groups. The policy problems related to disabled persons require that we also consider the dignity and social inclusion of these types of social assistance cases. The issue of welfare dependence cannot be explained entirely in economic terms for all categories of clients.

Conclusion

Relief for the poor originally took the form of charity in New Brunswick and was heavily influenced by the British poor law tradition. Progressively (and particularly after the Great Depression), the provincial and federal governments increased their involvement in the support of the poor. In the 1960s, under the Robichaud Liberal provincial government, the social assistance system was centralized at the provincial level. The 1990s witnessed the introduction of the current NB Case computer system.

In recent years, a public engagement exercise led to reforms that had a significant effect on the development of income support policies in New Brunswick. Public engagement leveraged important changes to structural employment barriers including the creation of additional childcare spaces, the extension of health insurance coverage to former recipients now in the labour force, and the reduction of the wage clawback rates for income support recipients. These reform initiatives respect the important contribution of non-economic factors, such as poor health and the presence of children, to the patterns of income support participation in New Brunswick. A comprehensive set of programs designed to mitigate non-economic barriers to employment are available to compliment policy interventions aimed at encouraging full-time labour market participation of individual citizens.

References

Canada Revenue Agency. 2012. *CCTB Calculation Sheet*. Ottawa: CRA. Accessed September 19, 2013. http://www.cra-arc.gc.ca/bnfts/cctb/cctb_clcfrm12-eng.pdf.

New Brunswick. 2009. *Overcoming Poverty Together: The New Brunswick Economic and Social Inclusion Plan*. Fredericton: Communications New Brunswick. Accessed September 19, 2013. http://www.gnb.ca/0017/Promos/0001/pdf/Plan-e.pdf.

New Brunswick Department of Human Resources Development. 1997. *1996–97 Annual Report*. Fredericton: Queen's Printer.

New Brunswick Department of Social Development. 2011. *Annual Report 2010–2011*. Fredericton: Communications New Brunswick.

New Brunswick Department of Social Services. 1978. *1977–78 Annual Report*. Fredericton: Queen's Printer.

New Brunswick Department of Social Services. 1980. *1979–80 Annual Report*. Fredericton: Queen's Printer.

New Brunswick Office of the Auditor General. 1998. *1998 Auditor General's Report*. Fredericton: Auditor General. http://www.gnb.ca/OAG-BVG/1998/1998-e.asp.

Provencher, Ysabel 2004. "L'aide sociale au Nouveau-Brunswick: Évolution historique et perspectives contemporaines." *Canadian Review of Social Policy / Revue canadienne de politique sociale* 54: 18–33.

Service Canada. 2013. *Connecting Canadians with Available Jobs*. IN-473-12-12E. http://www.servicecanada.gc.ca/eng/about/publication/ei/ccaj.pdf.

Statistics Canada. 2013. *2011 Census of Population*. Ottawa: Statistics Canada. http://www12.statcan.gc.ca/census-recensement/2011/dp-pd/index-eng.cfm.

Torjman, Sherri, and Ken Battle. 1993. *Breaking Down the Welfare Wall: Commentary*. Ottawa: Caledon Institute of Social Policy.

twelve

Social Assistance in Nova Scotia: Mainstreaming "Employability" and Cutting Costs in a New Single-Tier System

STELLA LORD

A brief history of welfare in Nova Scotia

Nova Scotia had a two-tier welfare system until 2001 when the Employment Support and Income Assistance (ESIA) Act came into effect. The two-tier system the act replaced divided welfare between municipal assistance for the "able bodied," who were expected to seek employment, and provincial assistance for the disabled and lone parents deemed worthy of longer-term and slightly more financial aid.

Municipal assistance can be traced back to eighteenth- and nineteenth-century poor laws and associated settlement laws that made the indigent poor the responsibility of local authorities, mostly through "indoor relief." Until the Poor Relief Act was abolished in 1958, some municipal poor houses or farms were still in use. After 1967, municipal assistance was cost shared with the province under Canada Assistance Plan (CAP) arrangements, but each municipality set its own welfare rates, which varied significantly. Provincial assistance began with the mothers' allowances and various disability programs developed in the pre- and postwar periods, which, in the post-CAP context, were merged to create provincial social assistance and the Family Benefits program (FB) in 1977 (Blouin 1989, 1992; Fay 2005).

Boychuk (1998) argues that the Family Benefits program (FB) shifted the welfare system from a "market/family enforcement" system characterized by very low welfare rates for both women and men and strict employment requirements to a "conservative" regime that provided slightly better benefits for single mothers with dependent children and more protection from work requirements. Boychuk rightly considers both regimes patriarchal—before CAP, the system reinforced women's dependency on marriage, and after FB, their role in childcare—but protecting lone mothers from employment-seeking requirements was not unreasonable within the context of a labour market marked by discrimination and gender inequality and a gendered social policy regime that provided little affordable, regulated childcare; few skills or job development programs; and weak pay equity legislation. Protection from work requirements was only partial, however.

Once dependent children left school or reached adulthood, single parents were returned to municipal income assistance, which had more strictly enforced employability requirements and lower benefits, at least outside of metropolitan areas (Blouin 1992).

The concept of "vocational rehabilitation" for persons with disabilities had been incorporated within the 1977 Family Benefits Act, and, under pressure from women's organizations, a voluntary career-planning program to assist single mothers to transition to employment developed in the early 1980s. However, a turn towards the market in federal policy after 1985 directed labour market activation, through a new federal-provincial Employability Enhancement Initiative, toward single parents (Federal-Provincial-Territorial (FPT) Conference of Ministers of Social Services 1985). As programs directed to social assistance recipients were implemented under the Canada-Nova Scotia agreement between 1987 and 1996, new employability expectations and practices were gradually integrated within Family Benefits, creating the basis for an employability delivery infrastructure. Labour activation proposals in the 1993–94 federal social security reform initiative helped to develop the knowledge, rationale, and political support required to restructure Nova Scotia's social assistance system (Human Resources Development Canada 1994). In 1994, the Nova Scotia government embarked on a six-year process to harmonize income assistance and create a single-tier welfare system (Lord 2009, 136–81). The demise of CAP, federal cuts to social program transfers, and the shift to block funding in 1996 provided another catalyst for change. Yet it was the development of a system of federal and provincial child benefits that laid the groundwork for regime change based on a universally applied welfare to work principle.

Welfare system restructuring: 1994–2000

Welfare system restructuring occurred in several stages (Lord 2009). Between 1994 and 1998, municipal income assistance delivered to "employable" recipients under more than 50 different municipal policy arrangements was gradually harmonized and put under provincial administration. Benefits were restructured and equalized, resulting in increases for some recipients in municipalities outside of metropolitan Halifax, but decreases in the city itself. After federal and provincial governments agreed to develop the National Child Benefit (NCB) in 1996, the Nova Scotia government began to integrate common employability policies within the newly harmonized Income Assistance (IA) program and the Family Benefit (FB) program. With increased federal investments in the NCB after 1998 and a clever offset arrangement that would enable the province to develop a new Nova Scotia Child Benefit (NSCB), the province began preparing to reform the FB program in 1998 (Nova Scotia Department of Community Services 1998, 1999; Nova Scotia Advisory Council on the Status of Women 1999). By 2000 the province was able to dispense with family benefits and introduce a single-tier system under the ESIA Act (2001) that supported the welfare-to-work principle.

By removing the clawback from federal child benefits (CCTB and NCBS) and adding the NSCB to a package of child benefits for very low-income families, regardless of their source of income, the Nova Scotia government claimed the new ESIA system would "take children off welfare." Though this claim was not strictly true, of course, the income-based arrangement did remove a financial barrier for single parents to move from welfare to work (Lord 2009, 291–373). ESIA regulations were also based on a universal "gender neutral" employability assumption that required participation in transition-to-employment processes as a condition of eligibility, but imposed a two-year limit on participation in educational and skills development programs. Dispensing with the old two-tier welfare system arguably made welfare fairer in that benefits and regulations were the same across the province, but the extent to which the new system improved overall conditions or ensured better outcomes for recipients is highly debatable. Unless a disability prevented employment, regulations imposed employability requirements on single parents with children over the age of one year. Single employable recipients in metropolitan areas and single parents and persons with disabilities previously receiving family benefits experienced benefit reductions that had still not improved in real terms by 2012 (Tweddle, Battle, and Torjman 2013, 26).

Recent developments: 2001–2015

Welfare system restructuring had been contested terrain within and outside the legislature between 1994 and 2000 (Lord 2009). With the erosion of benefits, stricter welfare-to-work rules, and limited educational options to transition to employment, contestation surrounding the Act and ESIA program did not abate after new regulations came into effect in 2001.

Regulations making single parents ineligible for income assistance if they attended postsecondary programs of duration longer than two years (which had been allowed under the FB program) were challenged by women's and student organizations early on. An evaluation of Employment Support Services (ESS) in 2007 also demonstrated that single parents in particular were not benefiting as much as they might from employment services (Goss Gilroy Inc. 2007). As a result, the Nova Scotia Department of Community Services (DCS) introduced Career Seek as a pilot project. This project allowed a limited number of female clients to enroll in certain postsecondary programs of more than two years duration (e.g., business, nursing, social work) as long as they had a viable employment plan and took responsibility for seeking a grant or student loan to cover tuition, books, and childcare. Although uptake has been low, the program was subsequently extended to other marginalized groups, and, at the time of writing, DCS was considering other changes.

Recognizing ESIA should be part of a broader, more holistic approach to poverty after a poverty reduction strategy (PRS) was introduced in Newfoundland and Labrador in 2006, community organizations and the Liberal and NDP opposition parties proposed a similar strategy for Nova Scotia. In October 2007, following a community-based forum on the idea, an ad hoc coalition presented, in a report entitled *Framework for a Poverty Reduction Strategy in Nova Scotia*, several proposals for a PRS, including a liveable income as a long-term goal (Lord, Ross, and Gaunt 2007). In December, the Liberals obtained government support for a working group made up of community, business and labour groups to develop recommendations for such a strategy (e.g., Bill 94, An Act to Establish a Poverty Reduction Working Group in Nova Scotia). The working group's report, submitted to government in June 2008, recommended a comprehensive PRS that included ways to move income assistance away from a system of "last resort," as well as action to improve current ESIA policies (Nova Scotia Poverty Reduction Working Group 2008). Just before a provincial election in April 2009, the government published *Preventing Poverty, Promoting Prosperity* (Nova Scotia Department of Community Services 2009). In this publication, the government promised to consult with stakeholders and to coordinate action on three major poverty reduction goals: enabling and rewarding work, improving support for those in need (including overhauling the welfare system), and acting on issues affecting children.

In April 2009, an NDP government was elected with a large majority. Given that party's opposition to the ESIA Act and support for improving the welfare system while it was out of government, there were high expectations that a more developed PRS which included welfare reform would emerge. Some promising signs surfaced during the early part of the NDP mandate: a poverty reduction coordinator was appointed, an interdepartmental poverty reduction committee co-chaired by the ministers of Community Services and of Higher Education and Workforce Development was established, and the government contributed to a community-led conference on poverty. At the conference, the DCS Minister Denise Peterson-Rafuse stated she intended to move ESIA toward a more respectful, case-based, restorative approach, and officials responded positively to ideas to reduce stereotypes of people living in poverty (Health Promotion Clearinghouse 2011). A comprehensive PRS, however, did not appear. By early 2012, it was clear there had been a retreat from stronger action on poverty reduction and there was seemingly little support within government for improving the ESIA program.

In June 2012, the DCS minister cited growth in expenditures and hinted at system abuse to justify new restrictions within the Special Needs Program, serving to reinforce the negative stereotypes of welfare recipients that government officials had earlier promised to remedy. As these regulation changes worked their way into the department's policy manual, front-line agencies and some physicians registered concerns about the effects on people with chronic illnesses and disabilities (Wuite, Saulnier, and Lord 2013). In the run-up to the 2013 election, the government backed down on some of the regulation changes, and the opposition Liberal party promised to reverse them. Interpretations of the regulations, however, became more restrictive.

Despite failing to strengthen the PRS proposals and the lack of significant improvements to the welfare system, the NDP government did make an effort to *alleviate* poverty over its four-year term (2009–13) especially in ways that encouraged labour market activation.

The Canada-Nova Scotia Agreement on Labour Market Development (Canada 2008) and the Labour Market Agreement (Canada 2009) facilitated the development of somewhat more capacity and flexibility to deliver job readiness and skills development programs for the chronically unemployed, marginalized groups, and persons with disabilities, including those on income assistance.

Beginning in 2010, on recommendations of the Minimum Wage Review Committee, the government agreed to increase the minimum wage through annual increments until it reached the LICO rate for an individual working full time in Sydney. Subsequent increases have been indexed to the cost of living. Subsidized childcare spaces increased, as did the amount and income threshold for the NSCB. An Affordable Living Tax Credit for low- and modest-income families and a Poverty Reduction Tax Credit for individuals on income assistance who had no dependents were introduced in 2011. These latter developments established an important principle because the tax credits are income based and not considered chargeable income for welfare purposes. Moreover, recipients may continue to benefit if they leave IA as long as income remains below the established income thresholds—admittedly very low in the case of the Poverty Reduction Tax Credit and the NSCB in particular.

Some modest improvements were also made to the ESIA program. The flat-rate earnings exemption increased from $150 to $300 for those in the

Table 12.1 Comparison of Nova Scotia Welfare Incomes with Various Income Measures

	Single Employable	Person with Disability	Single Parent, One Child	Couple, Two Children
Total Welfare Incomes	$7,316	$9,970	$15,916	$22,554
LICO	$16,573	$16,573	$20,170	$31,335
Poverty Gap	$-9,437	$-6,603	$-4,254	$-8,781
Welfare Income as % of LICO	43.1	60.2	78.9	72.0
MBM	$16,804	$16,804	$23,764	$33,608
Poverty Gap	$-9,259	$-7,223	$-6,242	$-11,901
Welfare Income as % of MBM	42.3	55.0	72.5	63.3

Source: Tweddle, Battle, and Torjman (2013, Tables 3, 4, 5, and 6).

Support for Persons with Disabilities program and from $100 to $150 for all other IA recipients. Allowable cash asset levels doubled to $1,000, making eligibility for welfare slightly easier, and, between 2009 and 2013, the personal allowance increased by 22 per cent—though there has been no increase in the shelter allowance since 2001 (Nova Scotia 2013). Despite these measures, real welfare incomes stagnated in part due to increases in housing, energy, and food costs. In 2012, these incomes remained below recognized measures of poverty (see Table 12.1).

Though the government's record on poverty reduction was only one of several contributing factors, in October 2013, the NDP experienced a humiliating defeat at the polls and a Liberal government came into power. Just 18 months into their term, it is perhaps too early to fully assess the current government's record on poverty reduction and welfare policy, but the government's austerity measures froze DCS funding two years in a row. This has resulted in significant cuts to community organizations and no increases in welfare benefits or tax credits for the poor in either the 2014 or 2015 budgets. Given a recently announced benefits review, a three-year ESIA transformation process, and changes to the department's administration and operations structure, early indications are that the government will continue to focus on system changes that seek to reduce the caseload by removing financial barriers to employment and through service-based labour market activation protocols that take a more pro-active case management approach.

Institutional features of the ESIA program in Nova Scotia

The legislative authority for the welfare system in Nova Scotia is found in both the Employment Support and Income Assistance Act (2000), officially called "An Act to Encourage the Attainment of Independence and Self-Sufficiency through Employment Support and Income Assistance," and the ESIA regulations (effective August 1, 2001 and revised March 12, 2007). The purpose of the act is "to provide for the assistance of persons in need and, in particular, to facilitate their movement toward independence and self-sufficiency" (ESIA Act, Article 1).

Aims and values

The aims of the ESIA Act and regulations have been translated into value statements, objectives, and operating principles in an ESIA policy manual that guides administration of the program. It states that "employment support and income assistance must be effective, efficient, integrated, coordinated and financially and administratively accountable" (Nova Scotia Department of Community Services 2013, 10). In its details, it illustrates the tension and contradictions between real income requirements and actual provision based on "need," and between human service and regulatory enforcement. These inconsistencies are typical of income assistance programs that view poverty and "need" as temporary phenomena to be rectified primarily through the labour market. There is, therefore, no statement of the causes of poverty, but it is clearly not viewed as a failure of public policy.

Although the policy manual recognizes that some require assistance to develop the skills and abilities necessary for economic and community participation "so far as it is reasonable for them to do so," overarching program values stress full participation and achieving economic independence through employment (10). At the same time, "the principle of need must be paramount in determining eligibility," and the program should "strive to provide . . . a level of assistance adequate to meet basic needs for shelter, food, clothing and personal care" (12). Yet addressing poverty should not be the responsibility solely of government; this responsibility should be shared with individuals, the community, and the private sector. Indeed, guidelines state that "income assistance must be combined with other forms of assistance to provide effectively for Nova Scotians in need," a statement that is perhaps intended to support a "charity model," which has strong roots in Nova Scotia (10).

Service delivery arrangements and operating principles

All policies, benefits, and programs apply provincially (see Table 12.2) and the provincial head office is responsible for policy and program development, service standardization, and monitoring. Day-to-day administration, however, is through regional offices, which provide coordination and oversight for district and local satellite offices that managed cases at a local level. Until April 2015, when several administrative and operational changes were announced, there were 4 regional offices and 36 district and satellite offices. In an effort to reduce costs, streamline services, and strengthen central reporting, several local offices have been closed or hours reduced, regional offices have been reduced to three, and the emphasis for managers is to shift away from case management toward service delivery and provider relationships (Hartwell, 2015).

As the name of the program implies, IA and ESS are currently organized as separate divisions. In large regions, such as the central region (which includes the Halifax Regional Municipality), ESS staff members are separate from IA staff, but, in some regions, staff may have responsibility for both IA and ESS clients. Interpretation of regulations and policies and access to programs have varied somewhat on a divisional, regional, or even local basis. This variation has been identified as a problem by DCS, especially in regard to clients with special needs. This discretionary policy is likely to change under the new administration and operations regime.

ESIA operating principles state that decision making should be at the point of client contact and ensure client confidentiality. The aim is to have understandable rules that treat clients "with compassion and respect" and to administer these in the "least intrusive and non-judgmental manner" (13). The program should provide "fair and responsive services" that take account of systemic barriers and socioeconomic disadvantages related to disability, racism, sexism, and agism (12). Clients should also be informed of their rights and obligations, including their responsibility to provide information and pursue other sources of support. Principles also mention employee training and a supportive work environment, as well as the need to coordinate with other government departments and community-based organizations to link recipients to programs and services (Nova Scotia Department of Community Services 2013, see policies 2.1.1–2.1.11).

Employment support services

Given the emphasis on moving recipients into employment, IA applicants and spouses are required to undergo an employability assessment as a condition of eligibility at intake and, unless excused due to disability, to engage in the development of an employability plan. The plan establishes goals for participation in employment services, which are administered by the ESS division. ESS assists clients to access services and programs aimed at achieving employment or enhancing employability and quality of life.

The strong employment requirements are somewhat mitigated by the definition of "employability"; by the factors that need to be taken into account to assist a person to become more self-sufficient or employable; by the resources in the community; and by the availability of transportation, childcare, and personal supports (Nova Scotia Department of Community Services 2013, see policy 4.1.1).

Services are provided by DCS itself or by an approved service provider and may include assistance with job searches, resume writing, and job preparation; employment referrals and entry supports or placements; personal development (to facilitate progressions to self-sufficiency); work or volunteer experiences in the community; or referrals to address life and health situations. Under certain circumstances, participants may attend educational upgrading to attain grade 12, take a core job-training program of up to two years at the Nova Scotia Community College (Educate to Work), or, if eligible, participate in two or more years of postsecondary education through the Career Seek program (Table 12.2).

Welfare incomes

With the emphasis on employability has come a trend toward supplementing low incomes, regardless of their source, through fully refundable tax credits or benefits. As non-chargeable income for welfare purposes, this facilitates transitions from welfare to work. Though income supplementation is also a way for governments to keep basic welfare benefits low (see Table 12.2), refundable tax credits, if indexed to inflation, have several positive elements. As they are delivered through the tax system rather than the welfare system, they are not subject to the same intrusive protocols as welfare and could be considered entitlements. They could also make increases to welfare incomes more palatable and reduce the potential political exploitation of divisions between the working and non-working poor.

In Nova Scotia, all IA recipients are eligible for the income-based Nova Scotia Affordable Living Tax Credit (NSALTC), which, in 2013–14, provided a base amount of $255 per annum for individuals and couples and of $60 for each child. Low-income people without dependents and incomes below $12,000 are also eligible for the Nova Scotia Poverty Reduction Tax Credit (NSPRTC) of $250 per annum. Payments of both tax credits

Table 12.2 Main Regulatory Components of the Nova Scotia ESIA Program

Component	Policy
Eligibility Requirements (policies 4.4.1, 5.1.1, 7.3.1)	Nineteen years of age or older or 16 to 18 if unable to reside in parental home. Present in province at time of application. Deemed "in need" as determined by budget deficit (present if chargeable income less than budgetary allowances defined in regulations). Some income is non-chargeable but applicants must pursue NCB, CCTB, WITB, and all other feasible sources of income; provide required documentation to substantiate need; and applicant and spouse must participate in employability assessment. Applicants attending or returning to postsecondary education not eligible. Exceptions if approved under the Labour Market Agreement for Persons with Disabilities (LMAPWD) and Career Seek after six months on IA (policy 7.3.2).
Participation in Employability Assessments and Programs (policies 5.1.5, 5.1.6, 5.1.7)	Refusal to participate in employability assessment results in refusal of assistance. If deemed employable, must sign "Understanding of Participation in Employability Activity" form; participation in designated employment-related activities required for ongoing IA eligibility. Medical documentation may be required when applicant or spouse indicates that a disability or illness limits ability to participate. Applicant or spouse may be required to participate in case planning if potential for employment exists or if involvement in employment services would increase self-reliance.
Basic Benefits (policy 5.5.1)	Personal allowance (food, household items, clothes, energy costs, and other living requirements): Adult = $255 ($150 if in hospital for 30 days or more; $81 if in residential rehabilitation program). Dependent children are assumed to be covered by NSCB and NCB. If not in receipt of these, allowance is $133 for child under 18 and $255 for child aged 18 to 20. Shelter allowance (rent or own home) is determined by family size: 1 = $300; 2 = $570; 3 or more = $620.
Shelter Allowance in Some Circumstances (policy 4.1a)	Shelter allowance of up to $535 may be allowed for a single person who 1) is disabled; 2) is fleeing an abusive situation; 3) has a chronic mental, cognitive, or physical condition that limits participation in employment services and is 55 years of age or over; and 4) is a youth aged 16 to 18.
Retention of Wages (policies 5.8.1, 5.8.2)	Employed recipient or spouse can retain the first $150 plus 30 per cent of net wages. A person whose physical, mental, or cognitive abilities may limit financial self-sufficiency and is engaged in supported employment may retain the first $300 plus 30 per cent of remaining net wages. Recipient or spouse participating in seasonable horticulture may retain up to $3,000 combined income per fiscal year (April 1–March 31).

(Continued)

Table 12.2 (Continued)

Component	Policy
ESIA Pharmacare; Transitional Pharmacare; Low Income Pharmacare for Children (policies 9.1.4, 9.1.5)*	Recipient, spouse, and dependents may access ESIA Pharmacare if without access to public or private drug plan. Flat co-pay fee of $5 per prescription unless eligible for exemption. Only medications and supplies approved and in the Nova Scotia Formulary are considered. Transitional Pharmacare may be provided for one year if recipient ineligible due to transitioning to employment. May request activation within one year of leaving assistance. Other conditions same as ESIA Pharmacare. Low Income Pharmacare for Children may be provided to families eligible for the Nova Scotia Child Benefit. Other conditions are the same as for ESIA.
Special Needs for Medical and Employment Expenses	May cover medical needs not covered by MSI (medical equipment and some dental, vision, and foot care); special diets (up to maximum of $150 a month); and bus passes for medical appointments. Medical verification may be required. Covered are eligible expenses associated with working or looking for work (childcare, transportation, work clothes, tools, etc.).

Source: Nova Scotia (2013).
* Extended Pharmacare was discontinued on December 15, 2014. Existing beneficiaries of the program were grandfathered as long as they remained eligible. Others previously eligible would be referred to the Health Department's Family Pharmacare, which involves income-based deductibles and co-pays. The Extended Pharmacare Program provided Pharmacare if total chargeable income exceeded total allowable expenses or a budget deficit existed when average monthly drug costs were included as expense.

are made four times a year. Those with dependents also receive the Nova Scotia Child Benefit (NSCB). This benefit is issued monthly with the National Child Benefit (NCB). Table 12.3 illustrates the income effects in select cases.

The nature and evolution of the caseload

The income assistance caseload traditionally varies with the unemployment rate, which, besides the general state of the Canadian economy, has historically been affected by the seasonality of employment in Nova Scotia. In the late 1980s and early 1990s, a general economic downturn was exacerbated by a significant decline of the ground fishery. As in other provinces, Nova Scotia also had relatively high numbers of lone mothers on income assistance. In March 1995, the total estimated SA caseload stood at 104,000, the highest in Atlantic Canada (National Council of Welfare 2005). The decline in the total caseload and the percentage of

Table 12.3 Total Welfare Incomes in Select Cases in Nova Scotia, 2012

	Single Employable	Person with Disability	Single Parent, One Child	Couple, Two Children
Basic Social Assistance	$6,402	$9,222	$9,642	$13,044
Additional SA Benefits				$150*
Federal Child Benefits			$4,734	$6,819
Provincial/Territorial Child Benefits			$584	$1,390
GST Credits	$257	$271	$648	$783
Provincial Tax Credits	$477	$477	$309	$368
Total Income	$7,136	$9,970	$15,916	$22,554

Source: Tweddle, Battle, and Torjman (2013).
Note: Increases in personal allowances and the NS Child Benefit in July 2012 have been prorated.
* Assumes one 10-year-old and one 15-year-old child, so School Supplies Supplement applies.

Table 12.4 ESIA Average Monthly Caseload in Select Fiscal Years by Family Composition

Family Composition	2000–01	2004–05	2008–09	2012–13
Single, no children (%)	18,049 (49.8)	19,629 (60.9)	18,189 (66.9)	20,113 (69.1)
Single, with children (%)	13,347 (36.9)	8,502 (26.4)	6,031 (22.2)	6,092 (20.9)
Couple, no children (%)	2,080 (5.7)	2,138 (6.6)	1,723 (6.3)	1,578 (5.4)
Couple, with children (%)	2,732 (7.5)	2,136 (6.6)	1,256 (4.6)	1,308 (4.5)
Total	36,209	32,245	27,199	29,091

Source: Nova Scotia Department of Community Services. Data acquired in 2013 from the DCS Policy, Planning and Research Branch on request from author.

single parents on welfare after 2001 (see Table 12.4) suggests that the new "gender neutral" system and stricter regulations and employability requirements have had an impact. Women have disproportionately been clients of ESS, and single parents appear to have been targeted for labour market activation. Because more than 85 per cent of single parents in Nova Scotia are women, it should be noted that this strategy has aligned with the expansion of relatively low-paying jobs in the service and personal care sectors—jobs typically performed by women. Though the numbers are smaller, a similar relative decline is evident for two-parent families with dependent children, but the decline has been somewhat less for couples with no dependents. Similar reductions have not occurred for those who are single and without dependents; their numbers have remained relatively stable and increased after 2008–09. In 2012–13, they represented 69.1 per cent of the caseload, compared with 49.8 per cent in 2000–01.

The introduction of more income-based tax credits and of more supports through transitional and extended Pharmacare, childcare subsidies, and job-development programs, as well as the gradual increase in the minimum wage, has likely contributed to the increase in single parents transitioning from welfare to work since 2001.

Disability cross-cuts all family types, so caseload statistics no longer treat "disabled" as a category. Disability, however, is recorded at intake for the purposes of assessing employability. Though the nature of their disabilities is not known, in October 2013, 12,134 clients (about 40 per cent of the caseload) reported some kind of disability. The high number of applicants citing disabilities is consistent with the relatively high percentage of persons with disabilities in the province and with the aging of the Nova Scotia population. There are also anecdotal reports that some recipients considered marginally employable may be encouraged to report a disability so they are eligible for the higher shelter allowance. Despite recent attempts to improve employability, the number of persons with disabilities on income assistance is likely to remain high unless employers improve workplace accommodations.

The future evolution of social assistance in Nova Scotia

The 2001 ESIA Act, the shift toward a single-tier system, stronger employability policies, and the introduction of supports such as transitional Pharmacare and subsidized childcare have institutionalized labour market activation as the organizing principle of the Nova Scotia welfare system. Including low-income people and families in tax measures such as the NCB, the NSCB, and, more recently, the Nova Scotia Affordability Tax Credit, regardless of whether their incomes are from low-paying jobs or social assistance, has also been tailored to foster employment. At the same time, low earnings disregards and high clawback rates continue to be barriers to supplementing welfare income through contract or part-time employment.

The ESS program and federal-provincial labour market agreements have supported the expansion of educational upgrading and other interventions, so more people—especially single parents—have been able to move off assistance more quickly than in the past, but there is no data on how many return. Meanwhile, some programs for IA recipients funded under federal-provincial labour market agreements were cut in 2014 as a result of new federal job-training priorities under the Jobs Grant program, access to two-year skills development through Educate to Work is rationed, and longer postsecondary education through Career Seek is restricted. If these latter programs were mainstreamed and restrictions lifted, more people could reap long-term benefits. More viable transitions to employment are also hampered by the limited available subsidized childcare spaces, high unemployment rates, low wages, and the low-income ceiling for NSCB eligibility.

As in other provinces, welfare in Nova Scotia has always been a political football, and welfare recipients have, at times, been stigmatized by some politicians and in the media. This has not changed. When he was leader of the opposition, the current Liberal premier of Nova Scotia was an advocate for poverty reduction but with a commitment to balance the budget and reduce the deficit through austerity measures, the development of a comprehensive PRS is definitely on the back-burner. Though the income ceiling for NS Child Benefit eligibility increased in 2014, welfare incomes have been frozen for two years. As it moves forward with the benefit review and system transformation in a context of austerity, all indications are that the main purpose of the changes is to cut welfare costs and strengthen the welfare-to-work model. It is uncertain at this stage to what extent the government will do this through positive measures, such as adding improved employment incentives, enhancing refundable tax credits, and improving employment supports, or through more cuts and punitive measures. Although the benefit review has been welcomed by poverty activists, as Kneebone and White (in this volume) demonstrate, welfare incomes have declined in real terms since the early 1990s, and it will require significant investment to improve the situation. Indeed, as the 2012 report of the Nova Scotia Participatory Food Costing Project (2013) demonstrates, income assistance recipients experience significant budgetary deficits in relation to real living costs, and many must depend on food banks because personal allowances to cover food go to higher rents and energy costs.

Though the government is tackling long waiting lists for the Support for Persons with Disabilities program and there have been rumours that DCS might develop a disability allowance, some advocates are concerned that categorization could lead to intrusive regulations regarding medical certification. Shifting the benefit system toward tax benefits to create a basic income has the potential to reduce intrusiveness and remove the stigma associated with the bureaucratic rules, regulations, and control welfare exerts over people's lives (Citizens for Public Justice 2008; Young and Mulvale 2009). In spite of growing interest within the welfare advocacy community about the potential of the upcoming benefit review, in a process driven by cost savings, the devil will lie in the details. Moreover, unless there is increased investment on the part of the federal government, speculation about a broader approach that could benefit all low-income people is unlikely to be realized.

Indeed, it must be remembered that, in the welfare field, changes for the better (and more recently for the worse) have, since the 1960s, largely been driven by federal intervention. The federal cuts to welfare, the shift to the block-funded Canada Social Transfer (CST) after 1995, and the abandonment of the national childcare program after 2001 reduced resources and served to hinder positive income assistance reform in Nova Scotia. Limiting the CST to a 3 per cent yearly increase, the new per-capita funding formula for health care based on GDP, and the loss of funds under federal-provincial labour market agreements will further strain provincial resources for social programs. Fiscal pressures, austerity measures, population aging and decline, and persistently high levels of unemployment could lead to further pressures on the program, as well as offloading to the non-profit sector. Despite what appears to be a growing awareness and concern about poverty at the community level, restraining welfare incomes and tightening welfare-to-work regulations, while recipients are left without the support they need to transition into or re-enter viable jobs in the labour market, could become the order of the day. This scenario does not augur well for the prospect of progressive social assistance policy in Nova Scotia.

References

Blouin, Barbara. 1989. *Women and Children Last: Lone Mothers on Welfare in Nova Scotia*. Halifax: Women's Action Coalition of Nova Scotia and the Institute for the Study of Women, Mount Saint Vincent University.

Blouin, Barbara. 1992. *Below the Bottom Line: The Unemployed and Welfare in Nova Scotia*. Halifax: Nova Scotia Association of Social Workers.

Boychuk, Gerard. 1998. *Patchworks of Purpose: The Development of Provincial Social Assistance Regimes in Canada*. Montréal: McGill-Queen's University Press.

Canada. 2008. *Canada-Nova Scotia Agreement on Labour Market Development*. Ottawa: Government of Canada.

Canada. 2009. *Canada-Nova Scotia Labour Market Agreement*. Ottawa: Government of Canada.

Canada-Nova Scotia. 1987. *Letter of Understanding on Enhancing the Employability of Social Assistance Recipients*. Ottawa: Government of Canada.

Citizens for Public Justice. 2008. *Towards a Guaranteed Liveable Income*. Ottawa: Citizens for Public Justice.

Fay, Jeanne. 2005. "The 'Right Kind' of Single Mothers: Nova Scotia's Regulation of Women on Social Assistance, 1956–1977." In *Mothers of the Municipality: Women, Work, and Social Policy in Post-1945 Halifax*, ed. Judith Findgard and Janet Guildford, 141–68. Toronto: University of Toronto Press.

Federal-Provincial-Territorial (FPT) Conference of Ministers of Social Services. 1985. *Agreement Regarding Enhancing the Employment Opportunities for Social Assistance Recipients*. Ottawa: Government of Canada.

Goss Gilroy Inc. 2007. *Evaluation of Employment Support Services: Final Report*. Prepared for the Policy, Planning and Research/Employment Support Services, Department of Community Services, Government of Nova Scotia. Ottawa: Goss Gilroy Inc. http://www.novascotia.ca/coms/department/documents/ESS-Goss-Gilroy-Evaluation-2007.pdf.

Hartwell, Lynn. 2015. Department of Community Services. Address to Staff. https://www.youtube.com/watch?t=15&V=1cqLV1iV-8U.

Health Promotion Clearinghouse. 2011. *Building Wellbeing and Prosperity Together: Taking Action on Poverty*. Halifax: Health Promotion Clearinghouse.

Human Resources Development Canada. 1994. *Agenda–Jobs and Growth: Improving Social Security in Canada, A Discussion Paper*. Ottawa: Government of Canada.

Lord, Stella. 2009. "The Politics and Processes of Social Assistance Gender Regime Change in Nova Scotia: From Voluntary 'Rehabilitation' to Compulsory 'Employability,' 1980–2011." PhD diss., Carleton University.

Lord, Stella, Rene Ross, and Lorely Gaunt, eds. 2007. *Framework for a Poverty Reduction Strategy in Nova Scotia*. Halifax: Nova Scotia Poverty Reduction Strategy Coalition.

National Council of Welfare. 2005. *Welfare Incomes 2004*. Ottawa: Government of Canada.

Nova Scotia. 2013. *Poverty Reduction Actions and Initiatives*. Halifax: Government of Nova Scotia. http://www.novascotia.ca/coms/poverty/.

Nova Scotia Advisory Council on the Status of Women. 1999. *Rebuilding the System: Response of the NS Advisory Council on the Status of Women to the Department of Community Services' Social Assistance Restructuring Initiative*. Halifax: Council on the Status of Women.

Nova Scotia Department of Community Services. 1998. *Rebuilding the System: A Discussion Paper*. Halifax: Government of Nova Scotia.

Nova Scotia Department of Community Services. 1999. *Rebuilding the System: Progress Report*. Halifax: Government of Nova Scotia.

Nova Scotia Department of Community Services. 2009. *Preventing Poverty, Promoting Prosperity*. Halifax: Government of Nova Scotia.

Nova Scotia Department of Community Services. 2013. *Employment Support and Income Assistance (ESIA) Policy Manual*. Halifax: Government of Nova Scotia.

Nova Scotia Participatory Food Costing Project. 2013. *Can Nova Scotians Afford to Eat Healthy? Report on 2012 Participatory Food Costing*. Halifax: Mount Saint Vincent University.

Nova Scotia Poverty Reduction Working Group. 2008. *Report of the Poverty Reduction Working Group*. Halifax: Department of Community Services.

Tweddle, Anne, Ken Battle, and Sherri Torjman. 2013. *Welfare in Canada 2012*. Ottawa: Caledon Institute of Social Policy. http://www.caledoninst.org/Publications/PDF/1031ENG.pdf.

Wuite, Sara, Christine Saulnier, and Stella Lord. 2013. *Cornerstone Compromised: A Critical Analysis of Changes to Special Needs Assistance in Nova Scotia*. Halifax: Canadian Centre for Policy Alternatives–Nova Scotia.

Young, Margot, and James P. Mulvale. 2009. *Possibilities and Prospects: The Debate Over a Guaranteed Income*. Halifax: Canadian Centre for Policy Alternatives–Nova Scotia.

thirteen
Social Assistance in Newfoundland and Labrador

MATTHIEU MONDOU

Introduction

The place of social assistance and of social protection more generally is particularly central in Newfoundland's society and history. Composed of "outport" fishing communities on an island isolated from the British or Canadian "mainland," Newfoundland has had to cope with more than its fair share of hard times. Communities and households were the primary source of assistance in this setting, until the people of Newfoundland voted with a small plurality to join the Canadian federation in the hope of raising their standard of living.

The story of welfare reform in Newfoundland is, in fact, a series of failed attempts to improve standards of living through industrialization and economic modernization. Surprisingly, the story ends with a success. This chapter will start with an overview of the history of social assistance in the province, focusing on the period starting in 1949, when Newfoundland joined the Canadian federation, up to the global financial crisis in 2008–09.[1] The following section will describe the social assistance programs and services, their evolution, as well as their guiding values. The last section will examine the reasons for the recent revival of the welfare state in Newfoundland and conclude on the challenges ahead.

A brief history of social assistance in Newfoundland

Historically, the evolution of welfare in Newfoundland has been linked to two main factors: global economic shifts in the resource sector and changing federal-provincial relationships.

The relationship between the welfare of the people of Newfoundland and the waning global economic demand for commodities that they produce was evident even before Newfoundland became part of Canada. During the Great Depression, Newfoundland was particularly hurt by the

1 For a rendition of pre-1949 politics see Noel (1971); Dyck (1996, 58–62).

collapse in the demand for fish. It was estimated that between one-quarter and one-third of the people of Newfoundland received in-kind public relief during that period (Dyck 1996, 59–60; Overton 2000, 4). The sole reliance on fisheries to secure the economic subsistence of the population naturally brought the will to diversify and modernize the economy. Newfoundland's belated and reluctant joining of the Canadian federation was, in many ways, linked to this political project. Newfoundland's champion of the "pro-Confederation" campaign, Joey Smallwood, explicitly connected his successful bid to the idea that social welfare and the potential for industrialization would increase after union with Canada. A Liberal, Smallwood sold the fact that, as Canadians, Newfoundlanders would enjoy the advantages of the Canadian family allowance, unemployment insurance, and the old age pension (Dyck 1996, 61; Summers 2001, 27). Premier Smallwood's (1949–72) economic modernization initiatives were, however, fraught with rampant clientelism and marked by repeated failures. Nonetheless, social policies expanded in the new Canadian province during Smallwood's time as premier, as cash benefits were given to vulnerable populations such as the elderly and mothers. The general push had the effect of moving the province's economy toward a cash economy, as opposed to a credit and barter economy based on seasonal fishing (Hardy-Cox 1997). A provincial ministry of public welfare was created, and, in 1949, several provincial social laws were passed: the Mothers' Allowances Act, the Dependents' Allowances Act, and the Disabled Persons' Act. The provincial programs included Old Age Assistance, the Blind Persons Allowance, and Relief to Persons with Disabilities. Social coverage was thus substantially increased, notably for people with disabilities and for women, including lone mothers and divorced women—an innovation for which women mobilized (Hudson 2013, 351; Locke and Rowe 2009, 7–9; McGrath 1996).

When the Conservatives came to power in 1972, the province's civil service was reformed in an effort to move away from Smallwood's patronage style. In this context, several transitions happened, which affected the way social policies were implemented. The province's social assistance program was formalized in the 1977 Social Assistance Act. Provincial social assistance moved from in-kind benefits in the form of food, housing, clothes, and fuel vouchers, to cash benefits (Locke and Rowe 2009, 17; McGrath 1996). Also, social assistance started moving toward what would today be called an "active labour market" type of policy. Recipients were offered basic skills training and massively referred to federal "make work" programs. These federally funded work opportunities provided short-term employment income but, more crucially, created unemployment insurance eligibility (Human Resources Development Canada and Newfoundland and Labrador 1996, 3–4; Locke and Rowe 2009, 17). The scheme, combined with a boom in the fisheries due to Canada's 1977 unilateral declaration of an Atlantic fisheries management zone of 200 nautical miles (Summers 2001, 36), had the effect of substantially reducing provincial social assistance caseloads in the late 1970s.

The 1980s and early 1990s were marked by an attempt to reorient social assistance toward the "pre-Confederation era" value of self-reliance and to steer growth strategies toward regional development. Under both Conservative and Liberal governments, social benefits and public services were scaled down because of budgetary constraints (Hudson and Close 2011; Overton 2000; Summers 2001, 41). Budgetary pressures were mounting throughout the 1980s, as overfishing had depleted the stocks. The pressures culminated in 1992 when the cod moratorium was declared by the federal government. This declaration single-handedly caused between 30,000 and 40,000 workers to lose their jobs—in a province with a population of 580,000 at the time[2] (Locke and Rowe 2009, 20–28; Newfoundland and Labrador Statistics Agency 2013; Summers 2001, 41).

The province's 1986 Royal Commission on Employment and Unemployment (RCEU) did not put on white gloves when it pointed at the province's economic and unemployment problems. Its report suggested tripartite (government-business-labour) consultation and regional labour market boards, recommendations that continued the push toward the active labour market policies initiated in the 1970s (Mondou 2009, 29). It also reaffirmed the principle of self-reliance. This self-help vision entailed encouraging the household production of goods. Logging, hunting, and growing vegetables in "outport communities" were seen as ways to supplement seasonal work and reduce existing state assistance (Hudson and Close 2011, 80). This orientation was formalized in the 1990 reform of the Social Assistance Act, which contained restrictive eligibility definitions as well as penalty and offence provisos.

In the 1990s under a Liberal government and the early 2000s under a Conservative government, attempts from the provincial government to scale down social benefits prompted a response from the community sector.

The first opening for the community sector in social policymaking happened in 1993. Pursuing its vision of local "economic recovery," the Liberal government wished to create an "economic infrastructure" through its 1992

2 Incidentally, the population of the province has since declined to approximately 527,000 persons in 2013.

Strategic Economic Plan. However, government reformers, in their desire to "flatten and lighten" organizational structures, were at odds with the labour movement and the civil service (House 1999). Government plans were counterbalanced by the community sector's call for a complementary "social infrastructure." Liberal Premier Clyde Wells (1989–96) responded by initiating consultations with the community sector in 1993 through his announcement of a Strategic Social Plan. It was not until 1996 when the Social Policy Advisory Committee (SPAC), an independent board composed of community organization representatives, was charged with the task of running a province-wide consultation that the idea of social planning really started to materialize.[3] Based on the SPAC's recommendation, new Liberal Premier Brian Tobin (1996–2000) created the Premier's Council on Social Development (PCSD) to implement the "social infrastructure" vision that had been approved by his predecessor. The PCSD was widely acknowledged by government and community sector participants alike as an "extremely successful experiment in participation" (Woodford 2006, 232). Although the concrete social policy outputs of this turn toward community-sector policymaking participation were meagre, it brought a sea change in terms of social policy thinking (Mondou 2009, 30–34; see also Mondou and Montpetit 2010).

In parallel, the promise of revenues from offshore oil drilling was starting to materialize. Newfoundlanders were naturally skeptical of the project, having seen past economic failures; but it seemed that, this time, they would "get it right" and reap the benefits of their efforts. Progressive Conservative prime ministerial candidate Brian Mulroney had struck an election campaign deal with Conservative Premier Brian Peckford (1979–89) to share the management and revenues of offshore oil drilling with the province, a deal that materialized in 1988 (Dyck 1996, 71; Summers 2001, 38). In 1997, the first oil well, Hibernia, started commercial production. Since then, oil production has soared, and oil prices were high and rising throughout the 2000–08 period, creating a massive source of revenue for the province (Canada–Newfoundland and Labrador Offshore Petroleum Board 2014). According to the Canadian Association of Petroleum Producers, oil and gas constituted 31 per cent of government revenues in 2009–10 and 34 per cent of provincial GDP between 2004 and 2009 (CAPP 2010).

3 Former Premier Kathy Dunderdale (2010–14) was at the time active within community organizations involved in the process.

Newfound oil prosperity: A recent turn in the history of social assistance

Confident that oil revenues would grow in the future, Conservative premiership candidate Danny Williams pledged in 2003 that, in 10 years, he would move the province from the one with the most poverty to the one with the least poverty. The first two years of the Williams government (2003–10) were marked by confrontation with the labour movement and civil service over substantial cuts in departmental budgets and increased user fees. As oil production started to become substantial, and as protests accumulated, culminating in a civil service strike and blockades of the provincial legislature and of the island's harbours, the premier changed target and decided to confront Ottawa (Hudson 2013, 359–61; Marland 2010). His gambit to slash the provincial bureaucracy and cooperate with Conservatives in Ottawa had failed. The Harper minority federal government could not deliver on its promise of excluding oil revenues from the interprovincial equalization formula. Williams doubled down by swapping allies and adversaries. Williams organized a vigorous ABC (Anything But Conservatives) campaign against the federal government and practically galvanized the whole province. During this process in which the provincial government was rallying support at home, the community sector secured input on social policymaking. Although community actors were uncertain about whether they were better off collaborating with the government or keeping a critical distance, in the end, most of them decided to collaborate. They wanted to move beyond a window-dressing role and offer real input in social policymaking (Hudson 2013, 354–64).

The new role for the community sector had a powerful effect on social assistance. The values of the community sector were embedded in social legislation starting in the early 2000s. In particular, the preamble of the Income and Employment Support Act of 2002 clearly exhibits the trace of community-sector mobilization, as the next section shows (Hudson 2013; Woodford 2006, 233). Also, the regulations ancillary to the 2002 act substituted the restrictive definitions of eligibility of the 1990 Social Assistance Act for more generous provisions. The 2002 legislative reform was the culmination of a review process of the province's social security program (called Social Assistance initially and then Income Support). This review was undertaken in the late 1990s. More concrete social policy gains followed in the form of a "Poverty Reduction Strategy," adopted unanimously by the Newfoundland and Labrador House of Assembly in 2006. The plan substantially increased the rate and coverage of social assistance, as well as those of other low-income benefits. It created benefits for "active" recipients who enter education or training programs or find a job. An important budgetary item of the strategy was the increase in coverage of the province's prescription drug program to include social assistance recipients and low-income households. In line with a general movement in the Canadian provinces, the plan announced the government's intention to raise the minimum wage in progressive stages. Adult basic education, abuse prevention centres, and women centres were also better funded.

Institutional architecture and the evolution of the social assistance caseload

The recent opening for the community sector in social policymaking layered a more generous coat onto an otherwise minimal core of provincial welfare institutions. The preamble of the 2002 Income and Employment Support Act—the legislation regulating social assistance in the province—illustrates this layering in the statement of the act's objectives:

WHEREAS the promotion of self-reliance and well-being, participation in community life and the alleviation of poverty are social policy goals;

AND WHEREAS the delivery of income and employment support programs shall respect the dignity and privacy of the individual and be equitable, accessible, co-ordinated, and fiscally responsible;

AND WHEREAS people encounter circumstances that affect their self-reliance and may require income support to assist with meeting their basic needs;

AND WHEREAS people may benefit from a variety of supports and services to help develop the skills and abilities necessary to prepare for, access, and keep employment;

AND WHEREAS it is recognized that persons with disabilities face unique barriers to employment;

AND WHEREAS partnerships between government, people, and community groups are desirable to ensure that appropriate income and employment support services are developed and maintained [.]

The main component of social assistance in Newfoundland is delivered through the Income Support program, which is two tiered. A benefit for basic needs (food, shelter, and clothing) can be supplemented by special allowances for disabilities, municipal tax payment, medical transportation, childcare expenses related to employment or training, and fuel costs related to place of living. Applicants are assessed according to an extensive application form evaluating household assets and income, family and accommodation situation, health coverage, disabilities, and employment-related expenses. Income Support beneficiaries may also be referred by department staff to additional opportunities corresponding to their specific employment, education, or family needs (Newfoundland and Labrador Auditor General 2012, 60). These programs include the Job Start Benefit, which grants cash assistance for up to 12 months to those moving into employment, the Child Benefit and Mother-Baby Nutrition Supplement for low-income families, and Adult Basic Education for beneficiaries with fewer educational credentials. Other programs help support low incomes in the form of subsidized housing; tax credits, such as the Low Income Seniors' Benefit and the Home Heating Rebate; and cash transfers, such as the Newfoundland and Labrador Child Benefit and the Child Care Subsidy Program. New families also benefit from the Progressive Family Growth Benefit, a single cash transfer, and the Parental Support Benefit, which grants monthly benefits of $100 during one year.

People with disabilities, in addition to their access to the supplemental allowances embedded in the Income Support program, have access to funding to adapt their homes and for regular personal care, as well as wage subsidies for employment. They also have access to opportunities under the auspices of the federal-provincial Labour Market Agreement for Persons with Disabilities. These include employment counselling and funding for education and for employment access-related equipment and training (Newfoundland and Labrador Minister of Advanced Education and Skills 2012). To assist in supporting people with disabilities, the province's Executive Council has a dedicated Office of Employment Equity for Persons with Disabilities. In addition, the provincial government announced in 2012 the establishment of the Disability Policy Office, which works with disabled people to advocate and raise awareness in government offices and the general population on disability issues.

Delivery of the services related to the Income Support program is provided by employees of the Department of Human Resources, Labour, and Employment (HRLE). The department's staff has grown substantially, from approximately 500 employees in 2005 to 700 employees in 2010, most of whom are women (Newfoundland and Labrador Department of Human Resources, Labour, and Employment 2006, 2010). In the previous 20 years, several department initiatives worked to alleviate the social stigma associated with receiving social assistance. Since the mid-1990s, the department has abandoned the practice of home visits because they did not "add significant value to ensuring that only eligible clients actually received benefits" (Newfoundland and Labrador Auditor General 2005,

334). In the early 2000s, the department also planned to move toward a client-centred approach to service delivery (Gruber 1987, 13–24), a plan that was fully implemented only by the late 2000s. Services—over programs—were emphasized in internal management, and a tailored approach was adopted to develop the employment and human capital potential of recipients, in line with the global trend toward active labour market policies (see Cox, in this volume). In-office interviews were replaced by cross-checking measures as a way to ensure the accuracy of information provided by Income Support applicants (Newfoundland and Labrador Auditor General 2005, 334). In-office meetings were instead used as a way of referring recipients to additional employment and educational opportunities. The implementation of a toll-free telephone application process removed the obligation to travel to district offices to receive income support. While enhancing the privacy and dignity of recipients, this move also allowed the department to cut the number of district offices from 46 to 28 in 2004 (Newfoundland and Labrador Auditor General 2005; Newfoundland and Labrador Department of Human Resources, Labour, and Employment 2006). Since the implementation of the Poverty Reduction Strategy (PRS), several improvements have been made to social policies. Income support levels are now automatically adjusted for inflation. A program covering prescription drug expenses has been expanded to low-income residents and new entrants to the job market. The strategy also enhanced collaboration with the community sector. HRLE increased funding for women centres active in violence prevention and gender issues and for local organizations addressing homelessness. These special place-based services are thus delivered by the community sector, and department employees are present on these organizations' administrative boards.

An Income and Employment Support Appeal Board (formally known as the Social Services Appeal Board) was created in 1993 to hear grievances related to the administration of any of these programs. The board is composed of three standing members, one of whom is a current or former beneficiary of Income Support.

With regards to the goals and values embedded in its social assistance legislation and programs, Newfoundland has a legacy that is heavily tilted toward emphasizing self-reliance. The human geography and economic circumstances in Newfoundland are such that households and the community sector, more so than the market or the state, have historically borne the costs of maintaining social welfare. The historical weakness of municipal governments in the province has also contributed (Dyck 1996, 57–58). For example, in the 1930s, the Newfoundland Adult Education Association promoted self-help education for land settlers to grow their vegetables and raise their farm animals (Locke and Rowe 2009, 6–7; Overton 1997); a call which was later echoed during attempts to reform social policy in the 1980s and 1990s (Hudson and Close 2011). Yet input from the community sector in social policymaking during the early 2000s, as described here, has introduced the counterbalancing values of dignity, respect, inclusion, and partnership into the official mission of the Department of Human Resources, Labour, and Employment. Thus, social assistance now operates under the recognition that social and economic development are tied together and that poverty is a complex phenomenon that creates barriers to employment, which the department's programs can help to alleviate.

Nature and evolution of caseloads

Table 13.1 shows the monthly rates for basic needs income support, exclusive of supplemental benefits.

Figure 13.1 shows the average annualized level of benefits received by the two categories of recipients compiled by the province's statistical agency. These figures relate to the right axis. The average yearly duration of income support has hovered around 9.2 months since 2004, up from an average duration of 6.8 months in 1992. The last decade has seen an evolution in the distribution of household types receiving income support. Couples with children have massively moved out of the Income Support program (and presumably started receiving other government benefits and fiscal incentives), while single parents—most of whom are women—have increasingly moved into the program during the last decade. The bulk of beneficiaries are still single adults (Newfoundland and Labrador Department of Human Resources, Labour, and Employment 2006, 2010).

Table 13.1 Monthly Rates for Basic Needs Income Support

	Maintaining a Household or Living with Non-Relatives	Living with Relatives
Single Adult	$509	$308
Couple without Dependent Children	$720	$611
Single Parent with Dependent Children	$661	$543
Couple with Dependent Children	$707	$707

Source: Newfoundland and Labrador Department of Advanced Education and Skills (2014).

Interestingly, though benefit levels have risen in the previous 20 years, the number of people receiving income support concurrently fell, from 100,000 individuals in the early 1990s to 50,000 individuals since 2008. Figure 13.1 exhibits this evolution of income support and low income in the province through the past 20 years. The diamond-dotted line shows the percentage of the population that falls below the after-tax low-income cut-off (LICO), as calculated by Statistics Canada. The square-dotted line shows the percentage of the population that received anywhere between 1 and 12 months of income support during each given calendar year, regardless of age. These two lines report measures of poverty and relate to the left axis. The evolution of appeals to the Income and Employment Support Appeal Board similarly show a strong decreasing trend. Hovering between 200 and 300 during the late 1990s and early 2000s, appeals went down to approximately 50 in the last few years (Newfoundland and Labrador Department of Advanced Education and Skills 2011).

Figure 13.1 Evolution of Income Support Incidence Benefit Levels, 1991–2011

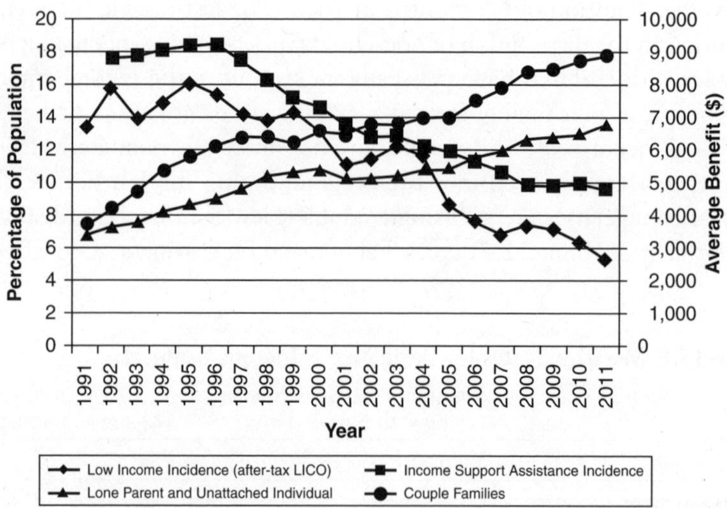

Source: Graphical presentation by author based on numbers compiled by the Community Accounts Unit (Newfoundland and Labrador Statistics Agency) and Statistics Canada. Numbers are provided by the Department of Advanced Education and Skills and Statistics Canada, CANSIM database, Table 202–0208.
Notes: Raw data on average benefits merge "lone parent" and "unattached individual" categories. For the two incidence lines, denominator numbers include all age cohorts. For income support assistance incidence, numerator numbers include dependents.

Discussion

The political-economic history of Newfoundland in the twentieth century is marked by numerous attempts to move away from an economy based on resource extraction (e.g., fishing, mining, and logging). Industrial modernization and economic diversification strategies held the promise of greater welfare for the province's inhabitants. Acknowledging the failure of these initiatives, provincial leaders returned to a traditional resource focus by the end of the century, assuming the role that the province could play as a provider of energy.

But oil production is not the *deus ex machina* of the story of welfare reform in Newfoundland. The province's sinking poverty rates and renewed welfare state result from several convergent forces. The influx of petrodollars in Newfoundland's economy would not have flowed toward welfare state programs without community sector mobilization and tripartite government, business, and labour involvement in resolving age-old questions of wealth production and redistribution in the province. Community sector enrollment in the tripartite focus eventually led to a form of corporatism that was consciously inspired by Ireland's experience. Though the province's coordinative institutions share some similarities with those found in Québec, notably regarding community sector involvement, they more closely resemble those of Newfoundland's cross-Atlantic cousin. Ireland, an island with a similar tradition of being cut off from mainland wealth, shares a common cultural heritage with the province. It seemed to offer a natural point of comparison when reformers sought a policy solution. By the early 2000s, the "Celtic Tiger" experience epitomized visions of success that Newfoundland politicians had been discussing for decades, if not for the whole twentieth century. Emulating Ireland's social partnership institutions entailed additional input from the province's labour and community sectors into policymaking (Donaghey and Teague 2007; Roche 2007). Concurrently, corporatist cooperation between former opponents within the province was facilitated by the strategic leveraging of the province's "sense of place" in the context of a heightened level of conflict with the federal centre of power during the mid-2000s (Hudson 2013; Marland 2010).

Thus, examining the recent experience of social policy renewal in Newfoundland reveals that changes in social assistance are not but a mere by-product of global economic shifts in the resource sector and changing federal-provincial relationships. A third factor appears: community sector and labour movement mobilization. In this respect, many of the Poverty

Reduction Strategy's initiatives, which are the bedrock of social policy renewal in Newfoundland, are the direct result of community and labour demands. Seen in this light, the revaluation of the welfare state appears as a wilful carving out of newfound oil prosperity from the community and labour sectors in the broader context of federal-provincial frictions. The gains from community and labour opting into the government's Poverty Reduction Strategy were substantial: greater input into labour market and social policymaking and greater involvement in service delivery (along with the resources needed for implementation). The ostensible effects of the PRS were no less important: higher levels of social assistance benefits, lower incidence of social assistance, a sizable reduction in poverty rates (see Figure 13.1), less contentious social policymaking and implementation, and the mitigation of social and labour conflicts.

Conclusion: Future developments amidst the economic downturn

Since the global financial crisis of 2008–09, the economic outlook for Newfoundland, though still sunny, has been moderated. The price of oil has dropped to levels that are much less profitable for offshore production. Production levels—and consequently government revenues—have adjusted downwards, but government expenses are still rising due to additional social and labour market policy commitments. Though the reduction of production levels might prolong the period of oil-induced prosperity, the spectre of economic dependency on the resource sector has resurfaced. How will the province keep up with its social policy commitments if the oil fields have lost their value? Drops in oil prices bring back the imperative of economic diversification. Yet, until now, concrete diversification initiatives reinforce Newfoundland's role as an energy exporter. The project to export hydroelectricity from lower Churchill Falls in Labrador does not part with a focus on resource extraction. Although the securing of a federal government–sponsored loan guarantee for power lines that will circumvent Hydro-Québec's grid in 2011 was a demonstration of masterful leveraging of federal-provincial relationships, the question of Newfoundland's particular vulnerability to global economic demand for energy remains. How will the province keep up with its social policy commitments if global energy prices do not rise? The question is even more valid with the "shale gas revolution," which is exerting strong downward pressure on the price of energy.

Newfoundland's answer to this vexing question is to invest in human capital. Springboarding on the Poverty Reduction Strategy impetus, the province plans to invest in additional education and training initiatives, active labour market policies that match unused labour force with growing labour demand, and research and development efforts. The province is also pushing to further formalize its corporatist institutions through the Strategic Partnership, which seeks to coordinate these human capital investment initiatives. However, uncertainties remain, and the province has to confront several challenges: attracting and keeping skilled individuals in the province, training and sourcing civil service expertise on active labour market policies, and fostering innovative—non-petroleum based—industries.

References

Canada–Newfoundland and Labrador Offshore Petroleum Board. 2014. *Total Monthly Oil Production: Offshore Newfoundland and Labrador*. St. John's: Government of Newfoundland and Labrador. http://www.cnlopb.ca/pdfs/graph_ph.pdf.

CAPP (Canadian Association of Petroleum Producers). 2010. *Newfoundland and Labrador's Offshore Oil and Natural Gas Exploration and Production Industry: Contributing to a Strong Provincial Economy*. http://www.capp.ca/getdoc.aspx?DocID=176807.

Donaghey, Jommy, and Paul Teague. 2007. "The Mixed Fortunes of Irish Unions: Living with the Paradoxes of Social Partnership." *Journal of Labor Research* 28 (1): 19–42.

Dyck, Rand. 1996. "Newfoundland." In *Provincial Politics in Canada: Towards the Turn of the Century*, 3rd ed., 31–84. Scarborough, ON: Prentice-Hall.

Gruber, Judith. 1987. *Controlling Bureaucracies—Dilemmas in Democratic Governance*. Los Angeles: University of California Press.

Hardy-Cox, Donna. 1997. "Through the Looking Glass: The Emergence of the Newfoundland Welfare State and the Socio-Cultural Impacts of Confederation." In *Ties That Bind: An Anthology of Social Work and Social Welfare in Newfoundland and Labrador*, ed. Gale Burford, 57–64. St. John's: Jesperson Press.

House, J.D. 1999. *Against the Tide: Battling for Economic Renewal in Newfoundland and Labrador*. Toronto: University of Toronto Press.

Hudson, Carol-Anne. 2013. "Newfoundland and Labrador's Poverty Reduction Strategy: The Transformation of Government-Rural Community Relations, 1999–2009." In *Social Transformation in Rural Canada—Community, Cultures, and Collective Action*, ed. John R. Parkins and Maureen Reed, 347–67. Vancouver: UBC Press.

Hudson, Carol-Anne, and David Close. 2011. "From Neo-Liberal Populism to Inclusive Liberalism: The Politics of Newfoundland and Labrador's 2006 Poverty Reduction Strategy." *Canadian Review of Social Policy* 65/66: 76–91.

Human Resources Development Canada and Newfoundland and Labrador. 1996. *Formative Evaluation of the Strategic Employment Opportunities Program—Final Report*. Strategic Initiatives Evaluation SP-AH025E–03–96. Ottawa: Evaluation and Data Development, Strategic Policy, Human Resources Development Canada.

Locke, Fran, and Penelope Rowe. 2009. *Poverty Reduction Policies and Programs in Newfoundland and Labrador—Tracing a Path from the Past to the Future*. Social Development Report Series. Ottawa: Canadian Council on Social Development.

Marland, A. 2010. "Masters of Our Own Destiny: The Nationalist Evolution of Newfoundland Premier Danny Williams." *International Journal of Canadian Studies* 42 (42): 155–81. http://dx.doi.org/10.7202/1002176ar.

McGrath, Carmelita. 1996. *How Long Do I Have to Wait? Building a Social Safety Net.* A Joint Project of The Writers' Alliance of Newfoundland and Labrador and Cabot College Literacy Office. Newfoundland and Labrador Adult Basic Education Social History Series, 9. St. John's: Robinson Blackmore Printing: http://en.copian.ca/library/learning/social/book9/book9.pdf.

Mondou, Matthieu. 2009. "Les policy designs contre la pauvreté—Une analyse comparée des plans de lutte contre la pauvreté et l'exclusion sociale au Québec et à Terre-Neuve-et-Labrador." MSc thesis, Université de Montréal.

Mondou, Matthieu, and Éric Montpetit. 2010. "Policy Styles and Degenerative Politics: Poverty Policy Designs in Newfoundland and Québec." *Policy Studies Journal* 38 (4): 703–22. http://dx.doi.org/10.1111/j.1541-0072.2010.00380.x.

Newfoundland and Labrador Auditor General. 2005. *2.15 Income Support Program, Annual Report.* St. John's: Auditor General of Newfoundland and Labrador. http://www.ag.gov.nl.ca/ag/annualReports/2005AnnualReport/CH2.15.pdf.

Newfoundland and Labrador Auditor General. 2012. *Part 3.3: Income Support and Accounts Receivable, Department of Advanced Education, Annual Report 2012.* St. John's: Government of Newfoundland and Labrador. http://www.ag.gov.nl.ca/ag/annualReports/2012AnnualReport/3.3%20Income%20Support%20and%20Accounts%20Receivable.pdf.

Newfoundland and Labrador Department of Advanced Education and Skills. 2011. *Income and Employment Support Appeal Board: Activity Report, 2010–2011.* St. John's: Government of Newfoundland and Labrador. http://www.aes.gov.nl.ca/publications/annualreport/IESAB-Annual-Report-2010-2011.pdf.

Newfoundland and Labrador Department of Advanced Education and Skills. 2014. *Program Overview: Advanced Education and Skills.* St. John's: Government of Newfoundland and Labrador. http://www.aes.gov.nl.ca/income-support/overview.html.

Newfoundland and Labrador Department of Human Resources, Labour, and Employment. 2006. *Annual Report 2005–2006.* St. John's: Government of Newfoundland and Labrador. http://www.aes.gov.nl.ca/publications/annualreport/HRLEAnnual-Report05-06.pdf.

Newfoundland and Labrador Department of Human Resources, Labour, and Employment. 2010. *Annual Report 2009–2010.* St. John's: Government of Newfoundland and Labrador. http://www.aes.gov.nl.ca/publications/annualreport/HRLE2009_10annrep.pdf.

Newfoundland and Labrador Minister of Advanced Education and Skills. 2012. *Programs and Services for Individuals and Families—An Initiative of the Poverty Reduction Strategy.* St. John's: Government of Newfoundland and Labrador.

Newfoundland and Labrador Statistics Agency. 2013. *Annual Estimates of Population for Canada, Provinces and Territories, from July 1, 1971 to July 1, 2013.* St. John's: Economics and Statistics Branch. http://www.stats.gov.nl.ca/statistics/population/PDF/Annual_Pop_Prov.PDF.

Noel, S.J.R. 1971. *Politics in Newfoundland.* Toronto: University of Toronto Press.

Overton, Jim. 1997. "An Exploration of Social Work's Pastoral Conventions—Adult Education, Self-Help, Land Settlement and the Unemployed in Newfoundland in the 1930s." In *Ties That Bind: An Anthology of Social Work and Social Welfare in Newfoundland and Labrador*, ed. Gale Burford, 31–53. St. John's: Jesperson.

Overton, Jim. 2000. "Academic Populists, the Informal Economy and Those Benevolent Merchants: Politics and Income Security Reform in Newfoundland." *Journal of Peasant Studies* 28 (1): 1–54. http://dx.doi.org/10.1080/03066150008438757.

Roche, William K. 2007. "Social Partnership in Ireland and New Social Pacts." *Industrial Relations* 46 (3): 395–425. http://dx.doi.org/10.1111/j.1468-232X.2007.00475.x.

Summers, Valerie A. 2001. "Between a Rock and a Hard Place: Regime Change in Newfoundland." In *The Provincial State in Canada: Politics in the Provinces and Territories*, ed. Keith Brownsey and Michael Howlett, 23–48. Toronto: University of Toronto Press.

Woodford, Michael Ross. 2006. "Problematizing Participatory Policymaking: Tensions and Potential." PhD diss., University of Toronto.

fourteen
Social Assistance in Prince Edward Island

KATHLEEN FLANAGAN

Introduction

Prince Edward Island (PEI) is the smallest and most densely populated of Canada's provinces. With a total land area of approximately 1.4 million acres, "the Island" is 224 kilometres from its eastern to western tips and anywhere from 6 to 64 kilometres from north to south. It is said on the Island that, wherever you are, you are no more than 10 miles from the sea.

The Social Assistance Program in Prince Edward Island is a blend of financial assistance to enable individuals and families to meet the basic necessities of life and counselling, problem solving, and planning to achieve self-sufficiency through employment or other means of income. Over the years, PEI has taken some innovative approaches to the provision of social assistance—although the province has often been challenged by economic circumstances, competing or conflicting federal policies, or local demographics. Despite government's efforts, local advocates, such as the MacKillop Centre for Social Justice (see MacEwen 2011) and the PEI Working Group for a Liveable Income,[1] stress that poverty is a serious and ongoing issue in the province, that social assistance rates are inadequate, and that more must be done. Many point to those families "living on the edge"—where the family is one job loss, illness, or car breakdown from being in need of social assistance.

Social assistance in Prince Edward Island—then and now

The evolution of social assistance policy and programs in Prince Edward Island is shaped by local, national, and world events. During the early 1950s,

> [t]he Island had a makeshift arrangement for people in distress, configured according to basic English Poor Law rules from 1601. . . . Provincial welfare assistance was paid only to rural residents. People in need of assistance had to wait for a month-end meeting

1 See www.cooperinstitute.ca.

> of the "welfare advisory committee" of ministers, who would approve or reject their applications, decide what amounts should be paid, and possibly vary or terminate payments previously approved. (Green 2006, 290)

Outside of rural areas, municipalities were responsible to provide assistance to citizens—but, in reality, this responsibility was left to churches and religious organizations. Religious organizations were either distinctly Catholic or Protestant, and, as a result, PEI had both Catholic and Protestant orphanages, hospitals, schools, youth centres, and "even Catholic and Protestant drugstores, distinguished by the availability of condoms only in the latter" (Green 2006, 146).

During these years, funding and administration of any available social assistance programs were governed by the provisions of the Social Assistance Act of 1952: An Act to Provide for the Granting of Assistance to Certain Persons under Certain Conditions. The Mothers' Allowance Act (Prince Edward Island 1949/1951, 1952) outlined stringent (by today's standards) eligibility criteria for social assistance benefits. For example, if a mother with a child was deserted by her spouse, she would be eligible to receive benefits only after a two-year period following the desertion; if the parent or child was disabled, the individual must have become disabled while living in PEI; for children, there was a three-year PEI residency requirement before benefits could be provided—if the child was younger than three years old, the mother must have lived in PEI when the child was born, and the child must have resided in PEI since birth.

Federal government cost-sharing efforts during the 1950s and 1960s were intended to establish some measure of consistency across Canada in social standards, but such measures were often out of reach of the government of PEI, which was unable to afford its portion of the expense (Forbes and Muise 1993). However, the introduction of the Canada Assistance Plan in 1966 (see Boychuk, in this volume) had a significant effect on PEI's legislative approach to social assistance, as it moved away from a categorical approach to social assistance and provided for assistance that focused on the presence of need rather than the cause of need (PEI Department of Community Services and Seniors 2012c).

The introduction of the Canada Assistance Plan also meant that PEI was able to terminate a variety of programs and policies such as the former Mothers' Allowances, Disabled Persons' Pensions, Unemployment Assistance, Old Age Assistance, and Tuberculosis (TB) Assistance and create a more inclusive social assistance program (PEI Department of Community Services and Seniors 2012c).

The General Welfare Assistance Act of 1966 combined municipal and provincial social assistance programs within one general welfare assistance program. At that time, all payments to individuals were approved by a welfare advisory board consisting of five legislators who reviewed hundreds of files per month and made decisions using their own discretion, which resulted in arbitrary judgments (PEI Welfare Assistance Review Committee 1989, 6).

It was not until 1972 that PEI introduced a comprehensive set of policy guidelines with authority delegated to the Director of Financial Assistance. This change was followed by enactment of the Welfare Assistance Act and regulations in 1974, with responsibility delegated to five regions in 1975. Once the province assumed responsibility for the administration of social assistance, it soon became clear that many families applying for social assistance were facing multiple challenges, including lack of transportation, addictions, mental health issues, disabilities, and lack of skills for employment (Green 2006). In the late 1970s, the province adopted a case-management approach, followed by a growing emphasis on job creation and employment-skills training in the early 1980s.

In 1989, the province undertook a major review of the social assistance program resulting in a final report *Dignity, Security, and Opportunity*. The report recommended that the program be reoriented from a 1950s–1960s attitude that envisioned eligibility as an end in itself (most likely because eligibility was subjective and often based on political connections). The report recommended that the program more fully reflect its legislated mandate to foster and support an individual's or household's pursuit of economic security and self-sufficiency (PEI Welfare Assistance Review Committee 1989, 17).

In the early 1990s, PEI introduced a series of progressive improvements, including higher benefit levels, new types of special allowances, and improved supplements for school-related expenses and for disabled people living at home. This development is consistent with the evolution of PEI's social assistance regime, which went from a "residual" regime in the 1930s through to 1980 to a "redistributive" one in the 1990s (see Boychuk 1998).

However, the downturn in the economy had a devastating effect in PEI, and caseload size almost doubled between 1990 and 1993. In 1995, the federal government announced the end of the Canada Assistance Plan, introduced block funding (the Canada Health and Social Transfer), cut budgets, and announced a new employment insurance system that included stricter eligibility criteria for the receipt of benefits (see Boychuk, in this volume). Economic conditions and federal policy wreaked havoc with PEI's efforts to modernize and improve social assistance.

Institutional architecture of the PEI social assistance program

Legislative authority

The Social Assistance Act of 2005 defines social assistance as both "financial assistance" and "social services." Specifically, financial assistance is defined as including payment for food, shelter, clothing, fuel, utilities, household supplies, and personal requirements; for special needs as prescribed by regulation; for care in residential institutions; for travel and transportation; for funeral and burial; and for health-care services. Comfort allowances and allowances for the other needs of those in residential institutions are also included (Social Assistance Act 2005, Section 1(d.2) [i-vii]).

PEI's legislation also provides applicants and clients the right to appeal any decisions made regarding the "provision of financial assistance under this Act" (Social Assistance Act 2005, Section 5.1 [1]). The Social Assistance Act provides for the establishment of the Social Assistance Appeal Board "composed of not less than seven and not more than nine members with some relevant experience in human services" (Social Assistance Act 2005, Section 5[1]). The act describes the composition of the appeal board (which includes representation from all provincial counties, a former recipient of financial assistance, and at least one person who is bilingual in English and French), and sets out the process under which appeals may be made and reviewed.

Table 14.1 Social Assistance Legislation in Prince Edward Island

Act	Year(s)
Mothers' Allowance Act	1949, 1951
Social Assistance Act	1952
General Welfare Assistance Act (repealed the Mothers' Allowance Act of 1951 and the Social Assistance Act of 1952)	1966
Welfare Assistance Act (repealed the General Welfare Assistance Act of 1966)	1974
Welfare Assistance Act	1981 (amended); 1982 (proclaimed)
Welfare Assistance Act	1988
Social Assistance Act (repealed the Welfare Assistance Act of 1988)	2005

Benefits and eligibility

The Social Assistance Act gives the Lieutenant Governor in Council the power to establish regulations to carry out the scope and ambit of the act (Section 7 [a-u]) and to establish categories and rates of assistance that may be granted (Section 4.1[1]).

The PEI *Social Assistance Policy Manual* notes that the "Social Assistance Program is designed for the individual (family) who is unable to provide for him/herself the basic necessities (i.e., food, clothing, shelter), or meet special emergency situations of need" (PEI Department of Community Services and Seniors 2014, Section 1). Such financial service may also be supplemented by problem solving and appropriate referrals to other agencies for complementary services. Each client is supported in the development of an employment or training plan and is helped to explore alternative sources of financial support. Also, "there is a parallel expectation to ensure that preventive and rehabilitative measures are taken where possible to assist the applicant to return to, or to develop toward, some level of independent functioning" (PEI Department of Community Services and Seniors 2014, Section 3).

Principles to govern the relationship between the client (individual or family), the worker, and the Department of Community Services and Seniors are outlined in the PEI *Social Assistance Policy Manual* and include a focus on individual rights, respect for the dignity and value of each person, self-sufficiency, and the importance of family as a source of support. The roles and responsibilities of caseworkers are also detailed, and the manual emphasizes the importance of managing financial and human resources.

The social assistance caseload: 1990–2013

There are numerous challenges with respect to collecting data about social assistance caseloads in Prince Edward Island. Though some data are available for years between 1969 and 2007 (see Figure 14.1), recent annual reports published by the PEI Department of Community Services and Seniors present data in mixed fashion. For example, some reports provide data based on the number of "cases" per year, and define a "case" as an individual or a family unit. In other reports, each person in a family receiving assistance is counted as a "case," and data are presented as the total number of individuals being "supported." Still other reports describe both "distinct cases" and "individuals." As well, some data are reported on an aggregate number for the fiscal year, and other data are reported as an average monthly caseload. There is no doubt that data collection to determine the social assistance caseload (or any caseload, for either health or social services) is complex. The number of "cases" and number of "individuals" are two distinct categories. Monthly caseload figures do not correlate to annual figures unless there is further analysis regarding the duration of involvement with the social assistance (SA) program.

Figure 14.1 (Kneebone and White 2014, 8) shows a fairly steady decline in the percentage of individual Islanders benefiting from social assistance. The authors define the *social assistance rate* as the number of social assistance beneficiaries measured as a fraction of the population aged 0 to 64 years, deriving data for population figures from the Statistics Canada CANSIM database, Table 282–0001.

Related reports suggest that, although the number of Islanders in receipt of social assistance increased significantly in the early 1990s—from 8,600 in March 1990 to 13,100 in March 1994 (National Council of Welfare 1997)—this number started to decline in 1995, and did so until 2005.

In part, the number of families receiving assistance was reduced because of stricter policies regarding eligibility. For example, in July 1994, the government announced that GST rebates were no longer exempt from the

Figure 14.1 Social Assistance Rates in Prince Edward Island, 1969–2007

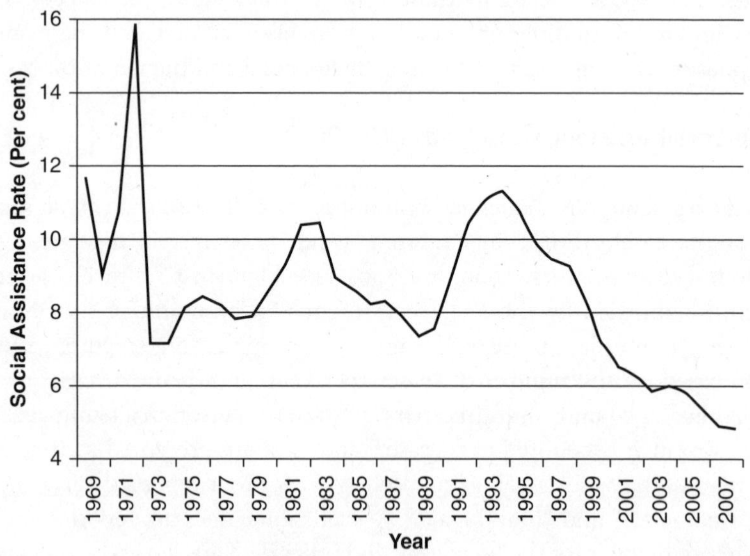

Source: Kneebone and White (2014, 8).

calculation of income, which translated into a dollar-for-dollar reduction in the calculation of eligibility and in social assistance payments. However, to understand and interpret such trends, we must first understand the full scope of related social service initiatives in the province. For example, as the National Council of Welfare reported,

> Between March 1994 and March 1996 the number of people on welfare in the province dropped from 13,100 to 11,700. The 1994 cuts probably contributed to the decrease but the number of unemployed people also fell during the period. According to the March 1995 provincial budget, the economy of Prince Edward Island continued to make strong recovery after leading the Atlantic provinces in growth in 1994. (1997, 17)

However, during this same time period (1995–2005), caseloads were also affected by the increasing number of social assistance recipients who participated in the Job Creation Program (JCP) and the Employment Enhancement Program (EEP). These programs were introduced in 1983 to support individuals in regaining financial independence. The EEP was designed to assist social assistance recipients by providing work and training opportunities that would help remove barriers to employment. The JCP was aimed at helping recipients retain or learn new work skills through short-term employment as they moved toward independence. The JCP placement provided a period of work experience, improved skills, and encouraged the possibility of gaining full-time employment.

In addition to the goal of creating financial independence, however, the program had another very simple and practical rationale. If funds from the PEI Welfare Assistance Program could be used to support eligible clients to seek paid employment, they would have employment earnings and, after a time, be eligible for unemployment insurance. Even though welfare assistance was a cost-shared benefit, the province did not need any matching dollars for federal unemployment insurance payments.

Annual reports from the PEI Department of Health and Social Services (2000, 2001, 2002) demonstrate that the steady increase in the number of social assistance clients registered for the JCP and EEP programs corresponds to the years that show a steady decline in the social assistance caseload (see Figure 14.1). Although fewer than 500 people were registered for these programs in 1993, more than five times as many were registered by 2001.

The Department of Community Services and Seniors reports that, over time, the number of Island households receiving support from the

Social Assistance Program has dropped from a high of 6,300 in the early 1990s to a low of 3,300 households in 2007. Since then, the number has risen slowly but steadily to just over 3,800 households involving almost 5,900 Islanders in 2011. This number represents approximately 4 per cent of the Island's population—a figure that is the lowest in the Atlantic provinces.

The recession in 2008 did not demonstrate immediate effects on the social assistance caseload. However, as noted in the 2011 discussion paper on poverty, the recession had consequences:

> Impacts however occurred including lower levels of employment, which were regained to record highs in early 2010. PEI also experienced a high proportion of unemployed Islanders eligible for Employment Insurance, increases in food bank use, and increases in social assistance (up 3% during 2009, from 3500 to 3600 households).
>
> Recessions tend to have a lag effect, with the impacts showing up sometime after the recession is officially over, especially among vulnerable groups. Unemployment rates rose and fell. Employment Insurance utilization in PEI remained high over the winter of 2010–11 while dropping in most other provinces. Food bank use increased by 13% in PEI from March 2009 to March 2010, and Social Assistance use is seeing a slight but steady increase. (PEI Department of Community Services, Seniors, and Labour 2011, 8)

The composition of the SA caseload mirrors that discovered through current research across Canada regarding populations more likely to be considered at risk for low income. Table 14.2 shows that, in PEI, about 700 single-parent families were receiving social assistance in May 2011, accounting for almost 20 per cent of the caseload. Demonstrating their greater vulnerability, 10 per cent of single-parent families in PEI receive social assistance versus 1 per cent of Island families overall. And, finally, single individuals make up a substantial share of SA recipients in PEI and account for much of the increase over the past years. In May 2011, almost 2,800 single individuals were receiving social assistance, up from 2,650 in May 2010. In May 2011, 68 per cent of SA recipients had an identified disability. Almost 40 per cent of the heads of households receiving social assistance are permanently exempt from seeking employment, and another 13 per cent are temporarily exempt.

Table 14.2 Breakdown of 2011 Social Assistance Caseload by Family Structure and Living Arrangements

Family Structure	Number (rounded) of Individuals
By Family Type	
Singles	2,700
Single-Parent Family	700
Couples with Children	200
Couples without Children	200
Total	**3,800**
By Age Group	
Children	1,600
Seniors	400
By Residence	
Live in Rental Unit	2,200
Live in a Community Care Facility	500
Homeowner	300
Other	800
Total	**3,800**

Other related social services

Disability support

In October 2001, Prince Edward Island became the first jurisdiction in Canada to separate income security from disability support. The introduction of the Disability Support Program removed any disincentive for eligible persons with disabilities to earn income, as the earned income did not reduce receipt of supports related to the disability or the amount received. Eligibility and level of funding and support were based on assessment of "need," as opposed to strict criteria. Funding was available "to enable an individual with a disability to live as independently as possible or to obtain and maintain competitive employment, or to help a family with extraordinary child-rearing support needs directly related to their child's disability" (PEI Department of Community Services, Seniors, and Labour 2010, Section 1.1.4).

In 2007, government struck a Disability Services Review Committee; its final report included several policy related recommendations, including the establishment of the Disability Action Council, which includes 19 members representing advocacy groups, service organizations, government departments, businesses, and community members (PEI Disability Services Review Committee 2009). The Disability Action Council continues to work with government regarding recommendations from the 2009 review and in matters related to social assistance.

Program utilization has increased slowly but steadily since the program's introduction. In 2011–12, the average monthly caseload for persons accessing service through the Disability Support Program was 1,229, an increase of approximately 4 per cent since 2009–10.

The Child Care Subsidy Program

The Child Care Subsidy Program provides financial support to cover all or part of the cost of childcare for parents who meet both social and financial eligibility criteria. Childcare subsidy is a critical component in any policy or program attempts to encourage employment. Eligibility is determined by parental employment, training, or medical status, and there is an income test to determine full or partial subsidy support.

In 2010, Prince Edward Island introduced the "Preschool Education Initiative," an innovative approach to early childhood education and care. The initiative regulated fees, set by the age of the child. For the most part, regulated fees were lower than the fees that were charged at the time of the program's introduction. These fees became the maximum per diem subsidy rate for full-time participation in childcare. Thus, parents—who select an early-years centre for their child or children—are not required to pay any differential in the cost of childcare. In many jurisdictions, this "gap" between the actual cost of childcare (as set by the childcare centre) and the maximum amount of subsidy available is a significant barrier to parents being able to take advantage of available subsidies. Even so, the rate of utilization of the childcare subsidy in recent years has followed trends in other children's programs in PEI; it has declined. This may be due to decreased numbers of children in Island communities (PEI Department of Community Services and Seniors 2012a, 12), fewer five-year-olds in childcare following the introduction of full-day kindergarten in 2009, or the need to review the program's eligibility criteria for family income.

Minimum wage rates

Since 2006, minimum wage rates have steadily increased in Prince Edward Island, although such increases have generated both advocacy for an even higher minimum wage and claims from business that these increases are causing job losses and that an increase to PEI's basic personal exemption for income tax (the lowest in the country) would be a better way to support low-income earners. Between 2000 and 2012, PEI's minimum wage has nearly doubled—from $5.60 to $10.00.

Social assistance rates

In Prince Edward Island, levels of financial assistance are determined by family status (single with no children and employable, lone parent with one child or more, or two parents with one child or more) and family resources. A "budget deficit" method is used to determine the amount of a benefit, whereby the total of the financial resources of an applicant is subtracted from the total allowable costs for approved items, with the difference being the maximum amount that may be paid. Financial resources to be considered, as well as allowable costs for approved items, are explained and detailed in the *Social Assistance Policy Manual* (PEI Department of Community Services and Seniors 2012c). In 2011, the Department of Community Services and Seniors developed a *Social Assistance Handbook*, which it distributed to individuals receiving social assistance, so they could better understand the policies and procedures for calculating eligibility and benefits.

Data suggest that Prince Edward Island's rates for social assistance for families with children appear to be on par with measures of basic need, while rates for single persons are below. (See Kneebone and White, in this volume, for a fuller discussion on the calculation of such measures.) Since 2007, Social Assistance Program funding has increased by 16 per cent ($4.7 million). This includes increases in shelter rates (11 per cent), food (10 per cent), and community care (33 per cent). In 2013, annual funding for the Social Assistance Program was $34.1 million. In November 2013, the government announced an additional 5 per cent increase to food rates for single persons, effective January 2014.

However, until November 2013, shelter rates had not increased since 2010 (CBC News 2013; Prince Edward Island 2014). Nevertheless, the rates approved by the Island Regulatory and Appeals Commission (IRAC) for rental units in the province have increased by 10 per cent since that year.

At the same time, SA rates for food have not increased for couples or families with children since 2009. Tarasuk, Mitchell, and Dachner (2014) report that rates of food insecurity in PEI have steadily increased since 2005; data from 2012 indicate that PEI has the fifth highest rate of food insecurity in Canada. Prince Edward Island is one of five jurisdictions (others include Nova Scotia, New Brunswick, Saskatchewan, and Yukon) where rates of food insecurity for children (birth to 18 years) are over 20 per cent—higher than the Canadian average of 16.5 per cent (13).

The PEI Social Action Program

In 2011, the PEI Department of Community Services, Seniors, and Labour (2011) released a thoughtful discussion paper examining the incidence and effects of poverty in Prince Edward Island. The paper acknowledged the complexity of defining poverty, along with the broad-reaching impact of poverty on child development, health, educational attainment, and economic prosperity.

As a result of the Island-wide discussions and submissions to government regarding poverty issues, the Social Action Program was launched in May 2012. The plan includes two core goals: "to support people to move out of poverty by strengthening their educational and economic opportunities and their participation in the labour force; and to protect and enhance the standard of living and quality of life for those unable to participate in the labour force for whatever reason" (PEI Department of Community Services and Seniors 2012b).

The launch of the Social Action Program effectively embedded the Social Assistance Program within an integrated strategy to address poverty in Prince Edward Island. One of the immediate goals of the Social Action Program is to improve the Social Assistance Program. To that end, related policy decisions have had a direct impact. For example, in 2011–12 PEI finally ended the clawback of payments made through the National Child Benefit (NCB). This clawback meant that for every dollar that a family received from the federal government in NCB payments, those dollars were considered as income in the calculation of eligible social assistance payments. Although the funds realized by the reduction in social assistance payments were reinvested in other types of programs for young children, such as the Healthy Child Allowance, childcare subsidies, and dental care for children, there was considerable criticism both within PEI and nationally (see CBC News 2009). The elimination of the clawback allowed for a recalculation of income for social assistance and for related programs such as family health benefits, childcare subsidies, and children's dental programs for approximately 800 families with children.

Other policy decisions have focused on employment. Since June 2012, over 500 SA clients have been referred to Employment Support Services, a partnership between Community Services and Seniors, SkillsPEI, and Rural Development. The program assists Islanders who receive social assistance to connect to employment services within their community.

Discussion: Ongoing emphasis on self-sustainability

Social programs in Prince Edward Island have consistently taken the approach of maintaining dignity and respect for the individual, and they have sought to promote self-reliance and self-sustainability. As early as 1948, at the end of World War II, it was clear to the Island government that the economic boom seen during the war years would not be sustainable and that the Island needed to invest in its citizens. Despite limited financial resources and a growing drain on education budgets due to higher birth rates after 1948, PEI sought to improve educational opportunities. Even with its efforts, which included upgrading teacher qualifications and salaries, introducing new curriculum, and delivering correspondence courses using radio, by the end of the 1940s, per capita spending on education in PEI ($6.90) was the lowest in Canada (Forbes and Muise 1993). The authors note, however, that when considering the size of the population of jurisdictions in Canada, only Alberta spent more on education on a per capita basis (Forbes and Muise 1993, 330).

PEI's traditional approach to social assistance continues in the goals identified in the current Social Action Plan. Both emphasize investing in citizens, treating people with dignity and respect, and supporting individuals in their quest to develop the skills and knowledge they need to obtain employment and, therefore, to earn an income sufficient to support themselves and their families. As noted earlier, the Island is often challenged by national and international economic trends, demographics, in and out migration, and competing federal policies, especially with respect to employment insurance (EI). Given that the Island's economy is primarily seasonal in nature (farming, fishing, and tourism), recent changes to EI have resulted in a decrease in the number of Islanders deemed eligible, creating the potential for increased numbers of Islanders seeking help from the Social Assistance Program. In 2012, an average of 95.6 per cent of the unemployed on PEI were receiving employment insurance. During the first 10 months of 2013, that fell to an average of 80.6 per cent (CBC

News 2014). This is further compounded by the complete lack of public transportation for any Island communities outside the capital city of Charlottetown—a situation that limits the range of potential jobs for rural residents.

The current Social Action Plan integrates social assistance within a broad strategy of health, social, educational, and employment-related initiatives. The plan describes an integrated and aggressive approach to managing social assistance within the broader issue of poverty. Although the program policy rationale is sound, the reality of inadequate rates for food and shelter and of competition for resources from current and compelling social needs related to mental health and addictions presents significant challenges for PEI.

References

Boychuk, Gerard W. 1998. *Patchworks of Purpose: The Development of Provincial Social Assistance Regimes in Canada*. Montréal: McGill-Queen's University Press.

CBC News. 2009. "Stop Clawback of Child Benefits, P.E.I. Urged." *CBC.ca*. Last modified November 12. http://www.cbc.ca/news/canada/prince-edward-island/stop-clawback-of-child-benefits-p-e-i-urged-1.857177.

CBC News. 2013. "Social Assistance Falls Short." *CBC.ca*. Last modified April 25. http://www.cbc.ca/news/canada/prince-edward-island/social-assistance-falls-short-1.1354978.

CBC News. 2014. "Far Fewer P.E.I. Unemployed Getting EI." *CBC.ca*. Last modified January 7. http://www.cbc.ca/news/canada/prince-edward-island/far-fewer-p-e-i-unemployed-getting-ei-1.2470411.

Forbes, E.R., and D.A. Muise, eds. 1993. *The Atlantic Provinces in Confederation*. Toronto: University of Toronto Press.

Green, John E. 2006. *A Mind of One's Own: Memoirs of an Albany Boy*. Charlottetown: Tangle Lane.

Kneebone, Ronald, and Katherine White. 2014. *The Rise and Fall of Social-Assistance Use in Canada, 1969–2012*. SPP Research Papers 7 No. 5. Calgary: The School of Public Policy, University of Calgary.

MacEwen, Angella. 2011. *The Cost of Poverty in Prince Edward Island*. Halifax: Canadian Centre for Policy Alternatives. https://www.policyalternatives.ca/sites/default/files/uploads/publications/Nova%20Scotia%20Office/2011/01/Cost%20of%20Povery%20in%20PEI.pdf.

National Council of Welfare. 1997. *Another Look at Welfare Reform*. Ottawa: National Council of Welfare. http://publications.gc.ca/collections/collection_2012/cnb-ncw/H68-43-1997-eng.pdf.

Prince Edward Island 1949/1951. *Mothers' Allowance Act*. Charlottetown: Government of Prince Edward Island.

Prince Edward Island. 1952. *Social Assistance Act of 1952: An Act to Provide for the Granting of Assistance to Certain Persons under Certain Conditions*. Charlottetown: Government of Prince Edward Island.

Prince Edward Island. 2014. *Budget Address 2014*. Charlottetown: Government of Prince Edward Island.

PEI Department of Community Services and Seniors. 2012a. *Annual Report 2011–2012*. Charlottetown: Prince Edward Island Department of Community Services and Seniors. http://www.gov.pe.ca/photos/original/2011-12CSSARE.pdf.

PEI Department of Community Services and Seniors. 2012b. *Social Action Plan to Reduce Poverty*. Charlottetown: Prince Edward Island Department of Community Services and Seniors. http://www.gov.pe.ca/photos/original/css_sapspeech.pdf.

PEI Department of Community Services and Seniors. 2012c. *Social Assistance Policy Manual*. Charlottetown: Prince Edward Island Department of Community Services and Seniors.

PEI Department of Community Services and Seniors. 2014. *Social Assistance Policy Manual*. Charlottetown: Prince Edward Island Department of Community Services and Seniors. http://www.gov.pe.ca/sss/index.php3?number=1048987&lang=E.

PEI Department of Community Services, Seniors, and Labour. 2010. *Disability Support Program Policy Manual*. Charlottetown: Government of Prince Edward Island. http://www.gov.pe.ca/photos/original/DSP_Pol_Apr2011.pdf.

PEI Department of Community Services, Seniors, and Labour. 2011. *Preventing and Reducing Poverty in Prince Edward Island: A Strategy for Engagement*. Charlottetown: Department of Community Services, Seniors and Labour. http://www.gov.pe.ca/photos/original/cssl_povertyred.pdf.

PEI Department of Health and Social Services. 2000. *Annual Report 1999–2000*. Charlottetown: Government of Prince Edward Island.

PEI Department of Health and Social Services. 2001. *Annual Report 2000–2001*. Charlottetown: Government of Prince Edward Island.

PEI Department of Health and Social Services. 2002. *Annual Report 2001–2002*. Charlottetown: Government of Prince Edward Island.

PEI Disability Services Review Committee. 2009. *Disability Services Review: Final Report*. Charlottetown: Department of Social Services and Seniors. http://www.gov.pe.ca/photos/original/SSS-DSR-Final.pdf.

PEI Welfare Assistance Review Committee. 1989. *Dignity, Security, and Opportunity: Report of the Welfare Assistance Review Committee*. Charlottetown: Prince Edward Island Department of Health and Social Services.

Tarasuk, V., A. Mitchell, and Naomi Dachner. 2014. *Household Food Insecurity in Canada, 2012*. Toronto: PROOF.

PART III

Contemporary Issues and Challenges

fifteen
Gendering Social Assistance Reform

AMBER GAZSO

The relationship between gender and social assistance receipt has long been a focus in research on social assistance reform, with two primary projects easily discernible. One project has been demographic analyses of the rates of social assistance usage by gender and often also by family type, such as single or lone-parent or two-parent families (Dooley and Finnie 2001). For example, such analysis shows how the number of lone- and two-parent family cases in British Columbia (BC) has decreased since 1995 (BC Ministry of Social Development and Social Innovation 2013a). In 2013 and among those "expected to work," lone-parent family cases (6,021) were the second-largest number of cases on employment and income assistance following single men (16,422); single men consistently outnumber single women as recipients of social assistance. Publicly available statistics also reveal that lone parents on social assistance in Ontario are the second-largest group by family type, following single individuals (Ontario Ministry of Community and Social Services 2013a). Kneebone and White in this volume, however, observe that Ontario caseloads have been increasing since 2009. Changes in Canadian caseloads have been varyingly attributed to reforms made to social assistance policies and programs or, as in the case of the drop in the number of lone mothers, to a growth in the service sector of the labour market, which tends to employ more women than men (Murphy, Zhang, and Dionne 2012; see also Boychuk, in this volume).

A second project has been the qualitative study of women and men's experiences of social assistance receipt following reform (Breitkreuz, Williamson, and Raine 2010; Gazso 2007; Little and Morrison 1999; Pulkingham, Fuller, and Kershaw 2010). Scholarly interest in the different experiences by gender, especially the experiences of lone mothers, is rooted in the long-standing awareness that poverty is distinctly feminized (Pearce 1978; Townson 2005). According to the 2011 Census, lone-parent families in Canada are increasing in number and the majority of these families continue to be led by mothers (Statistics Canada 2012a). Lone-mother families also continue to experience among the lowest incomes in Canada. Those who access social assistance receive total benefit amounts that are below the low-income cut-offs (National Council of Welfare 2010).

My focus in this chapter is in line with research on the gendered experience of social assistance receipt following periods of reform. More than this, I am interested in how discourses (e.g., meanings, images, and statements) shape social relations of social assistance receipt, including subject positions and experiences (see, for example, Breheny and Stephens 2007; Hammersley 1997). I combine a critical discourse analysis of post-1995 reforms to BC and Ontario social assistance policy and programs with findings from qualitative studies of parents' experiences to show how discursive constructions of gender and citizenship are interwoven in reforms, especially the creation of desired citizen subjectivities and the introduction of welfare-to-work programs.[1] I make the argument that social assistance reforms must be understood as including shifts in the very conceptualizations of individuals' citizenship rights to social assistance, from social to market citizenship, and that these shifts are overlaid with gender and, therefore, have gendered implications. Social assistance policy may seem to have been (re-)written and reformed in monolithic and sometimes neutral terms, but it has gendered consequences that must be accounted for in future reforms.

The wider context: "Active" welfare states and the citizenship shift

Jenson and Sineau (2001) maintain that the postwar Canadian welfare state and its rules, logic, and conceptualization of social rights can be viewed as a social rights citizenship regime. This regime's emphasis on social rights and justice for all citizens also included recognition of individualism (but see Boychuk, in this volume). In some ways, this regime was more of a socially constructed ideal than an achieved reality as not all persons—and especially not Aboriginal peoples or refugees—shared equal recognition of social rights. As well, conservative and liberal political discourses differed in their view of whether and how the welfare state

1 In critical discourse analysis, efforts are made to embed critical social theory's emphasis on unpacking the social construction of phenomena in order to bring about social change; the aim is to—ideally—envision a socially just society and achieve it through merging theory and practice (Hammersley 1997). In analysing social assistance policy discourse critically (all publicly available discourse including acts, ministry annual reports, websites, paper bulletins), I first explored how market citizenship is constructed through dimensions of neoliberal and social investment discourses. I then analysed how social assistance policy contains implicit or explicit gendered assumptions that are tied up with market citizenship. Keeping with the epistemological assumptions of critical discourse analysis, my analysis should be understood as a reading of the relationships between gender, citizenship, and social assistance policy.

should be maintained. Nonetheless, the very fact that most social policies and programs were universal in design and an entitlement of all Canadian citizens suggested an agreement around collective and social responsibility for recognizing and protecting against income insecurity (Mosher 2006).

Toward the end of the 1970s and into the 1990s, fractures began to appear in the postwar social contract. Increases in unemployment, economic recessions, the emergence and persistence of a federal deficit, and forces of globalization, such as the greater need for transnational market competition and investment, were symptoms interpreted as signalling the unsustainability of the postwar welfare state. Neoliberalism emerged as a discourse with a particular economic doctrine and ideology (Hartman 2005), stressing individual—not collective—responsibility, self-sufficiency, a reduced role of the state in the economy, and greater free-market competition. Applying neoliberalism to social policy change would correct for individuals' dependence on the state and poor political and economic engagement, faults some politicians and policymakers associated with the "passive" Keynesian social contract (Brodie 1996a; Rice and Prince 2013).

The replacement of the national Canada Assistance Plan (CAP) with the Canada Health and Social Transfer (CHST) in 1995 spurred on the neoliberal reform of provincial social policies. The CHST eliminated the federal-provincial 50/50 sharing of the cost of social programs and was seen to encourage provinces to experiment with the design and objectives of these in view of greater economic uncertainty (Battle 1998). Peck and Tickell (2002) note, however, that neoliberalism has not meant simply the "rolling back" of social policy but also the "rolling out" of social policy ideas and actions around regulation after 1990. The contemporary welfare state is "active" in that it eschews dependency and promotes human capital development, individual responsibility, and labour market participation. If necessary, the active welfare state conditions individuals' receipt of state support according to these goals (Pulkingham, Fuller, and Kershaw, 2010). Previous ideas about using social policies to protect people are replaced with interest in "responsibilizing activities of individuals and groups in their own welfare and security" (Ilcan, Oliver, and O'Connor 2007, 80).

The shifts from collective to individual responsibility for risks, from protection to investment for the future, and from entitlement on the basis of need to employment are central to active welfare states. And, for Jenson and Sineau (2001), these characteristics suggest the current citizenship regime is more accurately named the social investment citizenship regime. Moreover, in Jenson's (2009) view, neoliberalism played a lesser role in the post-2000 welfare state architecture than did the discourse of social investment. Whereas neoliberalism focused on correcting problems associated with spending, social investment discourse prioritizes the future, particularly profits and outcomes associated with policy change. Instead of responding to risks such as poverty, the social investment regime invests in and facilitates the management of these risks by creating opportunities and providing resources in social policies such as education and employability programs. Rather than a "safety net," the welfare state provides a "trampoline" (Jenson and Saint-Martin 2003).

Citizenship has been reconfigured in the active welfare state. The hegemony of neoliberalism has meant that its market ethos permeates all facets of social life (Broad and Antony 1999; Harvey 2007), including relationships with social policies (Gazso 2007). The citizenship of active welfare states is constituted as self-reliance and autonomy (Ilcan, Oliver, and O'Connor 2007) and puts so much emphasis on paid labour participation that Brodie (1997) maintains that market citizenship has essentially eclipsed social citizenship. Need alone has increasingly been overshadowed with previous, actual, or future employability—or labour market activation—as a basis for claiming the right to support (Gazso and McDaniel 2010). Citizenship has thus become encoded with neoliberal and social investment discourses (Breitkreuz 2005; Brodie 1996a, 1997; Jenson and Saint-Martin, 2003; Orloff 1993).

Social assistance reform, market citizenship, and new subjectivities

In the mid-1990s, larger market uncertainties, crises in government spending, and growing caseloads were perceived through the discourses of neoliberal and social investment and so were thought to signal problems with existing social assistance policies and programs in BC and Ontario. Reforms were understood as needed to make social assistance policies and programs sustainable and befitting of the active welfare state, especially in view of the replacement of CAP with the CHST (see Boychuk, in this volume). Post-1995[2] discourses of neoliberalism and social investment have filtered through interconnected dimensions of reform—restriction, enforcement, and surveillance (see also Gazso 2007)—to create entitlement on the basis of market citizenship in BC and Ontario (see Pulkingham and Graefe, in this volume, for a less narrowly focused analysis of reforms).

2 It was in 1995 that major changes were introduced in British Columbia. Ontario followed in 1997. The CHST of 1995 was divided into the Canada Health Transfer and Canada Social Transfer in 2004.

Restriction of benefit amounts is a strategy used to reduce caseloads and emphasize that individuals are better off working for pay than receiving assistance (see Boychuk 1998). When the BC Benefits Act replaced the 1972 Guaranteed Available Income for Need Act (GAIN) in 1995, benefit amounts were cut by 8 to 10 per cent for recipients who were deemed employable and who did not have dependents (Klein and Montgomery 2001). An even more dramatic cut in benefit rates—by 21.6 per cent—occurred in 1997 with the introduction of Ontario Works (Coulter 2009; Mosher 2006). In 2002, BC Employment and Assistance replaced BC Benefits, and reforms included reduced shelter allowances, capped crisis grants, elimination of earnings exemptions, and further cuts to benefit rates and employment supports such as childcare (Klein and Long 2003).[3] And, in 2012, the Ontario provincial budget froze benefit amounts, introduced cuts to the Ontario Works Community Start Up and Maintenance Benefit—a benefit originally intended to assist recipients with costs such as home repairs—and capped the cost of health-related discretionary benefits (Monsebraaten 2012; Ontario Coalition Against Poverty 2012). In BC and Ontario, the introduction of child benefit programs meant that parents with children experienced dollar deductions in their social assistance benefits for every dollar they received through the National Child Benefit program.

Restriction of benefit amounts occurs in tandem with the restriction of access in BC. Under the Employment and Income Assistance Act, applicants must undergo a five-week waiting period, previously a three-week period, before they meet a caseworker (BC Ministry of Social Development and Social Innovation 2013b). Through this act, BC also became known for being the only province to limit the amount of time people could access benefits to two out of five years. In many ways, BC had adopted US-style reform measures such as those introduced by the Clinton administration in the Personal Responsibility and Work Opportunity Reconciliation Act of 1996 (Pulkingham, Fuller, and Kershaw 2010). In 2004, the BC Ministry of Human Resources (2004) reduced the harshness of this enforcement measure because of public protest by introducing 25 exemption criteria "designed to ensure that no one who is unable to work or who is actively seeking work will lose assistance" (1).[4] More recently, Premier Christy Clark announced that time limits would be eliminated (BC Office of the

3 As of 2012, the BC government promised to restore earnings exemptions (Klein 2012).

4 Here are just a few examples of the exemption criteria that time limits do not affect: persons with persistent multiple barriers, pregnant women, and lone mothers with a child under the age of three (BC Ministry of Human Resources 2004).

Premier 2012). Though time limits had not always been enforced, in theory their existence prioritized and enforced active, market citizenship through restriction of access.

The dimension of *enforcement* captures how persons who are designated as employable or "expected to work" (as in BC) receive benefits conditional upon their performance of market citizenship. This classification is based on various characteristics of recipients' lives, such as number of children and their ages, whether they have a spouse, and health conditions. Client action plans in BC or employment plans in Ontario mandate employable persons' participation in welfare-to-work programs that range from educational upgrading and employment-readiness training (e.g., skills building) to job searches or actual employment-related activities, such as community service, that are not paid (the latter of which some term "workfare"). Employment-related programming was first introduced under BC Benefits and, by 1997, was shifted from being recommended to being an obligation.[5] Under BC Employment and Income Assistance (BCEA), employable persons are responsible for seeking employment actively and participating in education or job-skills training. They "must be available for any job you [sic] are able to do" (BC Ministry of Social Development and Social Innovation 2013c).

The introduction of Ontario Works contained the requirement that all employable recipients participate in welfare-to-work programs to remain eligible for benefits (Gorlick and Brethour 1998). As Maki (2011) notes, the very name of social assistance denotes how financial assistance is provided in return for employment participation. Current recipients continue to be responsible for "participating" in and "complying" with programming (Ontario Ministry of Community and Social Services 2013b). As noted in an OW bulletin, "The goal of Ontario Works is to help you get into the workforce and become financially independent," and ". . . if you receive help from Ontario Works, you *have* to take part in opportunities that will help you find a job" (Ontario Ministry of Community and Social Services 2011, 2; emphasis added).

How employable recipients are subject to monitoring to ensure their continued eligibility occurs through the final dimension of *surveillance*. Individuals are to demonstrate and document their compliance with market citizenship through the completion of "monthly reports" (BC) or statements of "income" and of "changes" to personal circumstances (ON), and recipients must be willing to be subject to ongoing eligibility audits and

5 It is understood that both provinces experimented with some forms of welfare-to-work programming, albeit in different ways, before 1995 (Boychuk 1998).

fraud inspections at their caseworkers' discretion. Fraud control divisions introduced in BC and ON serve as a key surveillance mechanism used to ensure that individuals maintain their eligibility. The introduction of new technological databases to standardize case reviews and of bureaucratic tools such as the welfare fraud telephone "hotlines" and drug testing suggest the increase in surveillance of benefit recipients under Ontario Works (Maki 2011).

Restriction, enforcement, and surveillance dimensions work together to socialize market citizenship. Said differently, these interconnected dimensions of social assistance discourse teach benefit recipients that employment *is* better than social assistance. In their receipt of, or application for, assistance, employable individuals are subject to administrative and regulatory procedures that uphold and enforce social constructions of the primacy of paid work. Indeed, employable recipients are expected to conform to specific subject positions, what Giddens (1998) called the "responsible risk taker" or others have referred to as "worker citizens" (Pulkingham, Fuller, and Kershaw 2010). Individuals are to have citizenship relationships with social assistance policy predicated on their taking responsibility for correcting their income insecurity.

Social assistance reform and the social (de-/re-)construction of gender

Shifts in the conceptualization of citizenship within social assistance policy reforms are interconnected with gender at multiple levels (i.e., individual, interactional, institutional, and ideological levels).[6] Gender and family ideologies consistently structure individuals' citizenship relationships with policy, a finding revealed more implicitly than explicitly in a reading of social assistance policy discourse.[7] Historically and generally, social policies for families have been primarily based on the male breadwinner/female caregiver model of family life (Eichler 1997). For example, social assistance policy specifically provided lone mothers some protection from

6 I understand gender as a fluid concept that operates at multiple levels; others, such as Thompson and Walker (1995), have termed this the "gender perspective." Gender is performed in interaction with others. Gender relations are an institutional part of the wider social structure and so are mapped into social policy. Finally, dominant gender ideologies of patriarchy or egalitarianism, or some variation in between, inform everyday social practices.

7 Said differently, social constructions of gender are often latent rather than manifest in social assistance policy discourse, with the exception of specific regulations such as the "spouse in the house rule" in Ontario.

economic insecurity and did so by substituting for the role of the primary earner or husband in nuclear families as long as the mothers were considered deserving of support (Baines 1996). Boychuk (1998) notes that, under Ontario Mothers' Allowances, lone mothers were perceived as caregivers for the next generation. He classifies the BC and Ontario social assistance systems of the 1930s through the 1970s as conservative regimes because they categorized recipients as deserving or undeserving, treated women and mothers differently, and consistently reinforced "gendered familial-status hierarchies" (Boychuk 1998). Scott (1999) terms the current model of family and gender relations in social assistance policy the "gender-neutral worker-citizen" model to stress how citizenship rights are configured in accordance with gender-neutral employability expectations. As Evans (1996) observes, reforms made to social assistance in Ontario shifted a woman's basis for claiming state support from mother to worker. So too did the introduction of BC Employment and Assistance in 2002, though earlier reforms to social assistance also suggested this shift (Pulkingham, Fuller, and Kershaw 2010).

The coupling of market citizenship with gender neutrality in social assistance policy in BC and Ontario is not unusual given the current logic of the active welfare state and changes in families and gender relations. Especially since the 1970s, mothers with young children are increasingly employed and dual-earner families are more common and necessary to meet everyday needs (Ferrao 2010; Sussman and Bonnell 2006). The gender-neutral worker-citizen model acknowledges parents' equal responsibility for providing for themselves and their children and no longer assumes women's dependence on men.

Although gender-neutral assumptions may appear to underpin conceptualizations of market citizenship in social assistance policy, the administration of policy in BC and Ontario has gendered contradictions and implications. Specifically, gender intertwines with the enforcement and surveillance dimensions of social assistance policy discourse. Considering the dimension of *enforcement*, women or men who are the heads of families or benefit units[8] and are designated as employable are expected to participate in

8 The 2002 BC Employment and Assistance Act (BCEA) applies social assistance to a "family unit" in British Columbia, with family defined as the "applicant or a recipient and his or her dependents" (BC Ministry of Social Development and Social Innovation 2013) and can include a lone-parent family, a two-parent family, and a childless couple. The 1997 Ontario Works Act delivers benefits to families who are classified as "benefit units": "a person and his or her dependents on behalf of whom the person applies for or receives basic financial assistance" (Service Ontario e-Laws 2011).

welfare-to-work programming. In both provinces, the unequal distribution of caregiving associated with being a lone parent is acknowledged in the short term (Gazso 2009). Lone parents may care for their children and are not expected to participate in welfare-to-work initiatives until their youngest child reaches age three under the BCEA program or is of "school-ready" age under Ontario Works. And yet these rules of social assistance policy may not be enforced fairly or gender neutrally. In my own interviews with parents on social assistance in BC, I found that they perceived that their caseworkers held different and gendered assumptions about them depending on whether they were male or female. In parents' views, caseworkers' perceptions influenced their determination of parents' eligibility for assistance and expectations of employability. Lone fathers spoke about how they felt caseworkers did not readily accept their caregiving of children under three and instead assumed that fathers ought to be working for pay (Gazso 2009). Mothers who were not expected to work because of the age of their children perceived that caseworkers might recognize their caregiving responsibilities but additionally felt that they evaluated their mothering as "good" or "bad." This latter finding is one shared across studies of mothers' experiences of social assistance (see, for example, Little and Morrison 1999).

Once lone parents are classified as employable, caregiving responsibilities are effectively made devoid of gendered meaning (Brodie 1996b; Gazso 2007). This makes for several problems, including the emergence of Canada's patchwork of day-care policies. Evans (1996) argues that shifting the basis from which Ontario's lone mothers can claim support has not been matched with an awareness of how caregiving responsibilities associated with young children impede labour market attachment. McMullin, Davies, and Cassidy's (2002) interviews with Ontario lone mothers also reveal that any cuts to total benefit amounts received undermined mothers' capabilities to care for their children and made it difficult for them to find paid employment. Notably, because most lone parents on social assistance are lone mothers, the burden of balancing meagre incomes with childcare costs, participation in welfare-to-work programs, and caregiving *is* a gendered one.

Moreover, the enforcement of a paid work ethic through mandatory participation in welfare-to-work programming is not necessarily a guarantee of income security and has gendered consequences. As *women*, lone mothers who exit social assistance face job markets characterized by gender inequality in pay and lack of workplace or other social policies to support childrearing and caregiving (Caragata 2003). Mothers, whether lone or not, overwhelmingly choose part-time jobs that permit caregiving but do little to improve their economic security (Breitkreuz, Williamson, and

Raine 2010). Escaping poverty is rendered difficult by social assistance policy that pressures individuals to enter any kind of paid work and that does not provide the education and skills for them to obtain secure jobs (Herd, Mitchell, and Lightman 2005).

The crux of the matter, especially for mothers, is that, as Maki (2011, 57) argues, "workfare erases their social reproduction[9] done in the home, casting them as flexible workers." Analyzing their interviews, Pulkingham, Fuller, and Kershaw (2010) observe how some lone mothers on social assistance in BC even diminish their roles as mothers in trying to present themselves as conforming to the genderless "worker-citizen" subjectivity. And Gingrich's (2008) qualitative study reveals that mothers on Ontario Works note the absurdity of their paying someone to care for their children while they participate in mandatory welfare-to-work programs that place them in settings where they look after other people's children.

The *surveillance* dimension of social assistance discourse is also rife with gendered complications (Maki 2011). The "spouse in the house rule" under Ontario Works meant that any man who appeared to be living with a lone mother and her children, including as a roommate, was perceived to be her spouse and financially supporting her, unless proven otherwise (Little and Morrison 1999). Women discovered to be living with spouses experienced sanctions or were completely expelled from caseloads because their failure to report such relationships was considered fraudulent (Maki 2011; Mosher 2006). Under current policy, a woman's eligibility for benefits is reassessed if she has lived with a man for three months. This change was introduced in response to the Ontario Court of Appeal decision in a case regarding the "spouse in the house rule" (*Falkiner et al. v. Director, Income Maintenance Branch, Ministry of Community and Social Services and Attorney General of Ontario*). In response to a Supreme Court case over BC's similar "spouse in the house" law, the Employment and Assistance Act was amended to specify its definition of spouse: two persons, including persons of the same gender, are one another's spouses if (a) they are married to one another, or (b) they acknowledge to the minister that they are residing together in a marriage-like relationship (BC Ministry of Social Development and Social Innovation 2013).

Although both provinces introduced a time period to establish the existence of spousal relationships in response to court decisions, the endurance of the "spouse in the house" rules nonetheless permits the continued surveillance of especially women's morality and sexuality. These rules rest

9 Social reproduction refers to the paid and unpaid work involved in the daily and generational maintenance of households and populations (Bezanson 2006).

on the inaccurate assumption that the only relationships women have with men (or now with women too, as in BC) are sexual and financially interdependent relationships. In addition, citizens can use Ontario's Welfare Fraud Hotline to report their perceptions of benefit recipients' fraudulent behaviour, such as a neighbour receiving income in addition to social assistance, so they are complicit in surveillance (Little and Marks 2006). Mosher (2011) finds that, though women and men can experience charges of fraud, women are more likely than men to be investigated for it on the basis of their intimate relationships with others.

Conclusion

As McDaniel (2002) has observed, neoliberal-infused social policy has a "one size fits all" approach that drowns out heterogeneity, especially differences related to race, class, or gender. Social assistance policy in particular has been (re-)written and reformed in monolithic and gender-neutral terms. Everyone on social assistance is actually, or potentially, a "responsible risk-taker." But gendered contradictions abound in the social assistance policies of BC and Ontario, especially because gender neutrality means overlooking how women experience greater economic marginalization and oppression than men (Breitkreuz 2005). Indeed, navigating expectations associated with responsible risk-taking precludes women's choices about caregiving and earning (Bezanson 2006; McMullin, Davies, and Cassidy 2002; Swift and Birmingham 2000). In gender-neutral social assistance policy underpinned by market citizenship, care is devalued and disregarded and is at the risk of disappearing (Gingrich 2008). The linking of benefit receipt to market citizenship has still other gendered implications, including contradictory enforcement and unfair surveillance.

This chapter concludes with a rather simple recommendation for how to consider, if not resolve, the gendered implications of gender-neutral social assistance policy in future reform: both the revival and mandate of gender-based policy analysis, a very specific tool initially designed by and for actual policymakers and analysts (Status of Women Canada 2013). Emphasis is placed on reviving and mandating this approach because provincial ministries have much discretion in choosing when and how to use it. This approach involves exploration of the potential, differential impacts of policies and programs on diverse groups of women and men. Requiring such an approach Canada-wide would mean that all future redesign of social assistance policies be seen through a gendered lens—so as to imagine the gendered implications of social assistance policy change *before* their actual experience.

References

Baines, Donna. 1996. "Rebel Without a Claim: Women's Changing Bases to Claim on the State." *Canadian Social Work Review* 13 (2): 187–204.

Battle, Ken. 1998. "Transformation: Canadian Social Policy Since 1985." *Social Policy and Administration* 32 (4): 321–40. http://dx.doi.org/10.1111/1467-9515.00119.

Bezanson, Kate. 2006. *Gender, the State, and Social Reproduction: Household Insecurity in Neo-Liberal Times*. Toronto: University of Toronto Press.

Boychuk, Gerald W. 1998. *Patchworks of Purpose: The Development of Provincial Social Assistance Regimes in Canada.* Montréal: McGill-Queen's University Press.

Breheny, Mary, and Christine Stephens. 2007. "Irreconcilable Differences: Health Professionals' Constructions of Adolescence and Motherhood." *Social Science & Medicine* 64 (1): 112–24. http://dx.doi.org/10.1016/j.socscimed.2006.08.026.

Breitkreuz, Rhonda S. 2005. "Engendering Citizenship? A Critical-Feminist Analysis of Canadian Welfare-to-Work Policies and the Employment Experiences of Lone Mothers." *Journal of Sociology and Social Welfare* 32 (2): 147–65.

Breitkreuz, Rhonda S., Deanna Williamson, and Kim D. Raine. 2010. "Dis-integrated Policy: Welfare-to-Work Participants' Experiences of Integrating Paid Work and Unpaid Family Work." *Community Work & Family* 13 (1): 43–69. http://dx.doi.org/10.1080/13668800902923753.

BC Office of the Premier. 2012. "Common Sense Changes Encourage Work, Protect Vulnerable Families." *Newsroom*. Victoria: Government of British Columbia. http://www.newsroom.gov.bc.ca/2012/06/common-sense-changes-encourage-work-protect-vulnerable-families.html.

BC Ministry of Human Resources. 2004. "Time Limit Policy to Protect People in Need [news release]." February 6.

BC Ministry of Social Development and Social Innovation. 2013. *Employment and Assistance Act*. Victoria: Government of British Columbia. http://www.eia.gov.bc.ca/publicat/VOL1/Part3/3-2.htm.

BC Ministry of Social Development and Social Innovation. 2013a. *BC Employment and Assistance Summary Report*. Victoria: Government of British Columbia. http://www.eia.gov.bc.ca/research/13/10-sep2013.pdf.

BC Ministry of Social Development and Social Innovation. 2013b. *Your Guide to Employment and Assistance*. Victoria: Government of British Columbia. http://www.eia.gov.bc.ca/publicat/bcea/BCEA.htm.

BC Ministry of Social Development and Social Innovation. 2013c. *Your Responsibilities and Rights*. Victoria: Government of British Columbia. http://www.eia.gov.bc.ca/publicat/bcea/rights.htm.

Broad, David, and Wayne Antony, eds. 1999. *Citizens or Consumers? Social Policy in a Market Society*. Halifax: Fernwood Publishing.

Brodie, Janine. 1996a. "Restructuring and the New Citizenship." In *Rethinking Restructuring*, ed. I.C. Bakker, 126–40. Toronto: University of Toronto Press.

Brodie, Janine, ed. 1996b. *Women and Canadian Public Policy*. Toronto: Harcourt Brace and Company.

Brodie, Janine. 1997. "Meso-Discourses, State Forms and the Gendering of Liberal-Democratic Citizenship." *Citizenship Studies* 1 (2): 223–42. http://dx.doi.org/10.1080/13621029708420656.

Caragata, Lee. 2003. "Neoconservative Realties: The Social and Economic Marginalization of Canadian Women." *International Sociology* 18 (3): 559–80. http://dx.doi.org/10.1177/02685809030183006.

Coulter, Kendra. 2009. "Women, Poverty Policy, and the Production of Neoliberal Politics in Ontario, Canada." *Journal of Women, Politics & Policy* 30 (1): 23–45. http://dx.doi.org/10.1080/15544770802367788.

Dooley, Martin, and Ross Finnie. 2001. *Differences in Labour Force Participation, Earnings and Welfare Participation among Canadian Lone Mothers: A Longitudinal Analysis*. Ottawa: Human Resources Development Canada, Applied Research Branch.

Eichler, Margrit. 1997. *Family Shifts: Families, Policies, and Gender Equality*. New York: Oxford University Press.

Evans, Patricia M. 1996. "Single Mothers and Ontario's Welfare Policy: Restructuring the Debate." In *Women in Canadian Public Policy*, ed. Janine Brodie, 151–72. Toronto: Harcourt Brace.

Ferrao, Vincent. 2010. *Women in Canada: A Gender-Based Statistical Report, Paid Work*. Catalogue no. 89–503-X. Ottawa: Statistics Canada. http://ywcacanada.ca/data/research_docs/00000186.pdf.

Gazso, Amber. 2007. "Balancing Expectations for Employability and Family Responsibilities while on Social Assistance: Low Income Mothers' Experiences in Three Canadian Provinces." *Family Relations* 56 (5): 454–66. http://dx.doi.org/10.1111/j.1741-3729.2007.00473.x.

Gazso, Amber. 2009. "Reinvigorating the Debate: Questioning the Assumptions about and Models of 'the Family' in Canadian Social Assistance Policy." *Women's Studies International Forum* 32 (2): 150–62.

Gazso, Amber, and Susan A. McDaniel. 2010. "The Risks of Being a Lone Mother on Income Support in Canada and the USA." *International Journal of Sociology and Social Policy* 30 (7/8): 368–86. http://dx.doi.org/10.1108/01443331011060724.

Giddens, Anthony. 1998. *The Third Way: The Renewal of Social Democracy*. Cambridge: Polity Press.

Gingrich, Luan Good. 2008. "Social Exclusion and Double Jeopardy: The Management of Lone Mothers in the Market-State Social Field." *Social Policy and Administration* 42 (4): 379–95. http://dx.doi.org/10.1111/j.1467-9515.2008.00610.x.

Gorlick, Carolyne A., and Guy Brethour. 1998. *Welfare-to-Work Programs: A National Inventory*. Ottawa: Canadian Council on Social Development.

Hammersley, Martyn. 1997. "On the Foundations of Critical Discourse Analysis." *Language & Communication* 17 (3): 237–48. http://dx.doi.org/10.1016/S0271-5309(97)00013-X.

Hartman, Yvonne. 2005. "In Bed with the Enemy: Some Ideas on the Connections between Neoliberalism and the Welfare State." *Current Sociology* 53 (1): 57–73. http://dx.doi.org/10.1177/0011392105048288.

Harvey, David. 2007. *A Brief History of Neoliberalism*. Oxford: Oxford University Press.

Herd, Dean, Andrew Mitchell, and Ernie Lightman. 2005. "Rituals of Degradation: Administration as Policy in the Ontario Works Programme." *Social Policy and Administration* 39 (1): 65–79. http://dx.doi.org/10.1111/j.1467-9515.2005.00425.x.

Ilcan, S., M. Oliver, and D. O'Connor. 2007. "Spaces of Governance: Gender and Public Sector Restructuring in Canada." *Gender, Place and Culture* 14 (1): 75–92. http://dx.doi.org/10.1080/09663690601122333.

Jenson, Jane. 2009. "Lost in Translation: The Social Investment Perspective and Gender Equality." *Social Politics* 16 (4): 446–83. http://dx.doi.org/10.1093/sp/jxp019.

Jenson, Jane, and Denis Saint-Martin. 2003. "New Routes to Social Cohesion? Citizenship and the Social Investment State." *Canadian Journal of Sociology* 28 (1): 77–99. http://dx.doi.org/10.2307/3341876.

Jenson, Jane, and Mariettte Sineau. 2001. "The Care Dimension in Welfare State Redesign." In *Who Cares? Women's Work, Childcare, and Welfare State Redesign*, ed. J. Jenson, 3–18. Toronto: University of Toronto Press.

Klein, Seth. 2012. "New BC Welfare Rules: Some Positive Steps Forward (and a Couple Steps Back)." *Policy Note: A Progressive Take on BC Issues*. Last modified June 12. http://www.policynote.ca/new-bc-welfare-rules-some-positive-steps-forward-and-couple-steps-back/.

Klein, Seth, and Andrea Long. 2003. *A Bad Time to Be Poor: An Analysis of British Columbia's New Welfare Policies*. Vancouver: Canadian Centre for Policy Alternatives.

Klein, Seth, and Barbara Montgomery. 2001. *Depressing Wages: Why Welfare Cuts Hurt Both the Welfare and the Working Poor*. Vancouver: Canadian Centre for Policy Alternatives.

Little, Margaret, and Lynne Marks. 2006. "A Closer Look at the Neo-Liberal Petri Dish: Welfare Reform in British Columbia and Ontario." *Canadian Review of Social Policy* 57: 16-45.

Little, Margaret Hillyard, and Ian Morrison. 1999. "'The Pecker Detectors are Back': Regulation of the Family Form in Ontario Welfare Policy." *Journal of Canadian Studies / Revue d'études canadiennes* 34 (2): 110–37.

Maki, Krystle. 2011. "Neoliberal Deviants and Surveillance: Welfare Recipients under the Watchful Eye of Ontario Works." *Surveillance & Society* 9 (1/2): 47–63.

McDaniel, S. 2002. "Women's Changing Relations to the State and Citizenship: Caring and Intergenerational Relations in Globalizing Western Democracies." *Canadian Review of Sociology and Anthropology* 39 (2): 125–50.

McMullin, Julie Ann, Lorraine Davies, and Gale Cassidy. 2002. "Welfare Reform in Ontario: Tough Times in Mothers' Lives." *Canadian Public Policy* 28 (2): 297–314. http://dx.doi.org/10.2307/3552330.

Monsebraaten, Laurie. 2012. "Ontario Budget 2012: Welfare Rate Freeze Really a Cut, Activists Say." *The Toronto Star*, March 27. http://www.thestar.com/news/canada/2012/03/27/ontario_budget_2012_welfare_rate_freeze_really_a_cut_activists_say.html.

Mosher, Janet. 2006. "The Construction of 'Welfare Fraud' and the Wielding of the State's Iron Fist." In *Locating Law: Race, Class and Gender Connections*, 2nd ed., ed. E. Comack, 207–28. Halifax: Fernwood Publishing.

Mosher, Janet. 2011. "Intimate Intrusions: Welfare Regulation of Women's Personal Lives." In *The Legal Tender of Gender: Law, Welfare and the Regulation of Women's Poverty*, ed. S.A. Gavigan and D.E. Chunn, 165–89. Portland, OR: Hart Publishing.

Murphy, Brian, Xuelin Zhang, and Claude Dionne. 2012. *Low Income in Canada: A Multi-Line and Multi-Index Perspective*. Income Research Paper Series No. 75F0002M–1. Ottawa: Statistics Canada. http://www.statcan.gc.ca/pub/75f0002m/75f0002m2012001-eng.pdf.

National Council of Welfare. 2010. *Factsheet: Welfare Incomes and Poverty over Time*. Ottawa: National Council of Welfare. http://www.ncwcnbes.net/documents/researchpublications/ResearchProjects/WelfareIncomes/2006WebOnlyData/factsheet17ENG.pdf.

Ontario Coalition Against Poverty. 2012. *OCAP Statement on 2012 Ontario Budget*. Toronto: Ontario Coalition Against Poverty. http://ocap.ca/node/994.

Ontario Ministry of Community and Social Services. 2011. *Ontario Works Provides the Help You Need*. Toronto: Ontario Works. http://www.docstoc.com/docs/26859232/Ontario-Works-provides-the-help-you-need.

Ontario Ministry of Community and Social Services. 2013a. *Ontario Social Assistance Monthly Statistics Report*. Toronto: Ministry of Community and Social Services. http://www.mcss.gov.on.ca/documents/en/mcss/social/reports/OW_EN_2013_09.pdf.

Ontario Ministry of Community and Social Services. 2013b. *Ontario Works Policy Directives*. Toronto: Ministry of Community and Social Services. http://www.mcss.gov.on.ca/documents/en/mcss/social/directives/ow/0201.pdf.

Orloff, Ann Shola. 1993. "Gender and the Social Rights of Citizenship: The Comparative Analysis of Gender Relations and Welfare States." *American Sociological Review* 58 (3): 303–28. http://dx.doi.org/10.2307/2095903.

Pearce, Diana. 1978. "The Feminization of Poverty: Women, Work, and Welfare." *Urban & Social Change Review* 11: 28–36.

Peck, James, and Adam Tickell. 2002. "Neoliberalizing Space." *Antipode* 34 (3): 380–404.

Pulkingham, Jane, Sylvia Fuller, and Paul Kershaw. 2010. "Lone Motherhood, Welfare Reform and Active Citizen Subjectivity." *Critical Social Policy* 30 (2): 267–91. http://dx.doi.org/10.1177/0261018309358292

Rice, James J., and Michael J. Prince. 2013. *Changing Politics of Canadian Social Policy*, 2nd ed. Toronto: University of Toronto Press.

Scott, Katherine. 1999. "The Dilemma of Liberal Citizenship: Women and Social Assistance Reform in the 1990s. In *Feminism, Political Economy, and the State: Contested Terrain*, ed. Pat Armstrong and M. Patricia Connelly, 205–35. Toronto: Canadian Scholars' Press.

Service Ontario e-Laws. 2011. *Ontario Works Act*. http://www.e-laws.gov.on.ca/html/statutes/english/elaws_statutes_97025a_e.htm.

Statistics Canada. 2012a. *Fifty Years of Families in Canada: 1961 to 2011*. Ottawa: Statistics Canada. http://www12.statcan.ca/census-recensement/2011/as-sa/98-312-x/98-312-x2011003_1-eng.cfm.

Status of Women Canada. 2013. *Gender-Based Analysis Plus Framework*. Ottawa: Status of Women Canada. http://www.swc-cfc.gc.ca/gba-acs/course-cours/eng/mod00/mod00-01-01.php.

Sussman, Deborah, and Stephanie Bonnell. 2006. "Wives as Primary Breadwinners." *Perspectives on Labour and Income* 7 (8): 10–17.

Swift, Karen J., and Michael Birmingham. 2000. "Location, Location, Location: Restructuring and the Everyday Lives of 'Welfare Moms.'" In *Restructuring Caring Labour: Discourse, State Practice, and Everyday Life*, ed. S.M. Neysmith, 93–115. Don Mills, ON: Oxford University Press.

Thompson, Linda, and Alexis J. Walker. 1995. "The Place of Feminism in Family Studies." *Journal of Marriage and the Family* 57: 847–65.

Townson, Monica. 2005. *Poverty Issues for Canadian Women*. Background paper prepared for Status of Women Canada. August. http://www.rapereliefshelter.bc.ca/sites/default/files/imce/Poverty%20Issues%20for%20Canadian%20Women%20-%20Background%20Paper.pdf.

sixteen
Entrenched Residualism: Social Assistance and People with Disabilities

MICHAEL J. PRINCE

Introduction

Disabilities include long-term physical, mental, intellectual, or sensory impairments that, in connection with various barriers, may impede a person's involvement in society. The politics of disability social assistance encompass numerous issues. For the purposes of program eligibility, how is disability to be determined authoritatively? How much financial support is to be provided to this group? What other benefits and services do eligible people with disabilities receive while on welfare? Which of these benefits and services, if any, should they continue to receive when leaving social assistance, and for how long afterwards? What assumptions are made about the work capacity of people with disabilities, and what supports are made available for employment? How do provincial disability social assistance benefits interact with other provincial and federal transfer and tax measures? What are the effects of social assistance programs on the identities and everyday lives of people with disabilities? How does provincial disability social assistance interrelate with social citizenship in the Canadian context?

The central argument of this chapter is that, for many Canadians with disabilities, provincial social assistance is effectively a first-resort program rather than a safety net. This social assistance is entrenched residualism: welfare is no longer a temporary and last-resort program. Disability social assistance occupies a prominent and notorious place in the Canadian income security system and too often operates in ways that infringe upon the dignity of applicants and clients. Because of the complexities of disability benefit systems, people with disabilities struggle in having their conditions recognized, in navigating programs, and in facing the effects of welfare state restructuring. A notable trend identified is "the rising proportion of the caseload comprised of persons with a disability" over the past 15 years or so (Stevens, Simpson, and Frankel 2011, 164; see also Kneebone and White, in this volume; and Stapleton 2011, 2012).

Provincial disability social assistance

Accounts of the historical development of disability-related social assistance are available in the literature (Jongbloed 2006; Prince 2001; Rice and Prince 2013), so only a brief history is presented here. The origin and form of modern disability social assistance in Canada, as shown in Table 16.1, is characterized by three movements. First, the establishment of distinct income assistance programs for the blind specifically and then for the disabled more generally took place in the 1930s and 1940s. This assistance was diffused across the country with the support of the federal government through cost-sharing agreements and then by specific federal laws in the early 1950s. In the context of mid-twentieth century Canada, social assistance was seen as an advance over more traditional forms of support to those in need, such as charity, and, indeed, public aid was considered by some as a social right or an entitlement. Second, these separate provincial programs for blind persons and disabled persons were absorbed into the more comprehensive Canada Assistance Plan (CAP), a federal cost-sharing policy introduced in 1966. Although some disability groups opposed the loss of separate programming for their constituency, by the mid-1970s, all provinces had transferred people with disabilities in these categorical programs to general, CAP-funded programs. Third, to the extent that social assistance for people with disabilities and other low-income individuals was a pan-Canadian program, this support ended with the termination of CAP by the federal government in 1996 and its replacement with the more general policy and less well financed Canada Health and Social Transfer (see Boychuk, in this volume). Since the decline and demise of CAP, five provinces have introduced specific categorical income assistance programs for people with disabilities, namely, Alberta in 1993, British Columbia in 1996, Ontario in 1998, Québec in 2007, and Saskatchewan in 2010. One or more provinces could follow.[1] The introduction of separate social assistance programs for people with disabilities indicates a variant of province building; it shows the autonomy and capacity of particular provincial governments to innovate in welfare policy and program governance.

---

1 New Brunswick considered adopting a separate social assistance program for people with disabilities in 2014. In the other direction on program design, a recent report in Ontario (Lankin and Sheikh 2012) recommended replacing the separate ODSP and integrating it with the general welfare program to have one social assistance system, with a disability supplement linked to the standard rate of social assistance.

Table 16.1 A Chronology of Major Disability Social Assistance Programs in Canada, 1930–2010

Date	Program	Level of Government
1930	War Veterans Allowance Act passed, which extended the means-tested benefits of the Old Age Pension Act of 1927 to burned out and disabled ex-soldiers	Federal
1937	Old Age Pension Act amended to provide for the blind and other persons with disabilities, aged 40–69, not covered by workers' compensation or veterans' benefits	Federal cost sharing with provinces on 75–25 basis
1947	Old Age Pension Act amended for blind pensions to remove the nationality criterion and lower the age threshold from 40 to 21 years	Federal cost sharing with provinces on a 75–25 basis
1951	Blind Persons Act to provide allowances to blind persons aged 18–69	Federal cost sharing with provinces on 75–25 basis
1952	Ontario introduces allowance for disabled persons	Ontario
1953	Alberta introduces allowance for disabled persons	Alberta
1954	Disabled Persons Allowance Act to provide allowances to disabled persons aged 21–69	Federal cost sharing with provinces on 50–50 basis
1966	Canada Assistance Plan—general program of income assistance and social services for low-income persons in need	Federal cost sharing with provinces on 50–50 basis
1990–95	A cap of 5 per cent growth per year on the federal share of CAP transfers to Alberta, BC, and Ontario	Federal
1993	Assured Income for the Severely Handicapped Act and program introduced	Alberta
1996	CAP terminated and replaced by Canada Health and Social Transfer (CHST) and a major reduction in federal cash transfers	Federal
1996	Disability Benefits Program Act	British Columbia
1997	Ontario Disability Support Act	Ontario
2002	Employment and Assistance for Persons with Disabilities Act	British Columbia
2004	CHST divided into the Canada Health Transfer and Canada Social Transfer	Federal

(Continued)

Table 16.1 (Continued)

Date	Program	Level of Government
2007	Social Solidarity Program (Programme de solidarité sociale) brings in allowances for those with "a severely limited capacity for employment"	Québec
2010	Saskatchewan Assured Income for Disability program	Saskatchewan

Three types of design for delivering disability social assistance are evident across the provinces. One type, already noted, provides specific, categorical programs of social assistance for people with disabilities. These are the Assured Income for the Severely Handicapped (AISH) program in Alberta, the Assistance for Persons with Disabilities (popularly called PWD) program in British Columbia, the Ontario Disability Support Program (ODSP), the Social Solidarity Program in Québec, and the Saskatchewan Assured Income for Disability (SAID) program. These categorical programs are anchored in specific laws or, in the case of Saskatchewan, in regulations under the general legislation for assistance. In a second type of design, the disability benefit is a distinct component yet is embedded within the general social assistance program. For example, Manitoba has a monthly income benefit for people with disabilities living in the community; New Brunswick has a disability supplement for some disabled clients on social assistance. The third type provides income support to people with disabilities through the regular social assistance system, as is the case in PEI.[2]

There are debates in Canada, historically and today, over adopting a categorical versus a general programming approach to income assistance for people with disabilities in a province's welfare policy (Guest 2003; Prince 2001). In the current period, thinking in some provinces favours the idea of a separate welfare program for people with disabilities. Motives

2 PEI has a general program that includes a medical assessment of an applicant to determine the nature, duration, and extent of an illness or disability. PEI has a disability allowance to support families in caring for adult family members with a disability who live in the home of the family member providing the care for activities of daily living. The allowance is up to a maximum of $150 per month. The province also has a needs-based Disability Support Program separate from the social assistance system, the aim of which is to assist people with disabilities with their personal planning and to help meet certain needs concerning a person's disability via personal and family supports, technical aids and devices, and employment and vocational supports.

for this approach include a desire to mitigate the stigma of traditional social assistance systems, to enhance the adequacy of income support for people with disabilities, and to create a new delivery system informed by a contemporary understanding of disablement. The political calculation is that it is more fruitful to seek positive change for low-income people with disabilities outside rather than inside provincial welfare programs. A separate categorical program may raise the public profile of the program and also the political influence of the constituency. Critics worry that separate social assistance programs for people with disabilities have fragmenting effects in at least two senses: one, separate programs divide the overall population of people living in persistent poverty and, two, such programs invariably splinter the population of people living with disabilities, creating a hierarchy of those in need, such as between persons with severe and prolonged impairments and persons with episodic disabilities (Lightman et al. 2009; Stapleton and Tweddle 2008).

Some disability advocates express caution about stand-alone categorical programs and suggest there can be a political cycle to this policy development.[3] Advocates acknowledge that separate programs initially may result in more adequate benefits and more sensitive delivery systems than previously existed for clients with disabilities. This improvement can result in an increase in the uptake and caseload and thus the budget. In turn, the growing budget leads to governmental concerns over perceived cost pressures, and these concerns prompt bureaucratic inclinations to make access to disability benefits more restrictive. This proposition, this trajectory of separate program assistance to people with disabilities, has garnered evidence—reported in case studies (Lightman et al. 2009; Vick 2012)—that warrants empirical analysis comparing types of program design, something that has not been done so far in the Canadian context.

The program elements of disability social assistance

According to Keith Banting (1987), the distinctive character of income security in the Canadian welfare state is that it is "a *direct* exchange between citizen and state" that bypasses other social institutions. "To the recipient," Banting says, "the role of the state in this field is direct, visible and, for many, crucial" (27, emphasis in original). To be sure, income

3 This discussion draws on my involvement with various provincial and national disability rights organizations over the last 20 years.

assistance, however inadequate current amounts may be, is essential to the lives of many disabled people. It is not clear that the exchange between provincial states and clients with disabilities is so direct or visible.

Provision of disability income involves several other institutions in society and the economy. Disability social assistance functions through interactions that can involve medical doctors, nurse practitioners and rehabilitation specialists, disability organizations, federal as well as provincial program officials, insurance companies, charitable meal agencies, community legal clinics and lawyers, employment service providers, emergency shelters and landlords, mental health services, and families and friends. For many Canadians with disabilities, these exchanges between the provincial state and themselves as citizens in need are difficult, convoluted, intrusive, and ambiguous experiences.[4]

Provincial disability assistance varies across the country by how disabilities are medically certified to determine eligibility; by benefit amounts; by whether benefits are indexed and how; and by the rules on allowable assets and exemptions, monthly earnings exemptions, and clawbacks. Other variations include the existence and extent of supplementary allowances and other special needs benefits or of training and transition to employment supports, whether an extension of health services is offered, how disability assistance interacts with other income programs and tax credits, and what reinstatement provisions and appeal structures are in place.

Among the distinctive features is that social assistance for persons with disabilities usually provides a somewhat higher payment than that for general social assistance and also includes an exemption from seeking work (OECD 2010, 49). People with disabilities are over-represented in annual average social assistance caseloads, a trend that one policy analyst has dubbed "the welfarization of disability"—a term emphasizing the significance of social assistance as a source of income for so many low-income Canadians with disabilities (Stapleton 2011, 2012). Caseload trends for people with disabilities are sensitive to the aging of the population and to the longer life expectancy for individuals with disabilities and severe health conditions. A study of social assistance caseloads in the later 1990s found that people with disabilities tend to remain on social assistance longer than do clients in other categories, tend to be an older clientele, tend to be unattached persons and couples without children, and tend to not have any outside income beyond social assistance (National Council of Welfare 1998).

4 This applies not only to social assistance programs but also to social insurance programs such as the Canada Pension Plan—Disability and EI sickness benefits as well as to tax measures for people with disabilities such as the disability tax credit or DTC (see Prince 2009).

Table 16.2 illustrates the "welfarization of disability" in a specific manner. Using survey data, this table shows the social assistance recipiency rate of working-age (16 to 64) people with disabilities and people without disabilities in all the provinces by low-income status.

The main message in Table 16.2 is this: overall, provincial social assistance programs serve mostly people with some degree of disability. Other data tell us that people with developmental and psychiatric disabilities are even more likely to be receiving social assistance than are people with disabilities in general (Council of Canadians with Disabilities 2010). Whether they are above or below low-income cut-off lines, *people with disabilities comprise the large majority of social assistance clients in Canada*. Among social assistance recipients with low income, three-quarters (74.7 per cent) had disabilities.

For this group of "worthy poor" in Canada, the true worth of social assistance benefits has diminished in recent decades (Kneebone and Grynishak 2011). Table 16.3 reports on the real value of annual disability benefits for each province for selected years, in other words, the value adjusted for inflation. *From 1994 to 2006, there has been a significant decline in the real*

Table 16.2 Social Assistance Recipiency of Working-Age People with and without Disabilities in Canada, by Low-Income Status, 2009

Social Assistance in 2009?			
All incomes	No	Yes	Total
With disability (%)	21.0	68.0	23.6
Without disability (%)	79.0	32.0	76.4
Total (%)	100.0	100.0	100.0
Low income (total income below the LICO)			
With disability (%)	29.1	74.7	40.2
Without disability (%)	70.9	25.3	59.8
Total (%)	100.0	100.0	100.0
Not low income (total income at or above the LICO)			
With disability (%)	20.3	62.4	21.7
Without disability (%)	79.7	37.6	78.3
Total (%)	100.0	100.0	100.0

Source: Based on Crawford (2013) analyzing data from the 2009 Survey of Labour Income Dynamics and employing the low-income cut-off (LICO) of Statistics Canada. The data are for the provinces but not the territories.

Table 16.3 Maximum Annual Provincial Disability Social Assistance Benefits (2006 Constant Dollars)

	NL	PE	NS	NB	QC	ON	MB	SK	AB	BC	Canada (Average)
1994	10,783	11,975	11,291	10,531	10,301	15,054	10,749	11,148	13,443	11,479	11,675
2000	10,175	10,330	10,566	8,182	10,410	13,846	9,548	9,948	12,871	10,999	10,688
2006	9,905	9,400	9,082	9,143	10,234	12,273	8,765	9,075	11,841	10,843	10,056
Real % change, 1994–2006	−8.14	−21.50	−19.56	−13.18	−0.65	−18.47	−18.46	−18.60	−11.91	−5.54	−13.87
% difference from national average, 2006	−1.50	−6.52	−9.68	−9.08	1.77	22.04	−12.84	−9.76	17.75	7.82	N/A
Provincial Average	10,068	10,274	9,963	8,913	10,316	13,341	9,437	9,860	12,194	10,907	10,527

Source: Adapted from Chen, Osberg, and Phipps (2013, 29).

value of maximum yearly disability social assistance benefits of 13.87 per cent. A recent assessment puts it this way: "governments in Canada continue to pay disability benefits that are now distinctly lower, in real terms, than twenty years ago" (Chen, Osberg, and Phipps 2013, 28). These data refer to the maximum amount; some clients receive less than that in financial assistance. The degree of difference by province between the highest annual benefit amount and the lowest amount has remained fairly constant over this period (the highest province's average being 1.4 to 1.5 times greater than the lowest province's average). The jurisdictions at either end of the differential have also remained fairly stable, with New Brunswick having the lowest benefit amount for most years until Manitoba assumed that position in 2006 and Ontario being the province with the highest disability benefit amount.

Provincial social assistance systems do not reveal a singular policy direction in benefits for people with disabilities. Three trajectories can be discerned from Table 16.3. One is of certain provinces—specifically, Newfoundland and Labrador, Québec, and British Columbia—closing or eliminating the gap between their disability benefit amounts and the provincial average, coming closer to the Canadian average. A second trajectory for some other provinces—namely, PEI, Nova Scotia, Manitoba, and Saskatchewan—is a widening gap between their maximum annual disability benefits and the provincial average, with benefit levels declining in relative terms. A third trend is that still other provinces are effectively maintaining their relative position, either below the average, in the case of New Brunswick, or above the average, in the case of Alberta and Ontario. Since 2006, there have been notable developments in social assistance for people with disabilities in some provinces; conspicuous examples are Saskatchewan launching a new income system in 2010 and Alberta implementing a major increase in AISH benefits of $400 per month in 2012, lifting the maximum monthly financial benefit to $1,588.

The larger disability income policy context

The stark reality is that the majority of Canadians with a disability who receive social assistance receive no other public income benefit at the same time (OECD 2010, 53). There is relatively little stacking or simultaneous adding together of benefits that would help offset "the low individual payments levels" of provincial social assistance for people with disabilities (OECD 2010, 54). If people with disabilities on social assistance do receive a second income benefit, it is most likely from the Canada Pension Plan–Disability program (CPP-Disability). Interestingly, this program is the only major example of intergovernmental cooperation in the disability income security system in the country. Since the termination of the CAP in the mid-1990s, the federal government no longer has a policy responsibility in the area of social assistance for people with disabilities or an explicit and direct financial role for these programs. Therefore, both orders of government shape the nature of social citizenship for people with disabilities through different income security programs.

The incredible importance of social assistance is due partly to the practice in the provinces of deducting, dollar for dollar, an effective tax-back rate of 100 per cent on payments that beneficiaries receive from regular employment insurance (EI) benefits and sickness benefits, CPP-Disability benefits, workers' compensation payments, and long-term disability benefits from a work-based plan. Indeed, "provinces routinely ask income-assistance applicants to apply for CPP-D" (OECD 2010, 50), treating that national program as the first payer of income benefits for people with disabilities with a recent attachment to the workforce (Stapleton and Procyk 2010). Provincial social assistance programs do partially exempt a level of earned income, an incentive that applies to some but certainly not all clients with disabilities.[5] Liquid asset exemption levels (i.e., cash, bonds, and personal savings) are typically higher for recipients with a disability than for other client groups; in particular, those groups deemed employable have low exemption levels (National Council of Welfare 2010). Also, social assistance programs usually fully exempt income from federal and provincial tax credits, such as the Canada Child Tax Benefit and the Registered Disability Savings Plan.

In terms of benefit expenditures, the significance of provincial disability social assistance is presented in Table 16.4. In addition to actual expenditures on disability social assistance for each province, the relative share of disability social assistance is given for total provincial disability income expenditures, for total federal and provincial disability income expenditures, and for total public- and private-sector disability income benefit expenditures.

By several measures, social assistance for people with disabilities features considerably in disability income policy spending in Canada. Provincial expenditures on disability benefits through social assistance programs totalled over $6.8 billion in 2010–11. In about half the provinces, social assistance spending for the disabled is the largest amount in their disability income

5 Monthly earnings exemptions in social assistance for people with disabilities vary widely across provinces, from a high of $800 in Alberta (the AISH program) and British Columbia to a low in PEI of $75 plus 10 per cent of net wages for a single adult with a disability. Some provinces, such as Nova Scotia and Ontario, contain work-related incentive in their earnings exemption policies for people with disabilities.

Table 16.4 Provincial Social Assistance Disability Benefit Expenditures, 2010–11

Province	Social Assistance Disability ($ in millions)	% of Provincial Disability Expenditures	% of Provincial and Federal Disability Expenditures	% of Private- and Public-Sector Disability Expenditures
British Columbia	777	52.8	25.7	20.3
Alberta	709	69.2	35.8	27.7
Saskatchewan	119	49.6	20.8	17.5
Manitoba	188	62.9	25.2	21.4
Ontario	3,500	60.3	36.8	29.1
Québec	1,304	38.2	28.9	22.7
New Brunswick	42	36.5	7.9	6.6
Nova Scotia	127	46.0	15.5	13.5
PEI	17	56.7	16.2	13.8
Newfoundland and Labrador	56	38.1	15.1	13.0
Provincial Average	683.9	51.0	22.8	18.6

Source: Author's calculations from data in Stapleton, Tweddle, and Gibson (2013), Annex 1, 43–53.
Note: Provincial disability income program expenditures include social assistance and workers' compensation and, in the case of Québec, the disability program of the Québec Pension Plan. Service programs and tax credits are not included. Federal disability income expenditures refer to CPP–Disability benefits, to EI sickness benefits, First Nations' social assistance for the disabled, and veterans' disability pensions and awards. Public sector disability expenditures are the sum of this federal and provincial disability income program spending. Private sector expenditures refer to work-based disability benefits, primarily long-term disability insurance.

systems. In both Alberta and Ontario, provincial disability social assistance represents about 36 per cent of the combined federal and provincial expenditures on disability income benefits. In several other provinces, disability social assistance spending accounts for around one-quarter of total federal and provincial spending on income support for people with disabilities.

Ideas on reforming social assistance for people with disabilities

In the Canadian disability movement, policy activists closely connect advocacy for disability rights with safety-net program reforms. Adequate income support is seen as central to social citizenship and as contributing to inclusion and dignity, which are both principles and intended outcomes of the disability rights movement. Where there is divergence in Canada's disability community is between those groups that focus particularly on social assistance reform and those who focus more broadly on income security reform. In any event, reform ideas on disability social assistance can be examined as one piece of a fuller project of public policy change.

To alleviate the high incidence of poverty among people with disabilities, national movement organizations and coalitions call on the federal government to reform several income programs. Recommended reforms are for making the non-refundable disability tax credit (DTC) a refundable tax measure; making those eligible for CPP-Disability benefits automatically eligible for the DTC; making CPP-D benefits non-taxable; expanding the EI sickness benefit from the current 15-week maximum duration to up to 52 weeks; expanding the Working Income Tax Benefit (WITB) disability supplement; and ensuring any new federal benefits for those on social assistance are not clawed back by the provinces (Council of Canadians with Disabilities 2010).

Three themes characterize the contemporary reform agenda on social assistance for people with disabilities in Canadian provinces. These are (i) administrative and governance changes that focus on such issues as improving access to information about a program, simplifying application procedures, investing in the appropriate training of staff, and improving accountability mechanisms; (ii) employment incentive and support measures for social assistance clients in job training and for entering the labour force; and (iii) poverty alleviation and the adequacy of income benefits.

Most attention certainly by disability groups and researchers has been on the theme of poverty alleviation. The Disability Without Poverty Network (2012), an association of disability, legal assistance, and social policy organizations in BC, recommends an increase to the monthly social assistance rate for a person with a disability from approximately $906 to a minimum of $1,200. The network points out that this better reflects the actual cost of living in the province and would ease poverty and enhance equity by bringing rates in line with income standards for other vulnerable groups, such as seniors under the Old Age Security (OAS) program. Research on the intergenerational effects of provincial disability benefits, which uses data from social assistance programs in Canada, finds "strong evidence that higher parental disability benefits lead to improvements in children's cognitive functioning and non-cognitive development, as measured by math scores in standardized tests, and hyperactive and emotional anxiety symptoms" (Chen, Osberg, and Phipps 2013, 1). In short, higher parental disability incomes have positive effects on child well-being.

A related recommendation is to index social assistance benefits to some measure such as the consumer price index. Only two provinces (Newfoundland and Labrador and Québec) have automatic indexation provisions for social assistance rates, so this proposal, too, is commonly heard across the country. This recommendation aims at ensuring that social assistance benefits keep pace with the cost of living, thus maintaining some modicum of adequacy and ending the stealthy decline in the real value of welfare payments that has occurred across provinces since the early 1990s.

> Allowing inflation to reduce the purchasing power of disability payments (or, indeed, any income-support payment) is simply poor public policy. Good public policy is made by policymakers who are forthright in stating and holding up to comment their judgments about what the appropriate level of income support offered to the disadvantaged and vulnerable in society should be. (Kneebone and Grynishak 2011, 17)

In provinces with low earnings exemption policies or stringent asset limits, these are frequently identified as items for change in social assistance for people with disabilities. These recommendations on poverty alleviation, as noted above, are frequently tied to a reform agenda that also addresses improved public service administration and enhanced labour market activation for people with disabilities.

Conclusion

Although there is some recognition in provincial welfare schemes of the additional costs and barriers faced by people with significant disabilities, the right of citizens to income support independent of labour force participation is greatly confined. As social assistance recipients, people with disabilities remain vulnerable and marginalized, struggling for a dignified and adequate standard of living. Provincial social assistance programs decide insiders and outsiders in eligibility and mark differences in public identities. A deep-rooted residual policy sector, social assistance for people with disabilities involves the distribution of a double stigma: a subordinate status as an individual who is dependent on state aid, like others on welfare, and a further stigma in the form of a spoiled identity as a person with an abnormal body or mind. Conceptions of disability may be shifting toward greater attention to the capacity and employability of many disabled people, yet this move takes place within a longstanding context of ideas about biomedical deficit, personal tragedy, and family responsibility. As long as these old beliefs prevail in practice, people with disabilities face limitations in their social rights, which include both income assistance and employment opportunities, and struggle within the entrenched residualism of social welfare programs.

References

Banting, Keith. 1987. *The Welfare State and Canadian Federalism*. 2nd ed. Montréal: McGill-Queen's University Press.

Chen, Kathy, Lars Osberg, and Shelley Phipps. 2013. *Intergenerational Effects of Disability Benefits—Evidence from Canadian Social Assistance Programs*. Canadian Labour Market and Skills Researcher Network, Working Paper No. 122. Vancouver: CLMSR.

Council of Canadians with Disabilities. 2010. *As a Matter of Fact: Poverty and Disability in Canada*. Winnipeg: Council of Canadians with Disabilities.

Crawford, Cameron. 2013. *Looking into Poverty: Income Sources of Poor People with Disabilities in Canada*. Toronto: Institute for Research and Development on Inclusion and Society (IRIS).

Disability Without Poverty Network. 2012. *Overdue: The Case for Increasing the Persons with Disabilities Benefit in BC*. Vancouver: Disability Without Poverty Network.

Guest, Dennis. 2003. *The Emergence of Social Security in Canada*. 3rd ed. Vancouver: UBC Press.

Jongbloed, Lyn. 2006. "Disability Income and Employment Policies in Canada: Historical Developments." In *Disability and Social Policy in Canada*, 2nd ed., ed. Mary Ann McColl and Lyn Jongbloed, 243–53. Concord, ON: Captus Publications.

Kneebone, Ronald, and Oksana Grynishak. 2011. *Income Support for Persons with Disabilities*. SPP Research Paper 4 No. 11. Calgary: The School of Public Policy, University of Calgary.

Lankin, Frances, and Munir A. Sheikh. 2012. *Brighter Prospects: Transforming Social Assistance in Ontario*. Toronto: Commission for the Review of Social Assistance in Ontario.

Lightman, Ernie, Andrea Vick, Dean Herd, and Andrew Mitchell. 2009. "Not Disabled Enough: Episodic Disabilities and the Ontario Disability Support Program." *Disability Studies Quarterly* 29 (3): 1–16.

National Council of Welfare. 1998. *Profiles of Welfare: Myths and Realities*. Ottawa: National Council of Welfare. http://publications.gc.ca/site/eng/428618/publication.html.

National Council of Welfare. 2010. *Welfare Incomes 2009*. Ottawa: National Council of Welfare. http://publications.gc.ca/site/eng/380994/publication.html.

OECD (Organisation for Economic Co-operation and Development). 2010. *Sickness, Disability and Work: Breaking the Barriers—Canada: Opportunities for Collaboration*. Paris: OECD. http://www.oecd.org/employment/emp/46093870.pdf.

Prince, Michael J. 2001. "Canadian Federalism and Disability Policy Making." *Canadian Journal of Political Science* 34 (4): 791–817. http://dx.doi.org/10.1017/S0008423901778092.

Prince, Michael J. 2009. *Absent Citizens: Disability Politics and Policy in Canada*. Toronto: University of Toronto Press.

Rice, James J., and Michael J. Prince. 2013. *Changing Politics of Canadian Social Policy*. 2nd ed. Toronto: University of Toronto Press.

Stapleton, John. 2011. "Social Assistance Disability Income Expenditures: Why Costs Are Going Up." Presentation for the Council of Canadians with Disabilities, Ottawa, Ontario, November 3.

Stapleton, John. 2012. "The Welfarization of Disability Programs." Presentation given at a Social Planning Council Workshop, Winnipeg, Manitoba, March 22.

Stapleton, John, and Anne Tweddle. 2008. *Navigating the Maze: Improving Coordination and Integration of Disability Income and Employment Policies and Programs for People living with HIV/AIDS*. Toronto: Canadian Working Group on HIV and Rehabilitation.

Stapleton, John, Anne Tweddle, and Katie Gibson. 2013. "What Is Happening to Disability Income Systems in Canada? Insights and Proposals for Further Research." Paper prepared for Council of Canadians with Disabilities. http://www.ccdonline.ca/en/socialpolicy/poverty-citizenship/income-security-reform/disability-income-systems.

Stapleton, John, and Stephanie Procyk. 2010. *A Patchwork Quilt: Income Security for Canadians with Disabilities*. Toronto: Institute for Work and Health.

Stevens, Harvey, Wayne Simpson, and Sid Frankel. 2011. "Explaining Declining Social Assistance Participation Rates: A Longitudinal Analysis of Manitoba Administrative and Population Data." *Canadian Public Policy* 37 (2): 163–81. http://dx.doi.org/10.3138/cpp.37.2.163.

Vick, Andrea. 2012. "Theorizing Episodic Disabilities: The Case for an Embodied Politics." *Canadian Social Work Review* 29 (1): 41–60.

seventeen

Immigrants on Social Assistance in Canada: Who Are They and Why Are They There?[1]

TRACY SMITH-CARRIER AND JENNIFER MITCHELL

Introduction

Canada is one of the most diverse nations in the world, defined and shaped by the hallmark of multiculturalism. Essential to the prosperity Canada has enjoyed over the years are immigrants who contribute immeasurably to building the social and cultural richness of Canada's mosaic. Arguably, Canada is quite skilful at attracting new talent to this country. The integration of these newcomers, however, has been far more challenging. Today, not all immigrants are faring well; beset by numerous barriers that restrict their full social and economic integration in society, some immigrants face conditions that could potentially lead to social assistance (SA) access.

The purpose of this chapter is to outline current trends in immigrant SA usage and to explore the potential reasons that immigrants may need to resort to SA in times of need. We begin by presenting our theoretical framework and proceed to highlight the limitations associated with obtaining suitable data to inform analyses on the immigrant SA population. We then discuss the context of SA access for immigrants and consider the factors that may influence immigrant SA participation. Next, we present data from Statistics Canada's Survey of Labour and Income Dynamics (SLID) to explore immigrant SA trends in Canada; this we follow with a case study examining immigrant participation in Ontario Works (OW). We conclude by providing several recommendations that seek redress to the barriers identified.

Theoretical framework

Recognizing that people see the world through different lenses, we understand the importance of acknowledging that we view the following discussion through a critical anti-racist lens. Henry et al. (1995) suggest that "democratic racism" is prevalent in Canada, a contradictory expression of

1 The opinions expressed are those of the authors alone and do not necessarily reflect those of the Ontario Ministry of Community and Social Services.

racism whereby notions of egalitarianism, justice, and fairness are embraced at the same time that racism is being manifested in social institutions, and people continue to rely on constructions of racial stereotypes to make sense of their everyday lives. Indeed the language used to depict immigrants cast them as "outsiders" (denoting exclusion or not belonging), "foreigners" (signifying strangeness), and "aliens" needing to be "naturalized," two terms suggesting abnormality (Dominelli 2008).

Anti-racist praxis includes efforts to achieve equality of opportunity by responding directly to the social relations that produce racism (Berman and Paradies 2010). A structural approach is adopted to explain how oppressed identities (e.g., based on gender and class) intersect with race to reproduce the structures of power and privilege that maintain inequality. The continuing racializing of social groups is exposed; processes that engender differential treatment (privileging those of white descent while prescribing unequal value to visible minorities) on the basis of presumed cultural, biological, or phenotypical characteristics (Li 2008).

The "data problem"

It is increasingly difficult to document SA trends, particularly for immigrants, as many sources of data have now been terminated (i.e., the National Council of Welfare, the long-form census) or transformed (e.g., the SLID has been abandoned and both the Canadian Income Survey and the Longitudinal and International Study of Adults [LISA] have been introduced). Several longitudinal databases collected by Statistics Canada have been suggested as sources of data: the Longitudinal Administrative Database (often involving significant cost and processing time), the Longitudinal Immigration Database (although it cannot be used to make comparisons with native-born Canadians), and the LISA (which, at the time of writing, has just been released).

Obtaining data at the provincial level is also challenging given the variability in provincial SA programs and data collection. Many provinces do not collect data specifically on immigrants, or, if they do, they may not collect data on all the immigration categories identified by Citizenship and Immigration Canada (CIC; e.g., Ontario). If data are collected on immigration status, they are often only recorded until participants attain citizenship, after which people may cease to be tracked as immigrants. These limitations make observing immigrant SA trends using only provincial data less than ideal. The paucity of suitable data on this population has likely contributed to the dearth of literature in this area.

Unpacking Canadian immigration

To set the stage for the discussion that follows, we must highlight the context of immigration today. Canada's Constitution Act of 1867 (originally enacted as the British North America Act) recognizes immigration to be a concurrent power, meaning that the federal and provincial governments share jurisdiction over immigration matters. In practice, however, the federal government has taken leadership for immigration policy and delivery, except for in the case of Québec (Dobrowolsky 2013). CIC (2012a) outlines three goals for immigration in Canada: *economic* (first), *family reunification* (second), and *humanitarian* (third), and the numbers of immigrants permitted entrance through these categories quite aptly reflect these objectives. Immigrants are admitted under one of two streams: *permanent residency*, a pathway to citizenship, and *temporary residency*, which involves short-term visitation or a study or work stay. There are several categories within the permanent residency stream. The first is comprised of economic immigrants (63 per cent of the 248,748 immigrants admitted in 2012), who enter through the following categories: skilled workers or skilled tradespeople, those with Canadian work experience (Canadian Experience Class), entrepreneurs, investors, the self-employed, provincial or territorial nominees, or live-in caregivers.[2]

Next, the family class, which includes spouses and partners, children, parents, and grandparents, represents 23 per cent of the permanent residents entering in 2012. This category is followed by those admitted as refugees, who account for 11 per cent of the total. Finally, the catchall "other" category (4 per cent) includes all other immigrants not already captured (Statistics Canada 2013a); these persons are accepted for exceptional reasons or because they fit humanitarian, compassionate, or public policy aims.

The area of highest growth, however, is through Canada's temporary residency stream (see Table 17.1), which includes immigrants admitted "to fill temporary labour and skill shortages when qualified Canadian citizens or permanent residents are not available" (CIC 2012b). In 2012, a total of 421,075 temporary residents entered Canada (Statistics Canada 2013a), many as "foreign" workers with work permits granted through Labour Market Opinions (LMOs) or free trade agreements and many as students. The surge in these numbers in recent decades demonstrates the shift toward temporary workers to meet (short-term) labour market needs rather than longer-term objectives met through permanent residency or

2 In 2013, economic immigrants also included those in the Start-Up Visa Program.

Table 17.1 Immigration in Canada, 2012

Permanent				Temporary Work/ Study Permit or Visa	Precarious Immigration Status
Economic	Family Class	Refugees	Other		
156,117 (63%)	56,449 (23%)	27,873 (11%)	8,305 (4%)	Foreign Workers 213,573 (51%) Foreign Students 104,810 (25%) Refugee Claimants 20,461 (.05%) Visitors 71,759 (.2%) Temp. Resident Permits 9,701 (.02%) Other Humanitarian 771 (.002%)	Betwenn 20,000 and 600,000 (Goldring et al. 2007)
Total: 248,748				Total: 421,075	

Source: CIC (2013b).

citizenship (Alboim and Cohl 2012). This trend is also visible in the now "permanently" installed super visa program (CIC 2013a), which transformed the family reunification program to allow families to be reunited with their parents and grandparents—but only temporarily—by establishing these relatives as long-term visitors (up to two years) and not as permanent citizens.

These numbers do not account for those with precarious immigration status, what some refer to as undocumented or illegal migrants. Estimates for this population in Canada range considerably, from a low of 20,000 to a high of 600,000 (Goldring et al. 2007).

Social welfare for immigrants

Across the globe, welfare retrenchment has resulted in increased demands on individuals with diminished state supports, generally hitting the most vulnerable (e.g., newcomers) the hardest. The vestiges of xenophobia and of racism, both historically pervasive in this country, continue to persist, with the social rights of citizens generally deemed to be reserved for just that group—citizens, or at least for those on a pathway to citizenship. Claims of "foreigners" abusing or taking advantage of Canada's "generosity" have been present for years but have witnessed a particular resurgence as of late, engendering limitations on immigrant welfare access. Countries with similar suspicions have done the same. The United States, for example, restricted non-citizens arriving after 1996 from receiving most types of public assistance; and, in Germany, immigrants without permanent residency may be denied entry or residency extensions if they access SA (Hansen and Lofstrom 2011). Although some clearly recognize the boost immigrants provide in driving Canada's economic performance, the concern of others appears to hinge primarily on the fiscal transfers needed to sustain them. Hence the normative proposition that immigrants produce an immense "fiscal burden" on Canadian taxpayers is often accepted unquestioned. Immigration, then, because of its historical place in the economic development of Canada, appears to be conceptualized as a "one-sided relationship, established on what Canada will gain economically from newcomers, not what it may have to provide for them" (Bhuyan and Smith-Carrier 2012, 215). In this context, any assistance to immigrants is viewed as a burden.

The recent brouhaha over the Temporary Foreign Worker (TFW) program, which was vividly played out in the Canadian press and prompted a brief moratorium on hiring from the TFW program in the food services sector, aptly demonstrates the one-sided relationship of immigration. Despite a complete lack of government oversight of the program and a business sector that has widely abused the program, TFWers have borne much of the criticism and will continue to shoulder most of the consequences of the fiasco; the Canadian business sector—that has profited tremendously from this pool of expendable, underpaid labour—largely has not. Arguably, the most vulnerable TFWers remain so precariously situated—both under the earlier, largely exploitative program and under the current overhauled program, which will likely make it more difficult for workers to obtain employment contracts—that they must accept often gruelling, unsafe, and potentially abusive jobs that take them miles away from their families, to whom some are returned once they become sick or injured (see Orkin et al. 2014 on "medical repatriation"). The jobs typically occupied by TFWers are ones that tend to be hard to fill or ones into which employers prefer to slot TFWers, knowing that they will be unlikely to leave suddenly (usually they leave only at the behest of the employer). Also, employers typically have paid less to TFWers in these jobs, at least until recently. Before 2013, employers were permitted to pay TFWers 5 to 15 per cent less than the going wage rate in the sector, driving down wages not only for TFWers but for all Canadians.

Though Canada continues to benefit from the precarious labour of immigrants, the health and social benefits it must provide for them is increasingly being restricted. Significant cuts were made in 2012 to the Interim Federal Health Program (IFHP) limiting health-care coverage for protected persons, refugee claimants, and others ineligible for provincial or territorial insurance plans (CIC 2012c). Following a court challenge in response to the IFHP cuts, temporary measures have been implemented by the federal government while it appeals the Federal Court's ruling that the changes to the program constituted "cruel and unusual" treatment to "individuals seeking the protection of Canada" under Section 12 of the Charter of Rights and Freedoms (Federal Court of Canada 2014). Furthermore, to curb SA utilization, Ottawa is pressing for the termination of benefits for "failed" refugee claimants (Keung 2013) under private member's Bill C-585, which would allow provinces to introduce residency requirements as an additional eligibility criterion; this move could potentially ban most refugee claimants and people without permanent resident status from accessing SA programs (Income Security Advocacy Centre 2014). Recent changes to the family sponsorship program have also reduced the scope of SA eligibility. Indeed, needing assistance at any point during the settlement process appears pernicious. "That's an abuse of Canada's generosity," stated Jason Kenney, former federal immigration minister responding to reports that increasing numbers of sponsored seniors are accessing SA. He went on to say,

> If you think your parents may need to go on welfare in Canada, please don't sponsor them. We're not looking for more people on welfare, we're not looking to add people as a social burden to Canada. . . . (Quoted in Fitzpatrick 2013)

Some argue, however, that these claims not only further incite (unwarranted) fears that immigrants, if unchecked, will overrun Canada's welfare system but question the contribution of particular immigrants—imputing they have little value.

Immigrant SA participation

Although overall SA participation declined dramatically from the 1990s to 2000s, it is unclear how much of this decline is attributable to the welfare reforms introduced or to the favourable economic conditions at the time (see Kneebone and White; Boychuk, in this volume). Research suggests these reforms significantly reduced the probability of SA participation across Canada, with estimates signalling they reduced participation for the immigrant population even more so (Berg and Gabel 2013). However, as will be shown, immigrant SA participation over the past decade has been increasing, if only slightly (likely, too, as a result of the Great Recession). Still, over the years, research has been mixed on who uses SA more—immigrants or the Canadian-born. Arguments promulgated in the mainstream media generally suggest that immigrants access welfare more. Lilley (2011) from the *Toronto Sun* notes that immigrants use SA more than their native-born counterparts, albeit recognizing that particular classes of immigrants access it far less. In SA research, Baker and Benjamin (1995, 650) find "no evidence that immigrants pose an excess burden on Canada's transfer programs," with immigrants in the late 1980s and early 1990s bearing lower rates of SA utilization at entry relative to the native-born (participation was found to rise as they "assimilated"). In contradistinction, Thomas and Rappak (1998) using SLID data showed that immigrants received more in certain government transfers, including SA, compared to the Canadian-born, who, on average, collected more in the form of child tax credits and employment insurance (EI). More recently, however, Ostrovsky (2012) finds no evidence of increasing rates of immigrant SA access (or EI usage) from 1993 to 2007, noting that immigrant participation actually declined during this period. That being said, some research shows that immigrants do tend to have slightly longer SA spells and decreased odds of exiting SA (e.g., OW) relative to the Canadian-born (Smith-Carrier, forthcoming).

Each provincial and territorial SA program is unique, applying different benefit amounts and eligibility criteria. Though various conditions exist that limit participant eligibility, many provinces and territories have opted not to limit eligibility on the basis of residency status, allowing citizens and permanent and temporary residents to apply. Governments do, however, generally restrict access for those lacking authorized immigration status and for some immigration categories (discussed below). Although some provinces allow temporary residents to access SA, in Ontario, only immigrants with permanent residency status are eligible, temporary residents are not. Other assistance, outside of SA, may also be available to immigrants fitting prescribed immigration categories, and Ontario's directives specifically note that sponsored immigrants (in the family class) are expected to receive any financial support necessary from their sponsors, not through SA. Convention refugees (sponsored by the federal government or a private sponsor) are eligible for settlement assistance from the federal government, and, while they receive this assistance, they are ineligible for SA. Furthermore, those wishing to make a refugee claim must obtain appropriate documentation to be able to apply for SA, namely, CIC verification that their claim is eligible to be heard by the Immigration and Refugee Board (Ontario Ministry of Community and Social Services 2013).

Rather than directing singular focus on caseload numbers, we are more interested in *why* people resort to SA in the first place, particularly in a context where emphasis is typically placed on individuals' failure to be "self-sufficient" and the burden they allegedly impose should they dare access the programs and services of the (post) welfare state—benefits that most[3] citizens can and do enjoy.

Contextualizing immigrant experiences in Canada

Although at one time the economic trajectory of immigrants in Canada was quite optimistic, the story has not been as positive in recent decades. For some, coming to Canada has fuelled a cycle of SA participation intermingled with periods of employment as part of the working poor (a trend also observed, however, among the native-born population). Though immigrants on SA remains an area largely under researched, in comparison, literature documenting the economic disadvantages and obstacles confronting immigrants is substantial. Still, it is important to note that immigration affects groups differently, yielding disparate outcomes for women versus men, and for particular groups of immigrants (by race or ethnicity, source country or immigration status) compared to others.

Low income and earnings differentials

In the 1970s, immigrants could initially expect to earn less than the Canadian-born. There followed a brief period of catch up (generally within a 10-year period) until they were on par or even surpassed their Canadian-born counterparts. More recent cohorts, however, are falling behind as the earnings gap continues to widen, with little evidence it will converge in the near future (Picot 2008). Recent immigrants[4] are thus two to three times more likely to experience low income (for at least a year) as compared to the native-born, and to experience it repeatedly (Palameta 2004).

3 We use the word "most" and not "all" in recognition that Aboriginal peoples, the longest standing residents in Canada, have generally not been privy to the same welfare provisions as other citizens in this country (see Papillon, in this volume, for further discussion on this topic).

4 CIC defines "very recent" immigrants to have been landed immigrants to Canada for five years or less, "recent" immigrants to have been landed immigrants between 6 to 10 years, and "established" immigrants to have been landed immigrants to Canada for over 10 years (for definitions, see Statistics Canada 2010).

Education and experience

Immigrants increasingly present higher levels of education than their Canadian-born counterparts. In 2006, 42 per cent of very recent immigrants had postsecondary education, up from 13.9 per cent in 1981 (Desjardins and Cornelson 2011). For principal applicants in the economic class or skilled worker category, the figure is higher still, at 79.5 per cent (Alboim and McIsaac 2007). Figure 17.1 depicts the employment and unemployment rates in 2013 for those with a university degree, and it shows that having postsecondary education does not translate into better outcomes for immigrants. Here we witness that very recent immigrants (landed five years ago or fewer) struggle most in their quest for employment, having an employment rate of 68.4 per cent and an unemployment rate of 11.6 per cent as compared to the Canadian-born who, also bearing a degree, have a comparatively low unemployment rate (2.8 per cent) and a high employment rate (90.9 per cent). This finding is particularly

Figure 17.1 Unemployment and Employment Rates by Immigration Status for Those with a University Degree, 2014

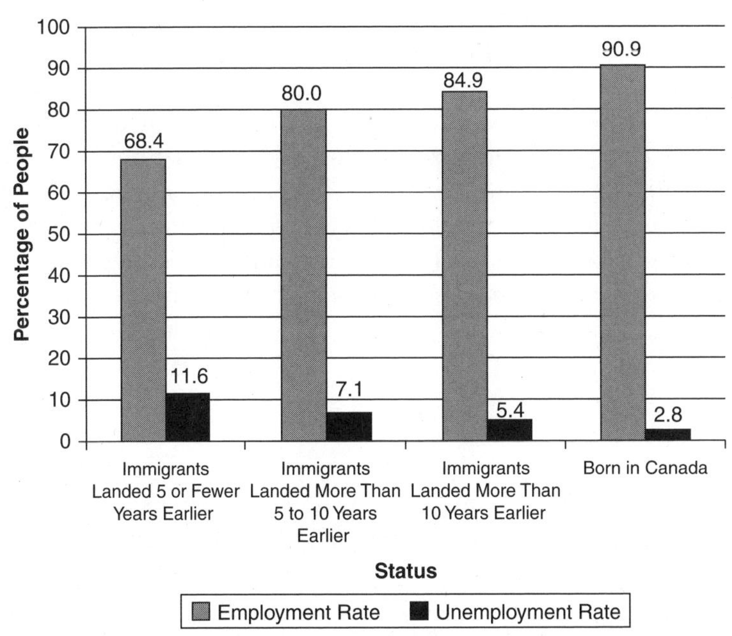

Source: Statistics Canada (2014).

disconcerting as one of the known escapes out of low income has traditionally been associated with the attainment of higher education.

There are several explanations given as to why postsecondary education has not yielded better outcomes for immigrants. Reitz (2001) argues that the education advantage immigrants once held has declined relative to that of the Canadian-born, the latter having benefited more from increases in postsecondary education. Moreover, Alboim, Finnie, and Meng (2005) estimate that education obtained abroad is discounted, worth only 70 per cent of Canadian education. Not only is immigrants' education discounted but their "foreign" work experience is as well, with a year of experience obtained abroad worth only one-third of what Canadian-born experience is valued (Alboim, Finnie, and Meng 2005). As a result, immigrants are often relegated to jobs with a lower status than their credentials and experience would dictate (Creese and Wiebe 2012).

Skills mismatch and credentials

It is well known that there is a skills mismatch issue in Canada. Indeed, Chen, Smith, and Mustard (2010) found that, four years after their arrival in Canada, over half (51.6 per cent) of immigrants were overqualified for their jobs based on their education levels, with the stereotype of the educated immigrant driving a taxi proving to indeed be true. In 2006, 53 per cent of immigrants driving taxis in Canada had postsecondary education (as compared to 35 per cent for Canadian-born taxi drivers), and one in three of these had degrees obtained in Canada (Xu 2012). The difficulty for immigrants of having their credentials recognized is widespread. Houle and Yssaad (2010) note that only 24 per cent of immigrants educated outside of Canada actually obtain a position in a regulated occupation that matches their training. Deskilling and churning (moving cyclically from one "survival job" to the next) are common, and form an employment path yielding little upward mobility (Mitchell, Lightman, and Herd 2007).

Unemployment

Earlier studies found that immigrants and non-immigrants tended to experience similar employment rates (see Thomas and Rappak 1998). Now, however, recent immigrants have higher rates of unemployment than the Canadian-born (Desjardins and Cornelson 2011) and tend to occupy low-paying seasonal or contract jobs offering few to no employment benefits.

Established immigrants have rates approaching the Canadian-born, but very recent immigrants have the starkest disparities, with an unemployment rate (13.6 per cent) that is well over double that of native-born residents (5.5 per cent) and an employment rate that is essentially 20 per cent lower than the rate for those born in Canada (Statistics Canada 2013b).

Health status

Immigrants, when they arrive, tend to have better health than the host population, a phenomenon known as the "healthy immigrant effect." This "effect" is largely due to an immigration system that places high priority on admitting young and healthy immigrants. The relationship between health and employment is important, particularly given that employment is deemed a key social determinant of health. Given a host of factors, not least of which includes a high unemployment rate, the healthy immigrant effect appears to be challenged after entry to Canada, resulting in growing numbers of recent immigrants experiencing significant (self-reported) health decline (Fuller-Thomson, Noack, and George 2011).

Discrimination

The composition of the incoming immigrant population has changed over the past few decades. Rather than migrating from "traditional source regions" (Europe and the United States), immigrants now tend to originate from Asia (China, India, and the Philippines). Immigrants entering from "non-traditional" source regions have been shown to have lower earnings at entry, even with experience and education equivalent to those born in Canada. Also, the rate of low income for immigrants (many of whom are members of racialized groups) has been steadily increasing (even in the 1990s, when it fell for the Canadian-born). This increasing rate of low-income affected immigrants across the board, regardless of age, education, or source-country origin, although it did not affect those from "traditional source regions" (Picot and Sweetman 2005). Given these factors, the hypothesis that racism and discrimination play a role in immigrant unemployment and SA access must be considered. A study by Oreopoulos and Dechief (2011) found that job applicants with English-sounding names on their résumés were 45 per cent more likely to be invited for an interview than applicants with Chinese or Indian names, regardless of both having comparable training and experience.

SLID data

The following section presents data from Statistics Canada's SLID from 2001 to 2011 (see Figure 17.2). The SLID sample is composed of two panels, each panel consisting of two Labour Force Survey rotation groups that include roughly 17,000 households (Statistics Canada 2012a). Though we cannot observe the total number of immigrants on SA from the SLID, we can observe trends using this sample. The total number on SA in 2011 was 2,666, of which 28 per cent were immigrants and 66 per cent were non-immigrants.

Although there have been few dramatic shifts in SA usage (for immigrants and non-immigrants alike), there does appear to be a steady increase of immigrants on SA over time, from 20 per cent in 2001 to 28 per cent in 2011 (perhaps suggesting that immigrants were more vulnerable in the recession); whereas the non-immigrant population tended to oscillate, from 67 per cent in 2001, increasing to 71 per cent in 2005, but back to 66 per cent by 2011. We now turn our attention to a case study highlighting important trends in Ontario.

Figure 17.2 SA Participation in Canada, 2001–2011

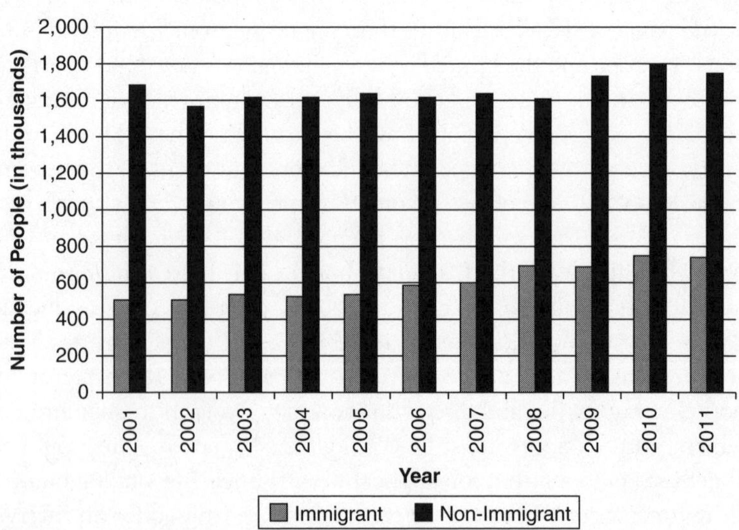

Source: Statistics Canada (2012b).
Note: SA payments are assigned to one family member only; therefore the amount for the economic family was used to determine if the person received SA.

Ontario as a case study

SA in Ontario includes two programs: Ontario Works (OW) and the Ontario Disability Support Program (ODSP). To be eligible for either, applicants must be legally entitled to reside in Canada permanently. The following are *not* eligible:

- Tourists
- Visitors (unless making a refugee protection claim)
- Convention refugees accessing sponsorship or settlement programs
- Inland refugees (unless authorized to apply)
- Those under removal or deportation orders
- Temporary residents (Ontario Ministry of Community and Social Services 2013)

Ontario's Ministry of Community and Social Services (MCSS) collects data on particular categories of interest to CIC (not all categories defined by CIC are reflected in Ontario's SA database). As a result, the numbers that follow, though useful in providing an overall picture, may not precisely capture the entirety of OW's immigrant population. MCSS does, however, record a "foreign-born" variable that allows one to track immigrants in the caseload, regardless of whether they have immigration or citizenship status at the time the data are run.

In November 2009, the total OW caseload was 236,219 (126,861 females and 109,357 males), totalling, with dependents, 433,831. In the same month, the immigrant caseload included 23,233 applicants (10 per cent of the overall caseload), with two dominant categories: refugee claimants and sponsored immigrants (Smith-Carrier 2011). MCSS tracks sponsored immigrants to ensure sponsors maintain the obligations specified in their sponsorship agreement. Should they fail to meet the provisions, they may be required to repay the government for any SA payments received by the sponsored immigrant, and, potentially, they may be banned from sponsoring future relatives.

In January 2014, new sponsorship criteria were put into effect to "ensure that sponsors have the financial means to support parents and grandparents, while reducing the net costs to Canadian taxpayers by leading to less reliance on health care and social programs" (CIC 2013a). The age of children eligible for sponsorship under their parents' immigration application was lowered from 22 to 18; the minimum income required to be eligible to sponsor relatives was increased by 30 per cent, demonstrated over three years, not one; and the length of time of sponsorship was doubled from 10 years to 20 (CIC 2013). These changes are intended to reduce immigrant welfare access and, ultimately, will allow only wealthier immigrants to benefit from the family reunification program.

Broken down by program, immigrants comprised 38 per cent of the OW population in December 2011, and non-immigrants accounted for 62 per cent. Even fewer immigrants participated in ODSP (24 per cent) compared to non-immigrants (76 per cent). Combined, immigrants comprised 31 per cent of Ontario's caseload and non-immigrants 69 per cent (Tefera 2012). Returning once again to the SLID (Figure 17.3), we observe an upward trend over the past decade in Ontario for immigrants and non-immigrants alike, as numbers initially vacillate but then steadily increase in the mid-2000s, and this increase intensifies after the economic downfall in 2008. Here, immigrants represent a lower proportion on SA than do non-immigrants, although, when considering their demographic mass, immigrants on SA roughly mirror their share of Ontario's population. Immigrants in Ontario represented 28.5 per cent of the total population in 2011 (Ontario Ministry of Finance 2011); in the same year, the proportion of immigrants on SA accounted for 31 per cent (Tefera 2012). Conversely,

Figure 17.3 SA Participation in Ontario, 2001–11

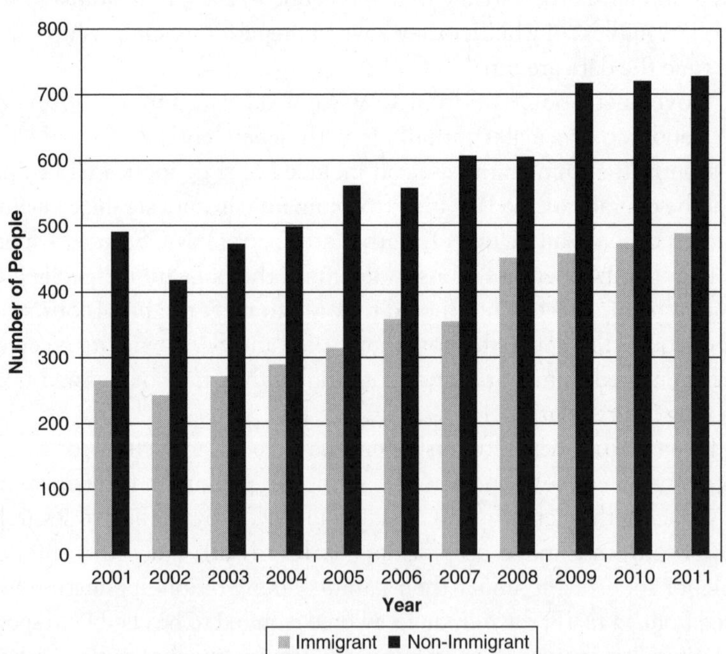

Source: Statistics Canada (2012b).

the proportion of non-immigrants in Ontario (71.5 per cent) was roughly equivalent to their share of the non-immigrant population on SA (69 per cent). The notion that Ontario's immigrants access SA more than their Canadian-born counterparts is thus questionable.

Several areas require redress to improve immigrants' future prospects. Many of these are not novel but have been well documented. They include the *provision of necessary employment supports* (i.e., childcare, transportation, and housing); the *delivery of higher-level language training* that fosters increased communication skills and occupation-specific language skills for the workplace; *expansion of bridge training, internship, and mentorship programs; education and support for employers*, particularly related to job shadowing, on-the-job training, and apprenticeships; *further work on credential recognition*; *investments in long-term human capital development strategies* focused on education, training, and skills rather than work-first strategies that exclusively focus on life skills, work habits, and job-search skills; *access to comprehensive and transparent data* to ensure that policymaking is not conducted within an evidence vacuum; and the *development of a national vision through broad-based dialogue* to define what the long-term goals of Canada's immigration system are and should be.

Rather than the constructed "burden to society" that people on SA are said to represent, we submit that SA participants, and immigrant SA participants in particular, recurrently "give, produce, and contribute" to society. We thus use SA "participant" rather than "recipient" (one who "receives") throughout this chapter in light of this understanding. We argue that Canada's present attention ought to focus less on immigrants' "problems" and more on the institutional structures needed to integrate immigrants effectively in society. Clearly, it is the institutional capacity that is inadequate, not the people.

References

Alboim, Naomi, and Elizabeth McIsaac. 2007. "Making the Connections: Ottawa's Role in Immigrant Employment." *IRPP Choices* 13 (1). http://irpp.org/wp-content/uploads/assets/research/diversity-immigration-and-integration/making-the-connections/vol13no3.pdf.

Alboim, Naomi, and Karen Cohl. 2012. *Shaping the Future: Canada's Rapidly Changing Immigration Policies*. Toronto: Maytree. http://maytree.com/wp-content/uploads/2012/10/shaping-the-future.pdf.

Alboim, Naomi, Ross Finnie, and Ronald Meng. 2005. "The Discounting of Immigrants' Skills in Canada: Evidence and Policy Recommendations." *IRPP Choices* 11 (2). http://irpp.org/wp-content/uploads/assets/research/diversity-immigration-and-integration/new-research-article-4/vol11no2.pdf.

Baker, Michael, and Dwayne Benjamin. 1995. "The Receipt of Transfer Payments by Immigrants in Canada." *Journal of Human Resources* 30 (4): 650–76. http://dx.doi.org/10.2307/146226.

Berg, Nathan, and Todd Gabel. 2013. *Effects of New Welfare Reform Strategies on Welfare Participation: Microdata Estimates from Canada.* University of Otaga Economics Discussion Papers No. 1304. Dunedin, New Zealand: University of Otago. http://www.otago.ac.nz/economics/research/DP_1304.pdf.

Berman, Gabrielle, and Yin Paradies. 2010. "Racism, Disadvantage and Multiculturalism: Towards Effective Anti-Racist Praxis." *Ethnic and Racial Studies* 33 (2): 214–32. http://dx.doi.org/10.1080/01419870802302272.

Bhuyan, Rupaleem, and Tracy Smith-Carrier. 2012. "Constructions of Migrant Rights in Canada: Is Subnational Citizenship Possible?" *Citizenship Studies* 16 (2): 203–21. http://dx.doi.org/10.1080/13621025.2012.667613.

Chen, Cynthia, Peter Smith, and Cameron Mustard. 2010. "The Prevalence of Over-Qualification and Its Association with Health Status among Occupationally Active New Immigrants to Canada." *Ethnicity & Health* 15 (6): 601–19. http://dx.doi.org/10.1080/13557858.2010.502591.

CIC (Citizenship and Immigration Canada). 2012a. "Canada Facts and Figures. Immigration Overview Permanent and Temporary Residents 2012." http://publications.gc.ca/collections/collection_2013/cic/c1-8-2012-eng.pdf.

CIC (Citizenship and Immigration Canada). 2012b. "Fact Sheet—Temporary Foreign Worker Program." Last modified February 19, 2015. http://www.cic.gc.ca/english/resources/publications/employers/temp-foreign-worker-program.asp.

CIC (Citizenship and Immigration Canada). 2012c. "Reform of the Interim Federal Health Program Ensures Fairness, Protects Public Health and Safety." Last modified April 25, 2012. http://news.gc.ca/web/article-en.do?nid=670949&_ga=1.253381513.1067223158.1423258180.

CIC (Citizenship and Immigration Canada). 2013a. "Backgrounder—Action Plan for Faster Family Reunification: Phase II." Last modified May 17, 2013. http://www.cic.gc.ca/english/department/media/backgrounders/2013/2013–05–10b.asp.

CIC (Citizenship and Immigration Canada). 2013b. "Facts and Figures." Last modified March 19, 2015. http://www.cic.gc.ca/english/resources/statistics/facts2013/permanent/01.asp.

Creese, Gillian, and Brandy Wiebe. 2012. "'Survival Employment': Gender and Deskilling among African Immigrants in Canada." *International Migration (Geneva, Switzerland)* 50 (5): 56–76. http://dx.doi.org/10.1111/j.1468-2435.2009.00531.x.

Desjardins, Dawn, and Kirsten Cornelson. 2011. "Immigrant Labour Market Outcomes in Canada: The Benefits of Addressing Wage and Employment Gaps." *RBC Economics: Current Analysis.* December. http://www.rbc.com/newsroom/pdf/1219-2011-immigration.pdf.

Dobrowolsky, Alexandra. 2013. "Nuancing Neoliberalism: Lessons Learned from a Failed Immigration Experiment." *Journal of International Migration and Integration* 14 (2): 197–218. http://dx.doi.org/10.1007/s12134-012-0234-8.

Dominelli, Lena. 2008. *Anti-Racist Social Work.* 3rd ed. New York: Palgrave Macmillan.

Federal Court of Canada. 2014. *Canadian Doctors for Refugee Care, the Canadian Association of Refugee Lawyers, Daniel Garcia Rodriques, Hanif Ayubi and Justice for Children and Youth v. Attorney General of Canada and Minister of Citizenship and Immigration,* FC 651. http://cas-ncr-ntero3.cas-satj.gc.ca/rss/T-356-13%20Cdn%20Doctors%20v%20AGC%20Judgment%20and%20Reasons.pdf.

Fitzpatrick, Meagan. 2013. "Don't Bring Parents Here for Welfare, Kenney Says." *CBC News*, May 10. Accessed August 3, 2013. http://www.cbc.ca/news/politics/don-t-bring-parents-here-for-welfare-kenney-says-1.1351002.

Fuller-Thomson, Esme, Andrea M. Noack, and Usha George. 2011. "Health Decline among Recent Immigrants to Canada: Findings from a Nationally-Representative Longitudinal Survey." *Canadian Journal of Public Health* 102 (4): 272–80.

Goldring, Luin, Carolina Bernstein, and Judith Bernhard. 2007. "Institutionalizing Precarious Immigration Status in Canada." CERIS Working Paper No. 61. Accessed June 6, 2015. http://www.ceris.metropolis.net/Virtual%20Library/WKPP%20List/WKPP2007/ CWP61.pdf.

Hansen, Jörgen, and Magnus Lofstrom. 2011. "Immigrant-Native Differences in Welfare Participation: The Role of Entry and Exit Rates." *Industrial Relations* 50 (3): 412–42. http://dx.doi.org/10.1111/j.1468-232X.2011.00644.x.

Henry, Frances, Carol Tator, Winston Mattis, and Tim Rees. 1995. *The Colour of Democracy: Racism in Canadian Society*. Toronto: Harcourt Brace and Company.

Houle, René, and Lahouaria Yssaad. 2010. "Recognition of Newcomers' Foreign Credentials and Work Experience." *Perspectives on Labour and Income* 11 (9): 18–33. http://www.statcan.gc.ca/pub/75-001-x/75-001-x2010109-eng.pdf.

Income Security Advocacy Centre. 2014. "Bill C-585 to Restrict Refugee Claimant Access to Social Assistance." http://www.incomesecurity.org/documents/BillC-585-Backgrounder-Sept2014_000.docx.

Keung, Nicholas. 2013. "Welfare Cut to Failed Refugees Awaiting Deportation." *Toronto Star*, November 10. http://www.thestar.com/news/canada/2013/11/10/welfare_cut_to_failed_refugees_awaiting_deportation.html.

Li, Peter S. 2008. "The Market Value and Social Value of Race." In *Daily Struggles: The Deepening of Racialization and Feminization of Poverty in Canada*, ed. Maria A. Wallis and Siu-Ming Kwok, 21–33. Toronto: Canadian Scholars' Press.

Lilley, Brian. 2011. "Immigrants' Use of Welfare a Mixed Bag, Documents Show." *Toronto Sun*, January 11. Accessed October 3, 2013. http://www.torontosun.com/news/canada/2011/01/11/16850306.html.

Mitchell, Andrew, Ernie Lightman, and Dean Herd. 2007. "'Work First' and Immigrants in Toronto." *Social Policy and Society* 6 (3): 293–307. http://dx.doi.org/10.1017/S1474746407003636.

Ontario Ministry of Community and Social Services. 2013. *Ontario Works Policy Directives*. Toronto: Ontario Works. Last modified January. http://www.mcss.gov.on.ca/documents/en/mcss/social/directives/ow/0101.pdf.

Ontario Ministry of Finance. 2011. *2011 National Household Survey Highlights: Factsheet 1*. Toronto: Government of Ontario. Last modified July 2013. http://www.fin.gov.on.ca/en/economy/demographics/census/nhshi11–1.html.

Oreopoulos, Phillip, and Diane Dechief. 2011. *Why Do Some Employers Prefer to Interview Matthew, But Not Samir? New Evidence from Toronto, Montreal, and Vancouver*. Metropolis British Columbia Working Paper No. 11–23. Vancouver: Metropolis British Columbia Centre of Excellence for Research on Immigration and Diversity. http://mbc.metropolis.net/assets/uploads/files/wp/2011/WP11-13.pdf.

Orkin, Aaron, Morgan Lay, Janet McLaughlin, Michael Schwandt, and David Cole. 2014. "Medical Repatriation of Migrant Farm Workers in Ontario: A Descriptive Analysis." *CMAJ Open* 2 (3): E192–E198. http://dx.doi.org/10.9778/cmajo.20140014.

Ostrovsky, Yuri. 2012. "The Dynamics of Immigration Participation in Entitlement Programs: Evidence from Canada, 1993–2007." *Canadian Journal of Economics / Revue canadienne d'économique* 45 (1): 107–36. http://dx.doi.org/10.1111/j.1540-5982.2011.01689.x.

Palameta, Boria. 2004. "Low Income among Immigrants and Visible Minorities." *Perspectives on Labour and Income* 5 (4): 12–17. http://www.statcan.gc.ca/pub/75-001-x/75-001-x2004104-eng.pdf.

Picot, Garnet. 2008. *Immigrant Economic and Social Outcomes in Canada: Research and Data Development at Statistics Canada*. Ottawa: Statistics Canada. http://www.statcan.gc.ca/pub/11f0019m/11f0019m2008319-eng.htm.

Picot, Garnet, and Arthur Sweetman. 2005. *The Deteriorating Economic Welfare of Immigrants and Possible Causes: Update 2005*. Ottawa: Statistics Canada. http://www.statcan.gc.ca/pub/11f0019m/11f0019m2005262-eng.pdf.

Reitz, Jeffrey G. 2001. "Immigrant Skill Utilization in the Canadian Labour Market: Implications of Human Capital Research." *Journal of International Migration and Integration* 2 (3): 347–78. http://dx.doi.org/10.1007/s12134-001-1004-1.

Smith-Carrier, Tracy. 2011. "Challenging the Dominant Discourse of 'Welfare Dependency': A Multi-Episode Survival Analysis of Ontario Works Spells." PhD diss., University of Toronto.

Smith-Carrier, Tracy. Forthcoming. "Reproducing Social Conditions of Poverty: A Critical Feminist Analysis of Social Assistance Participation in Ontario, Canada." *Journal of Women, Politics & Policy*.

Statistics Canada. 2010. *Profile of Internationally-Educated Immigrants Aged 25 to 64*. Ottawa: Statistics Canada. Last modified September 9, 2010. http://www.statcan.gc.ca/pub/81-595-m/2010084/e2-eng.htm.

Statistics Canada. 2012a. *Recipients of Social Assistance by Immigration Status and Period since Immigration, 2001–2011*. Custom table R574129. Ottawa: Statistics Canada.

Statistics Canada. 2012b. *SLID Custom Cross-Tabulations*. Ottawa: Statistics Canada.

Statistics Canada. 2013a. *Employment and Unemployment Rates' Gaps between Immigrants and Canadian Born Aged 25 to 54, 2011*. Ottawa: Statistics Canada. Last modified June 19. http://www.statcan.gc.ca/pub/71-606-x/2012006/t035-eng.htm.

Statistics Canada. 2013b. *Labour Force Survey*. Ottawa: Statistics Canada.

Statistics Canada. 2014. *Labour Force Characteristics by Immigrant Status of Population Aged 25 to 54, and by Educational Attainment*. CANSIM Table 282–0106. Ottawa: Statistics Canada. Last modified January 30, 2015. http://www.statcan.gc.ca/tables-tableaux/sum-som/l01/cst01/labor90a-eng.htm.

Tefera, Aklilu. 2012. "Immigrants and Their Welfare Use in British Columbia and Ontario." Proceedings from the 14th National Metropolis Conference. Toronto, Ontario, March 1. Accessed October 3, 2013. http://www.ceris.metropolis.net/?p=3965.

Thomas, Derrick, and J. Peter Rappak. 1998. *Employment Stability and the Adjustment of Immigrants: An Examination of Data from the Survey of Labour and Income Dynamics*." Income and Labour Dynamics Working Paper Series. Catalogue no. 98–01. Ottawa: Statistics Canada. http://publications.gc.ca/collections/Collection/Statcan/75F0002MIE/75F0002MIE1998001.pdf.

Xu, Li. 2012. *Who Drives a Taxi in Canada?* Ottawa: Citizenship and Immigration Canada. http://www.cic.gc.ca/english/pdf/research-stats/taxi.pdf.

eighteen

Playing Catch-up with Ghosts: Income Assistance for First Nations on Reserve[1]

MARTIN PAPILLON

On June 12, 2013, Minister of Aboriginal Affairs Bernard Valcourt announced the details of a federal investment in skills training for First Nations youths on reserve. To "close the gap" with other Canadians, the government will invest $241 million in new funding "targeted at youth receiving Income Assistance, providing them with access to a range of training and career counselling programs that will help them get jobs." Aboriginal youths, the minister added, "should have the same opportunities as all Canadians to find, keep, and enjoy the benefits of a job" (AANDC 2013c).

The significance of this announcement should not be underestimated. First Nations and other Aboriginal peoples across the country, just as other Canadians, have long engaged in skills development and other related labour market integration incentives. This announcement marks the first time, however, that the federal government has created a pan-Canadian program establishing active measures as a condition for receiving income support for First Nations citizens living on reserves. It is also one of the first major reforms of the federal income assistance program on reserves since its inception in 1964.

The Income Assistance Program for First Nations individuals living on reserve is a bit of an anomaly in Canada. Income assistance is, after all, a provincial responsibility. First Nations recipients living on reserves are the only Canadians getting last-resort support through the federal government. All other Aboriginal peoples, including First Nations citizens living off reserve, are under provincial programs.[2] With close to 170,000 beneficiaries in 2012, the federal on-reserve program is the fourth largest income assistance program in Canada. It is also one of the most important sources

---

1 I would like to thank Samantha Eisleb-Taylor for her invaluable assistance in preparing this chapter.

2 The Canadian Constitution recognizes three groups of Aboriginal peoples: First Nations, Inuit, and Métis. Members of First Nations who are registered under the Indian Act are considered "Status Indians" and therefore benefit from a certain number of legislated protections, as well as from federally run programs, including social assistance. Other Aboriginal peoples are considered provincial residents for the purpose of social programs. The present chapter focuses primarily on First Nations people with status who live on reserves.

of income on many reserves, with the number of monthly beneficiaries (recipients and their dependents) averaging 34 per cent of the total on-reserve population and reaching up to 80 per cent on some reserves. By comparison, the average number of beneficiaries in all of the provincial programs combined is 5 per cent (AANDC 2013d).

The program is a bit of a hybrid too: services are funded by the federal government, but they are delivered mostly by First Nations agencies, following the rates and eligibility criteria established by relevant provincial authorities. The result is a highly fragmented policy regime in which the federal government has a limited capacity to establish substantive policy directions beyond tinkering with the funding structure, as local programs must be consistent with provincial income assistance models. First Nations implementing the program also face a certain disconnect as they navigate between the limited flexibility of federal funding and evolving provincial objectives and rates. It is in part to address this disconnect, and catch up with existing provincial programs, that the federal government announced new funding for activation measures.

That being said, in its attempt to address the dramatic conditions on reserves through labour market integration measures that are consistent with provincial practices, the federal government also risks catching up its own ghosts. The development of the income assistance for First Nations program largely echoes that of the broader welfare state, but it is also rooted in more complex, and controversial, policy logic associated with Canada's colonial past. Income support for First Nations people was originally justified, and explicitly designed, as a tool of cultural and economic assimilation. By providing individuals with some material support, it was hoped they would see the benefit of salaried work and eventually adopt the "civilized ways" of the dominant society (Shewell 2004). Though the assimilation paradigm is long gone, the dual historical role of social assistance as a last-resort measure and a powerful acculturation tool still resonates in many communities.

As I discuss in this chapter, for many youths in First Nations communities, the chronic lack of employment they face is compounded by other challenges, including dislocated families, violence, drug abuses, and other psychosocial obstacles to labour market participation. These compounding factors, many argue, are intimately linked with the trauma caused by colonial policies (Alfred 2009). The echoes of our colonial past also resonate with some of the assumptions at the heart of the recently proposed reform. Implicit in the minister's active measures announcement is the notion that First Nation youths need to catch up to the dominant society and adapt to its realities, notably through greater work flexibility and mobility. Although the language is not the same, the objective in this respect is not radically different from those of past policies—it is still to transform "the Indian" into a "good" working citizen.

To understand the many challenges facing the delivery of social assistance to First Nations, this chapter suggests we need to pay attention to these ambiguities at the very core of the program. If the ghosts of the past are not confronted head on, they will continue to haunt us. Addressing this complex legacy means developing a truly holistic and flexible approach to First Nations well-being, an approach that pays serious attention to the geographic, social, and psychological contexts of each community. It also means developing a program that resonates with First Nations and pays attention to the sometimes profound cultural disconnect between Indigenous world views and relationships to the land and the individualist logic of the market economy.

After providing a socio-economic portrait of First Nations communities, this chapter looks at the historical foundations of the on-reserve Income Assistance Program, focusing on the interplay between welfare and Indian policies that lies at its core. It then discusses the hybrid model of program administration that has emerged in the postwar period and concludes with a discussion of the potential and limits of current attempts at reforming income assistance.

A socio-economic portrait of First Nations communities

During his recent visit to Canada in October 2013, James Anaya, the United Nations special rapporteur on the rights of Indigenous people, painted a grim picture of the conditions facing First Nations and other Aboriginal peoples. Canada, he noted, consistently ranks near the top among countries with respect to human development standards, yet "amidst this wealth and prosperity, aboriginal people live in conditions akin to those in countries that rank much lower and in which poverty abounds" (Anaya 2013).

According to the 2011 National Household Survey, Aboriginal people now represent 4.3 per cent of the Canadian population. Sixty per cent self-identify as First Nations members, of whom approximately half live on reserves. The reserve population is young and growing, with a median age of 26, compared with 41 for the overall Canadian population. Forty-nine per cent of First Nations citizens on reserves are under 25 years old (Statistics Canada 2013). Table 18.1 presents a comparative snapshot of Aboriginal and non-Aboriginal Canadians along some of the key indicators of well-being. The statistics are telling.

Table 18.1 Comparing Aboriginal Peoples, First Nations Members, and Other Canadians

	Aboriginal People	Status Indians	Canadian Population
Urban population (%)	56	51	82
Median age	28	26	41
Under 25 (%)	46	49	29
Single-parent families (%)	34	37	17
Postsecondary diploma (working-age population) (%)	48	42	65
University degree (%)	10	8	26
Employment rate (%)	63	53	76
Unemployment rate (%)	14	22	6.50
Life expectancy at birth **	75	73	78.7
Living in crowded housing ** (%)	11	26	3
Living below low-income cut-off ** (%)	21	28	11

Source: Statistics Canada (2013); **Statistics Canada (2008).

Unemployment rates on reserves are more than three times that of the Canadian population. Twice as many Aboriginal people and almost three times more First Nations members on reserves live below Statistics Canada's low-income cut-off.

Aboriginal peoples are also unequally distributed across the country, thereby creating unique challenges in some regions, notably in the Prairies and in the northern territories, where they represent a very significant and growing proportion of the population. In Manitoba and Saskatchewan, for example, more than 15 per cent of the population self-identify as Aboriginal. The proportion reaches 52 per cent in the Northwest Territories and 80 per cent in Nunavut. In Ontario, where more than 20 per cent of all Aboriginal people live, they represent just above 2 per cent of the population (Statistics Canada 2013).

There are also variations in the living conditions and well-being of First Nations communities, depending on geography, economic opportunities, and access to resources and infrastructures. A small but growing number of communities have developed profitable economic activities or benefit from revenues streams resulting from land claims settlements and other type of agreements with governments or the private sector. Most communities, however, are faced with limited opportunities and rely heavily on state support. Not surprisingly, the federal Income Support Program is the most important source of direct government transfers to individuals on reserves (AANDC 2013d).

The historical foundations of income assistance for First Nations in Canada

The objectives and guiding principles of Indian welfare in Canada have followed a familiar path. From ad hoc charity and last-resort measures in the early twentieth century, income assistance for the First Nations evolved into a comprehensive welfare program associated with citizenship rights in the postwar period. Today, as is the case for provincial programs, social assistance for First Nations citizens is increasingly framed as a "social investment" measure (see Cox, this volume; Jenson and Saint-Martin 2006)—one aimed at fostering labour market integration for a population group considered at risk in the globalized market economy. But there is a darker side to First Nations social assistance. As Hugh Shewell (2004) argues in his masterful history of Indian welfare in Canada, from its early articulation as a temporary relief system to its comprehensive postwar iteration, social assistance was seen as an instrument of cultural and economic assimilation.

Early Indian policy in Canada was rooted in assumptions about the backwardness and idleness of First Nations and other Aboriginal peoples. The state took on as its burden their transformation toward eventual membership in Euro-Canadian society. This "civilizing" mission involved instilling in the Indian liberal values and the work ethic associated with a capitalist economy. As Shewell (2004, 41) argues, the distribution of early forms of social assistance, such as food and clothing rations, was an integral part of this mission. It ensured that the Indians would settle on reserves and adopt some of the ways of the dominant society. Rations were also seen as an effective way to contain belligerent communities at a time of relatively intense colonial settlement (Tobias 1976).

With time, what began as a last-resort measure turned into the main lifeline for a population group that was economically marginalized, stigmatized, and confined to reserves. By the 1930s, most First Nation adults living on reserves received one form or another of state support for their survival (RCAP 1996). Increased public exposure of these conditions led to growing criticisms of federal Indian policy in the 1940s and 1950s. A flurry of inquiries and reports on the living conditions of Status Indians recast the "Indian problem" from a question of personal character and culture to one of discrimination and exclusion from the full benefits of citizenship.[3] What Indians needed, suggested the emerging thinking of the time, was not a paternalistic special status but equal opportunities to join in the market economy. The integration of Indians into the mainstream citizenship regime and the progressive elimination of the Indian Act therefore became the driving rationale of postwar Indian policy (RCAP 1996, 245).

The extension of social rights on reserves was central to this integrationist agenda. First Nations people on reserves gained access to most federal social programs in the 1950s, including old age assistance, blind persons allowances, and unemployment insurance and family allowances. With a few exceptions, however, provinces resisted extending their social programs to those on reserves. Status Indians, they argued, were primarily a responsibility of the federal government, pursuant to section 91(24) of the Constitution Act, 1867.

The federal Income Assistance Program for First Nations citizens living on reserves was formally established in 1964. The assumption was that the program would be a temporary measure, until Indians joined the market economy and assimilated to provincial welfare regimes. To facilitate the transition, the Treasury Board approved the usage of provincial rates and eligibility requirements in the administration of income assistance on reserves. The notion that provinces would eventually take over First Nations income assistance was reaffirmed under the 1966 Canada Assistance Plan, which established the parameters of federal funding for provincial social assistance programs. Part II of the plan encourages the Minister of Indian and Northern Affairs to negotiate shared costs agreements with provinces to that effect. To this day, Ontario is the sole province to have agreed to take on responsibility for the delivery of on-reserve income assistance, pursuant to an agreement reached in 1965.[4]

Faced with stiff resistance from both provinces and First Nations, the federal government eventually shifted its focus and began to transfer the administration of social assistance and other social programs directly to band councils and other First Nations organizations. By the 1990s, 80 per cent of federal funds for First Nations social programs were administered directly in communities through various funding arrangements (Papillon

3 A special joint committee of the Senate and the House of Commons examined the situation of Status Indians in 1946–48 and again in 1951–53. It was instrumental in shaping the new policy thinking (Cairns 2000; RCAP 1996; Shewell 2004).

4 Under the 1965 Memorandum of Agreement Respecting Welfare Programs for Indians, Ontario assumes responsibility for the provision of provincial social assistance programs to First Nations people living on reserves. The federal government reimburses Ontario for approximately 95 per cent of its expenditures.

2012). Income assistance is no exception, as I discuss next. The objectives and the services covered by the program, however, have largely remained unchanged since 1964.

In its rush to foster integration into the fledging provincial programs in the 1960s, the federal government adopted a very narrow understanding of social development—one focused on individual rights, personal autonomy, and participation in the market economy through salaried work. As Shewell (2004) suggests, this conception of wealth, though common sense in the Canadian mainstream, collides with traditional Aboriginal understandings of well-being, which often rest on a more collectivist ethic and a sense of connection to the land and to traditional practices. It also assumes First Nations are eager to join in a market economy that many see as the main culprit in their struggle for cultural, social, and spiritual survival (Alfred 2009).

Under the guise of equality and citizenship rights, postwar welfare policies also indirectly perpetuated colonial practices by defining Aboriginal peoples as outsiders looking in. The income assistance program sent a powerful message to those at the receiving end of the state's benevolence: you are receiving state support not just because of your condition but also because of what you are. Combined with notions of entitlement derived from treaty rights, the perverse association of income assistance with the fact of "being an Indian" still resonates today in many communities, where the majority of the population receives income support (AFN 2012).

Income assistance for First Nations today

Aboriginal Affairs and Northern Development Canada (AANDC) currently spends approximately $1.4 billion annually on social programs for First Nations individuals and families living on reserves. In addition to the main Income Assistance Program, the department also administers four other social programs: the National Child Benefit Reinvestment, the Assisted Living Program, the First Nations Child and Family Services Program, and the Family Violence Prevention Program. The Income Assistance Program itself currently supports 162,925 families with a total budget of $838 million (AANDC 2013a). As mentioned, it is the fourth largest income assistance program in the country in terms of caseload.

A closer look at available data suggests dependency rates, defined by AANDC as the total number of beneficiaries (recipients and their families), declined in the late 1990s and early 2000s, following a pattern similar to that followed by other income assistance programs discussed in this volume. Reliance on income assistance on reserves nonetheless remains six times higher than the Canadian average. As Figure 18.1 suggests, the drop in dependency rates is also largely offset by population growth, meaning the actual number of people on reserves living on income assistance continues to increase to this day. Reliance on income assistance also varies from one region to another, with higher rates in northern and rural communities and in Saskatchewan and Manitoba, where the on-reserve population also happens to be growing fastest.

According to the most recent program manual, the purpose of income assistance is the same as it was in 1964: to "support the basic and special needs of indigent residents of Indian reserves and their dependants and support access to services to help clients transition to and remain in the workforce" (AANDC 2012, 12). Following a trend that started in the 1970s, the program itself is mostly delivered through band councils and other local or regional First Nations authorities. In 2011–12, 541 First Nations delivered the IA Program (AANDC 2012). The main exception is in Yukon where

Figure 18.1 Income Assistance for First Nations Citizens on Reserves, 1981–2011

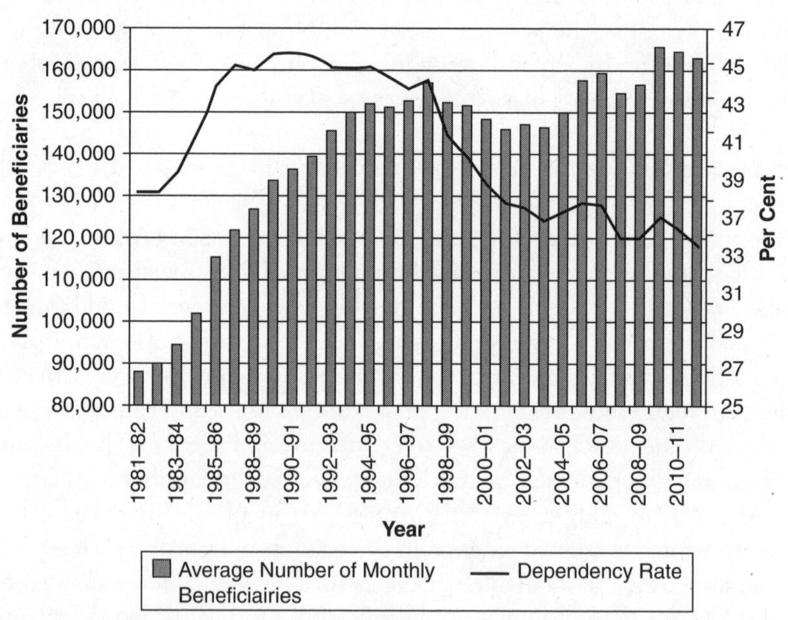

Note: The dependency rate is derived by dividing the number of income assistance beneficiaries by the total on-reserve population. Recipients are defined as those individuals who receive assistance payments whereas beneficiaries are all individuals who benefit from the payments.
Source: AANDC 2013a; DIAND 1996; INAC 2005.

the AANDC regional office administers the IA Program directly. Payments to clientele are determined on a needs base, and disbursements are paid out following the appropriate provincial and territorial fee schedule determined annually. Like most provincial programs, IA provides support for basic and special needs, based on the specific condition of each client. Basic needs account for 88 per cent of total expenditures, special needs for 5 per cent, and service delivery for about 7 per cent (AANDC 2013a).

As mentioned, Ontario has administered on-reserve income assistance on behalf of AANDC since 1965. Although AANDC retains funding authority, Ontario sets the terms and conditions of programming through Ontario Works. Like elsewhere in Canada, bands deliver the program in Ontario. Although the federal government has failed to convince other provinces to take on similar responsibilities, a number of bilateral and trilateral agreements were negotiated in recent years to facilitate coordination and to support the delivery of services on reserves, notably in British Columbia, Saskatchewan, Alberta, and Québec. Pursuant to some of these agreements, regional First Nations agencies, such as the British Columbia–based First Nations Social Development Society, now facilitate the coordination of services with provincial authorities and improve the capacity of local First Nations to deliver consistent and adequate services (AANDC 2012).

The program has faced several criticisms over the years. The Assembly of First Nations (AFN), among others, has called for a major overhaul of what it sees as a passive and overly complex program perpetuating a colonial form of dependency and keeping First Nations in poverty (AFN 2012). In a recent internal evaluation, the federal government also concludes that the income assistance program has failed to adapt to the contemporary challenges facing First Nation communities (INAC 2007). The report insists on the long-term unsustainability of the program in light of its escalating costs and on its failure to foster greater labour market participation among First Nations members. Part of the problem, it suggests, lies in the limited capacity of local First Nations in delivering services that are responsive to the needs of the communities. In many communities, there is often a single caseworker responsible for the entire range of services, from needs assessment to pre-employment support and follow-up, not to mention dealing with broader personal issues. The person often has limited training and is expected to make hard decisions that directly affect friends and relatives (AANDC 2013a; INAC 2007).

Although local capacity and independence are certainly relevant issues, the problem also lies with the history and the structure of the program itself. As discussed, it was initially designed as a temporary measure pending assimilation and an eventual transfer to the provinces. Since 1964, the program's main objective is simply to provide on-reserve services comparable to those of the relevant province. The federal government therefore casts itself in a relatively passive funding role while the delivery of the program is in the hands of First Nations and its policy content is limited to the mirroring of provincial practices. This amorphous regime, the Auditor General concludes in a 1994 report that is still relevant today, is "complex, cumbersome and difficult to manage." It is particularly difficult for local officials delivering services to follow federal budgetary constraints while "remaining fully knowledgeable and up-to-date on provincial standards" (Auditor General of Canada 1994, 3).

This structural tension was exacerbated by the Treasury Board's 1998 imposition of a 2 per cent cap on expenditure growth for Aboriginal Affair's social programming, including social assistance. Combined with population growth, this ongoing restriction on spending results in a significant reduction in actual per capita budget. This contraction in funding also corresponds with major shifts in provincial social assistance programs starting in the mid-1990s. Faced with their own budgetary crisis, provinces raised eligibility thresholds and lowered support payments, but they also established built-in back-to-work incentives and other measures to foster greater labour market integration among long-term welfare recipients.

Provincial income assistance programs have become more complex and layered with conditions that have little to do with the original welfare model that still largely informs the federal on-reserve program. The tensions resulting from this growing mismatch between the federal framework and provincial standards were put on full display recently in New Brunswick and Nova Scotia, where a group of First Nations challenged the federal government's decision to reduce the on-reserve income assistance rate to match the much lower basic rate of the two provinces. A federal judge granted the communities an injunction in light of the potential impact of such cuts. The problem, noted the judge, is that the basic provincial rate is now combined with additional measures and services for those willing to participate in employment programs. It is therefore almost impossible for on-reserve program providers relying strictly on basic federal funds to match what provinces are doing (CBC News 2012).

Are active measures the solution?

Faced with a costly, ineffective, and increasingly unmanageable program, the federal government has little choice but to change its approach to social assistance on reserves. In line with trends observed in other jurisdictions, AANDC is now increasingly defining income assistance as a developmental tool aimed at breaking the dependency cycle and "fostering greater autonomy" of individuals (AANDC 2013b; INAC 2007). A series of pilot projects have been established since 2003 to support better coordination and integration between the income assistance program and the various labour market integration measures available to First Nations (Kraneveldt 2011).

The 2013 budget announcement builds from these regional pilot projects and establishes two new pan-Canadian, on-reserve programs explicitly tying skills development and employment readiness to income assistance. The Enhanced Service Delivery program aims at developing a client-centred case management system for youth 18–24 and is focused on identifying individual needs and supports to overcome employment barriers. Participation in the program is to be enforced using incentives and disincentives modelled after those found in the related province (AANDC 2013b). The First Nations Job Fund adds to existing job training and readiness programming for First Nations youth and will be delivered through the existing Aboriginal Skills and Employment Training Strategy (ASETS) infrastructure, made up of local businesses and employers. For those First Nations that choose to undertake active measures programming, participation is mandatory for all "job-ready" recipients aged 18–24 (AANDC 2013b).

As it invests in activation measures, the government is also tightening its grip on program administrators. It is undertaking a "series of program compliance reviews" to ensure that First Nations are delivering the IA Program in step with provincial eligibility requirements, provincial rate schedules, and other program terms and conditions. Program compliance reviews, it suggests "will ensure program terms and conditions are being met and that appropriate income assistance benefits are being provided to eligible clients" (AANDC 2013b).

With the introduction of active measures as a condition for receiving IA, the program essentially realigns itself with most of its provincial counterparts. The tightening of administrative requirements along provincial lines also suggests the federal government intends to stay the course in terms of modelling its program to that of the provinces. Although this may ensure greater consistency in the services provided to First Nations and neighbouring communities, it leaves open the more complex issue of whether these programs are at all relevant to the unique context and history of the First Nations.

Many First Nation organizations support the introduction of active measures on reserves as a way to break the cycle of poverty and welfare dependency. They nonetheless insist that this type of measure must be accompanied with broader reforms to the way federal and provincial authorities approach social and economic development on reserves (AFN 2012; Kraneveldt 2011). To break with past practices and truly reconstruct income assistance as a development tool for communities, the federal government needs to do more.

For one thing, though highly decentralized, the current program remains very much organized along the lines of a classic top-down governance model: First Nations administer income assistance on behalf of federal authorities, yet they follow rules and objectives established by provinces. The recent measures reinforce this approach through greater compliance requirements and the multiplication of funding sources. One possible alternative to alleviate legitimacy and coordination problems would be to develop a more systematic tripartite approach to the IA Program. Tripartite governance models, in which First Nations organizations are engaged not only in the administration of services but also in the development of national, provincial and community-based strategies with both federal and provincial authorities already exist in other policy areas (Papillon 2012). This type of reform would go a long way in developing a sense of ownership and control over the program and in ensuring it resonates with the needs and expectations of the communities. It would also greatly facilitate coordination across jurisdictions.

A second essential element in recasting the program is the development of a holistic approach to social and economic well-being that goes beyond the current focus on labour market integration. Although addressing barriers to work is certainly important, training and skills development are not sufficient, especially in remote communities with limited job opportunities. Countless studies have insisted governments must stop working from within "silos" when they approach the multiple social and economic challenges facing Aboriginal communities. In a recent report, the First Nations Social Development Society of British Columbia identified multiple barriers to successful active measures in First Nations communities, including low literacy, addiction problems, family dysfunction, low mobility, and multigenerational trauma (Kraneveldt 2011, 12). Active measures, the report suggests, have limited impact if they are not coordinated with initiatives to address broader well-being issues. This means a more coordinated approach between the various authorities involved in health, education, welfare, and economic development, but it also means a long-term view of social and economic development that goes beyond the current focus on "catching up" with the mainstream population. It means developing goals that are consistent with Aboriginal peoples' own conceptions of well-being.

Paying greater attention to the cultural content of work and well-being is therefore a third dimension that deserves greater attention in developing a First Nations–driven program (see Jacob and Desautels 2013). As discussed, the cultural disconnect between First Nations citizens and income assistance has deep historical roots. Breaking this association is no easy task, but bringing in a cultural lens to program development would be an important step. Rather than assuming that all First Nation youths "want and deserve" the same job opportunities as any other Canadians, as the minister claimed in announcing the recent activation measures, the program could also make room for alternative economic activities that are consistent with local traditions and life-styles. There are already examples of this approach. Under the James Bay and Northern Québec Agreement, for example, Cree and Inuit hunters and trappers benefit from an income support program that recognizes their contribution to the community's cultural and social well-being. The program is not without its challenges, but it contributes to the reconciliation of salaried work and traditional practices by redefining the very notion of "productivity" in a way that could be emulated elsewhere (Papillon 2008).

Conclusion

Income assistance for the members of First Nations living on reserves has a troubled history. Welfare for First Nations people was originally justified, and explicitly designed, as a tool of cultural and economic assimilation. Its postwar recasting as a policy fostering greater integration into Canada's market economy did not fundamentally change the program's overall thrust. This historical narrative, this chapter suggests, still haunts us today as First Nations struggle with dependency rates eight times higher than the Canadian average and social and economic conditions comparable to that of third world countries.

The program's association with one of Canada's darkest chapters should not, however, lead us to conclude it is impossible to reform. Failure to make reforms would only serve to reinforce the deep feeling of disconnect between the First Nations and Canada's social architecture and citizenship regime. We also can't afford to fail. The growing and increasingly educated First Nation population is facing a bleak future if the cycle of poverty and dependency associated with income assistance is not addressed head on. The consequences are especially significant in regions of the country where the Aboriginal population constitutes an important demographic force.

Although welcomed by many as long overdue, recent reforms to the federal IA Program face numerous challenges. The fundamental structural problem of the program largely remains unaddressed—First Nations are still asked to run a program designed and funded by the federal government following expectations and objectives set by the provinces. The fragmented and inconsistent nature of services, not to mention the lack of First Nations input in developing objectives, is therefore likely to be reproduced. The program is also still largely driven by assumptions about well-being and economic participation that pay short attention to Indigenous identities and world views.

To be sure, there is no easy response to these challenges. This chapter nonetheless builds from the limited literature on the topic to suggest three priorities for future reforms. To move beyond its current ambiguous status, the program should first evolve into a true tripartite arrangement between First Nations, federal, and provincial authorities. A second element discussed here is the need for a greater coordination of social and economic development strategies toward a more holistic approach to well-being. The challenge in this respect is to move beyond the premise that First Nations simply need to catch up with the rest of Canada. This point leads us to the third element to consider, namely the development of a cultural lens that would instil greater flexibility in the program in terms of its objectives and instruments.

References

AANDC (Aboriginal Affairs and Northern Development Canada). 2012. *National Social Programs Manual*. Ottawa: Aboriginal Affairs and Northern Development Canada. http://www.aadnc-aandc.gc.ca/DAM/DAM-INTER-HQ-HB/STAGING/texte-text/hb_sp_npm_mnp_1335464147597_eng.pdf.

AANDC (Aboriginal Affairs and Northern Development Canada). 2013a. *Audit of the Income Assistance Program*. Project #12–07. Ottawa: Audit and Assurance Services Branch. http://www.aadnc-aandc.gc.ca/DAM/DAM-INTER-HQ-AEV/STAGING/texte-text/au_iap_1381490602693_eng.pdf.

AANDC (Aboriginal Affairs and Northern Development Canada). 2013b. Backgrounder—Income Assistance Reform: Enhanced Service Delivery. Ottawa: Aboriginal Affairs and Northern Development Canada. Last modified June 12, 2013. http://www.aadnc-aandc.gc.ca/eng/1371048267592/1371048310299.

AANDC (Aboriginal Affairs and Northern Development Canada). 2013c. *Harper Government Invests in Skills and Training for First Nation Youth*. Press Release, ref. #2–3811. Ottawa: Aboriginal Affairs and Northern Development Canada. Last modified June 12, 2013. http://www.aadnc-aandc.gc.ca/eng/1371048149693/1371048172737.

AANDC (Aboriginal Affairs and Northern Development Canada). 2013d. *Income Assistance: Key Facts*. Ottawa: Aboriginal Affairs and Northern Development Canada.

Last modified May 28, 2013. http://www.aadnc-aandc.gc.ca/eng/1369766807521/1369766848614.

AFN (Assembly of First Nations). 2012. *Active Measures Community Resource Guide*. Ottawa: Assembly of First Nations. http://www.afn.ca/uploads/files/social/active-measures.pdf.

Alfred, Taiaiake. 2009. "Colonialism and State Dependency." *Journal of Aboriginal Health / Journal de la santé autochtone* 5 (2): 42–60. http://www.naho.ca/journal/2009/11/07/colonialism-and-state-dependency/.

Anaya, James. 2013. "Statement Upon Conclusion of the Visit to Canada." United Nations Office of the Special Rapporteur on the Rights of Indigenous Peoples. Last modified October 15, 2013. http://unsr.jamesanaya.org/statements/statement-upon-conclusion-of-the-visit-to-canada.

Auditor General of Canada. 1994. *Report of the Auditor General of Canada 1994, Chapter 23: Indian and Northern Affairs Canada, Social Assistance*. Ottawa: Office of the Auditor General of Canada. http://www.collectionscanada.gc.ca/webarchives/20060304001712/http://www.oag-bvg.gc.ca/domino/reports.nsf/html/9423ce.html.

Cairns, Alan. 2000. *Citizens Plus*. Vancouver: UBC Press.

CBC News. 2012. "Judge Halts First Nations Welfare Cuts in Maritimes." *CBC News*, April 3. http://www.cbc.ca/news/canada/new-brunswick/judge-halts-first-nations-welfare-cuts-in-maritimes-1.1134656.

DIAND (Department of Indian Affairs and Northern Development). 1996. *Basic Departmental Data 1995*. Ottawa: Department of Indian Affairs and Northern Development. http://www.collectionscanada.gc.ca/webarchives/20071214083124/http://www.ainc-inac.gc.ca/pr/sts/bdd95/bdd95_e.pdf.

INAC (Indian and Northern Affairs Canada). 2005. *Basic Departmental Data 2004*. Ottawa: Indian and Northern Affairs. http://www.collectionscanada.gc.ca/webarchives/20071125233054/http://www.ainc-inac.gc.ca/pr/sts/bdd04/bdd04_e.pdf.

INAC (Indian and Northern Affairs Canada). 2007. *Evaluation of the Income Assistance Program*. Project 07/06, CIDM #1174769v11. Ottawa: Audit and Evaluation Sector, Indian and Northern Affairs.

Jacob, Steve, and Geoffrey Desautels. 2013. "Evaluation of Aboriginal Programs: What Place Is Given to Participation and Cultural Sensitivity?" *The International Indigenous Policy Journal* 4 (2). http://ir.lib.uwo.ca/iipj/vol4/iss2/1/.

Jenson, Jane, and Denis Saint-Martin. 2006. "Building Blocks for a New Social Architecture: The LEGO™ Paradigm of an Active Society." *Policy and Politics* 34 (3): 429–51. http://dx.doi.org/10.1332/030557306777695325.

Kraneveldt, Nene. 2011. *Active Measures Roll Up Report: 2010–2011*. North Vancouver: First Nations Social Development Society. http://www.fnsds.org/wp/wp-content/uploads/FINAL2010-2011AMRoll-UpReport.pdf.

Papillon, Martin. 2008. "Aboriginal Quality of Life under a Modern Treaty: Lessons from the Experience of the Cree Nation of Eeyou Istchee and the Inuit of Nunavik." *IRPP Choices* 14 (9): 1–26. http://irpp.org/wp-content/uploads/assets/research/aboriginal-quality-of-life/aboriginal-quality-of-life-under-a-modern-treaty/vol14no9.pdf.

Papillon, Martin. 2012. "Canadian Federalism and the Emerging Mosaic of Aboriginal Multilevel Governance." In *Canadian Federalism: Performance, Effectiveness and Legitimacy*, 3rd ed., ed. H. Bakvis and G. Skogstad, 291–315. Don Mills, ON: Oxford University Press.

RCAP (Royal Commission on Aboriginal Peoples). 1996. *Final Report of the Royal Commission on Aboriginal Peoples—Volume 1: Looking Forward, Looking Back.* Ottawa: Supply and Services Canada.

Shewell, Hugh. 2004. *"Enough to Keep Them Alive": Indian Welfare in Canada, 1873–1965*. Toronto: University of Toronto Press.

Statistics Canada. 2008. *Aboriginal Peoples in Canada in 2006: Inuit, Métis and First Nations, 2006 Census*. Catalogue no. 97-558-XIE. Ottawa: Statistics Canada.

Statistics Canada. 2013. *Aboriginal Peoples in Canada: First Nations People, Métis and Inuit, 2011 National Household Survey*. Catalogue no. 99-011-X2011001. Ottawa: Statistics Canada.

Tobias, John L. 1976. "Protection, Civilization, Assimilation: An Outline of Canada's Indian Policy." *Western Canadian Journal of Anthropology* 6 (2): 13–30.

nineteen
Aging and Social Assistance in the Provinces[1]

PATRIK MARIER AND ANNE-MARIE SÉGUIN

Introduction

Like the welfare systems of many industrialized countries, Canada's early social assistance programs did not really consider age as a special criterion. Family support, private charity, and local authorities constituted a last resort for individuals leaving the labour market, regardless of their circumstances (Myles 1989). For some older citizens, departure from the labour market resulted in a visit to the poorhouse (Quadagno 1988).

Beginning with the Old Age Pensions Act of 1927, the gradual involvement of the federal government prompted, over time, substantial improvements in the financial well-being of seniors. Federal involvement became an important part of the strategy, which was aimed at establishing the centre as the core facilitator of income redistribution (Banting 1987). Thus, instead of depending on provincial social assistance programs geared specifically toward working-age individuals, Canadians aged 65 and above now rely on less stigmatizing programs offered by Ottawa such as Old Age Security (OAS) and the Guaranteed Income Supplement (GIS). As a result, older Canadians now enjoy the lowest poverty rate among all age cohorts (RRQ 2004). This benefit structure is responsible for poverty alleviation outcomes akin to those of generous welfare states such as Sweden and Norway.

Beyond pensions, recent contributions have emphasized the importance of housing subsidies and home ownership to curb poverty among seniors (Ritakallio 2003). In Canada, the most notable element is the absence of taxation on capital gains when individuals sell their principle residence, a measure that favours individuals with substantial value in their own property. Although housing represents a core area for social policymakers (Carter and Polevychok 2004), federal intervention to ensure housing access for poor households occurred relatively late. The first legislation was adopted in 1932 and was quickly replaced

1 We would like to thank Corey Guitard for his research assistance and the editors for their comments and suggestions.

in 1935 by the National Housing Act, which sought to increase the construction of new housing developments to stimulate the economy. In the aftermath of World War II, the federal government committed itself to creating subsidized housing in 1949. However, this new policy did not feature predominantly in the social agenda of the government; the sums invested were modest, and the policy relied mostly on market-based mechanisms to supply living arrangements for poor households, regardless of the age of the potential occupants (Hulchanski 2002, 2007; Divay, Séguin, and Sénécal 2005). In stark contrast to the development of Old Age Security and the Guaranteed Income Supplement, for which the federal government assumed exclusive responsibility, the expansion of federal intervention in housing has consistently required a financial contribution on the part of the provinces. In addition, the federal government did not develop any significant programs targeting only older citizens in social housing, preferring instead to produce housing projects for seniors within existing programs. In 1993, the federal government withdrew its participation in the production of new social housing units, placing this responsibility squarely on the shoulders of provincial and municipal authorities. It is important to stress, however, that the federal government opted to fulfill its previous obligations in housing. This commitment remains important because social housing built between 1946 and 1993 supports close to 600,000 households (CMHC 2013).

This chapter is divided into three major sections. First, we introduce two sections featuring comparative analyses of current provincial dynamics with regards to financial support and housing programs for seniors, respectively. For each of these sections, we present a brief historical overview of the evolution of financial and housing social assistance programs targeted at older populations. Finally, the conclusion discusses future prospects for these programs and presents some international comparisons.

Social assistance for seniors

Before this section presents current efforts made by Canadian provinces to supplement the retirement income of poor older citizens, it gives a historical overview of social assistance programs geared toward seniors. Most substantial efforts to improve the retirement income of poor retirees have involved the federal government, and current provincial action consists primarily of offering top-up benefits to their citizens.

Historical background

For most of the twentieth century, growing old was synonymous with poverty for most Canadians. Prior to World War II, as in many other industrialized countries, Canada offered meagre retirement benefits (Myles 1989; Palme 1990). Canadian provinces had neither the means nor the desire to introduce pension programs that catered to the needs of the growing cohort of seniors living without financial support. Even after the introduction of the OAS and the GIS by the federal government, it took decades for cohorts of Canadians to enjoy noticeable increases in their retirement income.

The increasing industrialization and urbanization of Canadian cities have sparked a great deal of debate regarding the question of what should be done to alleviate poverty among older citizens. Municipalities, which provided mostly poor relief efforts in the early twentieth century, soon pressured provincial authorities to enact new measures to provide superior relief to an increasing number of seniors. Ontario, New Brunswick, Québec, and Nova Scotia had a well-developed network of poor houses by the late 1910s, although they were clearly insufficient to accommodate actual needs (Bryden 1974, 35).

A few provinces actually debated the introduction of province-wide financial assistance programs, but none saw the light of day (Bryden 1974, ch. 3). Interestingly, Newfoundland enacted a means-tested program in 1911. It is remembered as "the most blatantly gendered scheme for the needy elderly in the western world"; it was only available to men aged 75 and above despite the fact that women were living in far worse circumstances (Snell 1993, 86, 91). This discriminatory treatment of women continued until Newfoundland joined the federation in 1949.

Mounting pressures on provinces to act in this policy area remained unanswered for many years, eventually leading to a proposal by Ottawa to co-finance a means-tested program for individuals aged 70 and above. The Old Age Pensions Act of 1927 left the administration of the program to the provinces with a supervisory role granted to federal officials. This new pension was accessible to those who had resided in Canada for 20 years and in the host province for 5 years, but it excluded Aboriginals (Bryden 1974, 62). The initial enthusiasm for this program soon waned as individual negotiations with the provinces and multiple implementation issues began to undermine the potential for successful outcomes.

Rising living costs also led to calls for a more generous program (Bryden 1974, ch. 5). However, no other substantial policy change occurred before World War II. As a result, pension coverage and benefits remained marginal by the mid-twentieth century with close to two-thirds of Canadians aged 65 and above earning less than $1,000 in 1951 (Podoluk 1968, cited in Bryden 1974), which is comparable to an income of $8,790 in 2013 when adjusted for inflation.

With provinces facing many difficulties in the implementation of the 1927 program and with minor reforms accentuating the role of federal authorities in pensions, a constitutional agreement paved the way to a transfer of responsibility from the provinces to the federal government. This circumstance led to the adoption of the Old Age Security Act in 1951. It is important to emphasize the fact that Canadian provinces supported this federal intervention (Banting 1987). Provincial acceptance occurred because the federal government subsequently assumed full responsibility for this universal program, which originally provided $40 per month to individuals aged 70 and above.

Federal involvement in the provision of social assistance continued after the adoption of OAS. Between 1951 and 1970, the Old Age Assistance Act coexisted with OAS. It represented a continuation of the 1927 legislation for those aged between 65 and 69, but it was abolished in 1970 when the admissibility age for OAS was reduced to 65. A new "temporary" program, the Guaranteed Income Supplement (GIS) was instituted in the wake of the creation of the Canada Pension Plan (CPP), or Régime de rentes du Québec (RRQ), in 1966. The GIS was to provide assistance during the transitional years of the new contributory pension schemes. Like OAS, this program is financed and administered solely by the federal government and, in light of its tremendous political popularity, it became permanent in 1971 (Banting 1987, 13). The GIS has been increased on multiple occasions since and remains a core feature of today's pension system.

Contemporary provincial social assistance programs for seniors

The core programs providing social assistance to seniors remain federal, the OAS and GIS, and provincial assistance often serves to complement these two programs. Thus, it is imperative to begin with an overview of both the OAS and the GIS.

As of 2013, the OAS is a *near-universal* program for Canadian citizens aged 65 and above. There is a residency test of 10 years, and full benefits are granted to those who have resided in Canada for at least 40 years. For example, a low-income retiree who has resided in Canada for 30 years receives 30/40 (i.e., 75 per cent) of the maximum benefit. As of September 1, 2013, the maximum monthly amount is $550. Following reforms in the 1980s, a "clawback" gradually reduced the amount offered by the OAS program to those with incomes above $70,954. Once an individual reaches an income of $114,793 or above, he or she is no longer entitled to OAS. To mitigate some of the impact of the clawback and to benefit from higher rates, individuals now have the option to delay their receipt of the OAS until they reach age 70. These measures apply mostly to individuals aged 65 and above who remain in the labour market.

The GIS is the core social assistance program for low-income seniors. Rather than having to fill in a lengthy invasive questionnaire, as is the case for those applying to receive most kinds of social assistance benefits, potential GIS recipients are assessed for eligibility easily; the program is income tested, so all one has to do is attach an additional form to income tax filings. This application process is an extremely important instrument that helps to explain why the GIS has remained so popular. In fact, many Statistics Canada surveys lump both GIS and OAS together because many individuals do not understand how these two programs interact to provide a single pension cheque.

The GIS offers a maximum of $746 for single pensioners while couples receive $494 per person. Each retirement dollar received from various pension plans, including the CPP/RRQ but not OAS, reduces the amount of the GIS by 50 per cent. The ceiling for individual pensioners is currently set at $16,800.

In most cases, provincial support complements the GIS (see Table 19.1). This finding implies that provincial authorities utilize a similar formula to assess needs. With the exception of both Alberta and Saskatchewan, provincial assistance to seniors remains quite marginal and provides a meagre complement to the OAS and GIS combination.

There are nonetheless some interesting provincial variations. For example, Alberta and Saskatchewan provide less support to individuals in long-term care facilities, probably reflecting other subsidies and benefits given to these individuals. Alberta also requires a minimum of 3 months residency immediately before applying, and Ontario requires 12 months. Manitoba's support begins at age 55, five years before individuals have access to the GIS, and individuals receive a higher amount if they are in a relationship rather than single pensioners. Both New Brunswick and Newfoundland and Labrador give the same benefit regardless of the number of individuals in a household. Also, it is important to point out that Newfoundland and Labrador's benefit is available in full to citizens receiving double the ceiling of the GIS ($28,000). Interestingly, neither Québec nor Nova Scotia offers any GIS top-up.

In closing, it is important to emphasize that these social assistance top-up programs are not the only ones available to seniors. There is a panoply

Table 19.1 Provincial Top-up Programs for GIS, as of September 1, 2013

Province (Name)		Maximum Rate Per Couple	Minimum Age	Income Ceiling
BC (Senior's Supplement)	$49.30	$120.50	65	GIS
Alberta Seniors Benefit Program	$280.00* $190.00**	$420.00* $390.00**	65	$25,800 (including OAS)
Saskatchewan (Seniors Income Plan)	$250.00 $50.00***	$430.00 $100.00***	65	$4,560 /$912 (excluding OAS)
Manitoba (55 Plus Program)	$54.00	$116.00	55‡	Varies
Ontario Guaranteed Annual Income System (GAINS)	$83.00	$166.00	65	GIS
New Brunswick Low-Income Seniors' Benefit	$33.33	$33.33‡‡	60‡‡‡	Receive full benefit if some GIS
PEI—Financial Assistance Program	Must phone in regional social assistance office			
Newfoundland and Labrador—Low-Income Seniors' Benifit	$81.00	$81.00‡‡	65	$28,231

Source: Various governmental websites and information booklets.

Notes: Income ceiling is based on data for a single senior. This is the income at which a benefit is no longer available.

* For homeowner, renter, or lodge resident.

** Other residence categories.

*** Living in special care home.

‡ Individuals receiving income assistance are not eligible.

‡‡ Only one benefit is allowed per household.

‡‡‡ If the person receives the Federal Allowance benefit or the Federal Allowance for the Survivor benefit in 2012; 65 for GIS recipients.

of programs to increase income support for seniors. These involve special allowances for seniors with a disability, widows, and homeowners. For example, Québec has a special program for widows although the amount of the benefit is based on the RRQ contributions of the deceased and not on need. Also, the lack of substantive benefits offered by provinces should not be confused with a lack of provincial influence on federal social assistance programs. Prior to the recent reforms to push to 67 the age at which one becomes eligible for both the GIS and the OAS (starting in 2023), earlier attempts to decrease the generosity or accessibility to either of these programs faced strong opposition from provincial authorities and from aged-based interest groups such as CARP and Réseau FADOQ.

Housing support for seniors

Housing remains a significant expenditure for Canadians. Many low-income households spend a disproportionate portion of their revenue toward housing costs, which has an important impact on their overall living conditions. To assess the housing needs of its citizens, the Canadian government uses the core housing need indicator, which measures three things: *affordability*, or that costs for shelter, including rent, mortgage, and utilities payments, are less than 30 per cent of the household's before-tax income; *state of repair*, or that a dwelling is not in need of major repair; and *space*, or that housing is not crowded, meaning that it has sufficient bedrooms according to family composition (CMHC 2012; Engeland and Lewis 2004). By far, the most important factor is a lack of financial capacity, which makes it difficult to afford housing: in 2009, 91.2 per cent of urban households in core housing need were in need because they were unable to meet the housing affordability standard, either solely or in combination with the other two standards (CMHC 2012, 5-5). In 2006, statistics demonstrate that older homeowners faced more difficulties than other cohorts of owners, with 7.9 per cent, compared to 5.8 per cent for younger cohorts, being unable to meet core housing needs. The figures are much worse for older renters; 31.4 per cent of them had unmet core housing needs, which is above the 26.2 per cent for younger cohorts (CMHC 2012, A-19).

Historical background

From the initial involvement of the federal government in housing in 1935 to the termination of its responsibility for the production of new social housing units in 1993, low-income seniors' needs were mainly addressed within existing programs targeting families as well as retired and pre-retired persons. However, non-profit organizations and cooperatives embraced a different vision of public housing by constructing many public housing complexes tailored to the senior population.

The first federal laws established in the 1930s in the field of housing targeted families and, immediately after World War II, the families of workers and of soldiers involved in the war (CMHC 2011). In 1949, an important modification to the National Housing Act allowed the construction of public housing to satisfy the needs of poorer families. Despite this change, the construction of public housing remained very marginal between 1949 and 1963, with an average of 850 units being built annually across Canada with the financial support of the federal government (Hulchanski 2002, 9). During this period, some housing units were intended to house older people.

Starting in 1964, and for two decades after, the Canadian Mortgage and Housing Corporation (CMHC) would be highly active in developing many types of housing infrastructures: public housing, co-op housing, and non-profit housing. Many social housing projects for retired and pre-retired persons were constructed during this period. These actions followed from multiple initiatives to bolster the construction of social housing units targeting poor households. First, a 1963 joint federal and provincial program provided provinces with generous financing conditions up to 1978. The CMHC provided loans at preferential rates with lengthy amortization periods (CMHC 2011), and provinces created housing authorities, which assumed ownership, to manage the properties (Hulchanski 2007). Second, between 1963 and 1979, the federal government also spearheaded new programs to favour the creation of housing run by cooperatives, with complexes owned and managed by residents, and of housing run by non-profit organizations, with units built and managed by community groups (SHQ 1988). The first cooperative targeting seniors was built in 1969 in British Columbia (CMHC 2011, 145). During this effervescent period, the practice of having rent geared to income took hold, and most public housing authorities or corporations employed this policy tool. At the beginning of the joint program in 1963, rents were capped at 20 per cent of a resident's total income; they now range between 25 to 30 per cent depending on the province.[2] From 1978 to 1993, the federal government and the provinces also introduced a new form of assistance, which subsidized the costs of

2 Almost all households pay a rent geared to income. This type of subsidized housing is generally older than other types. Non-profit housing is rental housing built and managed by a community group. About two-thirds of this sort of housing is comprised of rent-geared-to-income units. Cooperative or co-op housing is owned and managed by the residents. About half of this housing is comprised of rent-geared-to-income units (the other units in this category are fixed at the local rent).

private apartments by reimbursing the difference between the market cost and the rent-geared-to-income ceiling (set at 25 per cent to 30 per cent of total income). This move represented a shift toward more market-driven mechanisms to provide affordable housing (CMHC 2011; SHQ 1988).

In 1993, at the beginning of a period of cutbacks, the federal government announced its withdrawal from the production of new subsidised housing programs, leaving this responsibility in the hands of provinces and municipalities. Following this decision, the Canadian government negotiated social housing agreements with seven provinces (Québec, PEI, and Alberta refused to sign). These agreements transferred to the provinces the managerial and administrative responsibilities for all programs in social housing, with the noticeable exception of cooperatives, which have had more complex arrangements. As part of the agreements, the CMCH provides an annual payment to cover a portion of the financing cost for projects approved for development in previous agreements ($1.7 billion in 2013; CMHC 2013). This amount is roughly equivalent to the amount of taxes foregone by authorities for capital gains obtained by owners when they sell their principal residence (Hulchanski 2002, 6).[3] This continuous and slow withdrawal of the federal government from housing results in having only 4 per cent of all households receiving some form of financial assistance (in full or in part) from the Canadian government (CMHC 2011). The federal government has not completely disappeared from social housing, but its involvement is now occasional, often as part of broad initiatives such as Canada's Economic Action Plan (2008–present). In this case, financial contributions were made to improve existing housing units, and $400 million was allocated in conjunction with the provinces to build more housing for low-income seniors (CMHC 2012, 5-3).

Subsidized housing for low-income seniors today: A fragmented portrait

Waiting lists to access social housing units remain lengthy across Canada, which has remained an issue since overall investments were far more substantial than they are today. This helps explain why provinces began accentuating their efforts in the 1970s by providing housing allowances, some of which targeted young families and older citizens. We are not referring here to the housing component of social assistance benefits, as in the

3 According to Hulchanski (2002, 6) and data provided by the Department of Finance of Canada in 2000, the exoneration of capital gains tax, when homeowners sell their principal residence, represented an annual housing-related subsidy of about $1.5 billion in 2000.

chapter by Michael Prince (Chapter 20), but to housing allowances for low-income households not receiving this benefit. This housing allowance formula was part of a global trend wherein the popularity of housing allowances had already been increasing in many countries such as France, Sweden, the Netherlands, Great Britain, and the United States (Finkel et al. 2006).

Currently, five provinces offer housing allowance programs (BC, MB, NS, PE, and QC), and three of them have targeted programs for older citizens (ranging in age from a floor of 52 years in Québec to 60 in British Columbia; see Table 19.2). The monthly allowances and the income ceilings vary across all three provinces, with Manitoba being far more generous than Québec. British Columbia has a variation scale, probably instituted to take into account the disproportionately high cost of housing in the Vancouver area. The assistance provided by both Québec and Manitoba, two provinces that have not experienced rising housing costs akin to those in BC, can also be considered as initiatives designed to assist poorer citizens that are not likely to re-enter the labour market.

Data concerning subsidised housing programs for older citizens are extremely difficult to gather because they are widely dispersed and information is ill-organized to conduct analysis. Complicating matters further, many programs offered by provincial and municipal authorities do not

Table 19.2 Housing Allowances for Seniors in Three Canadian Provinces, 2013

Province (Name)	Tenure	Maximum Allowance / Month	Minimum Age	Income Ceiling
BC (Shelter Aid for Elderly Renters)	Tenants	Variable*	60	Single $27,996** Couple $30,204**
Manitoba (RentAid Program)	Tenants	$230 maximum	55	Single $24,167 Couple $27,126
Québec	Tenants and homeowners	$80 maximum	52	Single $16,480 Couple $24,729

Source: Various governmental websites and information booklets.
Note: In housing allowance programs, households cannot benefit from other housing subsidy programs.

* The program reimburses part of the difference between 30 per cent of the total income and the paid rent. Regardless of the actual amount of rent paid, the program will only consider amounts up to maximum rent levels.

** These ceilings are provided for Vancouver. They are lower in the rest of the province.

target seniors specifically but can be made available to seniors. As a result, to determine the extent of the social housing effort devoted to seniors, we focused on data provided in official governmental publications (including websites) and on information obtained directly from professionals working within provincial agencies responsible for social housing programs.

In many cases, we were still unable to obtain accurate data due to the decentralized nature of housing programs. This is particularly significant in the case of a province such as Ontario, which has historically granted a lot of power to municipalities in this area.

Alberta, British Columbia, Prince Edward Island, and Québec provided sufficient information to generate a meaningful comparison and assessment. The data demonstrate that seniors benefit more than other groups from housing programs targeting poorer households. For example, in PEI there are 104 rent-supplemented units for seniors compared with 58 for younger families.[4] Among the 1,587 public housing units, 1,124 are for seniors. In Alberta, 10,400 community-housing units are for individuals and families, 1,400 for households with special needs, and 14,400 for seniors. Moreover, the province provides over 9,700 seniors lodges to low to moderate-income seniors who are functionally independent. In BC, 16,894 seniors received rent assistance against 10,379 families. In addition, 21,336 low-income seniors live in social housing units, surpassing the total number (19,662) of low-income families (British Columbia Housing 2013, 9). In Québec, of the 105,006 households receiving the housing allowance, 67,614 are composed of seniors. Also, out of the 21,806 households that have access to a dwelling from the programs Accès-Logis I and II, 10,952 are composed of senior citizens. From the 73,664 households currently living in Habitations à loyer modique (HLMs—public or private social housing), there are 37,403 households composed of seniors. Interestingly, seniors are far less reliant on Québec's rent supplement program. Only 1,742 out of 23,203 recipients are senior citizens.

Data from the CMHC on one-person subsidized urban[5] renter households in Canada corroborate these findings. In 2008, 38 per cent of single tenants receiving assistance were women aged 65 and above, and 11 per cent were senior men. This means that close to half of all single households receiving housing assistance were seniors (CMHC 2012, 85).

4 Data were provided by the professional staff of the Department of Community Services and Seniors.

5 Urban households are households living in census metropolitan areas (CMAs) or in census agglomerations (CAs).

What accounts for a proportionally higher use of housing programs by seniors? Poverty rates are now higher in younger age groups, but seniors rely more strongly on housing benefits. Although further studies are necessary, three potential explanations can shed light on this surprising outcome. First, the introduction of a housing allowance and the production of social housing occurred in the 1970s and in the beginning of the 1980s, when seniors experienced higher poverty rates. Despite relative improvement, seniors continue to benefit from this historical legacy. Second, seniors benefited during these years from a positive social construction and were thus considered to be "deserving poor" (see Schneider and Ingram 1993), making it easier politically to sustain or even extend housing benefits to them. Finally, during the 1970s and the beginning of the 1980s, senior populations were concentrated in the central and old neighbourhoods of large Canadian cities (Séguin, Apparicio, and Negron-Poblete 2013) in types of housing that were considered inadequate (Séguin 1996). Social housing was seen as offering a more adequate type of dwelling. In closing, it is also important to stress that the programs analyzed in this section are not the only ones available for senior citizens. There are many targeted programs such as subsidized housing for seniors living with incapacities, tax credits to ensure that seniors can remain in their own homes, and tax alleviation schemes to reduce the costs of municipal tax bills (Chouinard and Gagnon 2007).

Conclusion

This chapter presented a brief overview of the role of provinces with regards to social assistance programs for seniors by focusing on retirement and housing policies. Three interesting findings are worth highlighting. First, the role of the provinces is increasing in both fields. This finding is hardly surprising when it comes to housing policies, as the provinces never relinquished their responsibilities for these programs and the federal government has been steadily withdrawing its support since the 1993 budget. However, neither as severe a federal retrenchment nor as sustained a provincial role is the case when it comes to retirement policies such as pensions, and federal programs such as the OAS and the GIS have resulted in lower poverty rates. Yet eight provinces offer additional resources to poor retirees.

Second, the federal government has maintained its leadership in the field of pensions, assuming primary responsibility for OAS, GIS, and CPP. Although the rise in the retirement age to 67 in both OAS and GIS results in a transfer of costs toward provinces, which will have to extend their social assistance programs for two years, this change does not threaten existing arrangements. The situation is completely different in the field of the production of social and subsidized housing; the federal government has been exiting this policy area.

Finally, despite recent reforms to abolish mandatory retirement and permit more flexibility in terms of the age at which people retire, age remains a key determinant for poor individuals, as retirement benefits are far more generous than the social assistance programs provided by provincial authorities. The relative generosity of retirement benefits explains, in large part, why poverty rates fall strongly once individuals start to collect both GIS and OAS (RRQ 2004). However, factors other than being of retirement age affect the well-being of older Canadians in provinces that offer housing allowances. For example, two provinces (Québec and Manitoba) provide targeted housing assistance when individuals are in their fifties, and BC offers a senior housing allowance once someone reaches the age of 60. There are also many housing assistance programs that do not differentiate across age or status within the labour market, although seniors seem to be relying on these programs disproportionally compared to younger cohorts.

References

Banting, K.G. 1987. *The Welfare State and Canadian Federalism.* Montréal: McGill-Queen's University Press.

British Columbia Housing. 2013. *Annual Report: Housing Matters, 2012/13.* Victoria: BC Housing. http://www.bchousing.org/resources/About%20BC%20Housing/Annual Reports/2013/2012-13-Annual-Report.pdf.

Bryden, K. 1974. *Old Age Pensions and Policy-Making in Canada.* Montréal: McGill-Queen's University Press.

Carter, T., and C. Polevychok. 2004. *Housing Is Good Social Policy. Research Report F 50.* Ottawa: Family Network, Canadian Policy Research Networks.

Chouinard, Y., and R. Gagnon. 2007. *Inventaire des programmes provinciaux et territoriaux en habitation au Canada.* Québec: Société d'habitation du Québec.

CMHC (Canada Mortgage and Housing Corporation). 2011. *Canadian Housing Observer 2011.* Ottawa: Canadian Mortgage and Housing Corporation.

CMHC (Canadian Mortgage and Housing Corporation). 2012. *Canadian Housing Observer 2012.* Ottawa: Canadian Mortgage and Housing Corporation.

CMHC (Canada Mortgage and Housing Corporation). 2013. *Existing Social Housing.* Ottawa: Canadian Mortgage and Housing Corporation. http://www.cmhc-schl.gc.ca/en/inpr/afhoce/exsoho/.

Divay, Gérard, Anne-Marie Séguin, and Gilles Sénécal. 2005. "Le Canada." In *Politiques et interventions en habitation: Analyse des tendances récentes en Amérique du Nord et en Europe*, ed. Francine Dansereau, 13–44. Québec: Presses de l'Université Laval et Société d'habitation du Québec.

Engeland, J., and R. Lewis. 2004. "Exclusion from Acceptable Housing: Canadians in Core Housing Need." *Horizons* 7 (2): 27–34.

Finkel, M., C. Climaco, J. Khadduri, and M. Steele. 2006. *Housing Allowances Options for Canada*. Ottawa: Canada Mortgage and Housing Corporation.

Hulchanski, D.J. 2002. *Housing Policy for Tomorrow's Cities*. Canadian Policy Research Networks, Discussion Paper F27. Ottawa: CPRN/RCRPP. http://www.urbancentre.utoronto.ca/pdfs/elibrary/CPRNHousingPolicy.pdf.

Hulchanski, D.J. 2007. *Canada's Dual Housing Policy: Assisting Owners, Neglecting Renters*. Centre for Urban and Community Studies Research Bulletin 38. Toronto: University of Toronto.

Myles, J. 1989. *Old Age in the Welfare State: The Political Economy of Public Pensions*. Lawrence: University Press of Kansas.

Palme, J. 1990. *Models of Old-Age Pensions*. *Reprint Series*. Stockholm: Swedish Institute for Social Research.

Podoluk, J.R. 1968. *Incomes of Canadians, 1961 Census Monograph*. Ottawa: Queen's Printer.

Quadagno, J. 1988. *The Transformation of Old Age Security: Class and Politics in the American Welfare State*. Chicago: The University of Chicago Press.

Ritakallio, V.-M. 2003. "The Importance of Housing Costs in Cross-National Comparisons of Welfare (State) Outcomes." *International Social Security Review* 56 (2): 81–101. http://dx.doi.org/10.1111/1468-246X.00159.

RRQ (Régie des rentes du Québec). 2004. *Evaluation of the Québec System of Financial Security at Retirement in Relation to That of Other Industrialized Countries*. Québec: RRQ.

Schneider, A., and H. Ingram. 1993. "Social Constructions of Target Populations: Implications for Politics and Policy." *American Political Science Review* 87 (2): 334–47. http://dx.doi.org/10.2307/2939044.

Séguin, A.-M. 1996. "La construction sociale d'un compromis (1945–1970): Prélude à la rénovation urbaine dans le quartier Saint-Jean-Baptiste de Québec." *Urban History Review / Revue d'histoire urbaine* 24 (2): 12–24. http://dx.doi.org/10.7202/1016595ar.

Séguin, A.-M., P. Apparicio, and P. Negron-Poblete. 2013. "La répartition de la population âgée dans huit métropoles canadiennes de 1981 à 2006: Un groupe de moins en moins ségrégué." *Cybergeo: European Journal of Geography* 639. http://cybergeo.revues.org/25860.

SHQ (Société d'habitation du Québec). 1988. *Les programmes d'aide à l'habitation au Québec*. Québec: SHQ.

Snell, J.G. 1993. "The Newfoundland Old Age Pension Programme, 1911–1949." *Acadiensis* 23: 86–109.

twenty

Shelter and the Street: Housing, Homelessness, and Social Assistance in the Canadian Provinces

MICHAEL J. PRINCE

Introduction

Customarily social assistance is called the safety net of last resort in Canada, the final method of public support to those in dire circumstances. However, below this safety net are emergency shelters, transition houses, and soup kitchens, funded at times by provincial governments, to respond to the basic necessities of housing, food, and personal safety. People existing on the streets and in temporary shelters and those living in precarious housing situations are citizens at the bottom of the bottom income scale. The Canadian Homelessness Research Network (2012) provides an informative and multifaceted definition of homelessness:

> Homelessness describes the situation of an individual or family without stable, permanent, appropriate housing, or the immediate prospect, means and ability of acquiring it. It is the result of systemic or societal barriers, a lack of affordable and appropriate housing, the individual/household's financial, mental, cognitive, behavioural or physical challenges, and/or racism and discrimination. Most people do not choose to be homeless, and the experience is generally negative, unpleasant, stressful and distressing. (1)

This chapter focuses on the interplay of housing, homelessness, and provincial social assistance systems.[1] The evidence is clear that affordable housing has become a greater challenge than previously for many Canadians and that, in absolute numbers, the homeless population in

1 For information on the three territorial systems, see the National Council of Welfare reports on welfare incomes listed in the references for this chapter; as well, refer to the territorial government websites. For discussion of the federal government's role in homelessness policies, through the National Homelessness Initiative of 1999 and the Homelessness Partnering Strategy of 2007, which was renewed March 2013 for another five years to 2017–18, see Doberstein (2012) and Gaetz et al. (2013).

towns and cities across the country has increased considerably over the past 20 years (Canada 2009; Hulchanski et al. 2009). To explore these issues, this chapter proceeds in three parts. First, I discuss in general terms the place of housing or shelter in social assistance programs across the provinces. Second, I consider homelessness in Canada and the relation between people who are homeless and social assistance. Although some homeless people do not qualify for social assistance, it is a source of income for many people who are homeless. The limited Canadian research there is shows that social assistance is one source of income among several for people who are homeless and surviving on the streets. Third, the chapter offers concluding observations on the need for further enquiries on these topics and on the contradictory nature and the limited capacity of social assistance in tackling issues of homelessness and affordable housing. Social assistance policies have important effects on housing and homelessness, contributing to both the security and insecurity of shelter for many Canadians.

The place of housing in social assistance programs

Considerations of housing are built into welfare and other programs of Canadian social policy. When the Canada Assistance Plan (CAP) was in effect from the mid-1960s to the mid-1990s (see Boychuk, this volume; Prince 1995), one policy objective of that intergovernmental cost-sharing agreement was to support provinces in providing residential and institutional care for persons in need. That objective related to the program component in CAP that dealt with homes for special care, a relatively small component compared to the expenditures on general income assistance and welfare services. Specifically, this residential component included the funding of homes for the aged, nursing homes and hostels for transients, childcare institutions for orphans and children in custody, homes for unmarried mothers, and homes of other kinds for care and rehabilitation. Near the end of the CAP era, approximately 104,000 adults and children were in homes for special care, for which both levels of government shared costs. With respect to homelessness, across the provinces, there were 165 cost-shared homes for transients. Over the 1991–96 period, as part of a federal disability strategy, CAP funding also supported deinstitutionalization initiatives: that is, community-based living alternatives for people with intellectual and developmental disabilities contained in provincial institutions (HRDC 1995).

Across Canadian provinces, social assistance recipients have various housing arrangements and can be categorized as

- Homeowners
- Renting in the private housing market
- Renting social housing units
- Boarding in rooming and lodging houses
- Living with relatives
- Staying in emergency shelters and hostels for transient men and women
- Occupying transition houses and shelters from violence for abused women and their children
- Living in family shelters
- Living in shelters for youth
- Living in residential centres (often for people with disabilities)
- Staying in provisional shelters (e.g., hospitals, jails, detox centres)
- Living unsheltered or absolutely homeless

In all these living arrangements, there are people who receive social assistance. Even some who own and occupy their own homes are among those living in poverty in Canada, though most social assistance recipients across the country are renters in private-market housing (Canada 2009; National Council of Welfare 1998). These housing provisions vary in terms of community legitimacy, political support, public policies, funding sources, and support programs offered, as well as in terms of the clientele served (by age, ethnicity, and gender, among other markers of social identity). Of those individuals who are homeless on a given night, about half are estimated to be staying in emergency homeless shelters, about one-quarter are staying in women's shelters to escape violence (including transitional and second-stage housing), others are provisionally accommodated in hospitals, jails, or treatment centres, and still others are absolutely homeless and unsheltered, sleeping on heating grates, under bridges, on the streets, or in parks, alleyways, cars, dumpsters, and stairwells (Layton 2000; Rice and Prince 2013). The shelter arrangements for people who are homeless also vary in terms of reasons for service and for being turned away, the average length of stay, and the turnover rate of clientele (Allen 2000; Segaert 2012).

Basic social assistance is meant to include income support for food, clothing, and personal needs, as well as for shelter, utilities, and household needs. Most jurisdictions have an explicit shelter component in their basic benefit. The shelter component varies across and within jurisdictions by size of family and size of community—to reflect differences in cost of living. The shelter allowances in all the provinces have ceilings on rent. Most social assistance recipients obtain housing in the private rental market, so their rents are set by local market circumstances.

Authorities in several provinces reduce basic welfare benefits when it is known that individuals share housing. Consider three recent recommendations on social assistance reform in Ontario that deal with the interplay between living arrangements and welfare eligibility and rates. In recognition of the cost savings from sharing housing, the first recommendation is that "a person receiving social assistance who is living with one or more other adults [ought to] receive a modified rate, equal to 86 per cent of the standard rate." The second is that persons with a disability under the Ontario Disability Support Program "who live with their parents, and adults without disabilities who live with their parents where a parent is also receiving social assistance . . . should receive the modified standard rate." The third proposal is that "adults without disabilities who live with their parents, where the parents are not receiving social assistance, continue to be required to meet a test of financial independence, in addition to meeting other eligibility requirements, in order to be eligible for assistance" (Lankin and Sheikh 2012, 30–31). These examples illustrate the complexity of program design and of reform dialogue when social assistance systems endeavour to calibrate household arrangements with benefit rate structures.

The problem of finding affordable housing given the inadequacy of social assistance benefits has long been experienced by people with low incomes and has been noted in welfare studies. Most social assistance recipients rent in the private housing market and only a minority live in rent-geared-to-income social housing. Social housing refers to government-owned or -financed housing projects and non-profit (or third-sector) units and projects developed by cooperatives and other charitable agencies. In Canada, social housing represents about 7 per cent of the total housing stock. For social assistance recipients living in social housing, "rents are negotiated between welfare and housing officials, taking into account the amounts paid by the welfare system for different kinds of households" (National Council of Welfare 1993, 44).[2]

For many social assistance recipients, especially in urban areas, their actual shelter costs in the housing market exceed, at times by a large margin, what they have available for shelter in their monthly benefits. A report from Ontario suggests a new standard rate for social assistance that would not include a separate shelter amount. Thus, "rents for social assistance recipients residing in Rent-Geared-to-Income units [would] no longer be

2 More research needs to be done on how these rents are negotiated and, more broadly, on how the welfare, social housing, and market housing systems interact and what those negotiations and interactions mean for individuals and households.

based on rent scales, but rather on 30 per cent of household income (as it is for residents who are not receiving social assistance), including income from social assistance benefits, net of earnings exemptions" (Lankin and Sheikh 2012, 34). If the province were to introduce a housing benefit, the report recommends that the benefit be available to all people with low incomes, not solely to social assistance recipients (Lankin and Sheikh 2012, 32).[3]

Social assistance policies across the provinces have five housing-related and place-based elements: the shelter allowance components within the basic benefit, the reduction of benefits linked to household living arrangements, special assistance measures for household activities, fuel supplements for heat and utilities, and remote area supplements.

Maximum amounts for shelter allowances in social assistance are adjusted by locality within many provinces. Clients living in households in smaller municipalities, for instance, often receive lower benefits for the reason that shelter costs tend to be lower there than in large urban areas. Shelter allowance benefits are also targeted in some provinces for specific groups, such as families with children, persons with a disability, and those in private rental accommodations. Newfoundland and Labrador has a flat-rate shelter allowance for the disabled of $125 per month; to offset high shelter costs, New Brunswick has had (as of 2009) an income supplement benefit of $1,020 per year for families with children; and Québec has a monthly shelter allowance program for families with children of $960 per year. In Manitoba, there is a flat-rate shelter benefit of $35 per month for people with a disability and for singles and childless couples living in private rental accommodation and a benefit of $15 per month for those living in room-and-board housing.

Social assistance benefits are reduced in several provinces when it is known that unrelated individuals share housing or when a client lives in subsidized housing. In Québec, since 2005, "if an adult recipient lives with his or her mother or father who is not an employee-assistance recipient, the latter is deemed able to provide financial support [and] the adult's basic benefit will be reduced by $100 per month, or by $50 per month if the adult is the spouse of a student" (National Council of Welfare 2005, 10).

Several provinces include special assistance for additional supports related to shelter. These measures include funds for minor home repairs,

3 Québec and Saskatchewan provide low-income housing benefits. "Québec's program assists [to a] maximum of $80 per month based on the difference between the actual rent and 30 per cent of income. The Saskatchewan program assists low- and moderate-income families with children and people with disabilities with rental costs. Payment amounts depend on geographical location, family size, disability status, and income" (Lankin and Sheikh 2012, 90).

household furniture replacement, and moving costs. These special household benefits are usually available on a discretionary and one-time basis.

In some provinces, social assistance includes an auxiliary benefit for the cost of heat and utilities. Because many on social assistance live in a circumstance that other liberal welfare states call fuel poverty, this policy aims to enable people with low incomes to have warm shelters in cold weather conditions. Fuel supplements are intended to help compensate for the high heating costs experienced by social assistance clients who pay for heat separately (National Council of Welfare 2008); no doubt these high costs also reflect the poor insulation quality of some low-income housing. In New Brunswick, for example, a fuel supplement has been available over the period from November to April in six monthly payments or a one-time payment. New Brunswick also has an emergency fuel benefit for low-income households on social assistance. In 2004–05, Nova Scotia offered a one-time payment to defray the cost of heating fuel for people on social assistance. In a similar fashion, in 2004, Saskatchewan increased the amount for utility payments and then, in 2005, offered a temporary energy costs allowance, and Newfoundland and Labrador increased its fuel supplement from $25 to $50 per month at the end of 2005. Supplements for people living in out-of-the-way communities are another feature of social assistance programs in some provinces. These benefits "offer supplements to compensate welfare households living in remote areas [such as northern and rural regions] for higher living costs"(National Council of Welfare 2008, 13).

Recent public policy and budgetary decisions related to providing social assistance for housing reveal three patterns. One trend, which basically continues the restraint of the 1990s, is the nominal maintenance of shelter allowance rates in many jurisdictions.[4] Over time, of course, merely maintaining these rates effectively means a real decline in the purchasing power of benefits for shelter and a growing gap between shelter assistance and actual housing costs (Disability Without Poverty Network 2012). For example, Ontario implemented a 3 per cent increase to the maximum shelter allowance in 2005, the first increase since 1993, leaving the real value of the allowance well behind increases in shelter costs over that period. The maximum shelter rate under the Ontario Disability Support Program (ODSP) was raised in 2007. A second trend, starting in the early

4 A policy of maintaining shelter rates is at least not as regressive as actual reductions in the assistance for shelter costs, as was done by a number of provinces in the 1990s, for example, Nova Scotia, PEI, Québec, and New Brunswick (Prince 1998). Still, the nominal maintenance of shelter support is a tepid commitment to providing a decent standard of living for low-income Canadians.

to mid-2000s, has been the increase to particular housing-related elements of social assistance in many provinces. These include, as noted previously, increases to shelter benefits and to fuel supplements. To give a few other examples, in 2009, PEI increased both the basic rate and the maximum shelter allowance rate, and Saskatchewan enlarged the shelter component of assistance and made increases to the disability rental supplement and the family rental-housing supplement. These benefit increases tend to be of a modest amount. The third trend is the introduction by the provinces of new housing-related benefits in social assistance. In Manitoba, a new shelter benefit was introduced in 2006 that provides $50 per month for those social assistance clients living in private rental accommodation and $30 per month for those clients living in room-and-board lodgings. In a restructuring of shelter allowances, Saskatchewan introduced a family rental-housing supplement and a disability rental-housing supplement in 2005 (National Council of Welfare 2006, 2008, 2010).

Homelessness and social assistance

Like social assistance in general, homelessness is a politics of poverty, stigma, discrimination, and exclusion. Homelessness also entangles politically with the formal and social regulation of public spaces as well as with the criminalization and penalization of poor people by state authorities (Chesnay, Bellot, and Sylvestre 2013; Gordon 2004; O'Reilly-Fleming 1998).

It is well to remember that people who are homeless are not a distinct and homogeneous population group. As a major research study reports, "the pathways into and out of homelessness are neither linear, nor uniform. Individuals and families who wind up homeless may not share much in common with each other, aside from the fact that they are extremely vulnerable and lack adequate housing, income and the necessary supports to ensure they stay housed." This same study offers a view of why homelessness has increased in the twenty-first century: "We do know that the homelessness crisis was created through drastically reduced investments in affordable and social housing in the 1990s, shifts in income supports and the declining spending power of almost half of the population since that time" (Gaetz et al. 2013, 4).

According to the Canadian Homelessness Research Network and the Canadian Alliance to End Homelessness, approximately 30,000 individuals experience homelessness on any given night in Canada; in a given year, at least 200,000 Canadians access homeless emergency services or sleep outside. However, the scope of homelessness in Canada is no doubt much greater than these statistics suggest:

> The actual number [of the homeless] is potentially much higher, given that many people who become homeless live with friends or relatives, and do not come into contact with emergency shelters. Recent data from a March 2013 Ipsos Reid poll suggests that as many as 1.3 million Canadians have experienced homelessness or extremely insecure housing at some point during the past five years. (Gaetz et al. 2013, 5)

That represents almost 4 per cent of the Canadian population having experienced homelessness or extremely insecure housing over a period that includes the recession of 2008 and 2009 and the slow economic recovery of its aftermath.

Over the course of a year, most people who are homeless are so for only a short time, often less than a month; these individuals are transitionally homeless. For others, homelessness is an intermittent occurrence; these persons are episodically homeless. For still other people, homelessness is a long-term situation; these individuals are the chronically homeless. *The State of Homelessness in Canada: 2013* projects the following numbers for these three types of homelessness: transitionally homeless 176,000 to 188,000, episodically homeless 6,000 to 22,000, and chronically homeless 4,000 to 8,000 (Gaetz et al. 2013, 28–29).

The social assistance system itself affects not only how many people become homeless and the nature of homelessness but also who among the homeless get financial and shelter support. One way this system has an effect is through its administrative prerequisites of identification, such as having potential clients submit an address, a health card, or social insurance number to support an application (O'Reilly-Fleming 1998). "Requests for extensive documentation virtually guarantee noncompliance since few homeless persons carry or maintain timely records. Securing documents may be difficult for the homeless, estranged from families and out of touch with agencies able to replace lost or misplaced [or stolen] items. Entitlements may be out of reach for homeless persons unless they are assisted by savvy and aggressive advocates in the pursuit of documentation or unless standard documentation requirements are waived" (Brickner and Scanlan 1990, 12–13). A second way homelessness is shaped by social assistance occurs when welfare offices fail to inform individuals of their entitlements or do not offer advice on opportunities for retraining or new safe housing (Morrell-Bellai, Goering, and Boydell 2000). A third way is through placing conditions on family shelter support. In at least one province, "eligibility for family shelter accommodation is based upon an application for, or being on, public assistance in order to qualify for family shelter support" (Waegemakers Schiff 2007, 138).

Published research exists on homeless people in Canada and their sources of income and ways of making money. Table 20.1 reports on seven studies that shed light on the shadows of welfare: the place of social assistance in the lives of people who are in shelters and on the streets in particular Canadian cities.

For the individuals and families in these studies on homelessness, social assistance occurs in a wider context of market setbacks, private troubles, and state actions and inactions. Provincial welfare and disability programs are found to be a source of income for a sizeable number of homeless men and women. An early study in Canada on 390 homeless youth in Toronto (McCarthy and Hagan 1992), most on the streets for at least six months, found that social assistance of a one-time nature was a common source of income, a form of assistance that required minimal identification and examination. Even when social assistance is a source of income, some homeless individuals generate cash from engaging in underground activities (drug dealing, shoplifting, breaking and entering, and prostitution), selling personal belongings, and asking for help from family and friends. Some users of shelters have jobs, commonly in low-wage and precarious employment. Thus, besides receiving any public transfer payments, the homeless engage in money raising behaviours that are at once illicit, entrepreneurial, informal, social, mundane, and dangerous. In the glare of these realities, the question of undue dependency on the welfare state fades into insignificance.

Conclusion

For the many people in many places who rely on social assistance, the shelter component of these safety-net programs has little correlation to the actual rents in the private housing market. Thus, they face a serious budget constraint because of paying a disproportionately large share of their monthly income on shelter, which means that other essential items such as food, clothing, and utilities are foregone. The scholarly literature and research studies reviewed here show that the homeless population is comprised of young and middle-aged people, households as well as individuals, women and men, and two-adult and single-mother families. The time has long passed that the image of the homeless is of older men on skid row or a few bag ladies on city streets. The diversity of homeless Canadians, in both their biographies and circumstances, points to the countless systemic elements of homelessness.

Table 20.1 Canadian Research on People Who Are Homeless and Select Income Sources

Author and Study	Time of Data Collection	Location	Homeless Population: Sample Size and Profile	Findings on Income Sources
Allen (2000)	1996	Downtown Eastside Vancouver	26 men and women in an emergency shelter agency	Nearly all (88%) said they had received welfare as a source of income in the previous month. Money from employment or employment programs (31%).
Bose and Hwang (2002)	2001	Downtown Toronto	54 street panhandlers	In addition to soliciting money from passers-by, 42 per cent received monthly income from welfare, disability, or other government payments.
Keenan, Maldonado, and O'Grady (2006)	1999	Toronto (downtown and suburbs)	233 street-involved youth and 14 shelters or service agencies for homeless youth	For 15 per cent of the street-involved youth in Toronto, social assistance was a way to make money in the preceding three months. Money from paid employment another 15 per cent.
McCarthy and Hagan (1992)	1987–88	Toronto	390 adolescents without permanent housing, staying in hostels or living on the street	Just over half (53%) had received social assistance since being on the street, usually one-time emergency welfare. Most (70%) had obtained employment, mainly temporary.

(Continued)

Table 20.1 (Continued)

Author and Study	Time of Data Collection	Location	Homeless Population: Sample Size and Profile	Findings on Income Sources
Morrell-Bellai, Goering, and Boydell (2000)	1996–97	Toronto	29 homeless adults who included shelter users and shelter avoiders (people who preferred the streets or were barred from shelters)	Just over a third (35%) received welfare or public benefits and some (14%) worked; other sources of income included panhandling and family.
Khandor, Mason, and Cowan (2007)	2006–07	Toronto	386 homeless adults at downtown shelters and meal programs	About half (48%) had public income benefits, primarily provincial welfare or provincial disability supports.
Waegemakers Schiff (2007)	2003–04	Calgary	23 homeless families in a shelter for parents and dependent relatives	Many families (48%) had earned income from work but several (38%) had no income. Social assistance is an important requirement for family shelter accommodation in some cities.

Social assistance has a dual relationship to housing and homelessness. On the one hand, social assistance is a public provision—the delivery of financial support to people in significant need and perhaps under threat of violence. This safety net program, however inadequate and flawed, is an important source of money to address basic necessities of living in shelter and on the street. On the other hand, provincial social assistance seems to be part of the problem—with its challenging documentation requirements for some homeless people, with its benefit reduction and claw-back conditions, and with its real decline in shelter support while housing costs rise over time.

Despite good work by several cities, community agencies such as the Réseau d'aide aux personnes seules et itinérantes de Montréal, and a few provincial governments, there remains a notable lack of information and policy analysis on social assistance, housing, and homelessness in Canada. Consider, for example, these unanswered questions. To what extent does social assistance cover the actual shelter costs of recipients in each province, and does the answer to this question vary depending upon whether recipients live in large urban areas, towns, or rural communities? After paying shelter costs, what is the disposable income of a social assistance recipient in each province? What housing-related costs are covered? How much help with shelter is on a discretionary versus a compulsory basis in social assistance programs? Further work would be helpful in better understanding what steps provincial officials now take, or ought to take, to prevent the homelessness of social assistance recipients, such as reaching out to those in marginal housing, for example. How many people without shelter are without income support? We have no public research on whether and to what extent homeless people who ask for social assistance are rejected outright, diverted to community services, or supported through the application process. Regrettably, the lack of data on these questions undermines both the equity and effectiveness and the transparency and accountability of provincial asocial assistance systems.

A final observation: there are profound limits to provincial social assistance as a policy vehicle for tackling the issues of housing and homelessness. The analysis in this chapter shows that provincial welfare programs do offer several forms of financial assistance for shelter costs and housing-related expenses. These forms of support are usually on a modest scale, and the core shelter allowances embedded in basic welfare rates are far from adequate. There is little doubt that basic and special assistance could be improved upon. With respect to housing and homelessness, the administration and delivery of social assistance could be enhanced, especially in relation to those persons in insecure housing or precarious living arrangements. For the largest part, however, the main public policy vehicles for addressing affordable housing and homelessness in Canada go well beyond the last-resort safety net to involve other income security programs as well as policies on private-market and social housing, disability-related supports, employment, mental health and public health, substance use and harm reduction, spousal abuse, and family safety.

References

Allen, Tom C. 2000. *Someone to Talk To: Care and Control of the Homeless*. Halifax: Fernwood Publishing.

Bose, Rohit, and Stephen W. Hwang. 2002. "Income and Spending Patterns among Panhandlers." *Canadian Medical Association Journal* 167 (5): 477–79.

Brickner, Philip W., and Brian G. Scanlan. 1990. "Health Care for Homeless Persons." In *Under the Safety Net: The Health and Social Welfare of the Homeless in the United States*, ed. Philip W. Brickner, Linda Keen Scharer, Barbara A. Conanan, Marianne Savarese, and Brain C. Scanlan, 3–14. New York: W.W. Norton and Company.

Canada. Parliament. Senate. Standing Senate Committee on Social Affairs, Science, and Technology. 2009. *In from the Margins: A Call to Action on Poverty, Housing, and Homelessness*. Report of the Subcommittee on Cities. 2nd sess., 40th Parliament. http://www.parl.gc.ca/Content/SEN/Committee/402/citi/rep/rep02dec09-e.pdf.

Canadian Homelessness Research Network. 2012. *The Canadian Definition of Homelessness*. Toronto: Canadian Homelessness Research Network.

Chesnay, Catherine T., Céline Bellot, and Marie-Eve Sylvestre. 2013. "Taming Disorderly People One Ticket at a Time: The Penalization of Homelessness in Ontario and British Columbia." *Canadian Journal of Criminology and Criminal Justice* 55 (2): 161–85. http://dx.doi.org/10.3138/cjccj.2011-E-46.

Disability Without Poverty Network. 2012. *Overdue: The Case for Increasing the Persons with Disabilities Benefit in BC*. Vancouver: Disability Without Poverty Network.

Doberstein, Carey. 2012. "Applying European Ideas on Federalism and Doing It Better? The Government of Canada's Homelessness Policy Experiment." *Canadian Public Policy* 38 (3): 395–410.

Gaetz, Stephen, Jesse Donaldson, Tim Richter, and Tanya Gulliver. 2013. *The State of Homelessness in Canada, 2013*. Toronto: Canadian Homelessness Research Network.

Gordon, Todd. 2004. "The Return of Vagrancy Law and the Politics of Poverty in Canada." *Canadian Review of Social Policy* 54: 34–57.

HRDC (Human Resources Development Canada). 1995. *Canada Assistance Plan Annual Report 1993–94*. Ottawa: HRDC.

Hulchanski, J. David, Philippa Campsie, Shirley B.Y. Chau, Stephen Hwang, and Emily Paradis. 2009. "Introduction: Homelessness—What's in a Word?" In *Finding Home Policy Options for Addressing Homelessness in Canada*, ed. J. David Hulchanski, Philippa Campise, Shirley B.Y. Chau, Stephen W. Hwang, and Emily Paradis, 1–16. Toronto: Cities Centre Press.

Keenan, Caroline, Vicky Maldonado, and Bill O'Grady. 2006. "Working the Streets: An International Comparative Analysis of Income Generation among Street Youth." *Canadian Review of Social Policy* 58: 25–42.

Khandor, Erika, Kate Mason, and Laura Cowan. 2007. *The Street Health Report 2007*. Toronto: Street Health.

Lankin, Frances, and Munir A. Sheikh. 2012. *Brighter Prospects: Transforming Social Assistance in Ontario*. Toronto: Commission for the Review of Social Assistance in Ontario.

Layton, Jack. 2000. *Homelessness: The Making and Unmaking of a Crisis*. Toronto: Penguin/McGill Institute.

McCarthy, Bill, and John Hagan. 1992. "Surviving on the Street: The Experiences of Homeless Youth." *Journal of Adolescent Research* 7 (4): 412–30. http://dx.doi.org/10.1177/074355489274002.

Morrell-Bellai, Tammy, Paula N. Goering, and Katherine M. Boydell. 2000. "Becoming and Remaining Homeless: A Qualitative Investigation." *Issues in Mental Health Nursing* 21 (6): 581–604. http://dx.doi.org/10.1080/01612840050110290.

National Council of Welfare. 1993. *Incentives and Disincentives to Work*. Ottawa: National Council of Welfare.

National Council of Welfare. 1998. *Profiles of Welfare: Myths and Realities*. Ottawa: National Council of Welfare.

National Council of Welfare. 2005. *Welfare Incomes 2004*. Ottawa: National Council of Welfare.

National Council of Welfare. 2006. *Welfare Incomes 2005*. Ottawa: National Council of Welfare.

National Council of Welfare. 2008. *Welfare Incomes 2006 and 2007*. Ottawa: National Council of Welfare.

National Council of Welfare. 2010. *Welfare Incomes 2009*. Ottawa: National Council of Welfare.

O'Reilly-Fleming, Thomas. 1998. *Down and Out in Canada: Homeless Canadians*. Toronto: Canadian Scholars' Press.

Prince, Michael J. 1995. "The Canadian Housing Policy Context." *Housing Policy Debate* 6 (3): 721–58. http://dx.doi.org/10.1080/10511482.1995.9521201.

Prince, Michael J. 1998. "Holes in the Safety Net, Leaks in the Roof: Changes in Canadian Welfare Policy and Their Implications for Social Housing Programs." *Housing Policy Debate* 9 (4): 825–48. http://dx.doi.org/10.1080/10511482.1998.9521320.

Rice, James J., and Michael J. Prince. 2013. *Changing Politics of Canadian Social Policy*. 2nd ed. Toronto: University of Toronto Press.

Segaert, A. 2012. *The National Shelter Study: Emergency Shelter Use in Canada 2005–2009*. Ottawa: Homelessness Partnering Secretariat, Human Resources and Skills Development Canada.

Waegemakers Schiff, Jeannette. 2007. "Homeless Families in Canada: Discovering Total Families." *Families in Society* 88 (1): 131–40.

twenty-one

Do Active Programs Work? A Review of Canadian Welfare-to-Work Experiments

KELLY FOLEY

The 1990s are frequently characterized as a period of welfare reform in Canada. During this decade, in response to legislative changes, economic conditions, and shifts in public opinion, provincial governments introduced several reforms to their social assistance (SA) programs. In varying degrees, these program changes emphasized "active" policies that encouraged or enforced work or job-related training (Daigneault 2015; see also Cox, in this volume).

The set of policies that can be defined as "active" is large. The range of active programs can include financial incentives, sanctions and mandates, and information and counselling. This spectrum of policy instruments has been described as "carrots," "sticks," and "sermons" (Bemelmans-Videc, Rist, and Vedung 1998; Daigneault 2014). The program reforms introduced in Canada during the 1990s span much of this policy space (Gorlick and Brethour 1998).[1]

Now that governments and policy analysts have the advantage of two decades of hindsight, it is worth asking whether active programs work. Because the definition of active is described as a range of concepts, it is not surprising that there are many different ideas of what "working" would mean, and about how one would know if a program was working. In the past, active programs in Canada have been assessed by drawing attention to general "lessons learned" (HRDC 2000) or by developing detailed inventories of the various provincial initiatives (Gorlick and Brethour 1998). There are also studies that examine changes in social assistance participation, entry, and exit rates in the years following the period of welfare reform (Boychuk 2006; Finnie and Irvine 2008). For a general discussion of the effect of policy on welfare rolls, see Boychuk as well as Kneebone and White in this volume.

Pilot projects have also been implemented in Canada to test the effectiveness of particular design features of active programs. In this chapter,

1 A large component of the Employment Insurance (EI) program in Canada involves active labour market programs, such as retraining. Since eligibility for EI necessitates accumulating considerable work experience, many social assistance recipients would not be eligible for these programs. Card, Kluve, and Weber (2010) offer a comprehensive international meta-analysis of active labour market programs.

I focus on two projects called the Self-Sufficiency Project (SSP) and the Community Employment Innovation Project (CEIP). Both SSP and CEIP were funded by the Canadian government, implemented in partnership with three provincial governments, and evaluated by the Social Research and Demonstration Corporation.[2] There are at least three reasons that a concentrated examination of SSP and CEIP will contribute to an understanding of whether active programs work.

First, to some degree, the programs feature all three aspects of active labour initiatives: "carrots," "sticks," and "sermons." CEIP was a direct employment program offering participants a full-time job for up to three years in a range of occupations and industries. CEIP represented on-the-job training opportunities and a small financial incentive because the wages in CEIP jobs were higher than minimum wages and sometimes higher than welfare benefits. SSP offered a generous earnings supplement to SA recipients who found a full-time job within a year and continued to work full time. The SSP earnings supplement was a "carrot," but the requirement to find full-time work within one year could also be regarded as a "stick." A smaller project, called SSP Plus, implemented within the main SSP study, delivered the "sermons" in the form of job-search services.

Second, both SSP and CEIP were implemented as random assignment experiments. Random assignment has often been referred to as the "gold standard" in evaluation (Shadish, Cook, and Campbell 2002). In a random-assignment design, project participants are randomly allocated to either a control group or a group that is enrolled in the particular program being evaluated. Random assignment is employed in evaluations because it ensures that, on average, the only systematic difference between the program and control groups is eligibility for the program. Thus, comparisons of group outcomes can be credibly interpreted as causal effects of the opportunity to participate in the program.[3] The difference between an average outcome within the program group and within the control group is often referred to as the "impact" of the program. I adopt that convention in this chapter.

Third, a common criticism of the evidence produced in random assignment experiments is that the findings may not extend beyond the population

2 SSP was initiated by the federal Department of Employment and Immigration and later fell under the portfolio of Human Resource Development Canada (Michalopoulos et al. 2002). The Community Employment Innovation Project was funded by Human Resources and Social Development Canada and the Nova Scotia Department of Community Services (Gyarmati et al. 2008).

3 The causal interpretation of experimental comparisons depends on two assumptions. First, the control group is not affected by the program. Second, there are no "spill-over" or general equilibrium effects.

studied (Hansen and Rieper 2009; Heckman 2001). In light of this potential weakness, the third reason to study SSP and CEIP is that they were conducted in three different Canadian provinces. CEIP was implemented in a region of Nova Scotia with high unemployment; thus, the findings from that project are more relevant to similar communities. SSP was implemented in the lower mainland of British Columbia and in New Brunswick. During the SSP experiment, the economy was more robust and the social assistance program was considerably more generous in British Columbia compared to New Brunswick. Despite these differences, the program impacts were quite similar in both provinces, suggesting that the findings from the SSP are robust across policy and economic environments (Michalopoulos et al. 2002).

To begin, I describe the programs and summarize the estimated causal effect of SSP and CEIP on employment and social assistance receipt. I then turn to a discussion of why the programs failed to cause a permanent increase in full-time employment. Although the impacts of these programs were short lived, I discuss in the next section whether CEIP and SSP might be viable as efficient mechanisms for government transfers. Finally, I summarize some of the conclusions that can be drawn from the evidence generated by the CEIP and SSP experiments.

The Self-Sufficiency Project

The Self-Sufficiency Project was implemented in 1992 and offered lone-parent social assistance recipients a generous earnings supplement if they left welfare for a full-time job within one year of entering the program. Once eligible for the supplement, participants could receive it when they worked full time in any of the subsequent 36 months. During the supplement eligibility period, failing to work full time in a particular month would not affect eligibility in subsequent months. However, if participants received SA, they would be ineligible for any future supplement payments.

The SSP study included three different experiments. The main study, referred to as the "recipient study," targeted long-term SA recipients. Specifically, over 5,000 volunteers[4] were recruited from among lone parents

4 Though random assignment ensures that, among the study volunteers, eligibility for the supplement offer was randomly determined, it does not mean that the volunteers were a random subset of all social assistance recipients. From among the SA recipients identified from administrative files as meeting the eligibility criteria (lone parents who had received SA for the past year), 90 per cent agreed to participate in the study (Michalopoulos et al. 2002). The extent to which results based on voluntary recruitment, followed by randomization, are generalizable depends on whether the program would be implemented on a larger scale on a voluntary or mandatory basis.

in British Columbia and New Brunswick who had received benefits in at least 11 of the previous 12 months. A second study, called SSP Plus, was implemented on a smaller scale in New Brunswick. SSP Plus combined the financial incentive along with a range of job-search and employment-support services. The final study, referred to as the "applicant study," was designed to test whether new SA enrolees, who were also lone parents, would remain on welfare to become eligible for the SSP earnings supplement. The applicant study was implemented only in British Columbia. In this study, applicants, who were randomly assigned to the program group, were informed that, if they remained on SA for 12 months, they would be eligible for the SSP earnings supplement. All three projects were evaluated using random assignment.

The SSP supplement was designed to reduce the disincentives to work by providing a relatively low marginal tax rate on earnings and by raising overall income. The SSP supplement was equal to half of the difference between a benchmark earnings level and the participant's gross earnings. In 1993, the earnings benchmark, which grew with inflation and changes in minimum wages, was $2,500 per month in New Brunswick and $3,083 in British Columbia. Among those who received the supplement, the average monthly payment was $820. To put the value of these payments in context, the average payment almost covers the average monthly expenditure on rent and groceries, $878 (Michalopoulos et al. 2002). SSP further encouraged work by making supplement eligibility contingent on an individual working for an average of at least 30 hours per week in a given month.

An important feature of SSP is the one-year time limit to initiate the supplement. The goal of SSP was to encourage full-time employment among people who would not have otherwise worked, rather than to pay people who were going to work full time even if the supplement had not been offered. In the control group, after 5 years, 44 per cent of the participants were no longer receiving welfare (Michalopoulos et al. 2002). Because many SA recipients will eventually leave welfare, the time limit was introduced to reduce the likelihood that supplements were received by individuals who would have worked in the absence of the program.

Impacts in the SSP recipient study

The SPP recipient study followed the lives of 4,852 project participants for 4.5 years.[5] During the first year, full-time employment growth in the

5 The initial project sample was 5,685. The response rate to the final survey was 85 per cent (Michalopoulos et al. 2002).

program group vastly outpaced that in the control group. By the end of the first year, 36 per cent of program group members had initiated their SSP supplement eligibility by working full time. At the one-year mark, SSP had doubled full-time employment, representing an increase of 15 percentage points. After the first year, full-time employment rates in the program group remained fairly constant. In the control group, full-time employment was growing slowly but consistently, which meant that the program's impacts eventually faded. After 51 months, program group members were only 1.5 percentage points more likely to work full time, a statistically insignificant difference. The program effects on SA receipt largely mirrored these employment effects.

On balance, what SSP appears to have accomplished is an acceleration of the transition from welfare to work. The program encouraged roughly 30 per cent of SA recipients to find full-time work within one year; the control group took four years to reach that level of employment. Much of this impact can be attributed to the one-year time limit to initiate the supplement (Card and Hyslop 2005).

Despite the program's impact on full-time employment, the majority of program group members did not initiate the supplement. Among those who failed to initiate the supplement, 27 per cent in British Columbia and 38 per cent in New Brunswick indicated that the main reason was their inability to find a full-time job (Lin et al. 1998). In both provinces, a further 15 per cent reported family responsibilities and 14 per cent reported health or disability concerns as the main factor preventing their participation. There were only small provincial differences in the percentage of those reporting these reasons for not taking up the supplement.

Impacts in the SSP applicant study

The SSP applicant study was designed to test whether the possibility of receiving the supplement created an incentive for new SA enrolees to remain on welfare long enough to be deemed "long-term" recipients. To investigate this possibility, the applicant study offered new SA enrolees in British Columbia the opportunity to receive the supplement if they remained on SA for 12 of the next 13 months. Other than this requirement, the program operated in the same way as the recipient study.

The SSP applicant study revealed only modest "entry" effects. Although roughly 57 per cent of the applicant program group remained on welfare for 12 months, long enough to qualify for the SSP program, this fraction was only 3 percentage points higher than in the control group.

The pattern of impacts noted in the applicant study is roughly similar to that observed in the main SSP study. The impact of the program is largest in the first year of supplement eligibility and gradually declines thereafter. A key difference is that these impacts are larger and persist longer in the applicant study in almost every important economic outcome. In the recipient study, SSP increased average cumulative earnings by $3,070. In the applicant study, the analogous increase was $7,370. SSP generated 656 additional hours of work experience for applicants compared to 499 hours among long-term recipients. Five years after the 12-month waiting period, the impact on the full-time employment rate among applicants was nearly 5 percentage points. Income assistance records were available for an additional year, and, by the end of the sixth year, the effect on SA receipt was not statistically significant. This finding suggests that, for those in the applicant study, program impacts were larger, more persistent, but ultimately not permanent (Ford et al. 2003).

The differences in the magnitude and duration of impacts can be attributed to differences in the characteristics of the applicant and recipient participants. Compared to the long-term recipients, the new SA applicants had more previous work experience and higher levels of education (Berlin et al. 1998).

Impacts in the SSP Plus study

The SSP Plus study offered a combination of the SSP supplement and a range of job-search services to a smaller subset of the participants in the recipient study in New Brunswick. The services, including résumé workshops, job coaching, and job leads, were available throughout the supplement eligibility period. The SSP Plus study involved a sample of 765 lone parents who were randomly assigned into three groups. Participants had an equal chance of being assigned to a control group; a program group, whose members were offered only the supplement; and an SSP Plus program group, whose members were offered both the supplement and the services. Comparing the group that was offered both the services and the supplement to the group that was offered only the supplement reveals the incremental effect of the services.

In the first three years of the program, adding services to the supplement did not have a detectable effect on full-time employment. In the fourth year, full-time employment in the group offered services was 7.4 percentage points higher than full-time employment in the group not eligible for these services. Although this impact declined during the next year, it remained large. Four and a half years after random assignment, the incremental impact of the services was 6.3 percentage points. This difference was not statistically significant in large part because the SSP Plus sample size was quite small. The combined impact on full-time employment of SSP Plus services and the financial incentive was 9.4 percentage points four and half years after the program began, a point in time when no SSP Plus group members were receiving either services or supplements (Michalopoulos et al. 2002).

The SSP Plus services enabled more welfare recipients to find full-time work within one year and thus to initiate the earnings supplement. One explanation for the delayed impact of the SSP Plus services is that these additional supplement takers were less job ready and, immediately after initiating the supplement, lost or left their jobs. The incremental impact of the services grew over time because the full-time employment rate among supplement-eligible SSP Plus group members was consistently between 30 and 35 per cent from the second year onward. In contrast, full-time employment declined steadily among regular SSP group members who were eligible for the supplement (Robins, Michalopoulos, and Foley 2008).

Cumulatively, adding services did not have an effect on the number of months of full-time employment that SSP Plus group members worked during the evaluation period. Yet, the services reduced the number of months that they received SA by almost three. This result implies that, when SSP Plus program members were not working full time, they did not return to the welfare rolls. Moreover, the availability of job-search services increased total earnings by $3,206. In SSP Plus, almost all of the additional employment created by the services was in jobs that paid a wage that was more than $2.00 higher than minimum wage (Michalopoulos et al. 2002). The combined impact of services and the supplement may have been persistent because the services helped participants find higher paying jobs.

The Community Employment Innovation Project

The Community Employment Innovation Project (CEIP) was designed in part to address the lack of employment opportunities for social assistance recipients. CEIP was implemented in six communities in Cape Breton, Nova Scotia. Unemployment in this region was, and remains, high, in part because of declines in the area's traditional industries, coal and steel. In 2000, when the project began soliciting volunteers, the unemployment rate in the region was over 15 per cent.

CEIP was designed to replicate traditional employment and offered SA and EI recipients jobs on locally developed community projects for which they would earn "community wages" (Gyarmati et al. 2008).[6] Participants randomly assigned to the program group were offered "CEIP jobs," which were full-time positions in a variety of roles that would last for up to three years. Participants could leave the CEIP job and return at any time during the three-year period, as long as they did not return to social assistance.

Although CEIP wages were not designed as income supplements or financial incentives, for some SA recipients, CEIP jobs would represent an increase in their income compared to SA.[7] The initial CEIP hourly wage rate was $8, which was roughly 43 per cent higher than the minimum wage of $5.60. Compared to the SSP supplement, which roughly doubled earnings from minimum-wage work, any financial inducement provided by CEIP jobs was modest.

An important difference between the CEIP jobs and many other direct employment programs is that CEIP offered a stable job lasting up to three years. Moreover, the jobs were new and were developed by a community board to address services required by the local community. Although many of the jobs were in service occupations, a large fraction of the jobs were in business, finance, administration, and natural and applied sciences occupations (Gyarmati et al. 2006).

The experimental evidence suggests that, when such jobs are available, the majority of SA recipients will voluntarily exchange their benefits for work. Within four months, 90 per cent of the program group was working full time, compared to only 14 per cent within the control group (Gyarmati et al. 2008). In the first 18 months of the program, program group members worked full time an average of 14 months, almost all of it in CEIP jobs (Gyarmati et al. 2006). Over three years, employment levels in the program group gradually fell to 80 per cent (Gyarmati et al. 2008). At the same time, full-time employment was slowly growing in the control group. Nonetheless, the impact on full-time employment ranged from 78 percentage points in month 5 to 51 percentage points in month 36.

When the CEIP jobs expired, full-time employment among program group members dropped to 20 per cent. Because roughly 65 per cent of the program group were employed in CEIP jobs, a full-time employment rate of 20 per cent after those jobs had expired suggests that a sizeable number of CEIP jobholders were able to transition immediately to regular employment. Nonetheless, in month 41, compared to the control group, program group members were roughly 10 percentage points less likely to be working full

6 Throughout, the results I cite refer only to the SA sample.

7 On average, during the first year of the program, annual individual income was $3,700 higher in the CEIP group (Gyarmati et al. 2006).

time. Over the next year, however, full-time employment rates increased among program members so that, by the end of the follow-up period, the difference in full-time employment rates between the groups was not statistically significant. CEIP did, however, allow program group members to accumulate an additional 2,500 hours of experience (Gyarmati et al. 2008).

Understanding why SSP and CEIP failed to produce permanent impacts

An important question that emerges from the SSP and CEIP evaluations is why these programs, which seemingly generated the intended short-run impacts, failed to deliver the anticipated long-term impacts on employment.

In the SSP recipient and applicant studies, wage growth was the mechanism with the most promise to generate long-lasting impacts. While accumulating more work experience, program participants might experience wage growth. If wages were permanently higher as a result of SSP, then impacts on full-time work might persist beyond the supplement eligibility period. Unfortunately, almost all of the additional employment was in jobs that paid within $2.00 of the minimum wage (Michalopoulos et al. 2002). For the most part, wages did not improve as hoped. Although program group members gained an additional 0.28 years of experience, this experience did not translate into higher wages. In general, it might be the case that, for low-skilled workers, wages grow very little as experience increases. If that is the case, the 0.28 years of additional experience attained by program group members was unlikely to have a produced a statistically detectable effect on wages (Card and Hyslop 2005).

Although CEIP jobs all paid the same wage, program group members accumulated many additional hours of work experience, and doing so might have allowed them to transition into better paying jobs. Despite the additional experience, by the end of the follow-up period, the difference between the average earnings of the groups was statistically insignificant (Gyarmati et al. 2008). Possibly, the three-year intervention was not long enough to overcome the employment barriers in an economy where one person in six was unemployed.

Features of the SSP program itself might have contributed to the lack of wage growth. In particular, the supplement's generosity may have created an incentive for SSP program group members to accept jobs with little or no potential wage growth (Connolly and Gottschalk 2009). The job-search services offered in SSP Plus might have helped participants overcome the incentive to take any job. On average, program members that were offered both the supplement and the services worked in jobs paying higher wages than those offered the supplement alone.

A structural analysis of all three SSP experiments further suggests that SSP Plus has the potential to generate permanent impacts. Ferrall's (2012) structural model specifies functional relationships between skills, wages, job-search activities, and individuals' utility or well-being. The model also incorporates differences in unobserved characteristics that would affect work and welfare receipt, including welfare stigma, impatience, and the propensity to report earned income to authorities. The model can be used to evaluate alternative policies or forecast results outside of the sample. According to Ferrall's (2012) model, the impacts of SSP Plus would persist to at least five years beyond the end of the supplement eligibility period.

The potential to overcome limitations in work-oriented programs by integrating services is also suggested by meta-analyses of welfare reform in the United States (Berlin 2002; Bloom and Michalopoulos 2001; Greenberg, Deitch, and Hamilton 2009). In these studies, it was commonly found that programs with "mixed" approaches produced larger and longer lasting effects when compared to programs that encouraged human capital development first and those that emphasized immediate transitions to work.

SSP and CEIP as an alternative to transfer-based social assistance

Although the impacts of CEIP and SSP were apparently temporary, the degree of their short-run success warrants consideration of whether these programs represent an improvement over transitional transfer-based welfare. Are earnings supplements or direct employment more efficient ways of transferring government funds? CEIP was a relatively expensive program because the government incurred payroll costs. The evaluators caution that any cost-benefit analysis should account for benefits to the community as a whole. CEIP may be an efficient way to target the well-being of an entire community (Gyarmati et al. 2008).[8] With that in mind, the CEIP model could be relevant to northern communities and First Nations reserves with persistently high levels of unemployment.

8 A common critique of community-based development programs is that they will discourage labour mobility from depressed economic areas to areas of growth. In the CEIP evaluation, there was no evidence of any impact on labour mobility (Gyarmati et al. 2008).

SSP, in contrast, was relatively cheap. On average, SSP increased the total incomes of program group members by $5,256 over a five-year period. The total cost was $2,700 per SSP program group. Because SSP increased employment, tax revenues offset some of its costs. Consequently, SSP was estimated to transfer a dollar at a cost of only 50 cents (Michalopoulos et al. 2002).

Some, including John Greenwood, the founding executive director of the Social Research and Demonstration Corporation (SRDC), have argued that SSP implemented at scale would eventually resemble the applicant study (SRDC 2006). If implemented on a province-wide basis, the program participants would eventually be drawn from the flow of new applicants rather than the stock of existing long-term recipients. If this were true, then the potential long-run cost-benefit analysis of an SSP-like financial incentive could be quite favourable. In the applicant study, it cost the government only 10 cents to raise a program group members' income by one dollar (Ford et al. 2003). SSP was so inexpensive in large part because, while participants are working, tax revenues help offset the expenditures. During the second year of the program, in the recipient study, SSP increased average monthly government transfers (including the supplement) by $57 but also increased tax revenue by $27 (Michalopoulos et al. 2002). In the applicant study, the effect of SSP on government transfers was statistically insignificant, but the average tax revenue collected increased by $72 (Ford et al. 2003).

Costs are also low for the SSP in part because the supplement was available only to individuals who found full-time work within one year. The time limit is an important way in which SSP differs from in-work tax credits, such as the Working Income Tax Benefit, that are available to all low-income workers. The "stick" represented by the one-year time limit played a large role in generating the full-time employment effects and, by extension, the cost savings (Card and Hyslop 2005). There are reasons to be cautious about implementing SSP at scale, however. In particular, spillover effects could change the relative balance of costs and benefits. By encouraging work among welfare recipients, SSP would increase the supply of labour in low-skilled labour markets. This could decrease wages, increase unemployment, or prolong the duration of job searches among unemployed individuals not receiving welfare. Evidence from a calibrated economy-wide model of SSP does suggest that wages would fall as a result of implementing SSP at scale. After accounting for the various feedback effects, Lise, Seitz, and Smith (2005) estimate that implementing SSP at scale would represent a net cost of nearly a million dollars.

What have we learned from SSP and CEIP?

Although the decades of policy changes since the 1990s have not revealed a magic-bullet program that addresses all of the issues that gave rise to welfare reform, the evidence generated by SSP and CEIP has answered many questions and challenged some common presumptions about the nature of welfare dependency. David Card, a designer of the SSP experiment, has argued that, at the outset, it was not obvious that long-term social assistance recipients would respond to a complicated financial incentive (SRDC 2006). SSP demonstrated that, although not all did, a large fraction of lone parents would work full time if that work were more financially rewarding.

Evidence from the CEIP experiment challenges the notion that SA recipients do not want to work. Even though, on average, the CEIP jobs represented a comparatively small increase in income, most program group members exchanged their welfare benefits for a job. In this case, making work mandatory would have been virtually redundant. It is worth noting that CEIP jobs were stable and offered opportunities in a variety of occupations and industries.

A similar conclusion can be drawn from the SSP applicant study. Even when remaining on welfare for one year would make participants eligible for the supplement, 43 per cent of the applicant program group left the welfare rolls at least once during the first year of the program. The possibility of receiving the supplement increased the probability of study participants remaining on SA for a year by only 3 percentage points (Berlin et al. 1998).

SSP also challenged the conventional notion that reducing the cost of social assistance programs necessitates lowering the incomes of program participants. In the applicant study, evaluators concluded that it cost only 10 cents to raise participants' incomes by one dollar. Compare this finding to some estimates that have traditional transfers costing as much as 1.5 dollars per dollar transferred (Ford et al. 2003). Moreover, SSP reduced the fraction of individuals living in poverty, as defined by Statistics Canada's low-income cut-off, by as much as 14 percentage points (Ford et al. 2003).

Though SSP and CEIP demonstrate what can work well, these program evaluations also shine a light on the limits to and pitfalls of active social assistance programs. In particular, the low-skilled labour markets into which social assistance recipients typically transition offer few opportunities. Even though CEIP program group members were able to accumulate several months of additional work experience, this benefit did not translate into a better chance of working full time without the CEIP jobs. The inability to find a full-time job apparently prevented many SSP participants from benefiting from the supplement. Moreover, working in low-wage jobs that offered little or no wage growth meant that the impacts of the supplement were short lived. These issues point toward the more promising approach of combining services and training with financial incentives, as suggested by the larger and more persistent improvements to employment and earnings achieved by the SSP Plus experiment.

References

Bemelmans-Videc, M.-L., R.C. Rist, and E. Vedung, eds. 1998. *Carrots, Sticks and Sermons: Policy Instruments and Their Evaluation*. New Brunswick, NJ: Transaction Publishers.

Berlin, G. 2002. *What Works in Welfare Reform: Evidence and Lessons to Guide TANF Reauthorization*. New York: Manpower Demonstration Research Corporation.

Berlin, G., W. Bancroft, D. Card, W. Lin, and P.K. Robins. 1998. *Do Work Incentives Have Unintended Consequences? Measuring "Entry Effects" in the Self-Sufficiency Project*. Ottawa: Social Research and Demonstration Corporation.

Bloom, D., and W. Michalopoulos. 2001. *How Welfare and Work Policies Affect Employment and Income: A Synthesis of Research*. New York: Manpower Demonstration Research Corporation.

Boychuk, G.W. 2006. "Slouching Toward the Bottom? Social Assistance in the Canadian Provinces, 1980–2000." In *Racing to the Bottom? Provincial Interdependence in the Canadian Federation*, ed. K. Harrison, 157–92. Vancouver: UBC Press.

Card, D., and D.R. Hyslop. 2005. "Estimating the Effects of a Time-Limited Earnings Subsidy for Welfare-Leavers." *Econometrica* 73 (6): 1723–70. http://dx.doi.org/10.1111/j.1468-0262.2005.00637.x.

Card, D., J. Kluve, and A. Weber. 2010. "Active Labour Market Policy Evaluations: A Meta-Analysis." *Economic Journal* 120 (548): F452–77. http://dx.doi.org/10.1111/j.1468-0297.2010.02387.x.

Connolly, H., and P. Gottschalk. 2009. "Do Earnings Subsidies Affect Job Choice? The Impact of SSP Subsidies on Job Turnover and Wage Growth." *Canadian Journal of Economics / Revue canadienne d'économique* 42 (4): 1276–304. http://dx.doi.org/10.1111/j.1540-5982.2009.01546.x.

Daigneault, Pierre-Marc. 2014. "Three Paradigms of Social Assistance." *Sage Open* 4 (4): 1–8. http://dx.doi.org/10.1177/2158244014559020.

Daigneault, Pierre-Marc. 2015. "Ideas and Welfare Reform in Saskatchewan: Entitlement, Workfare or Activation?" *Canadian Journal of Political Science / Revue canadienne de science politique*. (Online before print, April.) http://dx.doi.org/10.107/S0008423915000098.

Ferrall, C. 2012. "Explaining and Forecasting Results of the Self-Sufficiency Project." *Review of Economic Studies* 79 (4): 1495–526. http://dx.doi.org/10.1093/restud/rds008.

Finnie, R., and I. Irvine. 2008. *The Welfare Enigma: Explaining the Dramatic Decline in Canadian's Use of Social Assistance*. Commentary No. 267. Toronto: C.D. Howe Institute.

Ford, R., D. Gyarmati, K. Foley, and D. Tattrie. 2003. *Can Work Incentives Pay for Themselves? Final Report on the Self-Sufficiency Project for Welfare Applicants*. Ottawa: Social Research and Demonstration Corporation.

Gorlick, C., and G. Brethour. 1998. *Welfare-To-Work Programs: A National Inventory*. Kanata, ON: Canadian Council on Social Development.

Greenberg, D., V. Deitch, and G. Hamilton. 2009. *Welfare-to-Work Program Benefits and Costs A Synthesis of Research*. New York: Manpower Demonstration and Research Corporation.

Gyarmati, D., S. de Raaf, C. Nicholson, D. Kyte, and M. MacInnis. 2006. *Community Employment Innovation Project (CEIP)—Testing a Community-Based Jobs Strategy for the Unemployed: Early Impacts of CEIP*. Ottawa: Social Research and Demonstration Corporation.

Gyarmati, D., S. de Raaf, B. Palameta, C. Nicholson, and S.-W. Hui. 2008. *Community Employment Innovation Project (CEIP)—Encouraging Work and Supporting Communities: Final Results of CEIP*. Ottawa: Social Research and Demonstration Corporation.

Hansen, Hanne Foss, and Olaf Rieper. 2009. "The Evidence Movement: The Development and Consequences of Methodologies in Review Practices." *Evaluation* 15 (2): 141–63. http://dx.doi.org/10.1177/1356389008101968.

Heckman, James J. 2001. "Micro Data, Heterogeneity, and the Evaluation of Public Policy: Nobel Lecture." *Journal of Political Economy* 109 (4): 673–748. http://dx.doi.org/10.1086/322086.

HRDC (Human Resources Development Canada). 2000. *Reconnecting Social Assistance Recipients to the Labour Market*. Ottawa: Lessons Learned.

Lin, W., P.K. Robins, D. Card, K. Harknett, and S. Lui-Gurr. 1998. *When Financial Incentives Encourage Work: Complete 18-Month Findings from the Self-Sufficiency Project*. Ottawa: Social Research and Demonstration Corporation.

Lise, J., S. Seitz, and J. Smith. 2005. *Equilibrium Policy Experiments and the Evaluation of Social Programs*. Working Paper No. 1076. Kingston, ON: Department of Economics, Queen's University.

Michalopoulos, C., D. Tattrie, D. Miller, P.K. Robins, P. Morris, D. Gyarmati, C. Redcross, K. Foley, and R. Ford. 2002. *Making Work Pay: Final Report of the Self-Sufficiency Project for Long-Term Welfare Recipients*. Ottawa: Social Research and Demonstration Corporation.

Robins, P.K., C. Michalopoulos, and K. Foley. 2008. "Are Two Carrots Better Than One? The Effects of Adding Employment Services to Financial Incentive Programs for Welfare Recipients." *Industrial & Labor Relations Review* 61 (3): 410–23.

Shadish, W.R., T.D. Cook, and D.T. Campbell. 2002. *Experimental and Quasi-Experimental Designs for Generalized Causal Inference*. Boston: Houghton Mifflin Company.

SRDC (Social Research and Demonstration Corporation). 2006. *Making Work Pay Symposium November 15–16, 2005*. Ottawa.

conclusion
A Brief Survey of Welfare Reform in the Canadian Provinces

DANIEL BÉLAND AND PIERRE-MARC DAIGNEAULT

As this volume suggests, provincial social assistance remains a central yet changing component of Canada's social policy landscape. In this chapter, we stress key insights found in the previous chapters, relying on the three "I"s discussed in the introduction—ideas, institutions, and impacts—to structure the discussion. We then assess whether convergence in welfare policy among the provinces has been taking place since the late 1980s. A section on the future of research on social assistance in Canada concludes this chapter.

Ideas, institutions, and impacts

Ideas

Our introduction and Robert Henry Cox's chapter outlined several key social policy ideas and principles that have proven popular on the international policy stage over the last three decades. The goal here is to assess whether these ideas have entered the realm of provincial social assistance in a meaningful way, implicitly or explicitly. "Activation," summarily defined as the attempt to tighten the relationship between social policy and employment using a mix of policy instruments, is perhaps the most prominent and relevant idea in the field of welfare, along with the closely related idea of "social investment" (Jenson and Saint-Martin 2006). As Amber Gazso argues in her chapter (p. 275), "the contemporary welfare state is 'active' in that it eschews dependency and promotes human capital development, individual responsibility, and labour market participation." In fact, activation is more than an idea but rather a set of relatively coherent and influential policy ideas, that is, a "policy paradigm" (Daigneault 2014a, 2014b, 2015).

The influence of the activation paradigm on provincial social assistance is visible in many if not most of the chapters. First, the work expectations placed upon social assistance clients have been reassessed, and putting people back to work is now an official objective in many provinces. For instance, one of the purposes of Ontario Works is to "recognize individual responsibility and promote self-reliance through employment" (quoted in Graefe, in this volume, p. 116). The idea is to renegotiate the contract between citizens and the state so that it is based on mutual obligation. Two examples of this idea are the "plans" for employable clients in BC and Ontario, which "mandate employable persons' participation in welfare-to-work programs that range from educational upgrading and employment-readiness training (e.g., skills building) to job searches or actual employment-related activities, such as community service, that are not paid (the latter of which some term 'workfare')" (Gazso, in this volume, p. 278). Second, in the 1990s, the federal and provincial governments attempted to break down the "welfare wall" by introducing various tax credits and income supports for low-income workers, in particular parents. The 1998 federal National Child Benefit supplement (NCB) is a prominent example of these measures, although many provinces have eventually decided to let the NCB "flow through" to families on social assistance (Boychuk, in this volume).

The other side of the work incentives issue is bleaker, however. The idea, consistent with the activation paradigm, is to ensure that the real value of social assistance benefits remains low so as to not discourage work (Daigneault 2014). Not indexing the value of welfare benefits and thereby letting them be eroded by inflation is a clear example of "social policy by stealth" (Battle 2001). For instance, in Québec, the level of the benefits for those expected to work were not indexed to inflation for 1994–2004, and they were only partially indexed from 2004 to 2008 (Noël, in this volume). In some cases, even the absolute value of benefits is lower than it used to be. A single employable person in Ontario received less in 2013 than in 1993 (Graefe, in this volume). In the same vein are the two pilot projects aimed at "activating" social assistance clients Kelly Foley discussed in her chapter. One of those, the Self-Sufficiency Project (SSP), was implemented in 1992 and offered lone-parent social assistance recipients a generous earning supplement if they left welfare for a full-time job within one year of entering the program. Once eligible, participants would receive the supplement when they worked full time in any of the subsequent 36 months. The SSP was a relatively cheap way to improve the income of clients and had a positive, albeit temporary, impact.[1]

Institutions

Beyond the ideas and discourse surrounding social assistance, we need to look at welfare institutions, especially how eligibility rules and benefit

---

1 However, a pilot project called Action emploi, implemented in Québec in the first half of the 2000s, was found to have long-lasting impacts on reducing social assistance recipiency (see Lacroix and Vigneault 2013).

levels have evolved since the late 1980s. First, as Ronald Kneebone and Katherine White show in their contribution, one thing that has not changed dramatically since the early 1990s is that, with the exception of Newfoundland and Labrador, provincial social assistance benefits for single employable individuals are typically set well below what is needed to cover their most "basic needs." This is true even when using Sarlo's (2001) conservative definition of what such needs constitute, as Kneebone and White do. The picture is even bleaker when one uses less restrictive measures of poverty and low income, such as the Market Basket Measure (MBM). Even the more "generous" provinces of Newfoundland and Labrador, Saskatchewan, and Québec provided benefits to single employables in 2012 that amounted to only 64.3 per cent, 55.1 per cent, and 52.0 per cent of the MBM, respectively. This reality, reinforced by the supplementary evidence put forward in our provincial chapters, suggests that provincial welfare programs tend to be especially ungenerous toward single employable adults. On average, both lone parents and married parents fare relatively better, although this is much more the case in provinces such as Prince Edward Island, Québec, and Saskatchewan than in places such as British Columbia, Manitoba, and Nova Scotia. Clearly, welfare benefit levels in the first group of provinces named are more consistent with the logic of "social investment" (Jenson 2011) than these levels are in the last group mentioned. Considering this variation, we cannot talk about uniformity among the provinces regarding differences in the benefit levels they offer to single employable adults, lone parents, and married parents, although we note a certain convergence in the fact that provinces are generally more generous with families than with single employable adults.

An area where some convergence is taking place is disability benefits. As Michael Prince suggests in his chapter on the topic, in constant dollars, disability social assistance benefits have declined significantly in all the provinces except Québec, where the value of such benefits has remained relatively stable since 1994, with a cumulative decline of less than 1 per cent. Regarding this issue, however, it is crucial to stress the distinction made between temporary and permanent or severe disabilities, which can play a major role in the development and operation of provincial social assistance programs. A striking example of this reality is seen in Alberta, which enacted the Assured Income for the Severely Handicapped (AISH) in 1979. As Donna Wood explains in her chapter, an important aspect of this new program for the permanent and severely disabled is its clear institutional separation from the Alberta Works Income Support (AW-IS) program, which offers benefits to the other categories of Albertans living on provincial social assistance. A key characteristic of this separation is the large discrepancy in the benefit levels offered by each program: AISH is much more generous than AW-IS. This situation is probably related to the fact that, as opposed to the situation prevailing regarding other segments of the unemployed population, creating "work incentives" for the severely disabled by keeping their welfare benefits as low as possible is not seen as legitimate, economically, morally, or politically. More research on this topic could help test this hypothesis and explore whether this approach to benefits for the severely disabled will spread across Canada. Will other provinces follow Alberta's path-departing example?

Impacts

Institutional and socio-economic changes that have taken place since the 1990s have had a direct impact on provincial welfare recipients in Canada. In that regard, the most obvious shift is the overall decline in the average social assistance recipiency rate in Canada. Although this rate was higher than 12 per cent in 1995, it is now barely above 6 per cent, which constitutes a major change in provincial social assistance. In fact, the average recipiency rate in Canada is now roughly comparable to what it used to be in the late 1960s and early 1970s. This trend has been witnessed in every single province; the social assistance rate in all provinces is dramatically lower today than it was in the mid-1990s (Kneebone and White 2014). In this context, a true convergence has taken place, in the sense that so-called welfare dependency—admittedly a normatively loaded expression—has declined across the country. Though this decline in welfare recipiency is primarily explained by socioeconomic factors, policy changes should not be neglected (Boychuk; Kneebone and White, in this volume).

Another broad shift observed in the provinces concerns the changing weight of different categories of beneficiaries on welfare rolls. As suggested in Kneebone and White's chapter and in some of the provincial case studies, the proportion of single individuals on welfare rolls typically increased over the last two decades. At the same time, the number and percentage of single- and two-parent families on welfare rolls decreased over the same period. A dramatic example of this trend is found in British Columbia. In that province, as Jane Pulkingham shows, single women currently represent one-third of social assistance recipients and are now the most important category of beneficiaries ahead of single parents, who used to constitute the largest group. Taking place in several provinces, this type of change in the composition of caseloads is highly consequential, especially considering that, across Canada, welfare benefits for single (employable) people are by far the lowest available today.

This reality is problematic from the perspective of poverty alleviation and meeting the basic socio-economic needs of recipients. In fact, the growing weight of single employable adults on welfare rolls simply means that a growing share of such recipients are likely to face stronger economic hardship than before. Politically, this situation could make provincial social assistance programs even more vulnerable to attacks from the right, as able-bodied singles are less likely to receive public support than permanently disabled individuals or even parents, whose social benefits are at least partly justified by the logic of "social investment" (Jenson 2004) and the need to ensure the welfare of children, a vulnerable but "deserving" group. More generally, this reality, just like the much higher benefits offered to the permanently disabled in provinces such as Alberta, points both to what Brian Steensland (2008) calls "categories of worth" (how certain groups in society are perceived as more deserving of state support than others) and to what Anne Schneider and Helen Ingram (1993) label the "social construction of target populations" (how perceptions of beneficiaries shape how welfare programs are designed and perceived). These remarks show that, once more, ideas about welfare affect the social assistance landscape in Canadian provinces, a reality similar to the one prevailing in other advanced industrial countries (Béland and Waddan 2012; Cox 2001; Somers and Block 2005; Stryker and Wald 2009).

Beyond this situation, a more positive trend in Canada is the significant decline of poverty and low-income status that has affected several social categories since the mid-1990s. For instance, as Brian Murphy, Andrew Heisz, and Xuelin Zhang report in their chapter, although it remains unacceptably high at about 30 per cent, the low-income rate for lone-parent headed families is much lower today than it was two decades ago. As for seniors, Patrik Marier and Anne-Marie Séguin suggest in their chapter on aging that Canada's older citizens now face much less poverty on average than do those in other age groups, including children. Simultaneously, they point to a recent increase in poverty among the elderly, which could justify the current quest to improve both federal and provincial public pension programs.

Overall, however, poverty and low income have generally declined in Canada since the mid-1990s, a situation that should not hide a clear and significant increase in income inequality related to the fact that wealthy people in Canada are becoming richer and richer (Murphy, Heisz, and Zhang, in this volume). The growing, disproportionate economic power of the top one per cent has clear policy implications in terms of both tax fairness and social policy financing, an issue we return to in the next section.

Convergence and divergence: Variations on a theme?

As indicated by the international literature reviewed in our introduction and by Cox's chapter, the issue of policy convergence and divergence has been a major aspect of the comparative scholarship on social assistance (see also Bahle, Hubl, and Pfeifer 2011; Barbier and Ludwig-Mayerhofer 2004; Eichhorst and Konle-Seidl 2008; Gough et al. 1997; Kenworthy 2010; Serrano Pascual 2007). In Canada, the issue of convergence and divergence has been studied by social policy scholars who have found significant differences between provincial welfare regimes (Boychuk 1998; Bernard and Saint-Arnaud 2004; Haddow 2013; Proulx et al. 2011). In particular, claims about a possible "race to the bottom" in relationship to the replacement of the Canada Assistance Plan (CAP) with the Canada Health and Social Transfer (CHST) in 1996 have been examined and rejected (see Boychuk 2006). Gerard Boychuk comes back to this topic in his chapter and finds that the impact of CAP on welfare recipiency rates and benefit levels never materialized. Rather, he identifies deteriorating economic conditions and the previous federal offloading of responsibility for unemployment insurance as the main drivers of policy change in the field of social assistance. Furthermore, Boychuk argues that the cost-sharing agreement embedded in CAP and its subsequent demise affected provinces differently, depending on the political ideology of their governments and their fiscal capacity. We do agree with Boychuk that cost sharing did not prevent radical retrenchment of welfare for ideologically committed right-wing governments, but we nevertheless think that CAP's funding formula used to mitigate the incentive to embark on retrenchment and restructuring for most governments.

There are good reasons to believe that the significance of CAP's demise lies primarily at the symbolic level. Even if Boychuk is right in pointing out that the "right to assistance . . . was simply not an element in the central policy debates in this period" (in this volume, p. 37), the fact remains that CAP has been interpreted as such by many people over the years. Indeed, CAP epitomized a conception of citizenship that emphasized notions of universality, justice, and social rights along the lines of the entitlement paradigm (Gazso, in this volume; see also Daigneault 2015). Thus, when the less restrictive CHST replaced CAP, many believed that it was indicative of a shift in citizenship regime and policy paradigm that would have serious implications for provincial social assistance. We argue that provincial social assistance regimes have been characterized by similar transformations—in other words, they generally move in the same direction, although significant differences persist. Because provincial social assistance policies remain in flux, the objective here is not to offer the last word on convergence and divergence. Instead, we seek to contribute to the ongoing debate on social assistance convergence and divergence through concise remarks about the chapters featured in this volume.

Looking to the future

This volume provides a broad overview of social assistance reform in the Canadian provinces. No scholarship presents the final word, however, and more research is needed to improve our understanding of this complex and changing topic. In this final section, we outline several of the avenues and roadblocks facing future policymakers and researchers working in the area of social assistance in Canada.

The "data problem"

The first roadblock we want to discuss relates to the lack of comparable and timely data on social assistance. Indeed, the "data problem" was the main motivation behind this volume, which represents a modest attempt to solve it. High-quality data are essential to good governance. On one hand, decision makers (e.g., MPs and public managers) need data to make good decisions (Heinrich 2007). Let us not be naïve: decision making is a delicate exercise—some will even say an art—that also relies on values, judgement calls, and intuition. Yet appropriate (i.e., relevant and valid) evidence is also required to assess the situation correctly and act upon it. On the other hand, data allow opposition parties, think tanks, media, civil society, and citizens to know what is going on with respect to welfare, and to hold governments accountable for their decisions. However, many contributors to this volume lamented—and rightly so—the paucity of data on social assistance. Kneebone and White argue that it is surprisingly difficult to obtain information on who receives assistance and on how much they receive in each province. Wood also notes that the statistics for AISH are only available on request. Similarly, Smith-Carrier and Mitchell suggest that data on immigrants and social assistance are extremely difficult to obtain because many sources have been terminated or transformed and systematic information concerning the status of immigrants within provincial welfare rolls is lacking, as many provinces fail to collect data on the topic. To improve our knowledge of welfare reform and its impact, we must encourage all provincial governments to address this gap and collect data on immigrants within their respective social assistance programs. As for the federal government, recent developments during the Harper years, such as the elimination of the compulsory long-form census, the "muzzling" of federal researchers, and the abolition of the National Council of Welfare, have generated legitimate worries about a deliberate suppression of the data relevant for social policy experts and citizens. Because data availability is essential for informed policymaking, this trend bodes ill for both welfare reform and the future of social assistance research in Canada, but it does increase the pressure on the provinces and non-governmental organizations to compensate for flawed federal policies. Are these decisions part of a "strategy of obfuscation" according to which the government deliberately seeks to undermine available information to make retrenchment initiatives less visible and therefore less costly politically (Pierson 1994)? Although we are not keen on conspiracy theories, the trend is troubling, to say the least.

Comparative research and in-depth case studies

A fruitful avenue for future research on social assistance would be to compare Canadian provinces with each other and equivalent substate entities located in other federal countries such as the United States. In addition to large-N studies that could compare general trends in caseloads and benefit levels at the substate level in different countries, more small-N qualitative studies could compare discourses about, and the politics of, welfare reform in Canadian provinces and in their equivalents in other countries. This second type of study could help trace the diffusion and implementation of ideas such as "activation" and "social investment" at the substate level while comparing institutional dynamics in different countries. Although this type of research poses methodological challenges, if done properly, it could enrich our understanding of provincial social assistance by providing comparative and international perspectives. Another possibility is to compare social assistance in a particular province with the situation prevailing in a unitary state (see e.g., Morel 2003). This type of comparison is especially relevant if that country is located within the European Union.[2]

Simultaneously, beyond large-N comparative research, more case studies and in-depth analyses on provincial social assistance in Canada are clearly needed. Regarding case studies and comparative work involving two or several provinces, we think more research on smaller, less-populous provinces would be especially beneficial. Again, research on political discourse and ideas and on the drivers of provincial welfare reform would be welcome

2 On the relevance of the European Union for policy analysis in Canada, see Verdun and Wood (2013).

contributions because these provinces remain relatively understudied, at least when compared to Ontario, Québec, and British Columbia. As many of the provincial chapters included in this volume suggest, we can learn a great deal from smaller provinces, which are every bit as relevant for comparative analysis as their three larger counterparts (see, e.g., Daigneault 2015). More generally and at the risk of repeating ourselves, we need more nationwide data on provincial social assistance to foster better case studies and comparative projects in the future.

Although the contributors to this volume discussed the 10 Canadian provinces, the three territories were excluded from our analysis to keep this volume more focused. Though it is important to recognize crucial constitutional differences between the provinces and the territories (Atkinson et al. 2013), future research could examine the state of social assistance in the territories. This type of research, comparative or not, would be especially helpful if it considered the socio-economic status of Aboriginal peoples and their evolving relationship to social assistance.

The relationship between different populations and social assistance

A key area in urgent need of more research is the fate of Aboriginal peoples within Canada's social assistance system. For instance, as Martin Papillon shows in his chapter, federal welfare benefits for members of First Nations vary from province to province because Ottawa decided decades ago that it would not set national benefit levels for these populations, as it does for other social assistance programs such as the Guaranteed Income Supplement (GIS). A question future research could address is why Ottawa made the decision to make welfare benefits for Aboriginal peoples vary across the country based on *provincial* policy criteria, which is a rather puzzling decision when other policy areas such as old-age social assistance are considered. Overall, in light of the demographic growth witnessed within Aboriginal communities and the much higher levels of poverty they face, both within and outside reserves, increasing the scope of rigorous research on the Aboriginal–welfare reform nexus at the provincial and the federal level is more pressing than ever.

Considering the acceleration of population aging in Canada, more research is also needed on provincial old-age housing and pension supplements, which are understudied yet significant social programs, as Marier and Séguin point out in their chapter. Another related area in which new scholarship would be especially useful concerns the relationship between provincial social assistance for the working-age population and federal programs such as the OAS and GIS, which provide basic public support for seniors, especially low-income ones. With the 2012 decision of the Harper government to gradually increase the entitlement age of OAS and GIS from 65 to 67 between April 2023 and January 2029, this issue is more crucial than ever before. This urgency exists because observers and policymakers assume that raising the age at which older recipients move from provincial welfare to federal old-age assistance will put an additional burden on provincial welfare systems. Once the entitlement age for OAS and GIS starts increasing, measuring the additional fiscal burden on provincial treasuries stemming from this federal policy change should be a priority. Equally important, because combined federal and provincial old-age benefits for low-income seniors are higher, on average, than welfare benefits for working-age people, the impact of the change in OAS and GIS entitlement age on the socio-economic status of those staying longer on provincial welfare rolls could prove significant. Considering these remarks, researchers should explore this issue and measure the impact of such a significant change in pension policy on older recipients of provincial welfare benefits.

Beyond Aboriginal peoples and seniors, immigrants are another key category we should keep in mind when studying provincial social assistance. Canada is a country with a comparatively high rate of immigration. Its population is not declining largely because it welcomes a larger proportion of new immigrants every year than most other advanced industrial countries (Statistics Canada 2008). Yet, as Smith-Carrier and Mitchell argue in their chapter, immigrants face several enduring challenges, both within and beyond the provincial social assistance landscape. For instance, the authors stress the fact that discrimination remains rampant in the labour market, a situation that is likely to undermine the efforts of immigrants on social assistance to find regular employment.

The respective status of women and men within the world of social assistance is another major policy issue, and future research on provincial welfare reform should draw on the insights of feminist scholarship about gender inequality, as Gazso does in her chapter. The main message of her contribution—the fact that social assistance is experienced in gendered ways—is a key point for all students of social assistance and not only for scholars interested primarily in gender relations. In future research on provincial welfare reform and beyond, gender scholars and social assistance researchers should collaborate more systematically with one another, as it is difficult to understand the profound social and political implications of specific policy changes without understanding how they may affect women and men differently, or how they may challenge or reinforce traditional gender roles and labour market disparities.

Another social category that future scholarship on provincial social assistance should focus on is people with disabilities, who rely more on welfare benefits than those in other categories, on average, but are sometimes treated differently from one province to the next depending on whether they are severely disabled or not. A key policy challenge future scholarship could shed light on concerns the need to reduce the high level of poverty among people with disabilities, an issue Prince discusses in his chapter on disability and social assistance. Is providing a separate welfare stream for the severely handicapped—an idea associated with Alberta's AISH program and similar schemes adopted in other provinces—the best way to reduce poverty among people with disabilities, or should advocates and policymakers explore other avenues to reach this crucial goal? This is the type of question that future scholarship on the disability-welfare nexus in the provinces could tackle.

If improving the socio-economic situation of people with disabilities is a priority, so is tackling homelessness while, at the same time, exploring the relationship between welfare reform and housing policy. Any investigation of this relationship should include an assessment of the shelter component of provincial social assistance. Compared to many other advanced industrial countries, Canada provides only modest public housing, and, as Prince points to in his chapter on housing and homelessness, a large gap can appear between the shelter component of welfare benefits and the actual costs of the local housing market. This situation is a clear source of economic hardship that could be addressed through improved housing policies or increased shelter components. In the end, however, Prince reminds us that social assistance is not the main policy vehicle through which governments should tackle homelessness and housing affordability issues. These social and economic problems are so broad they require bold efforts from Ottawa, the provinces, and municipalities that transcend the field of social assistance, which is only one component of social policy's "big picture" (Béland 2010).

The "big picture"

Researchers and citizens alike who consider the breadth of Canada's socio-economic challenges realize that social assistance has only a limited capacity to meet these challenges. Canada's "big picture" problems, including the plight of Aboriginal peoples and of immigrants, inequality between men and women, and the economic vulnerability of people with disabilities, can only be solved by equally comprehensive initiatives. More generally, the need to tackle broad economic and social issues such as poverty, social inequality, and social inclusion requires broad policy efforts that transcend discrete policy areas such as social assistance, which typically provides modest and often inadequate benefits to some of our most vulnerable citizens. Social assistance is only one relatively modest component of the complex set of policy tools different levels of government have at their disposal to help people in need while fighting poverty and inequality. Increasing our knowledge about social assistance in the provinces and beyond is essential to guide future reforms aimed at improving the social and economic status of the long-term unemployed; however, in the long run, only larger policy initiatives and political coalitions that may include yet transcend welfare recipients are likely to make a real difference. As Keith Banting and John Myles (2013) suggest in a recent volume, broad coalitions and policy initiatives centred on the general fight against inequality are needed in Canada. In this context, both future research and policy initiatives about provincial social assistance could tie welfare reform into the "big picture" of rising inequalities. It is hoped this volume contributes directly to the social assistance side of this essential policy debate.

References

Atkinson, Michael M., Daniel Béland, Gregory P. Marchildon, Kathleen McNutt, Peter W.B. Phillips, and Ken Rasmussen. 2013. *Governance and Public Policy in Canada: A View from the Provinces*. Toronto: University of Toronto Press.

Bahle, Thomas, Vanessa Hubl, and Michaela Pfeifer. 2011. *The Last Safety Net: A Handbook of Minimum Income Protection in Europe*. Bristol: The Policy Press. http://dx.doi.org/10.1332/policypress/9781847427250.001.0001.

Banting, Keith, and John Myles, eds. 2013. *Inequality and the Fading of Redistributive Politics*. Vancouver: UBC Press.

Barbier, Jean-Claude, and Wolfgang Ludwig-Mayerhofer. 2004. "Introduction: The Many Worlds of Activation." *European Societies* 6 (4): 423–36. http://dx.doi.org/10.1080/1461669042000275845.

Battle, Ken. 2001. *Relentless Incrementalism: Deconstructing and Reconstructing Canadian Income Security Policy*. Ottawa: Caledon Institute of Social Policy.

Béland, Daniel. 2010. *What Is Social Policy? Understanding the Welfare State*. Cambridge: Polity Press.

Béland, Daniel, and Alex Waddan. 2012. *The Politics of Policy Change: Welfare, Medicare, and Social Security Reform in the United States*. Washington, DC: Georgetown University Press.

Bernard, Paul, and Sébastien Saint-Arnaud. 2004. "Du pareil au même? La position des quatre principales provinces canadiennes dans l'univers des régimes providentiels." *The Canadian Journal of Sociology / Cahiers canadiens de sociologie* 29 (2): 209–39.

Boychuk, Gerard W. 1998. *Patchworks of Purpose: The Development of Provincial Social Assistance Regimes in Canada*. Montréal: McGill-Queen's University Press.

Boychuk, Gerard W. 2006. "Slouching Toward the Bottom? Social Assistance in the Canadian Provinces, 1980–2000." In *Racing to the Bottom? Provincial Interdependence in the Canadian Federation*, ed. K. Harrison, 157–92. Vancouver: UBC Press.

Cox, Robert Henry. 2001. "The Social Construction of an Imperative: Why Welfare Reform Happened in Denmark and the Netherlands but Not in Germany." *World Politics* 53 (3): 463–98. http://dx.doi.org/10.1353/wp.2001.0008.

Daigneault, Pierre-Marc. 2014a. "Reassessing the Concept of Policy Paradigm: Aligning Ontology and Methodology in Policy Studies." *Journal of European Public Policy* 21 (3): 453–69. http://dx.doi.org/10.1080/13501763.2013.834071.

Daigneault, Pierre-Marc. 2014b. "Three Paradigms of Social Assistance." *Sage Open* 4 (4): 1–8. http://dx.doi.org/10.1177/2158244014559020.

Daigneault, Pierre-Marc. 2015. "Ideas and Welfare Reform in Saskatchewan: Entitlement, Workfare, or Activation?" *Canadian Journal of Political Science / Revue canadienne de science politique*. (Online ahead of print, April.) http://dx.doi.org/10.107/S0008423915000098.

Eichhorst, Werner, and Regina Konle-Seidl. 2008. *Contingent Convergence: A Comparative Analysis of Activation Policies*. Discussion Paper Series No. 3905. Bonn: Institute for the Study of Labor.

Gough, Ian, Jonathan Bradshaw, John Ditch, Tony Eardley, and Peter Whiteford. 1997. "Social Assistance in OECD Countries." *Journal of European Social Policy* 7 (1): 17–43. http://dx.doi.org/10.1177/095892879700700102.

Haddow, Rodney. 2013. "Labour Market Income Transfers and Redistribution: National Themes and Provincial Variations." In *Inequality and the Fading of Redistributive Politics*, ed. K.G. Banting and J. Myles, 381–409. Vancouver: UBC Press.

Heinrich, Carolyn J. 2007. "Evidence-Based Policy and Performance Management: Challenges and Prospects in Two Parallel Movements." *American Review of Public Administration* 37 (3): 255–77. http://dx.doi.org/10.1177/0275074007301957.

Jenson, Jane. 2004. "Changing the Paradigm: Family Responsibility or Investing in Children." *Canadian Journal of Sociology* 29 (2): 169–92. http://dx.doi.org/10.2307/3654692.

Jenson, Jane. 2011. "Redesigning Citizenship Regimes after Neoliberalism. Moving towards Social Investment." In *Towards a Social Investment Welfare State? Ideas, Policies and Challenges*, ed. Nathalie Morel, Bruno Palier, and Joakim Palme, 61–88. Bristol: Policy Press. http://dx.doi.org/10.1332/policypress/9781847429247.003.0003.

Jenson, Jane, and Denis Saint-Martin. 2006. "Building Blocks for a New Social Architecture: The LEGO™ Paradigm of an Active Society." *Policy and Politics* 34 (3): 429–51. http://dx.doi.org/10.1332/030557306777695325.

Kenworthy, Lane. 2010. "Labour Market Activation." In *The Oxford Handbook of the Welfare State*, ed. F.G. Castles, S. Leibfried, J. Lewis, H. Obinger, and C. Pierso, 435–47. Oxford: Oxford University Press.

Kneebone, Ron, and Katherine White. 2014. *The Rise and Fall of Social-Assistance Use in Canada, 1969–2012*. SPP Research Paper 7 No. 5. Calgary: The School of Public Policy, University of Calgary. http://www.policyschool.ucalgary.ca/?q=content/rise-and-fall-social-assistance-use-canada-1969-2012.

Lacroix, Guy, and Thomas Vigneault. 2013. "Subvention salariale et sortie de la pauvreté: L'effet du programme Action emploi." In *Le Québec économique 2012: Le point sur le revenu des Québecois*, ed. M. Joanis, L. Godbout, and J.-Y. Duclos, 283–310. Québec: Les Presses de l'Université Laval.

Morel, Sylvie. 2003. "La France et le Québec: Des logiques de réciprocité semblables entre l'État et les pauvres?" *Santé, société et solidarité* 2 (1): 55–68.

Pierson, Paul. 1994. *Dismantling the Welfare State: Reagan, Thatcher, and the Politics of Retrenchment*. Cambridge: Cambridge University Press. http://dx.doi.org/10.1017/CBO9780511805288.

Proulx, Christine, Samuel Faustmann, Hicham Raïq, and Axel van den Berg. 2011. "Internal Diversity in Social Policy Regimes: The Case of Canada's Four Major Provinces." In *Social Statistics, Poverty and Social Exclusion: Perspectives from Québec, Canada and Abroad*, ed. Guy Fréchet, Danielle Gauvreau, and Jean Poirier, 176–89. Montréal: Presses de l'Université de Montréal.

Sarlo, Christopher. 2001. *Measuring Poverty in Canada*. Critical Issues Bulletin. Vancouver: Fraser Institute.

Schneider, Anne, and Helen Ingram. 1993. "Social Construction of Target Populations: Implications for Politics and Policy." *American Political Science Review* 87 (2): 334–47. http://dx.doi.org/10.2307/2939044.

Serrano Pascual, Amparo. 2007. "Reshaping Welfare States: Activation Regimes in Europe." In *Reshaping Welfare States and Activation Regimes in Europe*, ed. Amparo Serrano Pascual and Lars Magnusson, 11–34. Brussels: P.I.E.-Peter Lang.

Somers, Margaret R., and Fred Block. 2005. "From Poverty to Perversity: Ideas, Markets, and Institutions over 200 Years of Welfare Debate." *American Sociological Review* 70 (2): 260–87. http://dx.doi.org/10.1177/000312240507000204.

Statistics Canada. 2008. *Population Growth in Canada*. Ottawa: Statistics Canada. Accessed April 28, 2014. http://www.statcan.gc.ca/pub/91-003-x/2007001/4129907-eng.htm.

Steensland, Brian. 2008. *The Failed Welfare Revolution: America's Struggle over Guaranteed Income Policy*. Princeton, NJ: Princeton University Press.

Stryker, Robin, and Pamela Wald. 2009. "Redefining Compassion to Reform Welfare: How Supporters of 1990s US Federal Welfare Reform Aimed for the Moral High Ground." *Social Politics* 16 (4): 519–57. http://dx.doi.org/10.1093/sp/jxp022.

Verdun, Amy, and Donna E. Wood. 2013. "Governing the Social Dimension in Canadian Federalism and European Integration" *Canadian Public Administration* 56 (2): 173–84. http://doi.wiley.com/10.1111/capa.12012.

postface
From Welfare Reform—to Welfare Reformulation

SHERRI TORJMAN AND KEN BATTLE

The primary purpose of welfare is to act as the program of last resort for individuals with no other means of financial support. It comes into play when all personal resources, including income and assets, have been exhausted.

Although welfare is often referred to as a single program, it actually is administered by different departments in 13 provinces and territories. Each jurisdiction sets its own rules regarding eligibility, amount of aid, type and level of special assistance, enforcement, and appeals.

Despite the variation, provincial and territorial welfare systems share a similar structure—and the same strengths and shortcomings.

Welfare recipients are at the mercy of an often harried and under-resourced bureaucracy, required to follow and enforce massive volumes of rules. The rules are so complex that virtually any recipient's files will contain several "errors." People on welfare live in perpetual fear of sudden and seemingly arbitrary decisions affecting their very capacity to feed their families.

Regardless of jurisdiction or family type, there is a clear bottom line. Welfare recipients in all provinces and territories have low incomes. We know this by comparing their incomes to *poverty measures* and *income measures*. Welfare incomes are only a fraction of the key poverty measures and of the after-tax average and median incomes of other Canadian households.

There is another problem related to adequacy. In addition to being low, welfare rates are not indexed, except in Québec and Newfoundland, leading to long-term decline in their real value—and resulting in savings to governments via a classic form of social policy by stealth.

Because of all the problems related to the complexity, intrusiveness, and inadequacy of social assistance, we produced a report in 1987 called *Welfare in Canada: The Tangled Safety Net* published by the (now defunct) National Council of Welfare. It made 55 recommendations for reforming welfare. For years after the publication of this report, we wrote and spoke about the need to raise welfare rates—through increases to their base amounts and through indexation to ensure that their value kept pace with the cost of living.

Subsequent studies that we carried out several years later brought to light a new problem.

One of our first studies at the Caledon Institute back in 1993 detailed the interaction of the welfare and income tax systems. This welfare-tax interface study found that welfare recipients who supplement their benefits by working can keep only a small fraction of these earnings.

Welfare recipients effectively pay back to government most of their employment earnings—mainly through welfare tax-back payments levied on recipients' earnings but also in income and payroll taxes and in foregone refundable credits. Another disincentive to work is the potential loss of "income in kind" such as supplementary health and dental benefits, which can be worth hundreds or even thousands of dollars for some households.

We described this problem in a Caledon report called *The Welfare Wall: The Interaction of the Welfare and Tax Systems*. "Welfare wall" refers to the conundrum that some welfare recipients can end up worse off financially if they leave social assistance for the workforce.

We realized in doing this analysis that, unlike the position we had taken several years earlier at the National Council of Welfare, continuing only to recommend improvements to welfare was not the most effective way to tackle poverty in the long run. The welfare wall analysis was a pivotal study. It subsequently became the foundation for our work on exploring ways to dismantle welfare piece by piece and replace it with more adequate and less intrusive programs of income support. Welfare basically would revert to the income program of last resort, as it was originally intended.

The proposal for the National Child Benefit became the first brick in a recommended new architecture of income security. The idea behind this bold initiative was to begin the reform of welfare by removing child benefits from social assistance and using the resulting financial savings to improve services and supports for all low-income families. For its part, the federal government boosted its child benefit to a level at which all low-income families—welfare poor and working poor alike—received the same maximum amount. Child benefits no longer would be part of the welfare wall.

Another way to help make work pay is to enhance the major earnings supplementation program in the country, the Working Income Tax Benefit. It can be built into a far more powerful instrument, both in terms of increasing benefits and covering more low-income workers.

The third major component of welfare that is ripe for reconstruction involves a basic income for persons with severe and prolonged disabilities, thousands of whom must rely on social assistance. They should qualify instead for a separate income program, ideally run by the federal government. As part of the redesign, the resulting provincial and territorial financial windfall should be reinvested to fund a comprehensive system of supports for persons with disabilities, whether working or on some program of income support.

In short, we need to enhance the programs that already have several positive features. They are federally delivered, portable, equitable, and employ the income tax system as an administratively elegant delivery mechanism.

Reconstructing the pieces of welfare is a practicable challenge that would improve dramatically the quality of life not only for the poorest of the poor but also for the majority of low-, modest-, and middle-income Canadians throughout the country.

From welfare reform—to welfare reformulation.

Index